Notable British Trials Ser

TRIAL OF

PERCY LEFROY MAPLETON

EDITED BY

Adam Wood

MANGO BOOKS

First edition published 2019 (Hardcover)
This edition 2019 (Softcover)

ISBN: 978-1-911273-29-5 (hardcover)
ISBN: 978-1-911273-60-8 (softcover)
ISBN: 978-1-911273-30-1 (ebook)

Notable British Trials imprint ©William Hodge & Company (Holdings) Ltd
Used with kind permission.

General Editors:
David Green - M.W. Oldridge - Adam Wood

Published by Mango Books
www.mangobooks.co.uk
18 Soho Square
London W1D 3QL

Notable British Trials Series No. 86

TRIAL OF

PERCY LEFROY MAPLETON

EDITED BY

Adam Wood

Percy Lefroy Mapleton
sketched at the Magistrates' hearing

Author's collection

CONTENTS.

THE TRIAL —

FIRST DAY — FRIDAY 4th NOVEMBER 1881.

SECOND DAY — SATURDAY 5th NOVEMBER 1881.

SECOND DAY — SATURDAY 5th NOVEMBER 1881 (Continued).

THIRD DAY — MONDAY 7th NOVEMBER 1881.

FOURTH DAY — TUESDAY 8th NOVEMBER 1881.

LIST OF ILLUSTRATIONS.

PERCY LEFROY MAPLETON.

INTRODUCTION.

I.

*'Gentlemen of the jury. Some day, when too late,
you will learn that you have murdered me.'*

The dramatic statement made by Percy Lefroy Mapleton moments after Mr Justice Coleridge had passed sentence of death upon him was perfectly in keeping with the way he had lived his twenty-one years – full of drama, high-flown ideas and pipe dreams.

So indifferent was Lefroy to the proceedings of his four-day trial at Maidstone Crown Court that he spent the majority of his time preoccupied with his hat; he had asked permission to wear his dress suit in court, purely to impress the jury. His counsel, Montagu Williams, would later write that Lefroy assumed a studious pose whenever he caught a newspaper artist preparing a sketch of the accused.

The reality is that Lefroy had been found guilty of the most horrific of crimes to the Victorian sensibility – murder on the London to Brighton express train, on 27 June 1881.

For the Victorians, the railways were a source of pride. As the British Empire had expanded at a great rate since the turn of the nineteenth century, so too had the population of the capital city which controlled it through its governing bodies, banks and merchant houses.

Workers, merchants and refugees alike flocked to London, its population doubling from a little over one million in 1801 to two million in 1851. By 1871, 3.9 million people were living in the capital, many refugees from poorer parts of the country, Europe and the colonies. It is estimated that a fifth of London's population consisted of Irish settlers escaping the Great Famine of the 1840s. As the vast majority of these immigrants were labourers, they were perfectly suited to working on the myriad construction projects underway in mid-Victorian London: Euston, Paddington, Fenchurch Street, Waterloo, King's Cross and St Pancras railway stations were all built during a period of a little over twenty years. London Bridge Station, a crucial scene in the story recorded in this volume, was opened in 1836; its line direct to Brighton opened five years later.

Lefroy.

The murder of Mr Gold – Lefroy's crime – was the first homicide on a British railway since that of Thomas Briggs some seventeen years earlier. The 1864 attack upon Briggs, perpetrated by a German tailor named Franz Müller, was the first time a murder had occurred on a train, and understandably shocked and alarmed the nation in equal measure.[2]

Prior to this, the railways had often been used by the public as a means of attending public executions, such as the hanging of multiple murderer John Gleeson Wilson at Liverpool in 1849, when it was estimated that almost a quarter of the 100,000 attendees came to the city by train.[3] The previous year, the notorious Swell Mob commissioned a train to take them to Norwich to 'enjoy' the hanging of James Blomfield Rush [NBT 45], only to be turned away by police at Attleborough.[4]

Following the murder of Thomas Briggs, the safety of passengers was widely debated. Railway carriages at the time could only be entered via the doors on either side, with no doors linking compartments or corridors allowing passengers to pass along the train.

In a small measure designed to allay fears and criticism, the South Western Railway installed small portholes in the dividing walls between compartments, supposedly so that passengers would feel more secure. These portholes, quickly christened 'Müller's Lights', had female passengers complaining of Peeping Toms.

The Railway Act of 1868 compelled railway companies to install a means of communication between passengers and 'servants of the company', resulting in the introduction of a rope equipped with a bell on either end. Unfortunately, these early communication cords failed to work more often than not.

Following the murder of Mr Gold, one frequent traveller, a City solicitor, wrote to the press recalling an incident which took place in the wake of the murder of Thomas Briggs:

> I was in the habit of going home by rail at that time, and I carried a strong umbrella as the best means of protection. On one occasion I got into a carriage without noticing that the only other occupant had what seemed to be a roll of paper in his hand. As the train commenced to move, I thought he held it in an attitude of readiness for attack, and I accordingly sat equipped with my umbrella, prepared for any emergency. I was sure he had a bludgeon concealed in the harmless-

2   See NBT 13: *Trial of Franz Müller*, edited by George Knott (1911), and *Mr Briggs' Hat: A Sensational Account of Britain's First Railway Murder* by Kate Colquhoun (2011).

3   See *The Victorian Railway Murders* by Arthur and Mary Sellwood (1979), an excellent account of locomotive crimes from 1864 to 1901.

4   *The Norfolk Ancestor*, Vol 7 Part 6, September 1994.

Introduction.

looking roll of paper, and he certainly looked excited enough for a deed of violence. Need I say that I breathed more freely when I reached my destination. I sent a letter, which was published, to a morning paper, detailing my 'narrow escape'. Next day I read in the same journal a letter from my fellow-traveller stating that he was really the aggrieved person, that my watchful, suspicious air, and the position of my weapon of defence, my umbrella, made him uneasy, and that his roll of paper was simply a cucumber which he was bringing home to his family.[5]

Commenting on the murder of Mr Gold, the *Dundee Courier* lamented the opportunity presented to potential murderers and thieves by the constraints of the existing railway carriage design:

> There is no wonder if people not quite nervous should eye their fellow-passengers in railway carriages, with some degree of interest, when there is the chance of their being shut up for an hour or so, and alone, with a madman perhaps, or a desperate robber and murderer. The perpetration of brutalities and atrocities in such circumstances, although that cannot be said to be positively common, is yet frequent enough to suggest a grave doubt as to whether we ought to adhere to our system of enclosing railway passengers in small compartments, in which, without chance of help, a woman may be exposed to the brutality of a ruffian, or an elderly gentleman, quietly reading his paper, and suspected of having a gold watch and some bank notes in his pockets, may be robbed and murdered. One of the great Peers of this country, the Duke of Sutherland, has been in the United States lately, making inquiries with a view to the introduction here of railway improvements adopted in America. Perhaps he may be prepared to recommend that we should have our carriages communicating with each other, so that a person could go from one end of the train to the other, as they have in America. This would be a considerable change from our present practice, but some considerable change is necessary.[6]

The introduction of American Pullman carriages to Britain in 1874, with their longer interiors and connecting corridors, had promised to resolve the problem, but these were initially only used on the Midland Railway, and would not be in general use until the 1890s.

Nevertheless, when the Brighton express departed London Bridge on the afternoon of 27 June 1881, the railways were still considered to be, in the main, crime-free.

---

5   *Reynolds's Newspaper*, 3 July 1881.
6   *Dundee Courier*, 30 June 1881.

Lefroy.

II.

The case of Percy Lefroy Mapleton was a comedy of errors, from his pocketful of Hanoverian medals and his ludicrous attempts at disguise to his delusional relationship with the actress Violet Cameron and the pathetic episode in which his victim's watch chain was spotted hanging limply out of his shoe.

One witness at Lefroy's trial claimed to have seen the attack itself from her cottage, despite being a hundred yards away, idly looking through a window as the train hurtled past. Another was adamant that Lefroy had been wearing a particular style of hat on the day of the murder, despite overwhelming evidence to the contrary; it transpired that the headwear stated matched that worn by Lefroy in a sketch produced for a wanted poster, when Lefroy's name had, finally, been on everybody's lips.

The limelight had taken some time to come to rest on Lefroy, but the often unflattering revelations of the six months between murder and trial only hinted at the trajectory of Lefroy's twenty-one years; it would be fair to say that he had led a dramatic life.

Before this, desperate for a career in journalism, he had had cards printed bearing the words 'Arthur Lefroy, Author and Journalist'. He had apparently had a spell writing for the local *Wallington and Carshalton Herald* on a contributory basis, penning biographical sketches of local celebrities and a series of theatrical notices.[7] He claimed to have then spent some months working for the *Herald and Mid Surrey Advertiser*, but the title he most aspired to write for was 'the actors' Bible', *The Era*. In fact, during the hunt for Lefroy and his subsequent incarceration, several newspapers, ravenous for information about the railway murderer, reported that he had worked as a journalist for that title, prompting the proprietor Edward Ledger[8] to deny the claims in a letter to the editor of the *Daily Chronicle*:

> Sir - In your published reports of the trial of Arthur Lefroy it is stated in the evidence of the witness Clayton that he believed the prisoner was on the staff of the *Era*. Will you permit me to say through your columns that the statement is altogether untrue? Lefroy had no connection whatever with the *Era*. A letter written by him, and having some reference to a musical relic (an unknown work of Offenbach) was some time ago inserted in my paper, but beyond that I know nothing of the unhappy man who has been found guilty of so terrible a crime. I

---

7   *Evening Telegraph*, 29 June 1881.
8   Edward Ledger succeeded to the editorship of *The Era* following his father's death in 1874, and held the post for forty-seven years until his own passing in 1921.

Introduction.

am, Sir, your obedient servant.

Edw. Ledger,
Wellington Street, Strand WC, Nov 11.[9]

In fact, Mr Ledger had overlooked a review of the entertainment on offer at the Theatre Royal, Croydon, which his newspaper had carried in January of that year. In it, praise was given to 'Mr Arthur Lefroy', whose 'witty lines run with much smoothness, and that gentleman may fairly be congratulated upon his first attempt at furnishing "Stanton's Annual."'[10]

This seems, at face value, to be a major moment of success for Lefroy. But, as was usually the case, there was more to this than met the eye. The less edifying truth emerged after the trial – Lefroy had insinuated himself into someone's favours, exploiting their commercial interests and escaping with a line of credit (financial rather than moral) which he had no intention of repaying:

> He went to Mr Stanton, the then manager of the Croydon Theatre, prior to last Christmas, and, on the ground that [Stanton's] family had in some mysterious way done [Lefroy's] family a service, offered to repay the kindness by gratuitously writing for the Croydon Theatre a pantomime, giving the lessee to understand that he was an author and journalist of extreme experience, and mentioning a well-known author and a well-known actress as his immediate relations. The pantomime purporting to be Lefroy's was produced, after being subjected to a good deal of clipping; but on Boxing Night, when the house was full, Lefroy borrowed £5 from the manager on the strength of his 'gratuitous' pantomime, giving Mr Stanton an IOU, which he is, of course, the possessor of till this moment.[11]

Lefroy, needless to say, remembered it differently, claiming that he had been commissioned by Alfred Stanton to write the pantomime, and that he received a cut of the Boxing Day profits.[12]

Also praising the Croydon pantomime was a writer who identified themselves only as 'a Friend of the Family' in a letter to the *Daily Chronicle*:

> With regard to his literary ability, at which so much sneering has been indulged in, as a writer of some slight reputation, I can, in common with more that one editor of undoubted judgement, assert that, considering his extreme youth, he

---

9   *Daily Chronicle*, 12 November 1881.
10   *The Era*, 15 January 1881.
11   *Daily Chronicle*, 15 November 1881.
12   See Lefroy's autobiography, Appendix XI.

displayed power and undoubted dramatic fire. It has never been so stated in print, but it is a fact he contributed to the *Argosy*, which would entitle him, independent of other things, to be saved from the obloquy that has been heaped on him as a pretended author and journalist. His pantomime at Croydon was stated to be good; his story, 'Two Boxing Nights', was, I know, very good, and the little sketch now being published, 'Released in Death', is most certainly not wanting in merit.[13]

The article in *The Argosy*, 'A Peep at Melbourne in 1881', appeared in June 1881, attributed to 'Anon'.[14] 'Two Boxing Nights' is published as Appendix XIII in this volume, affording the reader an opportunity to judge for themselves whether the work has any literary merit; 'Released in Death', supposedly the autobiography of a man held captive for thirty years in a Russian dungeon, was a magazine article previously rejected but which was published in late 1881 once the author's name became notorious. At the time of writing, no trace of it has been found.

The letter from Lefroy referred to by Edward Ledger was written on 22 March 1881, and had indeed been published in *The Era*, under the headline of 'An Offenbachian Relic', in their edition of 26 March:

To the Editor of the Era.

Sir,

It may interest some of your numerous readers to know that, in addition to the list of M. Offenbach's published and unpublished works already given in your columns, another production of the great opera bouffe composer is in existence, a fact not at present known to half-a-dozen persons. This opera-comique is in three acts, and is entitled *La Reine Lucette*, or perhaps more properly *Lucette*. It was written twelve years ago, and immediately on completion was privately purchased by Mr Frank Coppin, of Melbourne. The plot of the piece turns upon the adventures of a young French girl on an enchanted island, and the music has been pronounced by the few who have heard it to be in M. Offenbach's best vein; that is to say music more of *La Grande Duchesse* type than that of the *Tambour Major*. M. Offenbach, prior to his death, made strenuous efforts to re-purchase it from Mr Coppin, but without success, that gentleman having resolved to produce it, if possible, first of all in Australia. But, owing to the force of circumstances, he has abandoned this idea, and I have every reason to believe that during the coming autumn the London public and the Profession will have an opportunity of passing judgement upon one of the great French composer's favourite works.

13   *Daily Chronicle*, 15 November 1881.
14   *The Argosy*, vol. 31, no. 6, June 1881.

Introduction.

Apologising for trespassing on your valuable space,

I am, Sir, yours faithfully.

ARTHUR LEFROY.

The use of the name 'Arthur Lefroy' was a calculated ploy; the writer had used this pseudonym to avoid being recognised by the more correct 'Percy Lefroy Mapleton', as the latter appellation was already known to the readers of *The Era*. In September 1878, the newspaper published letters from a number of theatrical persons who had been contacted by a Mr Percy Mapleton, who said he had prepared a tour of various provincial theatres and was therefore assembling a company for three months, to start at the Theatre Royal, Gloucester on the sixteenth of that month. On arrival, the tour manager was nowhere to be seen, and the members of the company were told that he had unavoidably had to decamp to Paris. Whether a practical joke or, more seriously, an attempt at obtaining substantial door receipts from the opening night, the newspaper's correspondents were undecided. But one thing all were agreed on was that they would very much like to get their hands on Mr Percy Mapleton.[15] Although a warrant was issued for his arrest, the case collapsed as the authorities were unable to trace the fake theatre manager.

Trying his luck again three years later, in 1881, 'Arthur Lefroy' had another carefully-planned scam in place. The supposed undiscovered Offenbach work was, of course, entirely fictitious. But by offering exclusive rights to the deceased French composer's 'new' work with the supposed backing of the wealthy Mr Coppin, Lefroy was able to reel in the acclaimed tenor and theatre manager Henry Bracy, at the time stage manager of the Globe Theatre. Bracy befriended Lefroy, whom he believed to be the secretary to the fictional Mr Coppin, and at one point promised to try to stage a piece written by his new young friend.

Over the next few months, Lefroy laid his plans. He told Bracy that Mr Coppin had died, leaving his young assistant not only the opera, but also £1000 *per annum*, to be increased to £10,000 should he marry. Lefroy would later claim that he mentioned this condition in the hope that Bracy would introduce him to the actress Violet Cameron.

Promising to place the Offenbach work in Bracy's hands before the end of June, Lefroy had to enlist the services of some composer who could satisfactorily forge the piece. Unfortunately, he wanted £50, which Lefroy did not have. He did, however, have a trusted friend who owed him ten guineas, and who had

---

15   See *The Era* of 9 July 1881 for a collection of these letters, published following Lefroy's arrest for murder.

promised to pay it back on 24 July when he came into an inheritance. Moreover, the friend undertook to lend Lefroy an additional £100, which would solve all his problems.

To get himself through the month until then, Lefroy borrowed £6 from an old friend from Wallington, a Mr Gutteridge. In the meantime, he challenged the Strand Theatre Cricket Club to a game against a team of colonial journalists selected by himself. At the end of the match, it was discovered that players' bags had been mysteriously cut open while in the pavilion, and purses stolen; Lefroy borrowed six shillings from Mr Bracy to pay his share of expenses.[16]

As the weeks progressed and Lefroy edged closer to the conclusion of his scam on Mr Bracy, he found himself saddled with increasing financial burden:

> I need hardly say the things pawned by me represent the various stages of desperation I passed into. And so the month went on. I owed money right and left and had it not been for the hundred pounds I was to receive at the end of the month I should have been utterly lost. I need hardly say that such a life as I was living was most terribly trying, and I felt utterly broken down as the mental strain was so great.

> At last the prayed for 24th of June arrived and my liabilities were as follows. I owed about 30/s to Bracy, three pounds to Mr Gutteridge, a pound owed to my cousins. I had all my clothes to redeem, Bracy believed I was entering on possession of my thousand a year on the following Monday, June 27.

> In a day or two I had to put without fail (if I wished to keep up my false position) the opera in Bracy's hands and I could not do this unless I handed over to the composer £50 before the 28th of June while as if this was not enough I owed my subscription of three guineas to the United Arts Club of which I had been elected a member.

> It will thus be seen that in the event of my failing to satisfy nearly all these persons, utter ruin must have followed.[17]

On the fated day, Friday 24 June, Percy Lefroy Mapleton entered the first class waiting room at Charing Cross Station to meet his friend and receive the £100 he had been promised. He was handed a cheque by the generous benefactor, who shook his hand as he rushed out to catch a train.

When Lefroy presented the cheque at the Strand branch of Child & Co., it was instantly returned marked 'no effects'.

His life was in ruins.

---

16   *The Bolton Evening News* of 29 June 1881, reporting on the match, stated that Lefroy's side lost, contrary to his boast of winning.

17   From Lefroy's autobiography; see Appendix XI.

Introduction.

III.

It hadn't always been like this.

Lefroy's mother was Mary Trent Seale, eldest daughter of Lieutenant William Seale, Colonial Secretary at St Helena in the South Atlantic ocean. Her mother was Margaret Seale, from a renowned military family whose association with the island dated as far back as 1642.

In 1843, at the age of eighteen, Mary married Captain Henry Mapleton at Jamestown, St Helena. Mapleton was some fifteen years older, and had joined the Royal Navy in 1825. By 1832, he was a Master of Sloops of War and Smaller Vessels, and it was claimed that he was the youngest master in the Royal Navy by 1840. He was ordered to accompany Sir James Ross on his exploration of the Antarctic, but, by the time he arrived in England from the West Indies, Ross had already sailed, and Mapleton had to secure another vessel, the *Eliza Scott*, in an attempt to catch up with Ross. In late 1840, during a severe storm near Tristan da Cunha, the *Eliza Scott* suffered substantial damage and Mapleton was obliged to dock at St Helena for repairs, abandoning the pursuit of Ross.[18] Henry Mapleton remained on the island, and was recorded in the 1841 census as Harbour Master.

During this time, an observatory was being established on St Helena by Lieutenant John Henry Lefroy who, alongside Lieutenant Eardley Wilmot, had been tasked with undertaking magnetical observations in various parts of the British Empire. Lefroy sailed for St Helena on HMS *Terror* on 25 September 1839, arriving on 31 January 1840. He remained until July 1842, when he was transferred to the observatory at Toronto. During his stay on the island, Lefroy assisted with the disinterment of Napoleon Bonaparte's remains: they were returned to France in October 1840, nineteen years after the Emperor's burial.[19]

Following their marriage in 1843, Henry and Mary welcomed two daughters, Mary[20] and Eliza.[21] Henry's career continued to blossom, and by 1847 he was appointed Summary Judge at St Helena, a position apparently created for him.

But during the 1850s dark clouds began to gather. Henry Mapleton's mental powers began to desert him. He began to suffer hallucinations and other delusions. He apparently attempted suicide, and later tried to smother his wife. By the late 1850s, his mental problems were causing concern, and it was said

---

18   See the Central News clipping detailing Henry Mapleton's naval career held at the National Archives (TNA: PRO HO 144/83/A6404/94).

19   *Dictionary of National Biography*, 1885–1900, Volume 32.

20   Mary Katerina Emily Beauchamp Mapleton (1845–1917).

21   Eliza Julia Travers Mapleton (1848–1915).

that on more than one occasion Sir Edward Hay Drummond-Hay, the Governor of St Helena, begged Mapleton's friends to persuade him to resign to prevent him being dismissed from his post.[22]

This pressure seemingly told, and the Mapleton family left the colonial island for the heart of the empire – London – where a son, Percy, was born on 23 February 1860 in Peckham, South London. The boy was baptised at St Mary Magdalene Church on 30 March and given the middle name of 'Lefroy' in honour of John Henry Lefroy, who had worked on St Helena's observatory at the time Percy's parents became involved with one another; they had presumably met the great colonial administrator.[23]

The boy was, by all accounts, a sickly child. The family's doctor, Dr Thomas Green of Parliament House, Peckham, would later write that Mary Trent Mapleton suffered with both heart and lung problems, and that her son had hereditary lung disease.[24]

With Henry Mapleton still employed in the Royal Navy, his wife Mary and their three children went to live with her brother Archibald Seale, a retired Superintendent of Lands for the East India Company based at St Helena, his wife Sarah and their children Francis and Annie; the 1861 census, taken a year later, captures this new family idyll. Even after Henry Mapleton retired and moved to a house in New Cross, South London, and his wife and daughters went to live with him, Percy Lefroy Mapleton remained with his uncle, aunt and cousins due to the delicate nature of his health, it being agreed that his aunt, Sarah Seale, could provide better care for the fragile child than his mother, who was herself ill. This remained the situation for the next fourteen years, Lefroy forging an unbreakable bond with his cousins Frank and Annie Seale.

Before he was ten years old, Lefroy's mother and uncle had died. Despite his delicate disposition, he received a good education, but the lack of any parental authority in his life resulted in his childish habit of lying going unchecked. His father Henry Mapleton showed no interest in his son, and went to live first with youngest daughter Julia at Islington in North London, where she was following a career as a nurse, and then with eldest daughter Mary, who by now had married, at West Drayton, west of London. Lefroy, his aunt Sarah and cousins Frank and Annie lived at 1 Alexandra Villas, Lausanne Road, just off Queen's

---

22   A covering note above a Central News clipping detailing Henry Mapleton's naval career held at the National Archives (TNA: PRO HO 144/83/A6404/94) avers that Henry Mapleton's brother-in-law George Voteur Seale could confirm the allegations as to Henry's mental health.

23   Following his arrest, some newspapers claimed that Sir John Lefroy was Percy's godfather, but there is no evidence of this.

24   Letter from Dr Thomas Green, dated 26 October 1881 supporting the petition to reprieve Lefroy on the grounds of insanity. TNA: PRO HO 144/83/A6404/56.

Introduction.

Road in Peckham.[25]

Following the completion of his education in August 1876, Lefroy seems to have floated along, lacking any firm direction. He attempted to start a career in journalism but was unable to find a break, and it seems that he began making a habit of obtaining money through deception from this time.

His health continued to cause him problems; he had reportedly been confined to his bed for more than a month with some form of lung disease.[26] On doctor's orders, at the end of 1877 he travelled to Ventnor, on the south coast of the Isle of Wight, spending several months there in the hope that the warmer climate might afford some relief from both bodily ailments and, worryingly, moral dilemmas. While there, Lefroy wrote a letter to cousin Annie in which he made reference to being tempted several times 'by the devil'. It was a strange letter, which would be used as evidence of an apparent unsound mind following his conviction for murder.

The following year it was decided that he should travel to Australia, again supposedly for the good of his health, but the timing of his departure – December 1878 – is close enough to the theatre scam of the previous September to allow us to question whether it was a coincidence, and indeed Lefroy himself admitted to the pangs of a burdened conscience. 'Until the vessel was actually out at sea,' he later wrote, 'I seemed to recognise in every man who looked at me a detective, such is the effect of a guilty mind, and not until the white cliffs of Old England were mere clouds on the horizon did I breathe a sigh of relief …'[27]

Although provided with two very good letters of introduction to important figures in the Australian establishment, Lefroy presented neither; his claim that he 'did not care to face then the searching questions which I not unnaturally imagined might be put to me, as to my arrival and abrupt departure' lending further weight to the suspected reason for his leaving British shores.

Instead of taking the opportunity to forge a career for himself in a thriving city where he was unknown, Lefroy seems to have whiled away his time in Melbourne simply waiting for funds to be sent enabling him to return home. This soon came to pass, and he departed Australia on 5 July 1879, arriving back in England on 30 September. He had, in fact, spent as much time travelling as he had been on Australian soil.

Lefroy had been away for just a little over nine months, but a lot had changed. His father had died of cirrhosis on 5 August, while his son was on his

---

25   1871 census.

26   Testimony of Thomas Clayton, husband of Lefroy's cousin Annie, at the magistrates' hearing. *Daily Telegraph*, 22 July 1881.

27   From Lefroy's autobiography; see Appendix XI.

return voyage.[28]

Lefroy's eldest sister Mary, who had married John Brickwood in February 1870 and had gone on to have seven children,[29] had filed for divorce in April 1879 following at least two years of abuse, both verbal and physical, at the hands of her husband. Since the early part of 1878, Brickwood had been carrying on an affair with one Marion Green, openly boasting about the fact to his wife and family.[30] In March 1879, he had become increasingly violent to both his wife and children, until at last Mary engaged the services of solicitor Thomas Duerdin Dutton of Pimlico and filed a petition for divorce the following month. The young solicitor carried out his duties well,[31] and Mary Mapleton was awarded £2 per month maintenance, with John Brickwood also ordered to pay costs.[32] The family moved to Southend, on the Essex coast, before daughter Alice was born on Boxing Day 1879, and by the time of the 1881 census Mary had found work as a governess.

Percy's second sister Eliza Julia was following a successful career as a nurse, and would rise to the position of Matron at the Fever Hospital at Islington by the time of the 1881 census. However, in early 1879, she had given birth to a son, seemingly out of wedlock. The boy was named Leon Gordon Liebie, and was baptized under that name in May 1884 when five years old. The only clue to the father's identity is on the baptism record, which gives him the same first name – Leon – and the occupation of surgeon. He is recorded as deceased.[33]

Following his arrival back in England, Lefroy called first on his sister Julia in Richmond, and under the circumstances presumably asked where his cousins could be found. He was directed to Cathcart Road, Wallington, about eleven miles away, where Annie now lived with her husband Thomas Clayton: the couple had married in 1873, and had welcomed two children by the time of Lefroy's return from Australia. Lefroy was invited into the household, and took up lodgings in a shared room with his other cousin, Frank Seale, who was at this

28 Henry Mapleton's death certificate.
29 Mary (1870–1957), John (1872–1948), Vincent (1873–75), Margaret (1875–1953), Ruth (1876–1962), Robert (1878–1940) and Alice (1879–1965).
30 In the 1881 census, John Brickwood is listed as living at Yerbury Road, Islington, with Marion 'Brickwood', described as his wife. By 1901 he was living with Alice Knight, sixteen years his junior, also described as his wife. They married in 1909.
31 Dutton was thirty-three at the time of Mary Brickwood's divorce petition.
32 Divorce Court File: 6248. Appellant: Mary Emily Beauchamp Brickwood. Respondent: John William Parker Brickwood (TNA: PRO J 77/225/6248).
33 Interestingly, a note written to support the petition to reprieve Lefroy claims that Eliza Julia Mapleton volunteered her services to nurse soldiers wounded in the Russo-Turkish War of 1877–78, and travelled to Bulgaria with an unnamed doctor of the Protestant Deaconess Institute, Tottenham. When she returned is unknown, but her son was born in January 1879.

Introduction.

time thirty-nine years old and an unmarried clerk in the City. The two became inseparable.

Evidence of an unhealthy mind surfaced. Although he appears to have been aware of her before travelling to Australia, since his return to England Lefroy had developed an infatuation with the young actress Violet Cameron, almost to the point of obsession. It would later be revealed that he had never met Miss Cameron, but it seems that she had become the driving force in his life, and according to some newspaper reports he carried her portrait around with him and claimed to his relatives that he was actually married to her.[34] Miss Cameron, who had first appeared on the stage in 1870 in *Faust and Marguerite* at the age of eight, had appeared at Drury Lane and the Adelphi Theatre as a child actor and enjoyed a highly successful career into her early adulthood.[35] She was two years younger than Lefroy, and, until her name became connected with his during his trial, she was completely unaware of his existence.

When a General Election was called in early 1880, Lefroy, still seeking gainful writing engagements, took Thomas Clayton up on his suggestion and offered his services to the Mid-Surrey Liberal party, supporting candidates Sydney Stern and Joseph Napier Higgins.[36] It was reported in the press that the Liberal committee met daily at the King's Arms in Carshalton, and later claimed that, as a consequence, Lefroy was well-known in the hostelry, to the point of always occupying 'one particular corner'. The claim would cause the landlord, George Jackson, to put pen to paper and send a letter to the *Daily News* to refute the allegation. The King's Arms had been run by his father before him, since 1851,[37] and Mr Jackson knew the effect that a little notoriety might have on his business:

> I shall feel obliged if you will correct a misstatement which appears in your paper of today. It there mentions that Lefroy was 'well known' at the King's Arms, and that he always occupied 'one favourite corner'. Now since the General Election, some fifteen months ago, when the Liberal committee was sitting here daily, and Lefroy was engaged as a canvasser, I am certain that he has not visited this house more than twenty times, when I have always observed that he was particularly abstemious. Even these occasional calls were made generally for the purpose of acquiring scraps of local news for the Wallington Herald; and as for

---

34   *Morpeth Herald*, 3 December 1881.

35   See a resumé of Violet Cameron's career up to the time of Lefroy's execution in Pascoe's Dramatic List (accessed via *Dundee Courier*, 29 November 1881).

36   Stern and Napier Higgins failed to oust the incumbent Conservative Members of Parliament, Sir Henry Peek and Sir James Lawrence, who enjoyed a majority of 2,533 following the 1880 election.

37   Business Directories and census returns, 1820–1901.

his occupying a favourite corner, it is quite untrue.[38]

It was alleged that Lefroy showed his face at the King's Arms on the evening before the murder of Mr Gold, when he obtained 3d of brandy but left a halfpenny owing. He attempted to borrow a sovereign from Mr Jackson, saying that he was owed money by *The Era*. Wisely, George Jackson refused the loan.[39]

In the two years since his return from Melbourne, Lefroy's life had entered a steady downward spiral, concurrent with the break-up of his family and failed aspirations of a career in journalism. By the spring of 1881, he had begun pawning any possessions of value – both his own and those belonging to others – and had resorted to petty theft. His abjection even began to attract attention:

> Lefroy, in the neighbourhood of Wallington and Carshalton, has latterly borne the nickname of 'Ananias', and in some quarters he is equally well known as 'Sloomy' ...

> During the last few days of his residence in Wallington, Lefroy pursued a plan with nearly every person with whom he could claim more than a passing acquaintanceship. He invited them to dine with him at a restaurant in the Strand, there to meet some celebrated people. If the invitation was accepted, he immediately tried to negotiate a loan of a few shillings.[40]

Lefroy's need for ready money was forcing him down ever-more-desperate paths; the next step was murder.

IV.

By contrast, the victim in this story, Mr Frederick Isaac Gold, had enjoyed a successful life. In 1881 he was sixty-four years old.[41] He had been born to wine merchant Isaac Gold of Wynyatt Street, Islington, North London, and his wife Hannah, *née* Browne, in 1817.[42] Within five years the family had relocated to the East End, with Isaac setting up shop as a tea dealer at 14 Whitechapel Road.[43] More children arrived: Elizabeth was born on 25 October 1825,[44] then

---

38   *Daily News*, 2 July 1881.
39   *The Western Times*, 1 July 1881
40   *Gloucester Journal*, 2 July 1881. Ananias was the Biblical liar. The *Webster Dictionary* definition of 'sloomy' is 'sleepy or sluggish'.
41   Baptised at St James, Clerkenwell, on 21 September 1817.
42   The couple were married at St James, Piccadilly, on 13 November 1814.
43   *Pigot's Directories* for 1821 and 1825.
44   Married John Beart on 19 January 1843; died 1873.

High Street, Carshalton

High Street, Carshalton, with The King's Arms on the left.
It was here that Lefroy visited while working for the local Liberal Party
during the 1880 General Election. The landlord of The King's Arms,
George Jackson, provided police with a sketch of Lefroy.

Author's collection

Mr Frederick Isaac Gold

Author's collection

another son, Thomas,[45] and finally Emma.[46]

By the age of 22, Frederick Gold was already taking his first steps running his own business, being listed in *Pigot's Directory* for that year at 6 Mile End Road. Two years later, in the 1841 census, he is recorded as head of the household, a baker, with his parents and two sisters now living under his roof; and two years after that he was at 5 Wentworth Place, Mile End Road – an address he would retain for twenty-five years.

On 13 April 1845, Frederick Gold married Lydia Matilda Wood at Trinity Church, Stepney. The banns show her living at Montague Terrace, Mile End Road, but she had been born at Walworth in South London, where her parents still lived.[47] As he continued to expand his business, Frederick Gold would open a baker's shop close to his in-laws, on the busy East Street.

Following the lead of his fellow successful local businessmen, Gold was initiated into the Freemasons on 3 August 1848, becoming a member of the Yarborough Lodge which had been founded on 18 April that year and consecrated on 6 July. The lodge met at the George Tavern on Commercial Road.[48]

Thomas Gold, eleven years Frederick's junior, would also follow a career as a baker. In 1861, he was listed as a master baker employing three men[49] and, according to Lydia Gold's later testimony, would also help his brother's business by collecting the weekly takings from the various shops. This practice stopped because, according to Mrs Gold, her brother in law 'had not behaved well in money matters'.[50]

By 1869, Frederick Gold was casting an eye on retirement. He was still at the same address, now renumbered as 77 Mile End Road,[51] but had sold a number of a shops and kept just the single business going at 145 East Street, Walworth, managed by a Mr and Mrs Cross. Mrs Gold believed her husband may have been keeping the shop on for his fourteen year old nephew, Thomas's son Frederick.[52] He and Lydia decided to retire to leafy Preston Park, a mile north of Brighton on the south coast, with Frederick travelling to Walworth

---

45   Baptised 8 June 1828.

46   Born 11 October 1832.

47   Lydia Matilda Wood was born in September 1823 and baptised on 21 December that year. Her parents were Samuel Wood, a cloth-tractor, and his wife Elizabeth Cooper. An older daughter, Mary Cooper Wood, was born in 1814. The family lived at York Place, Walworth.

48   Until 1863, when it moved to the Green Dragon at Spring Garden Place, Stepney. Mr Gold appears to have stopped paying his dues after 1852. Information from United Grand Lodge of England Freemason Membership Registers.

49   1861 census.

50   *Gloucester Journal*, 2 July 1881.

51   *Post Office Directory* for 1869.

52   *Gloucester Journal*, 2 July 1881.

once a week in order to collect the takings. Although now in his fifties and (in 1880s-terms) deemed as 'elderly', Mr Gold was a strong, robust man who enjoyed very good health, albeit of a nervous disposition. Lydia Gold would later state that her husband's

> constitution was thoroughly sound, but at the least thing he got nervous. He was too nervous a man to carry firearms, and never did such a thing. The only firearms we had was an old blunderbuss, which has not seen the light for the last thirty-six years. My husband had a great fear of anyone getting into his bedroom at night, and he always locked the door.[53]

The couple were not blessed with children, but enjoyed a comfortable life and were cherished members of the community. By the time of the 1871 census, they were living at 1 Clermont Road, Preston Park, and establishing themselves in their peaceful, sedate surroundings, while Thomas Gold had moved to the long-standing baker's shop at 77 Mile End Road with his wife Harriet and their son Frederick.

The lives of Mr Frederick Isaac Gold and Percy Lefroy Mapleton could hardly be more dissimilar; yet it was almost fated that they should meet. And on the afternoon of Monday 27 June 1881, they did – in the most tragic of circumstances.

V.

That day began early, with Mr Gold walking the short distance from his home to Preston Park railway station in order to take the 8.09 am train to Brighton. From there, he caught the 8.45 am express to London Bridge, arriving at 9.45 am. It was the usual routine he followed on a Monday, and he held a first class season ticket. He was dressed in his usual way, and although it was a fine morning he carried an umbrella under his coat, hanging from the armhole of his waistcoat, as was his custom. As usual, he wore an eye-glass, and his white-faced gold pocket watch attached to a long old-fashioned chain which hung around his neck. Mr Gold was a man of routine.

As Mr Gold was rushing toward the capital, Percy Lefroy Mapleton was still lying in his bed at 4 Cathcart Road, Wallington. Thomas Clayton, the husband of Lefroy's cousin Annie, went to his room to ask when three items belonging to him which Lefroy had pledged at a pawnbroker's shop would be returned to him; Lefroy promised to redeem them before the end of the day. Frank Seale,

---

53   Lydia Gold's testimony at the inquest, as reported in the *Gloucester Journal*, 2 July 1881.

Clermont-Road and Preston-Station.

Clermont Road, where Mr and Mrs Gold lived.
In the distance is Preston Park Station.

Author's collection

Railway Terrace, Wallington.
In the middle is the stationery shop owned by Albert Ellis,
where Lefroy swindled shopboy Frederick Pink out of the contents of the till.

Author's collection

Introduction.

Annie Clayton's brother, shared the room with Lefroy, but he had already left for work at Messrs J. T. Hutchinson on Gresham Street in the City, where he was employed as a clerk.

Clayton departed for his own job as a distiller's clerk, and Lefroy was left alone. He desperately needed money, and fast.

Just before ten o'clock, nearby stationer Albert Ellis received a visit from one of Annie Clayton's children.[54] The child handed Mr Ellis a letter requesting his attendance at 4 Cathcart Road; Mr Ellis recognised Lefroy's hand, having known him as a regular customer for eighteen months. The missive asked Mr Ellis to take an order from Annie Clayton, who was heavily pregnant. Not unreasonably, the stationer went to nearby Cathcart Road as requested, leaving his young assistant Frederick Pink in charge of the shop, which was close to Wallington railway station.

On arrival, Ellis was greeted by the Claytons' servant Joanna Chamberlain, and was handed a letter supposedly from Annie but in fact again in Lefroy's handwriting. As he read the note, Mr Ellis heard the gate click and, looking out of a window, saw the top of Lefroy's hat as he left the house.

When Ellis arrived back at his shop a few minutes later, the seventeen year old Pink told him that Lefroy had just left, having apparently settled his outstanding account of £1 7s 6d with two sovereigns which were given to him in a sealed envelope bearing Mr Ellis's name. Pink gave Lefroy all the money in the till – thirteen shillings – as change.

Mr Ellis opened the envelope. It contained two sovereign-sized worthless Hanoverian medals – thousands of which were issued in the wake of the Battle of Waterloo – a solitary shilling, and a blank piece of paper.

At Lefroy's trial, the gullibility of Frederick Pink was commented on by counsel – 'Are you often left alone in the shop?' – which drew laughter from those in court. That Mr Ellis usually sent his assistant to sell newspapers at the entrance to nearby Wallington station rather than trusting him behind the counter should not be a surprise.

But by the time Ellis emptied the paltry contents of the envelope into his expectant palm, Lefroy was long gone, next to be seen at London Bridge.

VI.

Mr Gold, meanwhile, was at his bakery shop in Walworth. He had arrived

---

54   This is how the messenger was described at the trial, but as two of Annie Clayton's three children were less than three years old, it is probable that the visitor was seven year old Melville, a particular favourite of Lefroy's.

at around 10.30 am. The manager of the shop, Mrs Catherine Cross, handed over the takings for the previous week, the amount – £38 in gold, five shillings in silver and a penny – written on a pink slip and deposited into a small bag. Bidding Mrs Cross a good day, Gold left the shop. She believed he was going to order some flour.

Whether he did so is unknown. What is certain is that Mr Gold headed north towards Whitechapel, where he retained an account with the London County and Westminster Bank at 130 Whitechapel High Street. Had he taken the most direct route, along Borough High Street, he would have passed Messrs Adams and Hillstead, a pawnbrokers at number 25, where at that moment Lefroy was redeeming a pistol.

Mr Gold entered the bank at around 1.00 pm, being attended by cashier Alfred Gilbert. He paid in £38, and made no withdrawal. The week's business complete, he prepared himself for the return journey to Preston Park. But, at some point, while in the vicinity of Whitechapel – either before or after visiting the London County and Westminster Bank – he was seen on the nearby Minories in deep conversation with his brother Thomas. This seemingly brief exchange would later present trouble for the younger brother.

He next appeared at 1.50 pm, at London Bridge railway station. Ticket collector William Franks knew Mr Gold well, and spoke to him on the platform as he was about to board the 2.00 pm Brighton express train, which was ready to depart. Mr Gold took his seat in the first class compartment of a composite carriage at 1.55 pm. He settled himself into the middle seat, facing the engine.

At two minutes to two, Percy Lefroy Mapleton appeared on the platform, walking briskly towards the front of the train and looking in through the carriage windows as he did so. In the front carriage, he saw a lady and a gentleman speaking, so he turned on his heel and walked back to the previous carriage, where Mr Gold was sitting. He fumbled with the door, and ticket collector Franks opened it for him. Lefroy offered up his ticket, a single from London to Brighton. Franks closed the door and watched Lefroy take the seat in the off-side corner, his back to the engine.[55]

Two minutes late, the train slowly pulled out of London Bridge.

At the first stop, East Croydon, guard Thomas Watson got out of the engine and stood on the platform. He had been employed by the London, Brighton and South Coast Railway for twenty years. He looked into the first class compartment

---

[55] This version of events is taken from William Franks' testimony at the trial, but in his autobiography Lefroy states that he sat first in a different carriage, where his intended victim was a man eating strawberries, only to be put off by the man's demeanour and change carriages at East Croydon to that in which Mr Gold was travelling. See Appendix XI. The strawberry-eating passenger, George Austin, later corroborated Lefroy's claim. See Appendix XII.

East Street, Walworth.
The frontage with the white canopy to the right of
The Rising Sun is No. 145, site of Mr Gold's baker's shop.

The London County and Westminster Bank,
130 Whitechapel High Street, where Mr Gold deposited the week's takings
before returning to London Bridge station.

By permission of Historic England Archive

and saw Mr Gold, whom he had known for the best part of a decade, sitting with a large white handkerchief loosely thrown over his head. This was not unusual: 'He used to travel by himself, or with very few people, as he said people would talk to him,' his wife later admitted. 'He also had a habit of closing his eyes to prevent people talking to him. He used to remove his hat and put a small cap on his head.'[56]

As the train entered the Merstham tunnel around ten minutes later, a Brighton chemist named William Gibson, travelling with his young son in the compartment next to Mr Gold's, heard four or five loud bangs, which he took to be fog signals. The reports followed one after the other, all in the space of five or six seconds.

The train continued on its journey.

VII.

At twenty minutes past three the train pulled into Preston Park station, a mile from Brighton. It had travelled non-stop from East Croydon, although it had slowed down just north of Hassock's Gate for a brief period in response to a stop signal.

As the train ground to a halt, ticket collector Joseph Stark approached the second composite carriage. Inside, alone, sat Percy Lefroy Mapleton. His face and neck were smeared with blood, and there was a clot beside one ear. There was blood between his fingers, blood upon his clothes, blood in the carriage, and blood upon the train's footboard, which also bore the marks of bloody fingerprints. The carriage was otherwise empty.

Lefroy stepped from the carriage, and asked for help. A second ticket collector, Richard Gibson, approached. The stricken passenger said he had been attacked by two men, one an elderly gentleman and the second a 'countryman', and was desperate for medical attention. Guard Watson left the train and joined them. Scanning Lefroy's clothing, he noticed a length of chain, between four and seven inches long, hanging from one of his shoes. Taking the end between his fingers and giving it a gentle tug, a small gold watch popped out. Lefroy appeared to be as surprised as anyone at the appearance of the watch, but it would later be claimed that he had concealed it there for its own safety - and his - when he entered the carriage and saw his two travelling companions. At the eventual trial, defence barrister Montagu Williams would offer a different, even more bizarre explanation.

Lefroy repeated his story of having been 'murderously assaulted' and,

56   *Gloucester Journal*, 2 July 1881.

Lefroy.

indeed, shot at, and appeared oblivious to Watson's attempt to hand back the watch, so the guard placed it on the seat.

Station master Alfred Hall arrived and ordered Gibson to escort Lefroy to Brighton, where he could be seen by the superintendent there. The passenger and the ticket collector got into the bloody carriage, and the Brighton express resumed its journey toward its original intended destination.

Mrs Lydia Gold, sitting at home less than half a mile away on Clermont Road, had quite possibly heard the train pull into Preston Park station. It was the service which her husband usually caught after completing his business in London. Perhaps she boiled some water for a pot of tea, and waited.

VIII.

As Lefroy was being escorted to Brighton, a platelayer employed by the London, Brighton and South Coast Railway Company named Thomas Jennings was walking through the Balcombe tunnel with his young nephew. By the light of their naphtha lamp, they saw the body of a large man laying on its back. The face, which had been badly beaten, was partly covered by a coat. The right arm was crossed over the left breast, and the left arm folded underneath the back. One boot remained on the body; the other was missing. Jennings thought the body felt slightly warm to the touch.

The nephew, William Jennings, went to telegraph news of the gruesome discovery, and shortly afterwards PC George Lewis of the Sussex Constabulary duly arrived and searched the body and the surrounding area. In the pockets of the coat he found a pocket-book, a rail season ticket and two receipts. The knees of the trousers were torn and bloodied. Six yards from the body, Lewis found a broken eye-glass. His pocket-watch, that fundamental accessory of the Victorian gentleman, was missing.

The body was removed from the tracks and taken to the stables at the Railway Inn near Balcombe station, where it was seen by local doctors Byass and Hall, along with Scotland Yard's divisional surgeon Dr Thomas Bond, who would give details of the injuries:

> There were excoriations and bruises, and the skull was badly fractured. The fracture was such as might have been caused by the body coming into violent contact with the ground. The left hand and face were badly cut, as if by some sharp instrument. These cuts must have been inflicted during life, and have bled freely. There was a wound in the corner of the left eye, about half an inch deep, and the mucous membrane of the eye was very much injected with blood. There was a bullet mark under the ear, and a bullet was extracted from the spine, into

Top: The approach to London Bridge Station

Bottom: Hassock's Gate Station, where the Brighton express slowed
and Lefroy claimed his attacker escaped.

Author's collection

Top: Preston Park Station
Bottom: Brighton Station

Author's collection

Introduction.

which it had passed. It was a small bullet such as would fit a small revolver. Such a bullet passing into the neck would cause momentary insensibility. The immediate cause of the death of Mr Gold was syncope, coming from the shock and loss of blood. There would be little loss of blood from the shot, but a great deal from the knife wounds, of which there were fourteen on different parts of the body.[57]

It was clear that this man had not been knocked down by a train; rather, he had been attacked while on board, and either fell or was pushed out of the carriage door as it passed through the Balcombe tunnel.

IX.

During the short journey to Brighton with Gibson, Lefroy elaborated on his story. He had been fired at three or four times, he said, and pointed to a wound on the top of his head where he said he'd been struck with a blunt instrument. His assailant had been the countryman, and not the elderly gentleman. He did not know what had happened to either. Lefroy gave Gibson his ticket, and also his name and address: Arthur Lefroy, of 4 Cathcart Road, Wallington.

On arrival at Brighton, Gibson took his injured charge to Superintendent Anscombe's office. There they saw Mr Hooper, the clerk, to whom Lefroy once more related his tale. Brighton platform inspector Mr Everett[58] came into the office, followed shortly afterwards by Thomas Watson, who had examined the carriage once it had arrived at its destination and was taken into sidings. In his hand he had two false sovereigns – Hanoverian medals similar to those found by Mr Ellis in an envelope at the stationer's shop in Wallington – which he'd found in the carriage, one under a seat and the other in a hole of the coconut matting on the floor. He offered them to Lefroy, who refused to take them, saying they were not his. Watson handed them to PC James Martin, who had by now joined them in the superintendent's office. Lefroy complained of feeling unwell and asked to see a doctor; the officers were ordered to take him to the Town Hall, where there was a police office at which he could make a statement before being taken for medical attention.

There, Lefroy gave a statement to police clerk Samuel Thompson, and said he was visiting Brighton to see Mrs Nye Chart, owner of the Theatre Royal.

---

57 *Berrow's Worcester Journal*, 12 November 1881; *The Newcastle Courant*, 11 November 1881.
58 Mr Everett had his fifteen seconds of fame when he was called to give evidence on the third day of the trial. However, when it was discovered that he was the wrong Mr Everett – he was Joseph Everett, a platform inspector from Argyle Road in Brighton but the court wanted Joseph Everett, a ticket collector from London Bridge – the witness was asked to step down without giving any testimony at all.

Lefroy.

He was then taken to the Sussex County Hospital, where he was seen by acting house surgeon Benjamin Hall. PC Martin set off to see Mrs Nye Chart.

After Lefroy's wounds were cleaned, it became apparent that the extent of his injuries was comparatively minor. There was a contusion about the size of a shilling on his forehead, a graze at the back of his right ear, and six small cuts on the crown of his head. Dr Hall believed the wounds could have been caused by an umbrella, or the barrel of a small pistol. Lefroy told the surgeon that he had been quietly reading his newspaper when he was suddenly shot at. This time, his assailant was described as an old man, with the countryman taking no part in the attack. After wrapping a bandage around Lefroy's head, Dr Hall suggested that he should remain in the hospital overnight as a precaution, but the injured man was having none of it; he had important business back in London that evening, he said.

Lefroy was returned to the Town Hall police office, where he was searched and further questioned. He now refused to see Mrs Nye Chart: 'Not in this state'. Chief Constable James Terry told Lefroy that Mrs Nye Chart was 'a very nice lady, and she would not mind seeing him,' but the wounded man refused, again saying he had an appointment that evening. They returned to Superintendent Anscombe's office at Brighton Railway Station, where Lefroy was asked whether he was badly injured. 'I should think I am, having four or five bullets in my head,' was the reply.

Detective Sergeants George Holmes and William Howland of the Metropolitan Police, attached to the London, Brighton and South Coast Railway, set about examining the possessions of their strange guest. In Lefroy's left hand coat pocket were twelve or fourteen shillings; in his trouser pocket, a white-faced watch smeared with blood. A leather pocket-book was also found, and, as Holmes was about to take a look inside, Lefroy exclaimed, 'That is my private property'. The detective quietly returned the notebook. Also found in his coat pocket were two or three Hanoverian coins. With similar coins having been found in the carriage, the question was begging to be asked – what did Lefroy know of them? Quick as a flash, the reply came: 'I know nothing about them. I must have got them when playing whist last night with my friends.'

The interrogation over, Lefroy was allowed to return to Wallington. He was escorted by Detectives Holmes and Howland, and the trio boarded the 6.10 pm train to the capital.

*

Mrs Gold, meanwhile, was still awaiting her husband's return. He had not

Introduction.

been on the 3.20 pm train, nor the 6.15 pm, and she began to get anxious. At about 8.00 pm, she walked the short distance to Preston Park Station to find out whether there had been an accident, but was told by the station master that there had not been. She returned home to recommence waiting.

At five minutes past ten, she received a telegram from the station master at Balcombe informing her that a man had been found dead, with papers on him in the name of F. I. Gold. She went to Balcombe immediately, accompanied by family friend Mr Thomas Lee Hollis. Despite the horrific injuries it bore, he had no trouble identifying the body.

*

On the train to Wallington, Detective Sergeant George Holmes rode with Lefroy in a first class carriage, while Detective Sergeant Howland travelled in the guard's brake so that he could more easily make enquiries at each stopping station along the way.

At Balcombe, Howland stepped onto the platform and spoke with the station master. He approached the carriage in which Holmes was sitting and broke the news that a body had been found in the tunnel. Just a few moments after Lefroy and the detectives had departed from Brighton, a telegraph had been received at Superintendent Anscombe's office breaking the news of the discovery. The Superintendent immediately telegraphed the station master at Balcombe.

The station master at Three Bridges, Mr Brown, had also been informed of the discovery and was waiting to board the train at Balcombe. He entered into conversation with Holmes – but still the train continued on its route.

It eventually stopped at East Croydon, and Lefroy and Holmes got out. The station master passed a telegram to the detective, which read: 'Tell Inspector Holmes to take number of watch on wounded man in 6.10 up train, as man found had no watch.'

Lefroy and Holmes took a cab from East Croydon to Lefroy's lodgings at Cathcart Road. Lefroy nonchalantly commented that, 'It is a very sad affair, and I hope the man will be caught. The Scotland Yard people should be informed at once.'

The men went into the house and entered the drawing room. It was, by now, 9.00 pm. Holmes asked Lefroy for a statement, which this time was written down. Thomas Clayton entered the room. Acting on the telegram received at East Croydon, the detective asked Lefroy for the serial number of his watch, receiving the confident answer, '56312'. Unfortunately, when the watch found in his shoe was opened, it revealed an entirely different number.

Lefroy.

Sergeant Holmes took down an address where Lefroy might be found the following day, and then bade him and Thomas Clayton a good evening. He left the house and walked the short distance to Wallington Station.

When he arrived, he was handed a telegram ordering him in no uncertain terms not to lose sight of Lefroy. Holmes hurried back to Cathcart Road, and stood guard outside number 4 until Detective Sergeant Howland and Sergeant Charles Tobutt joined him. One went to the back door, the other inside to apprehend Lefroy. They returned empty-handed. George Holmes had been absent from 4 Cathcart Road for six minutes, and Percy Lefroy Mapleton had vanished into thin air.

X.

Three days later, a little after eleven o'clock on the morning of Thursday 30 June, the dishevelled fugitive knocked on the door of 32 Smith Street in Stepney - this was, for the East End, a quiet road, and it was comprised of tidy two-storey terraced houses. He had seen a notice in a window offering a room to rent, and after some negotiation with the landlady, Mrs Sarah Bickers, he agreed to take the room that afternoon. It was to be his sanctuary for eleven days.

Where Lefroy had been between slipping away from Cathcart Road and arriving at Smith Street is uncertain, although in his autobiography, written while awaiting his execution, he claimed to have walked from Wallington to Fleet Street, arriving around 1.00 am and spending the night in the Sussex Hotel under the name of 'Lee'. He apparently spent Tuesday 28 June wandering aimlessly around Victoria Park and slept that night at a coffee house close to Blackfriars Bridge, with Wednesday bringing a day on Blackheath and Greenwich Park followed by a late return to Blackfriars Bridge, where he threw Mr Gold's watch into the Thames. The following morning, the Thursday, he meandered his way to the East End and the welcome anonymity of Smith Street.[59]

It was another astonishing coincidence: Lefroy had exited the bloody carriage five hundred yards from Mr Gold's home in Preston Park, and was now in hiding just half a mile from his victim's former residence on the Mile End Road.

Sarah Bickers was completely unaware of her new lodger's infamy. He had reinvented himself as Mr George Clark, claiming to have just arrived from Liverpool. He was an engraver, he said, who required a quiet room in which to continue his work free from disruption. He had no luggage, explaining that it would follow in a day or two (it never arrived). And, despite his claim to be

59   See Lefroy's autobiography in Appendix XI.

Introduction.

spending all hours working, nobody ever saw the engraving machine, which always seemed have been put away just as Mrs Bickers or her daughter entered the room with the lodger's meals.

Still, Mrs Bickers was no doubt used to the occasionally eccentric ways of those temporarily sharing her home. The family had lived at 32 Smith Street for nine years, and originally consisted of Mrs Bickers, her husband James and their three daughters. But James Bickers had passed away five years ago,[60] and elder daughters Sarah[61] and Caroline[62] had married – both apparently to former lodgers of number 32 – and moved a short distance away, so that by June 1881 it was just Mrs Bickers and her twenty-four year old daughter Jane[63] left at number 32 trying to make ends meet. They had taken in lodgers since the death of James Bickers, offering three rooms for rent, and at the time of the 1881 census (taken on 3 April, twelve weeks before Lefroy's arrival), these were occupied by a J. W. Goodfellow, a shorthand writer from Merthyr Tydfil, Mr Frederick Evans, a commercial traveller from Chelsea, and Harry Watlings, another traveller from London.[64]

'George Clark' settled into his room, upstairs at the front, and drew the blinds.

*

The inquest into Mr Gold's death was presided over by Wynne Baxter, the coroner for Sussex Eastern Division.[65] It had opened at Balcombe on 29

60 James Philip Bickers was born in 1822 at Millbank. He married Sarah Thompson on 20 August 1848 at St Martin in the Fields, Westminster, and the couple began raising a family at Chigwell, and had moved to Leinster Street, Paddington by the time of the 1861 census. In 1871, the family are recorded at Exmouth Street, Whitechapel, and around 1872 moved to 1 Providence Place, Bancroft Road, Mile End. James Bickers had a variety of jobs: he was a butler in 1861, a messenger in 1871 and a brewer's messenger at the time of his death on 27 February 1876, at 32 Smith Street. His death certificate records the cause of death as 'asthma exhaustion'.

61 Sarah Emma Bickers was born in 1854 at Chigwell, Essex. She married James Anderson, a brewery clerk from Berwick-on-Tweed, on 8 June 1878. The marriage register records both bride and groom as residing at 32 Smith Street. At the time of Lefroy's arrest, the couple were living nearby at 77 Whitechapel Road.

62 Caroline Bickers was born in 1855, also at Chigwell. She married William Farnworth, a customs officer from Liverpool, on 3 November 1877. Again, both were residing at the family home at the time. The couple moved just a mile away to Antill Road, Mile End.

63 Jane Bickers was born at Chigwell in 1856. She is often named 'Clara' in newspaper reports, but census returns clearly give her correct name as Jane, which is also how she signed the 1878 marriage record of her sister Sarah as a witness.

64 At least one of these gentlemen had, of course, left 32 Smith Street before Lefroy arrived on 30 June, creating the vacancy filled by the wanted man.

65 Wynne Edwin Baxter was born on 1 May 1844 at Lewes, Sussex. In 1868, he married Kate Bliss Parker, the union producing six children. He was called to the Bar in 1867, and in 1875 moved to London where he established a long-running solicitor's practice. He was elected coroner for East Sussex in January 1880,

June, two days after his murder, and concluded on Thursday 7 July, with the jury deliberating for just twenty minutes before returning a verdict of 'Wilful Murder against Arthur Lefroy, alias Mapleton'. Interrupting proceedings midway through the inquest was solicitor Thomas Dutton, who told Baxter on 4 July that he had been instructed by Mary Brickwood to watch proceedings on behalf of the family.[66] His smooth handling of her divorce two years earlier had evidently paid dividends.

Lefroy's victim, Mr Gold, had been finally laid to rest on 4 July, when he was buried at the Extra-Mural Cemetery just outside Brighton. Four mourning coaches followed the hearse on its sad journey through the streets of Preston Park. The blinds of many houses and businesses lining the route were drawn as a mark of respect. It was estimated that four or five thousand people witnessed the simple service given by Reverend Allan Freeman at the cemetery,[67] with many scattering flowers on to the coffin as it was lowered into the ground.[68]

On 30 July, probate was granted to the deceased's widow, Lydia; she would tell reporters that her husband had been rather secretive in money matters, and she might therefore have been surprised to learn that his personal estate was worth £1,690 9s 11d.

XI.

Meanwhile, the search for Lefroy was intensifying. Despite their best efforts, the police were unable to obtain a photograph of the fugitive and resorted to having a likeness drawn of their quarry. This was supplied by George Jackson, the owner of the King's Arms in Carshalton,[69] who certainly had had ample opportunity to observe the features of the wanted man. On the same day, it was widely announced that 'a medical man at Carshalton, who is a clever caricaturist, possesses a life-like sketch of Lefroy, showing him wearing his hat in his favourite fashion – at the back of his head'.[70]

The sketch, shown opposite, is most certainly in the style of a caricature.

---

a post he held for seven years. In 1885, Baxter was elected deputy coroner for the City of London and Borough of Southwark, and the following year as coroner for the County of Middlesex. His title changed in 1892 to coroner for the City of London (Eastern District) and the Liberty of the Tower of London, a post he held until his death in 1920. He presided over an estimated forty thousand inquests, including well-known cases such as Joseph Merrick, Miriam Angel (murdered by Israel Lipski - see NBT 84), and ten victims named in the Whitechapel murders files. See Wood, A., 'Inquest, London', *Ripperologist* 61 (September 2005).

66 *Evening Standard,* 5 July 1881.
67 *The People's Journal,* 9 July 1881.
68 *Lloyd's Weekly London Newspaper,* 10 July 1881.
69 *Derby Daily Telegraph,* 30 June 1881.
70 Ibid.

The caricature sketch of Lefroy.

from From City to Fleet Street by J. Hall Richardson

MURDER.

£200 REWARD.

WHEREAS, on Monday, June 27th, ISAAC FREDERICK GOULD was murdered on the London Brighton and South Coast Railway, between Three Bridges and Balcombe, in East Sussex.

AND WHEREAS a Verdict of WILFUL MURDER has been returned by a Coroner's Jury against

PERCY LEFROY MAPLETON,

whose Portrait and Handwriting are given hereon,--

and who is described as being 22 years of age, height 5 ft 8 or 9 in., very thin, hair (cut short) dark, small dark whiskers; dress, dark frock coat, and shoes, and supposed low black hat (worn at back of head), had scratches from fingers on throat, several wounds on head, the dressing of which involved the cutting of hair, recently lodged at 4, Cathcart Road, Wallington, was seen at 9.30 a.m., 28th ult., with his head bandaged, at the Fever Hospital, Liverpool Road, Islington. Had a gold open-faced watch (which he is likely to pledge). "Maker. Griffiths, Mile End Road, No 16261."

One Half of the above Reward will be paid by Her Majesty's Government, and One Half by the Directors of the London Brighton and South Coast Railway to any person (other than a person belonging to a Police Force in the United Kingdom) who shall give such information as shall lead to the discovery and apprehension of the said PERCY LEFROY MAPLETON, or others, the Murderer, or Murderers, upon his or their conviction; and the Secretary of State for the Home Department will advise the grant of Her Majesty's gracious PARDON to any accomplice, not being the person who actually committed the Murder, who shall give such evidence as shall lead to a like result.

Information to be given to the Chief Constable of East Sussex, Lewes, at any Police Station, or to

The Director of Criminal Investigations, Gt. Scotland Yard.

JULY 4th, 1881.

The handbill produced from the sketch.

from Masters of Crime by Guy Logan

Introduction.

Whether the 'medical man' had seen George Jackson's sketch of Lefroy and enhanced it, or simply produced his own independent depiction, is unclear, but somehow the drawing found its way into the hands of the *Daily Telegraph*, who decided to include a version of it in their edition of the following day, 1 July 1881. In doing so, they made history by publishing the first likeness of a wanted man.

From the first, reaction to the *Telegraph*'s decision to publish the drawing was mixed. The first published comment appeared in that evening's *Birmingham Mail*, who seemed supportive of its intentions:

> Rather a novel departure in London daily journalism is to be found in today's *Telegraph*. The railway murder is still the topic of the hour, and everything that relates to the supposed murderer Lefroy or Mapleton – whichever he may be called – is seized with avidity by the sensation-loving public; so today the *Telegraph* comes out with a sketch portrait of the fugitive by a gentleman who knew him, and is said to have had many opportunities of noting his characteristics. If this sketch is anything like the individual it is intended to represent, we are bound to say that Mr Lefroy, *alias* Mapleton, is not a prepossessing young man. The distinguishing features of the portrait are a low forehead, long straight nose, small receding chin, abnormal development of that part of the head where, phrenologists tell us, the animal passions lie, and a vacant, almost idiotic stare. The idea, though it may be objected to as imitating too closely the *Police News* style, is not a bad one, and as the assurance is given that the likeness is excellent, it may be made the means of assisting the detectives in their search for the culprit.[71]

In fact, alongside their sketch, the *Daily Telegraph* had also given a more detailed account of the fugitive's physical attributes, using a description provided by the police:

> Age 22, middle height, very thin, sickly appearance, scratches on throat, wounds on head, probably clean shaved, low felt hat, black coat, teeth much discoloured ... He is very round shouldered, and his thin overcoat hangs in awkward folds about his spare figure. His forehead and chin are both receding. He has a slight moustache, and very small dark whiskers. His jawbones are prominent, his cheeks sunken and sallow, and his teeth fully exposed when laughing. His upper lip is thin and drawn inwards. His eyes are grey and large. His gait is singular; he is inclined to slouch and when not carrying a bag, his left hand is usually in his pocket. He generally carries a crutch stick.

Scotland Yard resorted to using the *Telegraph* likeness in their reward poster,

---

71   *Birmingham Mail*, 1 July 1881.

Lefroy.

released on 4 July. Some £200 – half from the Government and half from the directors of the London, Brighton and South Coast Railway – was on offer to anyone who could provide information which resulted in the apprehension of Lefroy.

It did not take long for the novelty of the situation to cause problems. The offer of a reward, combined with the supposed means to identify the criminal, led to innocent members of the public, who had but a passing resemblance to the drawing, finding themselves in danger of arrest or even worse.

A reporter from the *Northern Echo* lamented:

> One of the police officials engaged in the hunt tells me that an incalculable amount of trouble has been given by the publication in the *Daily Telegraph* of an imaginary sketch purporting to be the portrait of Lefroy. This was drawn partly from memory by an acquaintance of Lefroy's and was touched up by a gifted artist. The result was a sketch of a very common criminal type, and it is positively appalling to find how many prototypes it has in real life. It was less like Lefroy than many innocent people to whose arrest it led, and, apart from the actual inconvenience to private individuals and trouble to authorities, it worked in the direction of defeating the ends of justice by withdrawing the public from the right scent.[72]

This 'inconvenience to private individuals' rapidly became commonplace.

On 5 July, four days after the sketch of Lefroy was published, an American gentleman walked into a police station and complained that he was constantly being watched on account of his supposed similarity to the drawing; he begged that he might be allowed to take up residence at the station for his own safety.[73]

A Mr Percy Harding was enjoying a walk in Kennington Park on the same day when he was spotted by two local officers, who thought he resembled Lefroy. Not satisfied with the name and address he gave, they took him to the nearest police station where he was able to convince them of his identity. Mr Harding seems to have been very like Lefroy; even his wife was surprised that such a mistake had not been made earlier.[74]

A rather more harrowing experience was supposedly endured by a Member of Parliament 'representing a Northern borough' who apparently looked like the wanted man. In the words of the London correspondent of the *Sheffield Independent*, who had his ear on parliamentary gossip, a striking similarity had

---

72 *Northern Echo*, 11 July 1881.
73 *Daily Telegraph*, 6 July 1881.
74 *Buckingham Advertiser and Free Press*, 16 July 1881. Harding took Detective Sergeant John Holmes to court for assault. Although he agreed to let the matter drop following an apology from Holmes, the detective had left the force in the week between arrest and court appearance – whether of his own volition was not reported.

been noted:

> He is tall, stoops a little, has a thin face, sallow complexion, and black moustache, and in other respects more or less faintly resembles that work of art, which the *Daily Telegraph* produced the other day. The Hon. Member, after the fashion common among our hard-working legislators, went out of town on Saturday, intending to spend Sunday at a watering-place on the south coast. On his arrival he immediately found himself the object of embarrassing attention on the part of the railway officials. The porters whispered amongst each other, and brought up higher officials to look at him. The cabmen on the ranks stood up on their boxes to inspect him, and when he walked into the town a crowd gathered at his heels. He was not long left in doubt as to the meaning of this attention, and made as quickly as possible for an hotel. But here again the same thing happened. The waiters stared at him, the chambermaids regarded him with visible apprehension, the landlord was dubious, and a crowd began to gather at the door. He took an early opportunity of communicating his name to the landlord, but this made no difference. Anyone could assume a well-known name. So, after waiting in his private room till the hour of the departure of the next train, he fled from the place, and spent Sunday at home, where he is better known.[75]

Conversely, the notoriety of the fugitive resulted, perhaps unsurprisingly, in some young men actually claiming to be Lefroy, despite the apparent danger which might result from such a foolhardy declaration. A Mrs Cook and her daughter were walking through Bostall Wood near Woolwich on Monday 4 July when a man suddenly appeared with a revolver and shouted, 'I am Lefroy!' He fired, and the bullet passed between the two women, who rushed back to the nearby cottage in which they lived. Assistance was swift in coming, and the young man was detained until a PC Gladwell arrived to take him into custody. The prisoner insisted to the officer that he *was* Lefroy, and while passing through Plumstead on the way to the police station repeated the claim to mystified onlookers. Once safely under lock and key, the truth was discovered. The young man was in reality Frederick Schwartz, an Austrian who had been employed at the Vienna Restaurant on the Strand before being dismissed for drunkenness. The cause of his problems had reared its head again, for it was revealed at the magistrates' hearing that Herr Schwartz's strange behaviour in Bostall Wood had been prompted by his consuming half a bottle of brandy.[76]

The continued absence of Lefroy himself led some to believe he may have

---

75   *Dundee Courier*, 11 July 1881. The whole tale was circumspectly qualified by the reporter, who nonetheless found it impossible to resist the urge to share it: 'There is a story current in the House which I would not like to vouch for. But if not true it is well invented.'

76   *Evening Citizen*, 6 July 1881.

committed suicide. A correspondent wrote to the *Daily Telegraph* to say that he knew Lefroy, and had met him at a restaurant near Charing Cross on 13 June, a fortnight before the murder. The writer claimed that Lefroy had shown him a small bottle of prussic acid, stating, 'If you're tired of your life, I've something here to suit you'.[77]

On the same day, a letter sent to *The Times* suggested that Lefroy, having considerable knowledge of the theatre, may have been escaping capture by dressing as a woman.[78]

Supposed sightings were made in the south coast towns of Folkestone, Shoreham and Littlehampton, and even in Calais. He was reportedly seen in Chester and Leeds in the north.

The truth was that nobody knew where Percy Lefroy Mapleton was.

The distress caused to numerous innocent young men purely because they looked like the missing murderer was neatly described in one newspaper editorial, under the heading 'The Effect of Publishing a Portrait':

> One of the circumstances connected with the railway murder which will be remembered with most astonishment is the number of young gentlemen with long noses, billycock hats and wounded heads developed by the crime. From all directions reports are arriving that persons closely resembling the description of Lefroy have been followed, or watched, or arrested. The very flattering portrait that appeared in the *Daily Telegraph* has generated an increased mob of long-nosed youths with receding chins and foreheads, wounded scalps, and unpleasant hunted looks. One could hardly suppose, after contemplating the pleasing portrait we have referred to, that the type of face attributed by the artist to Lefroy was a common one. Indeed, in the interests of the whole race of Englishmen, one would anxiously hope that the face was a quite impossible one. Yet, to judge by the arrests, it must belong to a great number of young gentlemen, and, what is stranger still, to young gentlemen with wounded heads. One curious hint, at all events, is furnished by this dark tragedy – *i.e.*, that if a man wants to look like a murderer he need only get a friend to sketch his face from memory, and publish the likeness in a daily paper.[79]

Another newspaper (reserving their thoughts until after the fugitive had been captured) voiced their own concerns over the *Telegraph*'s decision to publish the controversial likeness, and expressed the hope that Lefroy would not be immortalised in the obvious place for his kind:

---

77   *Daily Telegraph*, 6 July 1881.
78   *Glasgow Evening Citizen*, 6 July 1881.
79   *Newcastle Chronicle*, published in the *Dundee Evening Telegraph* of 5 July 1881.

Introduction.

As for the likeness of Lefroy which the *Daily Telegraph* glorifies itself for having procured, it was, they say, such a caricature that it was enough to throw the police off the scent. Now that he is disposed of, I hope we shall have no more sensational details on the trial; and as he is, after all, only a vulgar criminal we shall perhaps hear the last of him without that aggravation, a place on the Baker Street Chamber of Horrors.[80]

Lefroy's eventual appearance within the infamous room of wax models of murderers and thieves at Madame Tussaud's was a certainty, but at least the Baker Street attraction had the decency to wait until after the trial. Smaller provincial exhibitions, using the *Telegraph* drawing as their model, trumpeted their own displays, with Reynold's Waxworks on Liverpool's Lime Street leading the way with their wax figure of Lefroy displayed before he had even been captured; the *Bolton Evening News* reported that so realistic was the likeness that, on 8 July

one of the visitors, who was gazing at the figure with much bewilderment, bore such a strong resemblance to the figure himself as to excite the comment of the other visitors as well as of the officials of the place. But by far the most outstanding part of the business is that two astute police constables were said to have been so absorbed in the possibility of a 'clever capture', that they waited at the entrance of the waxworks exhibition until the fictitious Lefroy had finished contemplating his own likeness, and that they then followed him up the street.[81]

Needless to say, the exhibition-goer proved to be entirely innocent.

Madame Picketo's Waxwork at 147 High Street, Sunderland, proudly boasted their own wax likeness of 'Lefroy, charged with the Brighton murder' before the magistrates' hearing had been completed;[82] following the eventual guilty verdict, they smoothly edited their advertisement to describe him as 'the Brighton Murderer'.[83]

Tussauds finally confirmed their display a week after the trial ended,[84] with the *Western Daily Press* recoiling from the 'startling placards printed with red ink' with which 'Madame Tussaud announces that a portrait figure of Lefroy has been added to her collection'.[85] Inside, the tableau consisted not just of the wax figure of Lefroy himself, but also some pawn tickets and the pistol

80   *Southern Reporter* (Selkirk), 14 July 1881.
81   *Bolton Evening News*, 9 July 1881.
82   *Sunderland Daily Echo and Shipping Gazette*, 21 July 1881.
83   *Sunderland Daily Echo and Shipping Gazette*, 12 November 1881.
84   *The Globe*, 15 November 1881.
85   *Western Daily Press*, 19 November 1881.

supposedly used in the murder.[86]

There, Lefroy would stare down at interested visitors for more than fifty years alongside murderous contemporaries such as Charles Peace [NBT 39], Kate Webster [NBT 35] and, of course, his spiritual predecessor Franz Müller [NBT 13], until in the late 1930s an incident occurred which was perfectly in keeping with the story of Percy Mapleton. On 3 March 1938, a court heard how a seventeen year old boy named Leslie Williams had stolen Lefroy's revolver from its cabinet at the Chamber of Horrors, hiding it up his sleeve. He then used it during a rampage of crime, stealing a motor car, two suitcases and other items. He was caught and pleaded guilty to the thefts and unlawfully possessing a firearm. He was sent to Borstal for three years.[87] It had been a crime spree of which Lefroy would no doubt have approved. Lefroy's likeness would have a home in the Chamber of Horrors until 1997, cementing his terrible crime in the public's consciousness for 116 years.

Less fortunate in death was his victim, Mr Frederick Gold. While the murderer was presented in all his finery for the ghoulish denizens of London's West End to admire, Mr Gold was commemorated in a seaside display by a wax bust which showed his injuries, a cast of his head having apparently been taken after death. Thankfully, the signs of his suffering would not be gawped at for long.

A group of men visited the waxwork exhibition at Brighton's St James's Hall on Sunday 6 November 1881 - the rest day of Lefroy's trial - but one of their number, Harry Manser, was drunk and was accordingly refused admission:

> Later in the evening he evaded the vigilance of the proprietor and entered the exhibition, and afterwards overthrew a wax-work image representing the wounded head of Mr Gold, the victim of the Brighton Railway murder. According to the evidence of a witness he overturned the model, which was placed on a pedestal, and caused its destruction. [At the Brighton Police Court on 7 November] the proprietor of the Exhibition said the cast cost ten guineas, but he was willing to meet the Prisoner half way. The Stipendiary said he thought it was a case for a civil court, and discharged the Prisoner.[88]

The destruction of such a monstrous display might be deemed a good thing, but Harry Manser, walking free from court, almost stepped into a more dire predicament. News of his arrest for vandalism had reached the ears of Lefroy's defence counsel, who attempted to associate him with rumours of a man who, it

---

86   *Sporting Times*, 24 December 1881.
87   *Coventry Evening Telegraph*, 3 March 1938.
88   *London Evening Standard*, 8 November 1881.

was supposed, had fractured a leg falling out of a train during a struggle on 27 June: was this Lefroy's mysterious 'countryman', who, he claimed, had been responsible for the death of Mr Gold and an attack on himself?

The *Birmingham Mail* reported that

> Lefroy sat during most of yesterday [at his trial] as if utterly oblivious of anything that was passing around him. There was enough to move him, for not only was the summing up of the Judge proceeding, but a telegram had just been received by his counsel from Lewisham, which might have possibly awakened some hopes in his heart. It ran as follows:– 'Is man in custody at Brighton for breaking waxwork of Gold identical with ticket-of-leave man admitted June 27th Brighton Hospital, leg broken, reported himself London police as falling out of a train in struggle. Taken on crutches by police Guy's; examined Robert Perks; after man dismissed police noticed coincidence. Applied vainly to Perks. Sender known to juryman Harris.' Naturally, the counsel for the defence had telegraphed to Brighton Hospital for information, receiving presently, however, the following reply: 'Only one patient, Albert Duckett, crushed fingers, admitted to hospital on June 27. No fractured leg that day.'[89]

As we shall see, tracing the 'countryman' would prove extremely difficult.

But we are getting ahead of ourselves; at the time the *Daily Telegraph* published their version of the sketch of Lefroy, the whereabouts of the man himself was still unknown. In a short time, the fugitive would be captured, but the *Telegraph*'s decision to print the drawing of him led to a week which saw heightened public tension and excitement, wrongful arrests and innocent young men hounded in the street. It was a scenario repeated seven years later, when the decision to print a facsimile of a letter received from 'Jack the Ripper' fanned the flames of panic among the already skittish public.

In the same way, before Lefroy was even in police custody, he was already guilty in the eyes of the public, following trial by media.

XII.

Lefroy's time on the run eventually came to an end, in part due to his own reluctance to leave the lonely sanctuary of 32 Smith Street. He became increasingly desperate to get word to someone he trusted and, on Thursday 7 July, he asked landlady Mrs Bickers to go to the City to (he said) collect his wages. He complained that he was unable to go himself, as he had sprained his ankle getting out of bed that morning. When Mrs Bickers declined, he asked

---

89   *Birmingham Mail*, 9 November 1881.

her to send a telegram instead.[90] He wrote a draft which a neighbour named Mr Doyle took to the telegraph office. The message was a strange one: sent to J. T. Hutchinson's at 56 Gresham Street, it asked for his wages to be sent to him that evening – but he certainly was not employed by the firm. Instead, it was a ploy to establish contact with his cousin Frank Seale, who worked as a clerk for Mr Hutchinson.

Sarah Bickers had for several days felt an uneasiness about the strange Mr Clark, and when she found him wearing a coat belonging to another of her lodgers, she decided to go to nearby Arbour Square Police Station to make a complaint. The following morning, she sent her daughter to the Gresham Street offices identified by the telegram to see what could be learned about Clark.

There, Miss Bickers spoke with a young man with a 'light beard and curly moustache'[91] who told her that nobody by the name of Clark was employed there. She then related the suspicions which she and her mother had about the lodger. Having obtained a description of Clark, and the date he arrived at Smith Street, the young clerk put two and two together and realised who the mysterious man was. At the end of his working hours, he went to Scotland Yard with a colleague, where they met Inspector Donald Swanson. Telling the detective that they had information regarding a murderer who was currently on the run, they asked to see the officer in charge of the CID in order to claim the £200 reward on offer. Swanson took one of the men to Inspector Robson, who was in command of the CID by night. The informant secured a promise that the reward would be paid should his information lead to the arrest of the fugitive, and was assured that his identity not be revealed. The clerk declined to disclose his source but, reassured by the undertakings of the police, he said that the wanted man could be found in hiding at Smith Street, using the name 'Clark'.[92]

It was later reported in some newspapers that Miss Bickers had communicated the family's concern to Mr Hutchinson himself, and that it was he who informed Scotland Yard of Lefroy's whereabouts and demanded the reward, leaving the businessman feeling compelled to put the matter straight in a letter to the *Daily Telegraph*:

> It is stated as a fact that I saw Miss Bickers, and, to any ordinary mind, the natural inference to be drawn from what follows is that I was the gentleman who saw the authorities at Scotland Yard, and quibbled about the reward. In the first place, perhaps, I may be allowed to mention that Mr F. W. S. Seale, the second cousin

---

90 The *Birmingham Mail* of 9 July 1881 claims that Mrs Bickers was afraid to leave the house on her own.
91 *Sheffield and Rotherham Independent*, 9 July 1881.
92 Report by Inspector Frederick Jarvis, 7 December 1881 (TNA: PRO HO 144/83/A6404/24).

Introduction.

of Lefroy, is not, as stated at the inquest, my confidential clerk, but one of my general copying clerks; he has been in my service for about two years, and is, as far as I know, a most respectable and trustworthy man. When Miss Bickers called at my office she did not see me as stated, and I never even heard of her having called till some time afterwards. I was not, therefore, the person to whom she showed the copy of the telegram. The fact is she saw one of my clerks, and he informs me that, from certain facts she stated, he felt it his duty (as it clearly was) to communicate with the police.[93]

Frank Seale was told by his colleague that a visitor had called asking for him,[94] but said that he would have ignored the telegram anyway because he knew nobody by the name of G. Clark, and he and his family had received numerous nuisance letters at home in Cathcart Road since Lefroy had absconded. When interviewed by a reporter later, however, Seale confirmed that, had he known that the sender was his dear cousin Percy, he would have gone to him 'whatever the cost'.

If the informant was not Mr Hutchinson or Frank Seale, who was he? Because of his request for anonymity, details of his identity have remained sketchy – until now. His name was Joseph Mugford, a twenty-four year old clerk who had been born at Mutley, Plymouth. At the time of Lefroy's arrest he was lodging at the home of Mary and Elizabeth Bowen on New Union Street, Moorgate.[95]

Despite a claim from Mrs Sarah Bickers for part of the reward – she had, after all, kickstarted the sequence of events which led to the arrest – Joseph Mugford received the full £200 reward:[96] £100 from the Government and £100 from the directors of the London, Brighton and South Coast Railway. Several newspapers stated that they hoped a small portion of the windfall would find its way to Mrs Bickers, but this was not to be.

A letter from her son-in-law William Farnworth to Home Secretary William Vernon Harcourt underlined that, had it not been for Mrs Bickers' suspicions, her daughter would never have gone to Gresham Street, and therefore – but for her actions – the information would never have found its way to Scotland Yard.[97]

---

93   *Daily Telegraph*, 13 July 1881,
94   *Birmingham Mail*, 14 July 1881.
95   1881 census. Ten years later, in 1891, Mugford was an unmarried lodger at Dean Street, working as a general clerk. He married Annie Bayliss in March 1894. The couple moved to Fulham and had two children, one of whom sadly died at a young age. In 1911, Mugford was working as a law clerk, living at Sherbrooke Road, Fulham, with Annie and their son John. He died in 1930, aged 73.
96   Some £13,000 today.
97   Letter from William Farnworth dated 14 July 1881, sent from 32 Smith Street (TNA: PRO HO 144/83/A6404/15).

Lefroy.

The Home Office forwarded the letter to Scotland Yard; the newly-appointed Assistant Commissioner (Executive) Lt. Colonel Richard Pearson sent a reply which included a report written by Inspector Swanson explaining that he had received the information on Lefroy's whereabouts from Joseph Mugford. Swanson clearly felt sorry for Mrs Bickers, stating in his report: 'I have no doubt the matter has caused her considerable trouble and expense, which being a widow she can ill afford to bear'.[98]

Sensing that red tape might mean Mrs Bickers going unrewarded, on 22 November Director of the CID Sir Charles Howard Vincent personally intervened and suggested to the Home Secretary that she should be awarded a £20 gratuity for her part in bringing the murderer to justice. 'Should there not be any fund available at the Home Office out of which to pay such gratuity,' he wrote, 'I would beg to suggest that the Secretary of State's authority be issued to the Receiver for the Metropolitan Police District for the amount mentioned to be paid out of police funds.'[99]

The Home Office relented. A note written on Vincent's letter commented:

> This is unusual but Mrs Bickers seems to have a claim. The Treasury might perhaps direct their solicitor to pay this gratuity if the [Secretary of State] were to recommend it, but the easiest way would no doubt be to pay it from the Police fund.

Some three months later, the Treasury finally agreed to pay the £20 to Mrs Bickers, writing to inform her on 24 February 1882.[100] She had given up her home at 32 Smith Street, and had moved to 1 Jamaica Street, just around the corner. Perhaps she was seeking a little anonymity, just as Lefroy had done in the same neighbourhood not long before.

As for Joseph Mugford, his luck did not last long. Just two years after receiving the reward, he appeared at the City of London Bankruptcy Court owing creditors £42 11s 9d. He admitted that he was now employed as a clerk at the London and Westminster Loan and Discount Company on a salary of £2 per week, and solicitor Mr Mason, appearing for the creditors, sought to prove that Mugford could afford to pay considerably more than the two-shillings-in-the-pound (by instalments) which he had offered.

The clerk was asked whether it was true that his mother had given him her life insurance policy. Mugford replied that it was, but that he had sold it. Mr Mason then asked if it was true that the petitioner had received £200 over

---

98   Report with covering letter from Pearson dated 21 November 1881 (TNA: PRO HO 144/83/A6404/62).
99   TNA: PRO HO 144/83/A6404/121.
100   TNA: PRO HO 144/83/A6404/124. Sarah Bickers died in 1899 aged 72.

Introduction.

the capture of Lefroy, asking: 'That was the reward you received for being the means of arresting that notorious criminal and bringing him to justice? What did you do with it?' Mugford replied, to laughter from the court, that he had paid £10 of his debts with it, and 'made presents' of the rest to his mother, brothers and sisters. He himself had nothing left.[101]

*

Lefroy's liberty came to end on the evening of Friday 8 July, very soon after Joseph Mugford's visit to Scotland Yard. Although he had been oblivious to the movements of Sarah and Jane Bickers, he must have known that he would be found sooner rather than later.

At quarter to eight that evening, a cab pulled up in Smith Street. Inside were Inspectors Swanson and Jarvis, along with a PC Hopkins, who knew Lefroy from Wallington. It was again a very warm evening, continuing that fine, hot summer.

Swanson positioned Hopkins at the rear of the building. Suddenly, the detectives saw Miss Jane Bickers approach her home, and, as she opened the door, Swanson followed and entered at the same time. He was met by her mother, Sarah Bickers, whom the detective took into the parlour, stating the nature of his visit.[102] He was told that the man he was interested in was at that moment in his room on the first floor.

Swanson climbed the staircase, telling Inspector Jarvis to stay downstairs guarding the front door. He quickly opened the door to the first room, and saw a pale, thin man sitting in an armchair.

'Percy Lefroy Mapleton?'

'Yes; I expected you.'

Even before Lefroy confirmed his name, there could be no doubt that this was the wanted man. A newspaper account of the arrest gave a vivid description of the fugitive's appearance which this writer cannot better:

> It would have been impossible to have failed to see in the poor, weakly, inoffensive-looking creature the man whose sketch portrait, produced in the *Daily Telegraph*, and reproduced in the police circulars, had made his remarkable features familiar to the force from one end of the kingdom to the other. The appearance of the man, but for the terrible crime laid to his account, was such as might have moved to commiseration. As he sat in the chair he looked extremely weak, miserable,

101   *Trewman's Exeter Flying Post*, 23 July 1884.
102   Swanson's report on a letter from Mrs Bickers claiming the reward, 21 November 1881 (TNA: PRO HO 144/83/A6404/62).

and dejected. His emaciated appearance seemed to tell a tale either of want of food or inability to take nourishment. He offered no resistance, and was, indeed, incapable of offering any.[103]

Inspector Swanson continued:

'I am a police officer, and I arrest you for the wilful murder of Mr Gold on the Brighton Railway.'

'I am not obliged to make any reply, and I think it better not to make any answer.'

Swanson wrote this last comment in his notebook and read it back to Lefroy, who replied, 'I will qualify that by saying I am not guilty'.

Jarvis then entered the room and was told by Swanson that Lefroy had admitted his identity. Jarvis searched Lefroy, finding a solitary shilling, and the detectives then scoured the room. On top of a chest of drawers they saw a pipe, a bottle of arnica oil and a pair of scissors, which the suspect said he had used to cut off his moustache. Inside the drawers were a bloodstained black cloth waistcoat, two caps, three collars, part of a flannel shirt and a false moustache and beard. In a cupboard they found a light-coloured scarf and more pieces of material matching the flannel shirt.[104]

Swanson and Jarvis took the suspect downstairs, where Mrs Bickers was waiting. Addressing Lefroy, she said, 'I did not know that I had such a man as you in my house, or I would not have had you'.[105]

Lefroy was taken in a cab first to nearby Arbour Square Police Station, where his identity was confirmed, and then on to Scotland Yard. During the journey, Lefroy said:

I am glad you found me. I am sick of it. I should have given myself up in a day or two. I have regretted it ever since that I ran away. It put a different complexion on the case, but I could not bear the exposure. I feared certain matters in connexion with my family would be published. I suppose I shall be allowed to see a lawyer? I am glad you did not bring any of my so-called friends from Wallington with you.[106]

On arrival at Scotland Yard, Director of the CID Howard Vincent and Chief Constable Frederick Adolphus Williamson were waiting. The senior officers had

103   *Birmingham Mail*, 9 July 1881.
104   *London Standard*, 9 July 1881; *Sheffield Daily Telegraph*, 8 November 1881; *Hampshire Telegraph*, 13 July 1881.
105   Report by Donald Sutherland Swanson dated 21 November 1881 (TNA: PRO HO 144/83/A6404/62).
106   *The Times*, 11 July 1881.

CAPTURE OF LEFROY
FOR THE
MURDER on the RAILWAY.

LEFROY was apprehended on Friday Evening, at 33 Smith Street Stepney London, for the Murder of Mr. GOULD, on the railway.

Now for the shocking Railway Murder,
 On the London and Brighton Line,
A young man he has been arrested,
 For this cruel and cowardly crime ;
Full of fear and so dejected,
 He could not face his fellow man,
His guilty conscience did accuse him,
 When he carried out his wicked plan

CHORUS.

On the London and Brighton Railway,
 Mr Gould he lost his life,
By the hand of a coward,
 Who used the pistol and knife ?

No doubt money was the object,
 The murderer had in view,
When he killed this poor old man,
 And from the carriage his body
 threw.
The train was passing thro' the tunnel,
 At a very rapid rate,
Although it left behind the victim,
 The murder cannot escape.

'Twas shown the victim struggled hard
 To overcome his murderer ;
For blood was splashed about the
 carriage,
 And Lefroy's head was cut severe ;
They little thought when he told his
 story,
 He had killed his fellow passenger!

But when they found poor Mr Gould,
 Dead on the line, 'twas very clear ?

Lefroy escaped and went to London,
 And soon got into lodgings there,
Full of fear he drew the blinds down,
 His face he tried to hide with care ;
His landlady she felt alarmed,
 At his statement so it's said,
To the police she made known her
 suspicion,
 Which to his capture quickly led.

There they found the man they wanted
 Lefroy he was not surprised,
When the officers walked in,
 His person he had not disguised.
He expected there such visitors,
 So limly went away with them,
The neighbourhood was soon alarmed,
 As soon as they arrested him.

They took him by rail to Lewes prison,
 And passed the place where the
 victim fell,
Lefroy became somewhat excited,
 The fatal spot he knew too well ;
Now in his cell he is watched closely,
 While the victim's blood for ven
 geance crave,
The poor old man was shown no mercy,
 The song birds now sing o'er his
 grave,

Original handbill declaring Lefroy's capture.

Courtesy Dr Jan Bondeson

received news of the arrest by telegraph, and, after a brief interview with Lefroy, ordered that he be taken to King Street Police Station to be detained overnight. A Central News reporter, loitering at Scotland Yard with a view to gleaning some information about the capture, noticed Swanson and Jarvis descending a staircase with Lefroy between them. They got into a waiting cab and left for nearby King Street, where he was charged with the murder of Mr Gold. After a meal of sandwiches and coffee, the suspected murderer was placed in a cell and watched by no fewer than three constables.

At last, the police were able to compare the wanted man with the widely-circulated sketch, side by side. He did not display the imbecilic look displayed in the likeness, and several officers remarked that while there was a resemblance, they would probably have passed him in the street without suspecting that he was the man they were searching for.[107]

*

As news broke of Lefroy's capture, the usually sedate East End thoroughfare of Smith Street was crowded with the curious, the excitable and, of course, newspaper reporters. Although Lefroy himself had vacated the stage, there were still various players who had a part, and their stories made for enthralling reading, such as the following interview with J.W. Goodfellow, a fellow lodger at number 32, which appeared uncredited in the *Birmingham Mail*:

> Though my suspicions had been somewhat aroused by some peculiarities about our new lodger, and I had even mentioned them to a friend of mine, it certainly was a great blow to me on returning home [on Friday] afternoon to find that the docile and gentlemanly individual for whom I had conceived quite a liking, and who had been behaving so quietly, was the man Lefroy, charged with the frightful crime committed on the Brighton line. On reaching Stepney tonight I found my lodgings surrounded by a large crowd, among whom were many detectives and police, and inside the utmost confusion reigned. Lefroy had in my absence been arrested, and borne off to Scotland Yard. Our house is situated in a quiet and respectable street of Stepney, just opposite a church, and is very unlike the hovel in which it was expected that Lefroy would at length be discovered. ...
>
> On Friday morning [1 July 1881] I was introduced to him by Mrs Bickers. He had asked her for a latchkey, and she requested me to show him how to fit it into the door. I did so, for which he was much obliged, and expressed his thanks in a very genial way. He then returned to his room, where he remained – working at his

---

107   *Lloyd's Weekly London Newspaper*, 10 July 1881.

engraving, as it was supposed. I occasionally met him on the stairs, and used to exchange a few words with him. He did not at all appear to shirk my society, and always addressed me in a friendly way. I remember on one of these occasions, during the very hot weather, he said, 'It is very hot, is it not? I really think it is too hot to go out at all,' and back he went to his room, which had now almost become his prison, for there he incarcerated himself continually. ...

On one or two evenings he came down from his apartment about half past ten o'clock, and, letting himself quietly out, walked about the neighbourhood for an hour or so, smoking a well-coloured briar, for which he seemed to nourish a particular affection. No daily papers were taken in the house, and I do not think Lefroy had an opportunity of knowing the interest centred in the Brighton tragedy, and of judging the excellent likeness of him published by the *Daily Telegraph*, which gave a striking representation of his receding forehead and chin. Weekly papers, however, were in the house on Sunday, and these he may have seen. Until Sunday morning the landlady did not even know that the murder had been committed, and though in the afternoon of that day it formed a theme of some conversation, I need scarcely state no word was said pointing to Lefroy in the matter. The mystery hanging over him – the non-appearance of his luggage, his keeping to his room, and the story about the little machine that was always represented as ever working but could never be seen, aroused my suspicions at a time when my mind, like that of so many others, was full of the Brighton murder. I communicated these suspicions to a friend residing at Brixton, to whom I described our lodger. He said it tallied with the description given by the police. I had not seen the picture in the *Daily Telegraph*. If I had seen it I would most certainly have gone home and given Lefroy into custody. I believe this friend of mine has, by communicating with Scotland Yard, led to his arrest, and if so, I think I am entitled to some part of the reward. The day after his arrival Lefroy, while I was out, walked down stairs, and borrowed a book of mine from the parlour. It was a large volume of Cassell's, and furnished him with enough reading for several days. He had it still when arrested. When taking the book he said, 'It is very seldom I have time to read, but I should like to look at this'.

When I left home this morning [Friday 7 July] Lefroy had not come down to breakfast, but remained in his room. After the other lodgers had gone out this morning, I hear that Lefroy came down wearing one of their coats. I do not know if he intended to go out in it. Mrs Bickers is quite overcome at the arrest of her lodger, about whom the most she ever feared was that he would leave without paying his rent. It strikes everyone who knows Lefroy with surprise and wonder that a man apparently so mild in temper and so weak in frame could be the perpetrator of so great a crime as that with which he is charged.[108]

---

108 *Birmingham Mail*, 9 July 1881. According to the *South Wales Daily News* of 12 July 1881, Walter Goodfellow was well known in the Cardiff area, having been employed in offices there for a number of years. He apparently left for London in 1880.

Introduction.

By the time this interview appeared in print – two days after the arrest – the 'docile and gentlemanly individual' remembered by his fellow lodger had been spirited out of London by Inspectors Swanson and Jarvis, to be held at Lewes Gaol in Sussex, awaiting his committal hearing. He would never see the capital again.

Despite leaving King Street Police Station at the early hour of seven o'clock, word had spread of the imminent departure, and a large crowd gathered at Victoria Station to shout insults at the prisoner. The detectives hurried Lefroy into a first class carriage and drew down the blinds to screen him from the crowd, which by this time lined the platform. The train set off at 7.35 am. Lefroy chatted amiably with Swanson and Jarvis, sharing their cigarettes, and he generally seemed relaxed. As Mr Gold's body had been found within the Cuckfield Petty Sessional Division, and not within the jurisdiction of the East Grinstead magistrates as first supposed, the officers' destination had altered.[109] They changed trains at Haywards Heath to travel to Lewes instead of continuing to East Grinstead, and as the party stepped onto the platform, Lefroy was immediately recognised. Loud roars of disapproval rained down until Swanson, Jarvis and the prisoner boarded another first-class train, where once again the blinds were drawn.

The train left an hour later and arrived at Lewes just after half past ten; a cab took the detectives and their prisoner to Lewes Gaol. Throughout the journey, Lefroy appeared calm, but Swanson and Jarvis noticed that when travelling through Merstham and Balcombe tunnels he looked around and became excited.[110]

*

The ruling that a magistrates' hearing took place within the district where a body was found and not where the suspect had been arrested unexpectedly threw the spotlight on the Sussex village of Cuckfield, home to a community more usually concerned with agricultural matters.

On Friday 15 July, the prisoner was taken to the committal hearing, which was being held at the village's most suitable venue, the Talbot Hotel. His appearance - as it always did, now - drew a crowd of locals:

> The Cuckfielders gathered around, eyes wide open and mouth agape, for they felt something of surpassing interest to them was about to happen. That 'something'

---

109   *The Times*, 11 July 1881.
110   *Lloyd's Weekly London Newspaper*, 10 July 1881.

was at hand. In another minute a tall, thin, cadaverous young man, tightly held by the left arm by a sturdy policeman, supported, too, on the other side by another constable, and followed by four men in a line, passed through the doorway of the hotel.

It was not 'entrancing', yet it was distinctly painful. The wretched appearance of the central figure in that procession as it moved slowly down the principal thoroughfare of that dull village was such as was capable of moving the most careless mind ... There was no attempt at mobbing him; there were no shouts uttered; the unhappy prisoner was, if not exactly pitied, at least to a certain extent regarded with a feeling akin to commiseration – his looks were so depressing.[111]

Already in place was his lawyer:

The relatives and friends of Lefroy have decided that Mr T. D. Dutton, solicitor, who attended at the inquest on Mr Gold's remains, shall undertake the prisoner's defence. Lefroy, who knows Mr Dutton slightly, the latter having been his sister's lawyer, has also besought the services of that gentleman.[112]

Two miles of cable had been run up to the Talbot Hotel by the Post Office, in order that journalists could telegraph their reports back to their offices.[113] Inside, the hotel's function room on the first floor had been hastily prepared for the hearing, with three long tables arranged for the magistrates, lawyers and members of the press. Lefroy himself sat in an armchair, with the public standing at a cleared space partitioned from proceedings by a barrier constructed of timber. Through the half-open windows drifted the smell of nearby pigsties.[114]

After hearing evidence from more than fifty witnesses, the magistrates had no hesitation in sending the prisoner to trial. Having been held at Lewes Gaol throughout the hearing, Lefroy was transferred to Maidstone on 28 October, to appear at the Assizes there on 4 November.

The London, Chatham and Dover Railway, recognising an opportunity to benefit from the enormous public interest, announced that they would be running special trains from London to Maidstone for the duration of the trial.[115]

XIII.

The trial of Percy Lefroy Mapleton opened on Friday 4 November 1881,

111   *North-Eastern Daily Gazette*, 22 July 1881.
112   *Portsmouth Evening News*, 13 July 1881.
113   *Sheffield and Rotherham Independent*, 15 July 1881.
114   *Northampton Mercury*, 23 July 1881.
115   *North Devon Journal*, 3 November 1881.

The ivy-clad Talbot Hotel in Cuckfield,
scene of Lefroy's committal hearing.

Author's collection

Introduction.

with Mr Justice Coleridge presiding.[116] Leading the prosecution was Sir Henry James, the Attorney-General,[117] assisted by Mr Harry Poland and Mr A. L. Smith. The defence was led by Mr Montagu Williams,[118] aided by Mr Forrest Fulton and Mr Henry Kisch.

Sir Henry James, recognising that the jury could hardly have been left unswayed by the media coverage that the case had attracted, asked the twelve gentlemen to attempt to disregard everything they had read in the preceding months:

> I would earnestly ask you to allow any fact which may have impressed itself on your mind, or any opinion you may have formed on this case, to be cast entirely aside, and I trust that from your mind and from your memory you will banish any fact you have noted or any impression you have formed which is at all likely to be an ingredient in your consideration of this case.

He then went on to outline how he intended to prove that everything they had read about Lefroy was true.

Montagu Williams, feeling the sheer weight of circumstantial evidence against his client, did his best to introduce doubt into the minds of the jury, repeatedly asking them whether alternative explanations for certain aspects of the case were *possible*, if not altogether likely. This task would prove most challenging when it involved attempting to place Lefroy's supposed attacker into the carriage, as recognised by one reporter:

---

116 John Duke Coleridge, 1st Baron Coleridge (1820–1894). Lord Chief Justice of England 1880–1894. Presided over several notable cases, including R v Coney (1882), which ruled that bare-knuckle boxing was an assault occasioning actual bodily harm, regardless of the participants' consent, effectively ending the sport; R v Dudley and Stephens (1884), which established the precedent that necessity was not a defence against the charge of murder; and the Royal Baccarat Scandal of 1891, which saw the Prince of Wales enter the witness box (see NBT 56). Described in 1873 by the *Women's Suffrage Journal* as a 'firm and consistent' supporter of women's suffrage, Coleridge did not fare so well at the hands of the *Pall Mall Gazette*, whose obituary stated that 'On the bench he was dogmatic and sometimes inattentive, and his judgements, his summings-up, often, very often, varied from the forecasts of eminent and able lawyers. A rough, general sense of justice kept him, however, from going wrong. What most pleased his contemporaries was the air and fashion of his orations – for with orations he very frequently closed a case.' (*Pall Mall Gazette*, 15 June 1894.)

117 Sir Henry James, Q.C., M.P. (1828–1911). Knighted 1873. Liberal M.P. for Taunton 1869–1885, then Bury 1885–1895. Attorney-General 1873–1874, then 1880–1885. Sat on the Parnell Commission 1888-1889. 1st Baron James of Hereford 1895. Attorney-General to the Prince of Wales 1892–1895. Chancellor of the Duchy of Lancaster 1895–1902.

118 Montagu Stephen Williams, Q.C. (1835–1892). Called to the bar 1862. Junior Treasury Counsel 1879. Retired 1886, succeeded by Sir Charles Willie Mathews. Appointed Metropolitan Stipendiary Magistrate 1886; Queen's Counsel 1888.

Lefroy.

One of the great, if not *the* great difficulty, which the defence had to contend with was the mysterious 'countryman', who sprang into the train when it was travelling 50 miles an hour, murdered Mr Gold in the presence of Mapleton, robbed the old man of his watch, assaulted Mapleton, stuffed the gold watch into Mapleton's boot, flung the body out of the carriage, and then jumped from the train himself and vanished into space.[119]

Quite.

Mrs Ann Brown and her daughter Rhoda said that they were in their cottage at Horley – between Merstham and Balcombe tunnels – when the Brighton train thundered past. They claimed to have seen two men standing up with their arms waving above their heads; this was taken to mean that they had witnessed Lefroy and Mr Gold in the midst of a desperate struggle. Yet the train tracks were a hundred yards from the cottage, the train was travelling at speed and both witnesses were inside, looking out through a window. Did they really see anything?

Rhoda Lucas Brown had said at the inquest that she had thought little of it, but when her brother came home that evening and said there had been a murder on the line, both mother and daughter stated they had seen two men fighting on the train.[120]

The Browns' claims were given credence when a local architect named Thomas Winter gave evidence before Coroner Wynne Baxter. He had produced a plan of their cottage and measured the distance to the railway line; there was nothing to obscure the view, and he himself had observed several trains pass and said he could distinctly see everybody in the train.[121] Mr Winter was not called to give evidence at the trial.

Montagu Williams tested ticket collector William Franks's memory regarding what Lefroy was wearing in the few moments they had together when the latter boarded the train, including which coat was buttoned, from which pocket Lefroy produced his ticket – right down to how his hair was cut. Williams was trying to persuade the jury that Franks's evidence had been augmented by the newspaper reports that he had read. And there were indications that he may, indeed, have been following the right path, for the ticket collector had admitted at the inquest into Mr Gold's death that he had seen the *Daily Telegraph* sketch of Lefroy.[122]

119 *County Advertiser & Herald for Staffordshire and Worcestershire*, 12 November 1881.
120 *The Horsham Advertiser*, 2 July 1881. The brother was most likely twenty-two year old Edmund Lucas, an agricultural labourer living at home.
121 *The Horsham Advertiser*, 2 July 1881.
122 Ibid..

Introduction.

The influence of the *Telegraph* drawing was also explored during the testimony of Detective George Holmes, who had escorted Lefroy back to Wallington from Brighton. Although it had little bearing on his testimony, the legal point of whether the sketch could be admissible as evidence was raised by Mr Justice Coleridge, as reported by one newspaperman:

> By easy gradations, coming from one point to another, the learned counsel ascertained from the witness that he had seen in the *Daily Telegraph* an alleged likeness of Lefroy at the time he disappeared. Here a legal difficulty was raised by the Lord Chief Justice as to the advisability of such pictoral evidence. 'But, my Lord,' pleaded the Attorney-General, 'the coroner who held the first enquiry as to the cause of death handed to the witnesses a photograph of that picture in the newspaper'. 'The coroner made it evidence, did he?' slyly remarked his lordship, and the paper being handed to him he examined it, and next sent it over to the jury, who for the first time since they entered the box indulged in a laugh.[123]

Under cross-examination, Holmes had a far tougher time trying to explain why he had not taken Lefroy into custody after hearing him give an incorrect number for his watch, despite knowing that a watch was missing from a body found on the tracks at Balcombe, and that Lefroy had been wounded on a train on that very line; Mr Justice Coleridge was incredulous, and asked Holmes the same questions. George Holmes's stint in the witness box had proved to be very uncomfortable, and was neatly summed up by a reporter:

> When Mr Williams put the witness down the judge took him up, and upon the whole the unhappy detective endured on Saturday morning the most unhappy half-hour of his life.[124]

But the toughest reception of all was reserved for Thomas Clayton, who claimed to have vital evidence regarding the day on which the murder weapon was pledged at a pawnbrokers. Although it could have proved of great importance to Lefroy, potentially putting him in the clear, Clayton claimed he did not raise the matter at either the inquest or the magistrates' hearing, simply because he had not been asked about it; he had been reserving the information for the trial itself. To sensation in the courtroom, Clayton was angrily dismissed from the witness box by Mr Justice Coleridge.

It was not the first time that Thomas Clayton had crossed swords with the authorities over the Lefroy case. At the inquest, he had been forced to admit

123 *Birmingham Mail*, 5 November 1881. This legal discussion was not recorded in the trial transcript.
124 *Staffordshire Sentinel*, 7 November 1881.

to Coroner Wynne Baxter that he had sent a telegram of warning to Lefroy's sister Julia, bearing the words, 'If Percy calls tell him the police are after him'. Clayton claimed that his message was meant to encourage Julia to persuade Lefroy to hand himself in and to face the music, but, when he realised that to explain himself unambiguously would take the text over the permitted twenty words, he left it as it stood.[125] As many today have found with Twitter, Thomas Clayton was damned by the restrictive word limits of the medium of the age.

Ann Clayton followed her husband into the witness box, and faced a similar barrage of stinging questions as to how they knew Lefroy was at home all day on the twenty-first. Annie was positive, she said, because a neighbour had been confined on that day. The importance of the date was brought to her attention by a friend, claimed Annie; unfortunately, she was unable to recall that friend's name.

In his closing speech, the Attorney-General generously said that it was not unusual for the evidence of a relative of a prisoner to contain discrepancies. Montagu Williams leapt on the morsel offered and told the jury that it was proof that his client could not possibly have been the man who pledged the pistol on 21 June.

Equally murky avenues had been reconnoitred by the press, long before the trial. Did Lefroy know Mr Gold? It was claimed that a Limehouse businessman who was apparently well acquainted with Mr Gold and his family saw Lefroy in deep conversation with one of those relations at London Bridge Station on the morning of the murder. If true – and it surely cannot have been – it beggars belief that the witness to such an important incident decided not to inform Scotland Yard, reportedly because he did not want to be 'mixed up in the mess at all'.[126]

And yet, there was indeed a connection between Mr Gold and Wallington. His wife, Lydia Matilda Wood, had an elder sister named Mary Cooper Wood. According to the 1841 census, Mary was employed as a housekeeper by Mr Alfred Pill, a confectioner at 51 Cheapside, and her skills were obviously admired by Mr Pill, for the couple married in January 1847, and the union produced three children: Alfred Jr, Mary Jr and Elizabeth. When Mary Cooper Pill died in 1862,[127] Alfred continued working at Cheapside, but after the demise of young Alfred, aged just twenty, in 1875, Alfred Pill Sr retired to The Knowle on Manor Road, Wallington – minutes from the Claytons' house on Cathcart Road. Although Mr Pill had become well known in Wallington by 1881, he was, by this time, seventy-six years old and said he did not venture out often,

125 *Sunderland Daily Echo and Shipping Gazette*, 4 July 1881.
126 *Sheffield and Rotherham Independent*, 15 July 1881.
127 She was buried in the City of London and Tower Hamlets Cemetery on 22 April 1862.

preferring to tend his garden. Although he would not have known Lefroy had he seen him in the locale, there was a good chance that the murderer would have been aware of Mr Pill.[128] At the inquest, Pill's daughter, Mary Susannah Pill, said she lived with her father at The Knowle; and, although Mr Gold had visited them at Wallington, he had not been that year as the railway station was not on the main line. She said that she knew Cathcart Road, and that there was a school there, but did not know anyone by the name of Clayton, Mapleton or Lefroy.[129]

Several newspapers carried reports that Mr Gold had met his brother Thomas in the Minories on the day of the murder: was there, perhaps, some altercation with the brother who had 'not behaved well in money matters'?

Montagu Williams delivered quite possibly the finest speech of his career when closing for the defence, offering variant explanations for the most straightforward points, most unsubstantiated, but all designed to stoke doubt in the minds of the jury.

The twelve gentlemen of the jury might have been impressed, but they retired for just ten minutes before declaring Percy Lefroy Mapleton guilty of murder.

*

As the trial itself appears in full following this Introduction, we need not pick through the evidence line-by-line. What is worth noting, however, is the bizarre behaviour of Lefroy throughout his four days in the dock, as described by his defence barrister Montagu Williams:

> While the jury were being sworn, Lefroy stood listlessly with his hands behind him. Though self-possessed, it was clear that he was nervous.

> Before the Attorney-General commenced his [opening] speech, the prisoner placed his hat on a ledge at the side of the dock. He took it up again, and then once more returned it to the ledge. Apparently, he was loth to part with it. It subsequently transpired that Lefroy was a man of considerable conceit. On the first morning of his trial, he actually asked for his dress-coat, in order that he might wear that garment in the dock. He was, in a word, a man steeped in a kind of petty, strutting, theatrical vanity. Nevertheless, it was almost inexplicable that he should devote more attention to his hat than to the proceedings of the trial.

> It was curious to note the change that took place in Lefroy's bearing and demeanour whenever he caught sight of an artist from one of the illustrated

---

128   Alfred Pill died in August 1891 aged 86.
129   *Huddersfield Chronicle*, 2 July 1881.

papers in the act of sketching him. He suddenly brightened up, and, if I am not mistaken, assumed a studied pose for the occasion …

The proceedings apparently made little impression upon Lefroy, for beyond every now and then lifting his eyelids, he made no sign. At times, indeed, he seemed to be dozing.

On the third day of the trial, which was a Monday, the case for the prosecution closed, and, at about eleven o'clock, I rose to address the jury for the defence. My speech lasted for about three hours, and I do not think that I ever saw a jury more attentive than on this occasion. Some of them gave way to tears.

Once during the delivery of my speech, Lefroy shifted his chair a little, and seemed for the moment as though he really intended to wake up and listen. This was a mere spasmodic effort, however, and it soon died away. He either had not any interest in the business in hand, or he took care to disguise it.

During the absence of the jury, I noticed that the prisoner, whose life was hanging in the balance, showed symptoms of nervousness for the first time. His hands seemed to come mechanically to his face, his fingers twitched as he tugged at his moustache, and he moved uneasily in his chair, being evidently unable to control his emotion. Once or twice he got up from his seat, leant over the bars of the dock, and addressed a few words to his solicitor, Mr Dutton; then, as if by a great effort of will, he sat down again, and was comparatively calm.

When the foreman pronounced the word 'Guilty', up rose Lefroy, and, placing his hands behind him, advanced to the rails. He seemed to be altogether at ease, though pallid. There was a moment, however, when he grasped convulsively at the rails, and swayed to and fro, as though about to fall. But the weakness was only for a moment. The next minute he was himself again, and, folding his arms, he fixed his eyes intently upon the jury, and said: 'Some day you will learn, when too late, that you have murdered me'. Then, with a firm step, he retired, and disappeared from the public gaze.[130]

As will be seen in the Appendices later in this volume, Lefroy's self-belief – or was it self-delusion? – continued long after his conviction.

XIV.

Lefroy was taken back to Lewes Gaol – his unhappy sojourn to Maidstone over – and placed in the condemned cell. The date of his execution had been set for 29 November.

With three weeks to save his client from the hangman, solicitor Mr Dutton

---

130   Williams, M., *Leaves of a Life*, volume II (London: Macmillan & Co., 1890).

Introduction.

did what Victorian solicitors did in these circumstances: he drew up a petition for a reprieve on the grounds of insanity. Attempting to gather appropriate medical evidence, he wrote to Home Secretary Sir William Harcourt seeking permission for Doctors Forbes Winslow and Winn to visit the convict in his cell, in order to ascertain the state of his mental health. Forwarding the request to Harcourt, Assistant Under-Secretary of State Godfrey Lushington added a note which confirmed the Home Office's usual stance on such requests:

> There was, I believe, no evidence of insanity at the trial, as the line of defence was that he never did the act. It is stated in one of the letters that the Grandfather was insane & I am told the father died of drink – the Petition now being got up will probably contain some details on these points … Dr Winslow and Winn are the last persons to whom such an inquiry should be intrusted.[131]

Harcourt agreed, and declined the application.

Despite this setback, the petition duly arrived, and indeed included references to a strand of mental fragility running through the family. The sad demises of Lefroy's mother, father, grandfather and uncle were described, along with a letter from the doctor who had treated Mrs Mapleton during her labour with Lefroy, who stated that the child suffered from hereditary lung disease and as a result was physically weak.

Dutton argued that, had the prisoner been of sound mind, his instructions as to his defence would surely have been different: would he have adhered to the story of the third person in the carriage – the mysterious countryman – had he been able to realise that it was a version of events impossible to prove? And there was Lefroy's strange insouciance during the trial itself, belying an inability to grasp the gravity of his predicament.

Was Lefroy alluding to the family history of insanity when he told Swanson and Jarvis that there were 'certain matters' which he feared would be exposed?

Harcourt's response to the petition was withering.

> I don't think there is anything here to warrant medical enquiry. The father was a drunkard & the mother died of consumption & is said to have been subject to fits of melancholy & frenzy while with child of prisoner. Neither of these is insanity. As to the other relations said to have been insane there is not a particle of evidence. This is the oft repeated case of an afterthought defence not set up at the trial or even suggested & at the last moment fired at the S. of S. [Secretary of State] as a forlorn hope.[132]

---

131   TNA: PRO HO 144/83/A6404/41.
132   TNA: PRO HO 144/83/A6404/56.

Lefroy.

As one last desperate attempt to delay the inevitable, Dutton visited Lefroy and told him that, from information presented by his family and others, there was evidence to cast suspicion on him as the murderer of Lieutenant Percy Roper at Chatham Barracks in the February of 1881 – a case which was, at that moment, in the newspapers alongside Lefroy's, chiefly because a juicy reward of £600 had been offered for information leading to the capture of the perpetrator. Lefroy saw the opportunity to postpone his execution, and made a statement to the chaplain at Lewes Gaol, confessing to the murder.

Permanent Under-Secretary Sir Adolphus Liddell received the papers from the Reverend Cole and forwarded them to Home Secretary Harcourt, but not before adding his own thoughts: 'I think the execution should take place and the matter be enquired into afterwards'. Harcourt concurred.

With time running out and no sign of clemency on the horizon, Lefroy began to write his life story. In it, he confessed to the murder of Frederick Gold, and also confirmed that he had had nothing to do with the death of Lieutenant Roper.

His so-called autobiography, written and re-written several times in his cell at Lewes, is published here in its entirety for the first time (see Appendix XI). Liddell called it a 'curious production, written for effect and with considerable cunning and I believe no small amount of lying' – a view shared by Harcourt, who told him to keep it locked up. But with the benefit of the wealth of information at the fingertips of the modern researcher, it is interesting to note how much of Lefroy's version of events holds water. If he would fabricate journalistic engagements and theatre tour arrangements, why go to the trouble of including small details such as the name of the boatyard near which he contemplated suicide by throwing himself into the Yarra during his unhappy weeks in Melbourne? Or claim that, on his voyage out to Australia, he shared a cabin with a detective from Lincoln who was chasing a fugitive from the law, verifiable facts which can be – and have been – proved to be correct? Or was it a case of putting in just enough truth to persuade his readers of the veracity of his story? Either way, the autobiography makes for fascinating reading. We are pleased to present it here for your enjoyment. It is apparent throughout that Lefroy was completely driven by his delusional fixation on Miss Violet Cameron.

The final blow to Lefroy would be the very clear and public rejection by the object of his affections. Writing to the editor of the *Daily Telegraph* on the day before the execution of her unknown and unwanted suitor, she asked:

> As my name has been most unfortunately mixed up with the case of Lefroy, I beg that you will give an emphatic denial to the report that he was at any time known to me. I never saw him or exchanged a word with him in my life. But since his conviction he has written me a most painful and unaccountable letter, which is

MISS VIOLET CAMERON

STEREOSCOPIC CO1   COPYRIGHT

Author's collection

Introduction.

now in the possession of Mr Forbes Winslow.[133]

Lefroy's epistle to Miss Cameron had been written in his cell at Lewes Gaol on 14 November. In it, he confessed his devotion:

My dear Miss Cameron – a dying man is writing these few lines to you, lines which no person here will read but the Governor and the minister of religion, whose initials you will see on it, and in whose breast I need hardly say they will live for ever undisclosed, and as a dying man I ask you to read them, and forgive this hand, which soon will be still and cold in the grave, for penning them. When I first met and was introduced to you at the seaside in 1878, you were at Brighton, when I was introduced to you in another name than my own. I loved you. Don't be angry. I was not always what I am now. Several times after I saw you only to become madly, passionately fond of you. If I remember rightly, you were only there a week, and when you left all the light and brightness of my life seemed to pass away. You had given me no encouragement – why should you? I was only a boy or little more, and consequently you, in the springtime of your fresh young life, might naturally have thought, had you given it a thought at all, that it was only a boy's admiration of a pretty girl. But it was not. It was alone that has been the mainspring of my life ever since. Hopeless, unrequited as it might be, it was an intense, honest passion, and as such has saved me from many and many a sin I should otherwise have committed. From a distance I have watched your rise in your profession with mingled feelings. Feelings of delight, and at the same time of bitter despair. Delight at your well-deserved success; despair, as every upward step you took widened the gulf between us. But all the same I have lived on with the wild hope of winning you in the end. Trying to do right for your sake. And as you, with the world at your feet, loved by many and admired by all who know you and your brave unselfish life in your danger-beset profession, accept this last tribute, small and worthless though it may seem, of gratitude – aye, and hopeless love – from one whose life is quickly closing in. You have always been my ideal of what woman should be. Your face as I first saw it is ever by my side – aye, and will be to the bitter end. Cheering me, comforting me, not with hopes of what might have been, but what may be in the glorious future. God grant your life may continue as bright, as happy as it is now, and that your married life may be unsullied by any shade of grief or woe, and may your death be as happy as your life has been. Violet, my darling, I call you so for the first and last time on earth. God bless you. My love for you will cease only with my life, and the dearest, most precious treasure I have in the world is a faded rose you carelessly gave to

---

133   *Daily Telegraph*, 29 November 1881. Violet Cameron went on to achieve continued success on the stage, and married David de Bensaude in 1884, the couple having a child. Miss Cameron caused a scandal two years later by embarking on a widely-reported affair with Hugh Lowther, the 5th Earl of Lonsdale, bearing him two children.

Lefroy.

me nearly four years ago.[134]

*

Percy Lefroy Mapleton was executed at Lewes Gaol on Tuesday 29 November 1881. It was only the fourth hanging to take place there in the twenty-five years since the gaol had opened.

Newspaper reporters were admitted at 8.30 am and escorted to a yard where the gallows had been erected in the right-hand corner, a simple crossbeam over a pit into which the prisoner would drop. Forty feet to the left was a grave, already dug in readiness to receive the body. Apart from the press, the only people in the yard were Mr Bull, the Deputy Governor of the gaol, and William Marwood, the executioner. At five minutes to nine, Marwood went inside to fetch the prisoner:

> In two minutes the procession emerged from the door leading from the corridor in which the condemned cell is situated. First came the Chaplain, the Rev T. H. Cole, who as he came out began to read the Burial Service in clear and solemn tones, the only other sound being the clang of the 'passing bell', which had been tolling some ten minutes. The clergyman was followed by a warder, and then came Lefroy, pinioned and bare-necked, with a warder on either side, and the executioner close in the rear, supporting the convict by a slight touch of the elbow; not that the culprit seemed to require such assistance, as he walked with a set, steadfast face, moving as a man in a dream, his lips tightly closed, looking neither to the right nor left, stepping quietly in time with the remainder of the procession.

> Lefroy wore a suit of brown mixture, the same as on the examination at Cuckfield, and not the prison garb in which he has been attired since his conviction. In the rear of him came the Governor, the prison surgeon, one of the visiting justices, and the under sheriff, while the melancholy cortege was brought up by the under governor.

> It took but a moment to reach the scaffold, on to which Lefroy stepped without the slightest hesitation, a slight fixing together of the lips alone showing inward agitation. Then Marwood proceeded to his work, first placing Lefroy in proper position under the beam, testing this by laying the rope upon his shoulders, and afterwards fastening his legs with a broad leather strap. He then produced the cap for shrouding the convict's face from his pocket, and instantly placed it in position. As this was being done Lefroy slightly raised his eyes, but not a feature of his face relaxed its rigidity. His lips never moved in response to the clergyman, who all this time, in tones that showed the deep emotion he felt, was reciting the

---

134 *Birmingham Daily Post*, 8 December 1881.

selected portions of the service. As soon as he had drawn the cap over Lefroy's eyes, Marwood put the noose around his neck, and with dexterity and rapidity adjusted the rope.

Marwood stayed a moment to see that all was right, and then with a slight touch of his hand on Lefroy's right shoulder, but without going through the ceremony of shaking hands, he stepped back from the scaffold and stood by the lever that controlled the working of the drop. The next instant the minister recited the words "Lord have mercy upon us"; Marwood pulled the lever, and the doomed man dropped out of sight of the spectators. The surgeon made a short inspection of the body, but did not go into the pit. It was evident that death must have been instantaneous.[135]

Lefroy's body was left hanging for an hour. At 10.15 am, it was cut down and Richard Turner, the surgeon attached to Lewes Gaol, examined the body and pronounced life extinct. An inquest was immediately conducted under Wynne Baxter, and the fourteen jury members viewed the body, which by this time had been placed in its coffin, and returned a verdict that the law had been properly carried out. The coffin was then buried in the grave previously prepared.

The strange life of Percy Lefroy Mapleton was over.

XV.

Several of those involved in the Lefroy affair in an official capacity would have their expertise called upon in even more terrible circumstances; seven years later, Inspector Donald Swanson would lead Scotland Yard's hunt for Jack the Ripper, while Coroner Wynne Baxter presided over the inquests into the deaths of many of the Ripper's victims. Dr Thomas Bond would become known for his profile of the Whitechapel murderer, accepted by most as the first criminal profile.

Swanson was a particular beneficiary of the reflected glory of Lefroy's case: his capture of the notorious fugitive would catapult him into the limelight and see him handed cases of increasing importance. He was awarded £5 by the Commissioner for 'energy and zeal displayed in making numerous enquiries,'[136] and also received £5 from the London, Brighton and South Coast Railway.[137] His good fortune was perhaps not enjoyed by all, as reported by one newspaper: 'Inspector Swanson, whose name has been made so prominent in connection

---

135 *The Derbyshire Times*, 30 November 1881.
136 Swanson's Metropolitan Police file (TNA: PRO MEPO 2/2980).
137 Letter from the general manager of the London, Brighton and South Coast Railway dated 23 January 1882, held in Swanson family archives.

with the arrest of Lefroy, bears the soubriquet among his colleagues of "Lucky Swanson."[138] Inspectors Jarvis and Turpin also received £5 each.[139]

Montagu Williams, unsuccessful defence barrister this time around, would suffer a similar defeat the following year, when he failed to save George Lamson from the gallows for the murder of his brother-in-law Percy John [see NBT 18]. Williams resigned as Junior Treasury Counsel in 1886 due to a growth on the larynx which affected his voice, and was succeeded by Charles Mathews.[140] Before his death in 1892, he published his memoir, *Leaves of a Life*, which included a lengthy account of the Lefroy trial and, happily for this volume, a verbatim account of his closing speech to the jury.

Following the execution of her brother, Mary Mapleton emigrated to Australia with her children. They left London on 9 September 1883, on board the *Gauntlet,* arriving in Keppel Bay, Queensland, on 27 December 1883. They settled at Gympie, where Mary died in August 1920.

Percy's other sister, Eliza Julia Mapleton, remained in London for at least a decade, being recorded at Penge in the census of 1891. Two years later she and her son Leon seemingly made an attempt to start a new life in America, departing Liverpool on board the *Umbria*. They arrived in New York on 26 December. Mother and son are recorded in the New Jersey State Census for 1895 as Eliza and Leon Mapleton, residing at Plainfield, Union County. However, by the turn of the new century, they were back in England and were recorded in the 1901 census at Southampton. Eliza, aged fifty-one, was listed as a retired hospital matron, and Leon, now in his early twenties, as a French Correspondent. In 1911, Eliza, now calling herself Eliza Travers Liebie, was living alone in Liverpool Street, behind King's Cross Station, listening to the rattle of the trains as they set off out of the city. She died in January 1915.

Following the trial, it was reported that 4 Cathcart Road, where Lefroy had lodged with his cousins, had been left vacant, to be let on account of the morbid curiosity attached to the house.[141] In fact, the Claytons had relinquished the property while Lefroy was on remand, moving nearby to the ironically-named Melbourne Road in October 1881.[142] The family were still there in 1887. Annie Clayton died in 1913 aged seventy; Thomas Clayton followed her in 1932.

---

138 *The North-Eastern Daily Gazette*, 18 July 1881.

139 *The Worcestershire Chronicle*, 10 December 1881.

140 Charles Willie Mathews (1850–1920), later Sir Charles. Senior Counsel to the Treasury, and, from 1908, Director of Public Prosecutions, he appeared in several other cases covered in this series: see, for example, *Trial of the Stauntons* [NBT 11], *Trial of Adelaide Bartlett* [NBT 41] and *The Baccarat Case* [NBT 56].

141 *Sheffield Daily Telegraph*, 11 November 1881.

142 Tax Collection Rate Books, 1783–1914: Poor Rates (1881) LG19/3/4. Thomas Clayton is recorded as the tenant at 1 Melbourne Road on 15 October 1881.

Introduction.

Frank Seale, Lefroy's cousin who had such an impact on his early life, finally married in September 1890, to Eliza de Beauchamp, a widow following her first husband George's death the previous year. Frank's sister Annie was one of the witnesses.[143] In 1899, Frank died, aged sixty.

Mrs Lydia Matilda Gold, the unhappy widow, continued to live in Preston Park, close to the station at which her husband's murderer stepped out of the bloodied carriage, for a further twenty-nine years. She died on 27 February 1910, leaving more than £6000,[144] with a request that £150 of that amount be used to pay for the erection of a memorial plaque to Mr Gold and herself at St Peter's Church, Preston Park.[145] Her wish was fulfilled, and can still be viewed today in the form of a white marble plaque on a wall inside St Peter's bearing the following inscription:

> THIS TABLET IS ERECTED
> IN MEMORY OF
> FREDERICK ISAAC GOLD
> WHO DEPARTED THIS LIFE 27TH JUNE 1881,
> AGED 64 YEARS.
> AND OF
> LYDIA MATILDA, HIS WIFE,
> WHO DIED 27TH FEBRUARY 1910,
> AGED 86 YEARS.
> FOR MANY YEARS THEY WERE
> PARISHIONERS OF PRESTON
> AND REGULAR WORSHIPPERS IN THIS CHURCH.
> "I AM THE RESURRECTION AND THE LIFE."

By a strange coincidence, just weeks earlier, St Peter's was the scene for the funeral of Mr Robert Peel, who had been the driver of the Brighton express on that fateful June afternoon in 1881. He had been raised near Newcastle-upon-Tyne, and began a long career as an engine driver in 1845, having the distinction of driving the first Newcastle to London train. He moved south to join the London, Brighton and South Coast Railway in 1847. Perhaps unsurprisingly, taking into account his thirty-four-year career, he was involved in several exciting incidents. Twice he had had to leap from his engine to save his own life; less fortunate were the seven men and two horses he ran into and killed over the years. Mr Peel's testimony at the trial, indignantly refuting the suggestion

---

143   Marriage certificate of Francis Seale and Eliza de Beauchamp.
144   Probate was awarded to Mrs Gold's brother, Samuel Wood.
145   *Shoreditch Observer*, 30 April 1910.

Lefroy.

that he may have slowed the train long enough for an assassin to escape, had all the hallmarks of a man who had been in his job for a long, long time, and knew it like the back of his hand. Following the death of Mr Gold, Peel hung up his driver's cap and began a seven-year stint as foreman at Hastings Station, looking after their engines. He finally retired in 1888, aged sixty-nine, and was presented with a marble clock and an engraved gold watch, only for the latter to be stolen from him during a visit to London in 1904. He died on 8 January 1910, seven weeks before Mrs Gold.[146]

Percy Lefroy Mapleton lived his life as if in a dream, and from this remove, more than 135 years later, he seems an almost dream-like character: a parody, to some extent possibly even worthy of our sympathies. But the harsh reality is that Lefroy was a liar, a thief, a fraudster and, finally, a murderer – for which he paid the ultimate price.

It is worth pausing to reflect on the way in which coverage of the Lefroy case became increasingly sensationalistic in an attempt to attract readers – a ploy continued to this day, as seen with overwhelming and irritating online clickbait headlines.

As Lefroy provided newspapers with column inches for months, from the murder of Mr Gold, his escape and (short-lived) ability to avoid detection, and finally his appearance at the magistrates' hearing and his eventual trial, many reached for the ever-more lurid morning and evening editions. But some were aghast at the nature of the reporting, and one, the music hall newspaper *The Entr'acte*, was not shy in letting its readers know that it did not approve.

In his 'Gadfly' column of 16 July, proprietor H. J. Chawner commented:

> It is right and proper that there should be a public record made of the real facts of this sensational case, though I do not know that it serves any honest purpose to supply the public with those details which are calculated to invest it with the element of romance. For my own part, I do not want to know anything concerning the ordinary habits of a man who commits a murder; nor do I think that any benefit accrues from descriptions in print of how he looked when in the company of the gaoler, how many times he asked for refreshments, or his demeanour in his cell; all these details, I contend, help to give a colour of heroism to a man who is nothing more than a despicable wretch, too cowardly to get necessary bread and cheese by honest competition.

> But I find that what are objectionable and repellent morsels to one man are luxuries which another will roll over and over in his mouth. It may not entertain you nor me, my dear readers, to read in a morning newspaper that Mr Lefroy was in the best of spirits after he was arrested; that he playfully nudged Superintendent

---

146 *Brighton Gazette*, 12 January 1910.

Introduction.

Williamson in the ribs several times during a short stay at Scotland Yard; that he smoked a goodly number of cigarettes during a railway journey to Lewes, and that he was nice and chatty when he got to his destination; but, unfortunately, there are millions in this country to whom such details would bring much entertainment.

There are tremendous numbers of our fellow-countrymen and countrywomen who will persist in making heroes of the wrong people; let them but once see that justice has got a ruffian by the collar, and as quick as lightning their sympathies go with the possessor of the collar, never mind what the wearer's desserts may be. These are the folks who take a delight in reading that an accused murderer accepts his position with perfect sang froid; that his spirits are not one whit cast down, and that he was positively playful in cross-examining a witness; he is a hero in their eyes, and if he should but rebuke an opposing counsel, or ask that he might be allowed so much tobacco per diem to smoke in his cell, his heroism goes up one-hundred per cent at a bound.

It is deplorable that there are so many of these wrong-headed and wrong-hearted people about, but so it is; equally lamentable is it that there are journals – not many, I hope – that make a point of catering for them. These papers don't limit themselves to a report of facts; the plain melody does not satisfy them, and they play every kind of variation upon the theme; they tell us when Lefroy looked round the court, when he sighed, when he blew his nose, when he appeared to be interested in some evidence, and when he was indifferent.

The *Daily Telegraph* seems to me lately to have been catering pretty considerably for the class of person I refer to. The *D.T.* not only travelled somewhat out of its usual way in publishing a sketch of Mr Lefroy Mapleton, but it has followed up this policy by further efforts in the same direction; in fact, if this individual had been one of the greatest and best men that England has ever produced, I very much question whether the Peterborough Court organ would have permitted him to engross more of its columns day after day.

All this, I contend, is calculated to demoralise. We do not want to be informed by the *D.T.*, or any other paper, what the house is like in which Mr Lefroy Mapleton was arrested; he should not be made of this importance. In a case of this kind everything should be done in the direction of justice; no stone should be left unturned to place the responsibility of the deed on the right shoulders, care being taken to avoid advertising the man that all respectable people would like to forget.[147]

******

---

147   *The Entr'acte*, 16 July 1881.

Lefroy.

My appreciation must be recorded for the kind assistance given by the following people during the preparation of this volume: Neil Bell, Caroline Bunford, Kate Clarke, David Green, Mark Ripper (M.W. Oldridge), Lisa Ward of the Friends of St Peter's Church, Preston Park and Neil Watson.

Leading Dates in the Percy Lefroy Mapleton Case.

23 February 1860	Percy Lefroy Mapleton born in Peckham, south London. He lives with his mother and sisters at the home of his uncle and aunt, Archibald and Sarah Seale, and their children Annie and Frank Seale.
5 June 1866	Death of mother Mary Trent Seale. Her brother, Archibald Seale, dies two months later. Lefroy is raised by his aunt Sarah and begins attending school in 1867.
14 December 1878	Lefroy is sent to Australia for the good of his health, departing from London. He arrives in Melbourne on 12 February 1879.
5 July 1879	Lefroy leaves Australia, arriving in England on 30 September. He first visits his sister Julia in Richmond, then goes to live with his cousin Annie, her husband Thomas Clayton and cousin Frank Seale at 4 Cathcart Road, Wallington, Surrey.
21 June 1881	A pistol is pledged at pawnbrokers Messrs. Adams and Hillstead.
27 June 1881	
8.05 am	Frederick Isaac Gold leaves his home at Preston Park.
8.09 am	Train departs Preston Park for Brighton, arriving at 8.17 am.
8.45 am	Mr Gold departs Brighton on the express train to London Bridge, arriving at 9.45 am.
9.45-9.55 am	Stationer Albert Ellis receives a letter in Lefroy's handwriting asking him to call on Annie Clayton at 4 Cathcart Road. He goes, but waits just five minutes before returning to his shop.
c.10.05 am	Lefroy visits the stationer's shop and obtains 13s from Ellis's shopboy, Frederick Pink
c.10.30-10.40 am	Mr Gold visits his shop at 145 East Street, Walworth, departing at 10.45-10.55 am.
10.49 am	Probable train to London Bridge from Wallington caught by Lefroy, arriving at 11.32 am
11.00 am-12.00 pm	A pistol is redeemed at Messrs. Adams and Hillstead.
c.11.30 am-12.30 pm	Mr Gold meets his brother Thomas in the Minories.
c.1.00 pm	Mr Gold visits his bank at 130 Whitechapel High Street.
1.50 pm	Mr Gold arrives at London Bridge and boards the 2.00 pm Brighton train.
1.58 pm	Lefroy boards the train.
2.02 pm	The train departs.
2.32 pm	The train stops at Croydon.

Lefroy.

c.2.40 pm	The train enters the Merstham Tunnel. Passenger William Gibson hears what he took to be four or five fog signals fire out.
c.2.50 pm	The train passes Horley, where Ann Brown and her daughter see two men in the train standing up, giving the appearance of fighting or 'larking about'.
3.20 pm	The train arrives at Preston Park, where Lefroy alights.
3.30 pm	Lefroy is taken to Brighton to make a statement and receive medical treatment.
4.00 pm	A body is discovered in Balcombe Tunnel.
6.20 pm	Lefroy leaves Brighton accompanied by Railway Police Detective Sergeant George Holmes. When the train stops at Balcombe, Holmes is told that a body has been discovered.
c.9.00 pm	Lefroy and Holmes arrive at Cathcart Road, Wallington, where a further statement is taken.
c.9.30-10.00 pm	Lefroy leaves the house.
10.05pm	Mrs Lydia Gold receives a telegram from the station master at Balcombe informing her that a man had been found dead, with papers upon him in the name "F. I. Gold". She goes at once with family friend Thomas Lee Hollis, who identifies the body as that of Mr Gold.
29 June 1881	Inquest into the death of Frederick Isaac Gold opens.
30 June 1881	Lefroy takes a room at 32 Smith Street, Stepney, giving the name "G. Clark".
1 July 1881	The *Daily Telegraph* publishes a likeness of Lefroy.
4 July 1881	A £200 reward is offered for information leading to the capture of Percy Lefroy Mapleton.
	Frederick Gold buried at the Extra-Mural Cemetery near Brighton.
7 July 1881	Lefroy sends a telegram to "S. Seale, J.T. Hutchinson and Co., 56 Gresham Street".
	Inquest into the death of Mr Gold concludes with a verdict of murder against Lefroy.
8 July 1881	Lefroy is arrested at Smith Street by Inspector Donald Swanson.
9 July 1881	Lefroy is conveyed to Lewes Gaol by Swanson and Inspector Frederick Jarvis.
15-21 July 1881	Committal hearing at Cuckfield; Lefroy is remanded for trial.
28 October 1881	Lefroy transferred to Maidstone Gaol.
4 November 1881	Trial opens at Maidstone Crown Court.

Leading Dates.

8 November 1881	Trial ends; Lefroy is found Guilty.
	Lefroy is transferred back to Lewes Gaol to await execution.
17 November 1881	Solicitor Thomas Dutton writes to the Home Office seeking permission for Drs Forbes Winslow and Winn to examine Lefroy to ascertain his mental condition.
18 November 1881	The request is declined.
21 November 1881	A Petition for Lefroy's reprieve is submitted by solicitor Thomas Dutton.
22 November 1881	The Petition is declined.
24 November 1881	A pistol is discovered by railway tracks at Earlswood.
26 November 1881	Lefroy confesses to the murder of Lieutenant Roper at Chatham.
28 November 1881	Lefroy finishes writing his autobiography, entrusting the manuscript to prison Chaplain T. H. Cole.
29 November 1881	Lefroy confesses to the murder of Mr Gold and retracts his confession to the murder of Roper.
	Lefroy executed at Lewes Gaol by William Marwood.
13 January 1882	£200 reward paid to Joseph Mugford, the city clerk who identified Lefroy as the "Mr. Clark" lodging at 32 Smith Street and informed Inspector Donald Swanson at Scotland Yard.
24 February 1882	A gratuity of £20 is paid from Treasury funds to Lefroy's landlady at Smith Street, Mrs Sarah Bickers, following personal intervention from the Director of the Criminal Investigation Department, Howard Vincent.

MAIDSTONE CROWN COURT

Friday 4 November to Tuesday 8 November 1881

Before Mr Justice Coleridge

Percy Lefroy Mapleton
(otherwise Arthur Lefroy)
Indicted for the Wilful Murder
of
Frederick Isaac Gold.

Sir Henry James (The Attorney-General),
Mr Harry Poland,
and
Mr A. L. Smith
conducted the prosecution.

Mr Montagu Williams,
Mr Forrest Fulton,
and
Mr Henry Kisch
appeared for the defence.

First Day –
Friday 4 November 1881.[1]

Lord Coleridge took his seat in the Crown Court at ten o'clock this morning, and the prisoner Percy Lefroy Mapleton was immediately afterwards placed in the dock.

The prisoner, on being called on to plead by the Clerk of Arraigns, pleaded 'Not Guilty' in a very low voice. He was also called upon to challenge the jury, but he took no apparent notice of the names, and did not turn his head in the direction of the jury box.

The indictment, which was read to the prisoner, was that he did wilfully and of his malice aforethought kill and murder Frederick Isaac Gold at Balcombe, on the 27 June 1881. The name of the committing magistrate was Mr J. M. Norman, of Cuckfield. Prisoner was also charged on the coroner's inquisition with the wilful murder of the said Frederick Isaac Gold. Prisoner is described as being a journalist, aged twenty-two, well educated.

The Attorney-General, Mr A. L. Smith, and Mr Poland conducted the prosecution on the part of the Crown. The prisoner was defended by Mr Montagu Williams, Mr Forrest Fulton, and Mr Henry Kisch.

Opening Speech for the Prosecution

The ATTORNEY-GENERAL, whose opening sentences were very indistinctly heard in the gallery, said, — May it please your Lordship, — Gentlemen of the jury, — I am sure I need not do more than ask you to give me your undivided attention while I state to you the facts connected with this case. You have just heard that the prisoner at the bar is charged with murder, and of course you are aware of the consequences following upon a conviction for such a crime. Of course we are all aware that the circumstances of the case attracted much public attention when it occurred, some months ago, and I presume that the facts of the case are to some extent known to you. But I would earnestly ask you to allow any fact which may have impressed itself on your mind, or any opinion you

Attorney-General

---

[1]	Transcript of the day's proceedings amalgamated from the *Daily News*, Saturday 5 November 1881; *Brighton and Sussex Daily Post*, Saturday 5 November 1881; *Maidstone and Kent County Standard*, Saturday 5 November 1881; *Manchester Guardian*, Saturday 5 November 1881; *Sussex Evening Times*, Friday 4 November 1881; *West Sussex Journal*, Tuesday 8 November 1881.

Lefroy.

may have formed on this case, to be cast entirely aside, and I trust that from your mind and from your memory you will banish any fact you have noted or any impression you have formed which is at all likely to be an ingredient in your consideration of this case. I will now, without further preface, proceed to state to you very briefly, and without attempting to draw any argument from the facts I am about to place before you, the nature of the evidence which I believe will be laid before you in order to support this prosecution.

Gentlemen, you have heard that the prisoner at the bar is charged with having committed wilful murder on 27 June last upon the body of Mr Gold. Mr Gold was a gentleman who had retired from business. He was sixty-four years of age, and he lived at a place in the suburbs of Brighton. He had been engaged in business, but had retired from taking any active part in it either in London or elsewhere. He had, however, retained, I know not whether there was more than one, but certainly one shop in which he had a pecuniary interest, and which was managed by a person whom he had placed in it. It was his habit every week, that is to say every Monday, to proceed to London for the purpose of receiving from his manager the weekly payments of the shop. Sometimes he left the money he so received at his bankers in London, and sometimes he carried it with him to his home near Brighton.

Following his usual practice, upon Monday 27 June last, Mr Gold left his home at five minutes past eight o'clock to proceed by train to London. He left the station near Brighton at eight o'clock, and he would arrive in London shortly before ten o'clock. He took with him upon that day his ordinary wearing apparel, to some portion of which great attention will be called, and he also carried with him a watch with a white face, made by a person of the name of Griffiths, and bearing the number 16261. Having arrived in London he appears to have proceeded to his shop, which was managed by a person of the name of Cross, from whom he received the sum of £38 5s 1d. We next find him at his bankers, which was the eastern branch of the London and Westminster Bank, situated in Whitechapel. He there deposited the sum of £38, and though we have no information as to the sum of money he was actually carrying, yet so far as we know almost the entirety of the sum he received from his manager was deposited in the bank, and therefore he would be taking no considerable sum back with him to Brighton.

He was next heard of at the Brighton Railway Station at London Bridge, where he arrived shortly before two o'clock. Mr Gold was a season ticket-holder upon that line, and was well known to the officials engaged at the station. He started in the express train that leaves London Bridge at two o'clock, and he took his seat in a carriage which contained

The Attorney-General, Sir Henry James QC MP.

First Day – Friday 4 November 1881.

four compartments. The first was a second-class compartment, then came a first-class smoking, then another first-class, and lastly a second-class. It was in the first of the first-class compartments, and therefore a smoking compartment, that Mr Gold was seen by the collector to take his seat, and just before the train left a second person took his seat in that compartment. For that train there were only three first-class tickets issued from London to Brighton. Mr Gold, as I have stated, travelled with a season-ticket. A lady took two tickets, numbered 3179 and 3180, and both these tickets were given up and have been returned. The third ticket, numbered 3181, was issued to a person with whose identity I will deal hereafter, and that ticket will be produced before you.

The train seems to have reached Croydon station at twenty-three minutes past two, and I now purpose to continue the journey of that train, and to place before you certain facts connected with it, and it will be your duty to draw such inferences as suggest themselves to you. There is, after leaving Croydon, and at a distance of some eight miles from Croydon, a tunnel called the Merstham tunnel, which is a mile, or rather over a mile, being 1,830 yards long. As the train approached the entrance of that tunnel, the attention of a traveller, a Mr Gibson, a chemist, was attracted by the sound of four explosions. It occurred to him that they were fog signals, and having his son with him, a little boy of three or four years old, he reassured him as to what was the cause of the noise, and at that time there is no doubt that he seems to have been under the impression himself that it resulted from the fog signals laid down on the line. You probably will find that the explanation of those sounds, which were attributed to the explosion of fog signals at the time, resulted from the explosion of firearms.

The next incident is that, after the train had run a distance of eight miles, there is a place called Horley, and close to the line are some cottages. A Mrs Brown and her daughter were standing in front of the cottages at that time; and although I place very little reliance on the effect of this testimony, the fact is to be noted that, as the express train passed, witness and her daughter saw two persons standing up in the train, either struggling or, as their evidence goes, 'larking together'. A test has been applied as to whether persons in a train could be so seen from the cottages, and whether they could or not is not a very crucial matter in this case. But, if this evidence be true, we shall have this result: that the struggle probably commenced at the time the explosion was heard, and continued up to the time I have mentioned, and that the person who, without doubt, was killed on that occasion, was still continuing the struggle.

The next point, gentlemen, that is reached which is important in this

Lefroy.

case, is a place called Balcombe tunnel. It is some thirty-two miles from London, and therefore from the place where Mrs Brown and her daughter observed the struggle it would be seven miles distant. I now proceed to tell you what occurred. In the timetable, the train is set down as proceeding to Brighton without stopping; but without any notice given in the timetable – therefore, without the fact being brought to the knowledge of travellers – the train did stop at a spot called Preston Park, which is one mile from Brighton station. Upon the arrival of the train there, the ticket collector had his attention called to the prisoner at the bar, who was then riding in the same first-class carriage as that in which, without doubt, Mr Gold had commenced his journey from London. The prisoner was found in a condition that showed he had been subjected to force, the result of which must have attracted the attention of anyone. He was, if I may use the expression, fairly smothered in blood. He was suffering apparently from some injuries or wounds upon the head, and his collar was gone. The carriage was saturated with blood as well. The prisoner, in asking for a policeman, addressed himself to the ticket collector, and made certain statements to him. I wish to give you only the very general result of these statements; first, because several people are inclined to differ as to what was said, and second, because, from whatever cause, the prisoner had arrived at a state considering which it would be unjust to him were we to lay too much dependence on the exact words uttered by him. He certainly, at least, was not in a condition to judge of every word he said. But the result was that he stated to the officials with whom he came into communication that he commenced his journey from London with two persons in the same compartment as himself. One he described as an elderly man, and the other as a countryman about fifty years of age; and, as he was entering the tunnel, he says, he was attacked, as he believed, by the younger man, became insensible, and knew nothing of anything that occurred until shortly before the arrival of the train at Preston Park. A most material fact in the case is that, when he presented himself on the platform, attention was called to the fact that hanging from his shoe was the chain of a watch. The explanation given by the prisoner was that he had placed it there for safety, and when the chain was taken from the shoe, a watch was found attached to it. That watch was restored to him at the time, and I now repeat that the watch is a most material fact in the case.

I pass on to what occurred when the prisoner arrived at Brighton, and was taken to the town hall, where he made his statement. From the town hall he was taken to the hospital, and after remaining there in charge of two policemen, he was allowed to return to his place of residence at Wallington. I may also point out that in the carriage were found three

First Day – Friday 4 November 1881.

Hanoverian medals which bear some resemblance to sovereigns, and in the prisoner's coat pocket three more of these were found. I think, however, it would be well for us to not enter too minutely at this stage into the particulars of the conduct of the policemen on this occasion. Yet it is the fact – I will say no more of it – that the prisoner, being given in charge to the two policemen, was allowed to go home to the house of his second cousin.

Before I relate what happened there, there were one or two things which occurred in the meantime. About a quarter before four on the Monday evening, some three-quarters of an hour after the train had passed through Balcombe tunnel, a platelayer came upon the body of Mr Gold near the entrance to the tunnel. There is no doubt from the marks on the body that Mr Gold had been shot, for a bullet was found in his neck. There were marks also of injuries apparently inflicted with a knife on the body, showing that there must have been a long and deadly struggle between the dead man and whomsoever inflicted these wounds. If such were the case, it would rather corroborate the probability that they resulted from the struggle witnessed from the cottage, and that that struggle commenced when the explosions were heard in Merstham tunnel. Therefore, now we have this result standing before us, that whenever the struggle commenced, and by whatever means the wounds were inflicted, Mr Gold had arrived at his death before the train reached the middle of Balcombe tunnel. Again, at a quarter before five on this Monday, a platelayer found on the line itself, some distance near Brighton, an ordinary shirt collar. Gentlemen, I think you will come to the conclusion that that collar no doubt was the collar of the prisoner at the bar. When he arrived at Brighton he had no collar, and had to purchase one with the aid of a policeman, and you will find that that collar is of the same size as the one which was found – at least, there is a difference of half an inch, but that is very slight.

The next incident that occurred was that at five minutes past three, at a place below Burgess Hill, some forty-two miles from London, a hat was found on the up line. That hat must have been thrown from the carriage in which the deceased was travelling by someone besides himself. Later on, on 30 July, at a place called Hassock's Gate, a young woman was walking in a field which was some yards from the railway, and at the commencement of a place called Clayton tunnel, on the same Monday evening, about a quarter before seven, an umbrella was found, which proves to be the umbrella of Mr Gold. I think it will be well to call attention to the exact spot where the umbrella was found. Hassock's Gate is about forty-three and a half miles from London. A question will arise as to the speed at which the train was travelling at Hassock's Gate.

Lefroy.

Attorney-General

Whatever inference may be drawn from that, I ask you to bear in mind that two miles on the journey of the train below Hassock's Gate, Mr Gold's umbrella was found. That probably proceeded from the carriage in which he was riding, and at this time – two miles from Hassock's Gate and four and a half miles from Preston Park – a second person was riding, and evidently threw the umbrella out of the carriage to get rid to it. It may be assumed that the object was that by throwing the hat and umbrella out of the carriage, and everything else belonging to Mr Gold, when the train arrived at its destination, there should be no proof of another person having been there, and no traces of the identity of who had been there, and no traces of the identity of who had been such person who rode there. That hat and umbrella are got rid of before the train arrives at its destination, and the other article is, as I have shown you, a watch of a certain number, and as I shall be able to establish to you without the slightest doubt, that watch, which was taken from the shoe of the prisoner, is the watch of the murdered man.

I have stated to you the time – about five o'clock on the evening of Monday 27 June – when he went with a police constable to the house at Cathcart Road, Wallington. I will say nothing with regard to the position or habits of the prisoner; but, living at Wallington, it was his habit frequently to go to London. He had a second-class season ticket, and when he had not that ticket he probably travelled third-class. We have no trace, according to the evidence of Mr Clayton, that he travelled first-class before 27 June. There was an incident which occurred on the morning of the 27th, but I hope you will not suppose I mention it to suggest any reflections upon the moral conduct of the prisoner. Living at Wallington was a stationer named Ellis. On this Monday morning, a note was received by Mr Ellis purporting to come from Mrs Clayton, and requesting Mr Ellis to call upon her with regard to an account. Whilst he was at the house, prisoner left, and proceeded at once to the shop of Mr Ellis, whose absence had been secured by a promise to pay, and there the prisoner made a proposal to the boy that he would give him two sovereigns which were in an envelope, and receive 13s change to settle the account. The boy complied with the request, believing the envelope to contain two sovereigns, and the prisoner received 13s in change. As a fact the envelope contained two Hanoverian medals and one shilling. Whether the prisoner placed the shilling there to make the envelope heavier is for you to judge, but the boy received these two worthless pieces. I should not have mentioned this matter at all lest you should be indirectly influenced by it to suppose that the prisoner's moral sense is not of a high order, but the prisoner must undoubtedly have been that morning in a state of impecuniosity, and there can be no doubt

First Day – Friday 4 November 1881.

that he had Hanoverian medals on the morning of 27 June. You will find from the evidence that, when the Hanoverian medals were found in the carriage, he denied all knowledge of them, and said they never belonged to him, or words to that effect. He also, no doubt, intended the inference to be drawn that someone who had been in possession of those medals had been in that carriage.

Well, gentlemen, he does not appear to have left Wallington by an ordinary train after receiving the money. The boy from whom he had, by the means I have mentioned, obtained the money, was in the habit of selling papers at the station, and therefore, if he had gone from Wallington station, he would have seen the boy. There are stations in close proximity to Wallington, one of them being called Waddon. But, gentlemen, the matter of this inquiry as to what time he left Wallington for London brings me now to the statement of a witness most material in this case. I mentioned to you that Mr Gold was shot, and therefore whoever committed this murder must have had in his possession some firearm, a pistol probably, for the bullet was a very small one. Gentlemen, you will have evidence placed before you which, if you believe the witness, will establish to you that the prisoner had upon this day a revolver in his possession. At a shop in the Borough, there is a person named Creek, carrying on business as a pawnbroker. There had been certain articles pawned at that shop. On 2 June, a person of the name of William Lee had pawned a coat, and this person had given the address: 8 Southampton Street, Peckham. On 11 June, there had been a transaction by which a dress-suit was pledged for £1 5s in the name of James Lee, of 20 Southampton Street. On 21 June, some person, in the name of William Lee, had pawned a revolver, or pistol, for the sum of 5s. We now come to 27 June. On that day, at a time which is certainly answering, as far as we can judge, to the time when the prisoner would have arrived in London, this pistol was taken out of pawn. Gentlemen, in this matter you will have to deal with the direct evidence of the pawnbroker's manager, and that evidence will, I think, place it beyond doubt that the prisoner is the same person who pawned the clothes and who also pawned the pistol, and took it out on the morning of the murder. The pawn tickets were found in the coat of the prisoner, and you will find that the person who pawned the clothes and the person who pawned the revolver gave the same Christian name, the same surname, and substantially the same address, the only difference in the latter being a slight difference of numbers.

Well, gentlemen, we have the prisoner at the pawnbroker's shop at a time which I have shown is consistent with his leaving Wallington, and we now come to London Bridge. Mr Gold is there, and the booking

Lefroy.

clerk will tell you that about five minutes before two he delivered to a person who he believes to be the accused a single ticket from London to Brighton. I would not dwell upon that if it stood alone, but undoubtedly the clerk did issue a ticket numbered 3181, and that was found upon the prisoner. He is seen at the station, and there can be no question that he was in the same carriage with Mr Gold, even according to his own statement. You will have distinct evidence that he was seen to pass along the train and enter the carriage, and so far as we know there was no person in it besides the accused and Mr Gold.

Such was the way, gentlemen, in which this journey was commenced. I have narrated to you the incidents of the journey, and I have also narrated to you what occurred on the arrival at Brighton. There is only one other incident to which I would here draw your attention. There was found upon the line a hat other than Mr Gold's. I will not say to whom it belonged, but evidence will be produced to show that it was of the same shape and make as that which the prisoner wore, and that it fitted him almost exactly.

Well, gentlemen, there is one subject more. On this Monday night, the prisoner made a second statement to the constable who was with him, and produced the watch. The constable took down the number and the name of the maker, and Mrs Gold will tell you that that was the number of her husband's watch.

Only a few words more. In the course of the return journey with the two policemen, an official of the line entered the train, speaking in a voice which in his opinion was heard by the accused, and stated that a body had been found in the tunnel. The prisoner knew of that; and, directly the police quitted the house, the prisoner stated to a servant that he was about to leave in order to visit a surgeon in the neighbourhood; but you will find that he never went to any doctor at all. He left by the back part of the premises. This was on the night of Monday 27 June. As to what became of him during the next few days, I have no information to place before you; but on Thursday, the 30th, he makes his appearance at the house of a Mrs Bickers, at a small street, Smith Street, in Stepney. At this time there was, of course, a hue and cry after the prisoner. He had given a false name; he had stated that he had arrived from Liverpool, and was an engineer; and he remained from the Thursday until the Thursday of the next week alone, having no occupation, and only once or twice leaving the house.

While residing in Smith Street, the prisoner secured the services of a person to take a telegram to the telegraph office. The message was sent in the name of Clark[2] to a Mr Seale for the purpose of obtaining money,

First Day – Friday 4 November 1881.

and the place to which it was sent was an office in Gresham Street. The telegram, which I will read to you, is in the following terms: 'To Mr Seale, at Messrs Hutchinson's, 56 Gresham Street, from Mr Clark, 32 Smith Street. Please send my wages tonight without fail about 8 o'clock'. The prisoner, let me observe, had no wages there. The telegram continued, 'Flour tomorrow'. That is an expression the meaning of which does not transpire. The remaining portion of the telegram is, 'Not 33'. On the evening of the day on which that telegram was sent to Mr Hutchinson, information having reached the police,[3] two constables, Detective Swanson and another constable,[4] called at the house where the prisoner was residing, and took him into custody. In the room they found a false beard, which might be used to disguise a person.

I have now referred you, gentlemen, in general terms to the evidence that will be given before you. On the part of the prosecution, you have it shown that the prisoner was undoubtedly in the carriage in which this dangerous struggle took place. You have it shown that he had upon his person property of the murdered man. You have it put before you that he had the means of taking that man's life, there being no other person present in the carriage at the time when the murder was committed. These facts, I think, will lead you strongly to the suspicion that the prisoner is responsible for what took place. It is stated on behalf of the prisoner that there was a third person in the carriage when the murder was committed, and I am sure that the defence will be ably laid before you by his counsel. If the prisoner was merely tacitly present while some other person committed the murder, you have it that he (the prisoner) placed, according to his own account, the property of the murdered man in his shoe for the purpose of safety. The question is, what has become of that property? He took it on the night of 27 June, and where is it now? Can it be said on the part of the prisoner that the watch was not the property of Mr Gold; if so, why should he have retained it? Then again, if the prisoner ought to be in the position of the accuser, why was it that with the property of the murdered man in his possession he did not present himself to prefer the accusation? He did not do so, but took

---

2   Some sources give 'Clarke'. We have used the spelling contained in a report made by Inspector Donald Swanson, who led the case, and also letter from Mrs Bickers' son-in-law to Scotland Yard asking for information on the reward.

3   The telegram was sent on Thursday 7 July; it was on the evening of Friday the 8th that Lefroy was arrested. His landlady at Smith Street, Sarah Bickers, had that morning sent her daughter to Mr Hutchinson's offices at Gresham Street to see the lodger's supposed employer, where she spoke with a clerk named Joseph Mugford. It was he who realised that the mysterious Mr Clark was in fact Lefroy, and at the end of his work that day went to Scotland Yard.

4   Swanson was in fact accompanied by Inspector Jarvis and PC Hopkins.

Lefroy.

to flight, apparently to escape from those who were anxious to prefer a charge against him. There was something else that caused him to take the course he did.

I have thus placed the facts before you, and I ask you to judge of those matters according to your common sense. Of course, it is the desire of the prosecution that nothing should be unduly pressed against the prisoner, and, like every accused person, he is entitled to any doubt that may arise. If, on the other hand, the facts prove that he, and he alone (although no one saw this murder), was the person who took the life of Mr Gold, however painful that may be, you will not shrink from your duty in finding the prisoner guilty of the crime of which he is charged.

**Joseph
Goldsmith**

JOSEPH GOLDSMITH, examined by Mr POLAND.

I am an assistant in the engineer's office of the Brighton South Coast Railway. I produce a plan showing the railway line between London and Brighton. I have also measured the distance between the booking-office at London Bridge and the pawnbroker's shop of Messrs Adams and Hillstead in the Borough. It is 274 yards and 49 steps via Denman Street, and 299 yards another way.

From the booking-office at the station to the place where the train usually starts is about 150 yards? — Yes.

What is the distance from London Bridge to Croydon? — About 10 miles. I do not know the distance from Croydon to Merstham tunnel.

Cross-examined by Mr WILLIAMS.

The distance from London to Horley station would be 25 miles, 13 chains? — 25 miles, *35* chains.

To get from Merstham station to Horley, the train would pass through Redhill Junction and Earlswood? — Yes.

The next station after Horley would be Three Bridges, and that would be a distance of between 29 and 30 miles from London? — 29 miles, 14 chains.

Balcombe tunnel is 32 miles from London? — Yes.

The distance from Merstham tunnel to Balcombe tunnel would be about 13 miles, roughly? — 15 miles.

And the next station would be Haywards Heath: 37 miles, 53 chains from London? — That is right.

The next station would be Burgess Hill, is that right? — Yes.

And then would come Hassock's Gate: 43 miles, 36 chains from London? — Yes.

Between Hassock's Gate and Preston Park there are two tunnels. The first one is the Clayton tunnel, which is 2250 yards long and about 46

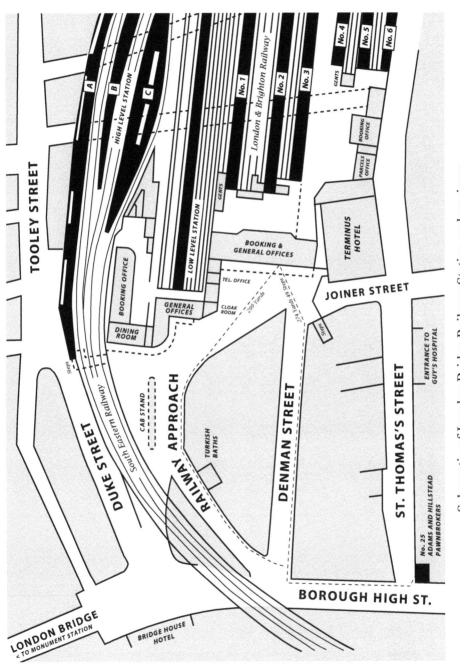

Schematic of London Bridge Railway Station and environs.

© *Adam Wood*

miles from London? — 46 from the south end.

What is the distance from the end of that tunnel to Preston Park station? — About 3¼ miles.

Then there is the Patcham tunnel, 484 yards long and about 3¼ from Brighton? — Yes.

LYDIA MATILDA GOLD, examined by Mr POLAND.

I am the widow of the deceased.

Were you living for some time at Titchfield, Preston, near Brighton. — Two years last June.[5]

Were you living there with your husband, Frederick Isaac Gold? — Yes.

Was he sixty-four years of age when he died? — Yes.[6]

Had he retired from business about eighteen years? — Yes.

Was he a strong man? — Yes, and a healthy man.

Your nearest station is Preston Park Station? — Yes, we were not five minutes' walk from it.

Had your husband a first-class season ticket to London? — Yes. He generally went there every Monday, and sometimes twice a week. He travelled by express train.

Had he a freehold shop at 145, East Street, Walworth? — Yes, it was a baker's shop.

He used to go there to collect the takings? — Yes.

Did he bring you money down for housekeeping expenses? — Yes.

Generally, when? — On the Monday preceding the first of the month.

And had you dividends payable to yourself? — Yes.

Did your husband bring you money down in anticipation? — Yes.

How much have you known him to bring down on the first? — £60, £70 or £80.

In what coin? — Notes and gold.

Had he brought money down on the Monday previous to his death? — I am not sure.

On Monday 27 June, did your husband leave early in the morning? — Yes. He left home about 8.05 am with the intention of going to Brighton by train. From there he would catch the 8.45 am express to London.

What time did you usually expect you husband to return? — Shortly after three. He generally came by the two o'clock train. But on the 27th

---

5   The 1881 census gives Titchfield House, Clermont Road, Preston Park. Before that the Golds are listed at 1 Clermont Road (1871 census) and 13 Clermont Terrace (1874 and 1878 Directories).

6   Frederick Isaac Gold was baptised on 21 September 1817 at St James' Church, Clerkenwell.

he did not do so. I thought he might then arrive by the 6.15 pm train. About eight o'clock I went to the station to ascertain if there had been any accident, but the station master informed me that no accident had occurred. At five minutes past ten I received the telegram [*produced*] from the Balcombe station master informing me that a man had been found dead, with papers upon him with the name F. I. Gold. I went on to Balcombe immediately, accompanied by Lee Hollis, who identified the body.[7]

On that Monday, was he dressed in the ordinary way? — Yes.

Did he take an umbrella with him? — Yes.

How did he carry it? — It had a large hook-like handle, and he used to hook it to the armhole of his waistcoat under his coat.

You were shown the umbrella before the magistrates? — I was.

Was that his? — Yes.

It had a piece of your work on it? — Yes; where I had darned it.

I think he also wore an eyeglass, and you were shown a portion of it before the magistrates? — Yes. I have identified it.

[*Inspector Swanson here produced the pieces of eyeglass, the purse, and the watch chain.*]

Did he used to wear a gold watch? — Yes.

Was that with a long chain? — An old-fashioned long chain.

Round his neck in the ordinary way? — Yes.

You formerly lived at Mile End? — Yes; some years ago.[8]

And you know that your husband purchased it then? — Yes; of Mr Griffiths, a watchmaker.[9]

You remember the watch? — Perfectly.

What sort of face had it? — A white face.

Do you recollect having that watch repaired some time in the present year? — Yes – in May, I think it was – at Market Street, Brighton, by Mr Boivin, who finally left it at our house.

And you gave it to your husband? — Yes.

Is this piece of chain part of what belonged to your husband? — Yes. He used to wear it round his neck.

---

7   Thomas Lee Hollis of 16 Clermont Road, Preston, a twenty year old assistant to a wine merchant who had known Mr Gold for ten years. He was known as Lee and signed himself 'Lee Hollis' after giving evidence to the inquest.

8   Between 1843 and 1860 Frederick Gold is recorded at 5 Wentworth Place, Mile End; the address was renumbered 77 Mile End Road and he is registered there as late as 1869 (*Post Office Directory*). Mr and Mrs Gold had moved to Preston Park by the time of the 1871 census.

9   Almost certainly John Widlake Griffiths, a watchmaker operating for many years nine doors down from Mr Gold at 15 Wentworth Place (1851 *Post Office Directory*), renumbered to 97 Mile End Road (1869 *Post Office Directory*).

First Day – Friday 4 November 1881.

Some articles of clothing were shown you before the magistrates. A hat which was shown you was your husband's hat? — Yes.

Had your husband a small purse? — Two; one for gold and one for silver.

To the best of your belief, is this purse the one your husband used to carry? — Yes, it is.

Now, the pieces of eyeglass? — Yes. I recognise them; also the memorandum book. There was another pocket-book in which he carried all his private papers. That I have not seen. In that pocket-book he would keep his railway ticket as well.

All your husband's collars were marked? — Yes. I used to mark them myself.

Your husband kept an account at the eastern branch of the London and Westminster Bank? — Yes.[10]

Cross-examined by Mr WILLIAMS.

Your husband was a broad, powerfully-built man? — He was. He looked very well indeed when he left me on the Monday morning.

He wore a double eyeglass, I believe? — Yes.

He also used to carry a skull cap? — Yes; and he must have had it with him on the morning in question, as I have searched for it and cannot find it.

How many shops had your husband? — He had only one shop in London. He formerly had three or four.

Did anyone collect his money for him from Preston Park? — No; for the last four or five years he used to collect the money himself. Before that his brother collected the shop takings.

Did the sums he brought home vary? — They did.

Re-examined by the ATTORNEY-GENERAL.

What material was the skull cap made of? — Silk.

Did you ever know him to carry firearms of any kind? — No; he never did. He was too nervous.

Mr Justice COLERIDGE: Anyone who knew his habits would know he would be carrying on Monday a sum of money? — Yes. Generally between £30 and £40.

---

10   Situated at 130 Whitechapel High Street. The building had its top floor removed and fascia remodelled following bomb damage in WWII. The London and Westminster Bank continued trading via numerous mergers until 1970, when it was merged with the National Provincial Bank to form the National Westminster Bank. A branch of NatWest continued to occupy 130 Whitechapel High Street until a few years ago. At the time of writing it is a venue for yoga and Pilates classes.

Lefroy.

KATE BOIVIN,[11] examined by Mr A. L. SMITH.

I am the daughter of Joseph Boivin, watchmaker, of Market Street, Brighton. Mr Gold was a customer of my father's.

Do you remember his watch being at your shop to be repaired? — Yes. I remember booking the receipt in our day book under the date 31 May of this year. [*The day book was produced showing the following entry: 'Mr Gold, Preston, gold English patent lever watch, to be adjusted and cleaned, 3s 6d.'*] The number of the watch was 16261. I made this entry from my own description of the watch. I believe the maker's name was Griffiths. It took about a week to repair, and then I gave it to my father to take to Mr Gold.

MATILDA BOIVIN, examined by Mr A. L. SMITH.

I am a sister of the last witness, and assist my father. On 31 May last, Mr Gold brought his gold, white-faced watch to our shop and left it to be repaired. It was repaired and I charged him 3s 6d. The watch was handed to my father.

JOSEPH BOIVIN, examined by Mr POLAND.

I carry on business at Market Street, Brighton, as a watchmaker. I knew Mr Gold as a customer for several years. I have repaired his gold watch several times. It was a gold English patent lever, open-faced, with white numbered dial. I remember my daughter Matilda drawing my attention to the watch when it was left with me to be repaired. I do not remember the maker's name.

What did you do with the watch? — When it was repaired I took it to Mr Gold's house, but as he was not at home I left it with Mrs Gold. Mr Gold afterwards called at my shop and paid me 3s 6d for the repairs. I then crossed it out of the day book. That was the last time I saw Mr Gold.

Cross-examined by Mr WILLIAMS.

What was the value of the watch? — About £8 or £10.

MRS CATHERINE CROSS, examined.

I am the wife of Charles Cross, of 145 East Street, Walworth. My husband managed a baker's shop there for Mr Gold.[12]

---

11   The family's name is usually given as 'Bovin' in newspaper reports, but the spelling used here matches their signatures in deposition papers.

12   In the 1881 census taken two months before the murder, Charles Cross is listed as a 'pawnbroker's manager'. This may have been to help out Henry Telling, a pawnbroker three doors along East Street at number 151, who in the 1881 census is registered at

First Day – Friday 4 November 1881.

Catherine Cross

Was Mr Gold in the habit of calling every week for the week's takings? — Yes.

Did he call on Monday 27 June last? — He did, between 10.30 am and 10.40 am.

Did you see him? — Yes.

Could you say whether he had an umbrella with him? — I do not remember seeing it.

Did you see his watch chain? — Yes.

What was the value of the takings that week? — I gave him £38 in gold, five shillings in silver, and one penny.

Do you know if Mr Gold had any other money about him? — I could not say.

Was the money put in a small holland bag? — Yes, with a memorandum of the amount, written on a small piece of pink paper [*produced*].

The previous Monday how much had you given him? — Almost the same amount.

How long did Mr Gold remain at the shop? — About a quarter of an hour.

When he left, did he say where he was going? — He did not say, but I believe he was going to order some flour.

Alfred Gilbert

ALFRED GILBERT, examined.

I am one of the cashiers at the eastern branch of the London and Westminster Bank, Whitechapel. Mr Gold kept an account at the bank. On Monday 27 June, Mr Gold paid in to his credit £38 in gold, and drew nothing out. That was about one o'clock in the afternoon.

William Franks

WILLIAM FRANKS, examined by the ATTORNEY-GENERAL.

I am a ticket collector at the London Bridge station.

Did you know the late Mr Gold? — Yes. He used to travel on the railway, and was a season ticket-holder.

You knew him well by sight and name? — Yes.

another pawnbroker's business at 41 The Grove. The same census lists the head of the shop at 151 East Street as twenty one year old Herbert Telling, Henry's brother, who is recorded as an 'assistant pawnbroker'. Catherine Cross is recorded at number 145 as a 'Shop woman', suggesting it was she who ran Mr Gold's shop from day to day. The *Nottingham Evening Post* of 4 July 1881 reports Mrs Cross as stating she had known Frederick Gold for four years, and that his brother Thomas had collected the takings on just one occasion three years ago. Charles Cross married Catherine Atkins in April 1871. He was working as a baker. In 1881 they lived at 145 East Street with their children Charles Jr (nine years old) and Rose (seven years old). Interestingly, they were still there in 1891 despite the death of Frederick Gold and presumably a change of ownership.

Lefroy.

William Franks

On Monday 27 June, did you see Mr Gold at the London Bridge station? — Yes, at about 1.50 pm. He seemed in very good spirits.

Where did you see him? — On the platform of the main line.

At that time, was the 2.00 pm express to Brighton made up and ready to start? — Yes, it was waiting in the station.

The first carriage was the usual brake? — Yes. Then came a composite carriage consisting of a second-class compartment in the front, next to which was a first-class compartment.

Did you speak to Mr Gold? — Yes. I asked him if he was going on by the express, and he said, 'Yes, my lad, I'll jump in in a moment.'

What compartment did he get into? — Into a first-class smoking compartment of the second composite carriage. I opened the door for him.

What time was it when Mr Gold took his seat? — About 1.55 pm.

Had you known the prisoner at the bar before that day? — Yes, sir.

How? — By his travelling on the line.

When did you first see him? — About two minutes before two o'clock.

Describe what he was doing. — He was walking very sharply along the platform towards the engine of the two o'clock express. He looked into the first carriage nearest the engine, where a gentleman and a lady[13] were talking, then turned round suddenly and walked back to where Mr Gold was sitting, looking into the windows as he went.

Well, what then? — When he got to Mr Gold's carriage, he tried to open the door but could not. I opened it for him, and he showed me his ticket. It was a first single express ticket from London to Brighton.

Was any other person in the carriage except Mr Gold? — There was not.

What time was it when the prisoner entered the carriage? — It was about one minute to two.

Did anyone else get into the carriage before the train started? — No.

Where were you standing? — Opposite the compartment.

If anyone had got in, would it have been your duty to see if he had a ticket? — Yes.

Where was Mr Gold sitting? — On the middle seat, facing the engine.

Where did the prisoner sit? — With his back to the engine in the off-side corner.

What is your impression as to the hat the prisoner was wearing? — A low felt hat.

Was the carriage locked? — The near side was locked, but I can't say whether the off side was or not.

13   According to the *Manchester Guardian* of 5 November 1881, the young woman was talking to her two brothers who had come to see her off.

Did the train leave on time? — It was about two minutes late in starting.

William Franks

Cross-examined by Mr WILLIAMS.

You say the prisoner was wearing a low felt hat? — I believe so.

Before the coroner, you said, 'He had a hard felt hat, low and rounded at the top'? — I described the hat as well as I could to the best of my recollection. I stated something similar before the magistrates.

Will you swear today that he wore a felt hat? — No, I will not.

You say he sat in the far corner with his back to the engine? — Yes.

You spoke as to his exact height, and went so far as to say that there were pockets at the side of his overcoat, which was unbuttoned? — Yes.

You said that the frock-coat he had on underneath was buttoned? — Yes.

That the colour of the frock-coat was black? — Yes.

That he took his ticket from the ticket pocket of his overcoat on the right-hand side? — Yes.

That his overcoat was not new? — Yes.

That his hair was cut the same as your own? — Yes.

You noticed all this in that time? — Yes.

Is it your duty to see that the passengers to all the trains have their tickets? — To a good many of them.

Would anybody else be in duty bound to look after persons getting into the train and ask for their tickets? — Yes.

How many? — One.

Did you say before the coroner, 'The next first-class compartment to that occupied by the two men was empty'? — Yes

Will you pledge yourself to how many persons were in the next compartment? — I will not.

How many trains do you see like that in the course of a day? — It all depends upon what duty I am on.

Had prisoner anything in his hand? — He carried nothing in his hand. His overcoat was open.

Some time previously, he had been reported for not giving up his ticket? — Yes; his name and address were taken in the ordinary way.

Were you the person who reported it? — I was not.

Were you the person who stopped him? — No.

Were you present when he was stopped? — Yes.

Did he on the day in question look into a carriage where there was a young lady? — Yes, but he passed that.

Did you know that a felt hat had been found on the line? — No.

Will you swear to that? — Yes.

Have you read an account of this in the papers? — I have looked into

Lefroy.

William Franks

the papers about it. I cast my eye over the papers, but took no particular notice of any of the evidence excepting my own.

When did you give your evidence before the coroner? — On 2 July.

Did you there see a likeness of the prisoner? — Yes, a picture was shown me by the coroner.

Did you remain in court after you had given your evidence to the coroner? — Only three or four minutes.

Were you in court with a man named Clayton? — No, I was not.

Were you there when he was examined? — No.

At Cuckfield, before the magistrates, did you remain in court after you had given your evidence? — No, I did not.

I suppose you have taken a great deal of interest in this case? — No more than it refers to myself.

Re-examined by the ATTORNEY-GENERAL.

When did you hear of Mr Gold's body being found? — The same evening. I went down to Balcombe and identified him.

Did the prisoner wear a moustache when you saw him? — Yes, I believe he did.

Was it in the *Daily Telegraph* that you saw the picture of the prisoner? — I don't know which paper it was from.

Henry Sewell

HENRY BOLTON SEWELL, examined by the ATTORNEY-GENERAL.

I live at 55 Adolphus Street, New Cross, and I am a booking clerk at London Bridge station. On Monday 27 June, at about 1.52 pm or 1.53 pm, I commenced issuing tickets for the Brighton express. I first issued two first-class tickets to a lady who returned and asked me to change them for two singles, which I did. The numbers of these single tickets were 3179 and 3180. I afterwards issued a third first-class single to Brighton to a person whom I believe to be the prisoner. The number of the ticket I gave him was 3181.

Did you issue any other first-class tickets except those three you mention? — No.

When the first-class ticket was issued, what money was paid for it? — A sovereign, and I gave him 7s 9d change.

Were there third-class carriages to the train? — No; first and second only. The return tickets are 17s 6d first and 12s 6d second.

Are any tickets issued for this train at Victoria? — Yes.

Do the trains join at Croydon? — I do not know whether they did on that day.

When tickets are given up by passengers what becomes of them? —

First Day – Friday 4 November 1881.

They are returned to the accountants' office.

Henry
Sewell

Cross-examined by Mr WILLIAMS.

You said before the magistrates, 'I don't think he had an overcoat on. To the best of my belief he had a high hat on. I told the coroner I did not notice his hat particularly'? — Yes, I did say so.

A first-class return ticket to Brighton is available for eight days? — Yes. A holder would be entitled to return any day between the first and the seventh.

Would a return ticket issued from Victoria be available to London Bridge and back? — Yes.

Would any person having a ticket issued from Brighton to Victoria between the 1st and the 7th be entitled to return with that ticket to London Bridge? — Yes.

And the same would apply to Worthing or any station beyond? — Yes.

EDWIN GARDNER, examined by Mr A. L. SMITH.

Edwin
Gardner

I am a booking clerk at East Croydon station. On 27 June, I issued three third-class singles to Brighton by the two o'clock express from London. I have my book here. They were numbered 8565, 8566 and 8567. They were the only tickets issued for that train; no first-class tickets, either single or return, were issued.

JAMES WOOD, examined by Mr A. L. SMITH.

James
Wood

I am a porter at East Croydon station. On 27 June, the two o'clock express from London to Brighton stopped at our station and three third-class passengers got in, all of them ladies. A gentleman came to see them off.

JOHN GEORGE AGER, examined by the ATTORNEY-GENERAL.

John
Ager

I am a clerk in the accountants' office at London Bridge. The two first-class tickets given to a lady passenger at London Bridge on 27 June were returned to this office. The next ticket, numbered 3181, has not been returned. The three third-class tickets issued at Croydon were also returned. I examined them all.

A JUROR: May I ask whether any tickets were issued for Worthing by that train? — There were no first-class tickets issued for Worthing.

The ATTORNEY-GENERAL: What time do you keep tickets after they are returned? — Three or four weeks.

You were not asked to keep the tickets, and all of them were destroyed? — Yes. There were a considerable number of tickets issued the week before 27 June.

Lefroy.

Cross-examined by Mr WILLIAMS.

What return tickets were delivered up that day at Preston entitling persons to travel to Brighton, you cannot say? — No, I cannot.

You can only speak of returns and singles issued by that train? — Yes. I can't say what return tickets were issued entitling persons to travel to Brighton.

WILLIAM HUMPHREY GIBSON, examined by Mr POLAND.

I am a chemist, living at 107 King's Road, Brighton.

Were you a passenger by the two o'clock train in question on 27 June? — I was.

Had you a second-class ticket? — Yes, a return ticket.

Had you a little boy with you? — Yes.[14]

Which carriage were you in? — It was about three carriages from the engine. I got into the second-class compartment, and I noticed that the compartment next in front of me was a first-class smoking carriage.

Did the train stop at Croydon? — Yes.

Did anything strike your attention after leaving Croydon? — Yes. Immediately on entering Merstham tunnel, I heard four or five reports, which at the time I took to be fog signals. I reassured the boy, who was alarmed by the noise.

Were they all fired at the same time? — Yes, they followed each other within five or six seconds.

Was there any other passenger in the compartment? — Yes. There was a gentleman. I don't know who he was.

Arriving at Brighton, did you see anyone get out of the first-class compartment immediately behind yours?[15] — Yes. I saw the prisoner get out.

You got out? — Yes.

Did you know him at all? — No. I did not speak to him.

Did you see blood on him? — Yes, he was smeared with blood.

Did you see anyone else get out of that compartment? — Yes, one of the officials of the railway got out with the prisoner.

Did you notice some marks of blood on the footboard of the carriage? — Yes; on the off side – or right side going towards Brighton.

Did you know Mr Gold? — I did not.

---

14   In his deposition, thirty-nine year old Gibson stated that his son was three and a half years old. According to the 1881 census, he and wife Ellen had four sons: twins Sidney and Arthur (five years old), Horace (three) and Alexander (one). It is therefore probable that the boy accompanying his father that day was Horace Gibson.

15   Mr Poland appears to be slightly confused here: the prisoner actually got out of the carriage in front of Gibson's. The witness nonetheless replies in the affirmative.

First Day – Friday 4 November 1881.

Did you, after this day, see his body? — Yes.

Where? — At Balcombe, on the first day of the inquest.

Did you recognise it? — I recognised it as the body of the gentleman I saw walking on the platform at London Bridge before the two o'clock train started. I saw him passing backwards and forwards while I was in my compartment.

Did you see the prisoner get into the train at London Bridge? — No, I did not.

Cross-examined by Mr WILLIAMS.

Did you say before the magistrate, 'I was riding in the compartment next to that where Mr Gold was. I sat with my back to the engine'? — Yes.

Did you also say, 'I did not see anyone standing by the carriages on the platform at London Bridge'? — I did.

Did you also say, 'I knew the witness Franks, the ticket collector. I did not see him when the train left. I did not notice him standing outside the carriages when the train left'? — I do not positively remember.

[*Question repeated.*] — I don't remember that I did see him.

Were you awake during the whole of the journey? — Yes.

Did you say before the coroner that you heard four shots? — Four or five, I won't say which.

Did you notice between Merstham tunnel and Preston Park any slackening of the speed of the train? — I did not. I think if there had been, I should have noticed it.

Re-examined by the ATTORNEY-GENERAL.

I was at London Bridge ten minutes before the train started. I stood on the platform five minutes, and then got in the carriage. I did not see any other ticket collector there besides Franks. I did not look to see if Franks was on the platform when the train left, but I know he was there shortly before, for he examined my ticket when I got into the carriage.

The Court here adjourned for luncheon.

MRS ANN BROWN, examined by Mr POLAND.

I live at King's Head Cottage, Horley. The cottage is on the London side of Horley Station, and about a hundred yards from the east side of the line. It is a five minutes' walk from the station. The trains can be

Lefroy.

Ann Brown

plainly seen from the front room.[16]

On Monday night, 27 June, did you hear of a body being found on the line? — I did.

Between two and three o'clock on the afternoon of that day, did you see a train pass towards Three Bridges? — Yes.

What did you see? — I saw two men standing up in a carriage. They seemed to be fighting or larking, I cannot say which.

Did you notice where the carriage was? — It was not the first, nor yet the last.

Can you tell nearer that that? — No.

Nor what sort of carriage it was? — No.

Was your daughter in the room at the same time? — Yes.

Cross-examined by Mr WILLIAMS.

Wherever your daughter was, you did not see her? — No; I was sitting close to the window. I did not notice her.

Then it is obvious she was not in front of you. What you saw was a hundred yards from the line, through a shut window? — Yes.

I believe you said before the magistrates you could not say how many people there were in the carriage? — I only saw two persons in the carriage.

Rhoda Lucas Brown

RHODA LUCAS BROWN, examined by Mr POLAND.

I am the daughter of the last witness.[17] On the afternoon of 27 June, I was in the front room of my mother's cottage. My mother was there too. I saw a train pass in the direction of Brighton.

Did you notice anything in the train? — I saw two men in it.

What were they doing? — They appeared to be fighting or playing with their arms.

Were they sitting down or standing up? — Standing up.

Did you see what part of the carriage it was? — No.

---

16 In her evidence before the magistrates at Cuckfield, Mrs Brown added that she was the wife of Daniel Brown, a farm labourer. Although she was aged fifty-six in 1881, Mrs Brown had only been married to sixty-three year old Daniel for just over four years; she previously had been widowed, her first husband James Lucas having passed away in 1869. The couple had ten children between 1847 and 1867. Although Daniel Brown is recorded in the 1881 census at King's Head Cottage, he was in fact at Wandsworth Lunatic Asylum, where he had been admitted on 11 January that year. He died there on 27 August 1883.

17 Rhoda Brown was the youngest child of James and Ann Lucas, baptised in March 1867. She was therefore fourteen years old at the time of the trial. She went into service before marrying William Strong in 1893, the couple having seven children. She died in 1932.

Cross-examined by Mr WILLIAMS.

Rhoda Lucas Brown

Where were you standing? In front of your mother? — No, I was standing close by the side of her – not in front of her.

I think you said before the coroner, 'I did not take much notice of it'? — Yes, I did say so because there are so many trains pass.

When you were examined before the magistrates at Cuckfield, did you remain in court after you had given your evidence before the court? — No.

THOMAS WATSON, examined by the ATTORNEY-GENERAL.

Thomas Watson

I am a guard in the employ of the London, Brighton and South Coast Railway. I have been in their service for twenty years. I was in charge of the front portion of the two o'clock express from London Bridge to Brighton on 27 June. There was another guard who rode in the rear brake. There were two composite carriages next to my brake, which was a third-class brake. These were carriage number 836, a composite; 385, a composite, in which the prisoner was riding; 645, a first-class; 134, composite; 425, a second-class; 1031, a third-class; and 314, a brake van.

You joined the train at London Bridge? — Yes; I was there half an hour before the time of starting. The train started at 2.01 pm.

Who was the ticket collector in charge of the front part of the train? — Franks. I cannot give the name of anyone else.[18]

Did you know Mr Gold? — Yes, I have known him as a ticket-holder for eight or ten years.

Did you see Mr Gold on 27 June? — Yes; he was on the platform, but I did not see him in the carriage.

After leaving London Bridge did the train stop? — Yes. At Croydon.

Did you then see Mr Gold in the carriage? — Yes.

Did you notice anyone else with him? — No.

Had Mr Gold anything on his head? — He had a white pocket handkerchief loosely thrown over his head.

Did you notice anyone else get into the carriage at Croydon? — No.

Did any other carriages join the train at Croydon? — No

Did you notice any explosion in Merstham tunnel? — No.

Did you hear fog signals at the entrance to the Merstham tunnel? — No. If fog signals had been used, I must have heard them. I am confident no fog signals were used.

Where did you stop next? — The train did not stop till we got to Preston.

---

18   The other collector was Joseph Stark.

Lefroy.

Thomas
Watson

What time did you arrive there? — [*Witness looked at his book.*] 3.20 pm. We were one hour and fifteen minutes travelling from London.

Did the train slacken speed between Croydon and Preston Park? — Yes, we slackened speed at the stop signal about 150 or 200 yards north of Hassock's Gate.

Can you tell the jury what you slackened speed to? — I should think down to four miles an hour.

What were you doing when the train slackened speed? — I was looking out of the glass window of the brake.

Does that command views of one or both sides of the train? — Both sides.

Did you see anyone leave the train at Hassock's Gate? — I am positive no one left the train there.

Why? — Because I looked out on both sides.

When you say you looked out of both sides, what opportunity have you of doing that? — There's a side light on each side. The glass projects six or seven inches.

Did you see anything thrown from the train? — No.

How high is the footboard from the line? — Nearly four feet, I should think. [*The ATTORNEY-GENERAL said the exact height would be proved to be three feet, ten inches.*]

We hear that the train stopped at Preston Park? — Yes.

Does that stoppage appear in the time tables? — Not in the public books. We stop there to detach the Worthing carriages, and also to collect tickets.

When you stopped was your attention called to the prisoner? — Yes, I saw him standing on the platform, close to the compartment in which he had been riding. He was talking to one of the ticket collectors.

When you first saw him, what was he wearing on his head? — Nothing whatever.

What coat had he on? — To the best of my recollection, a dark coat.

An overcoat or undercoat? — An undercoat.

Had he a collar on? — No.

What condition was he in with regard to blood? — He was completely smothered with blood: his face, his neck, and his hands.

Was any portion of his clothes covered with blood? — I did not notice his clothes.

Did you address yourself to him, or hear him speak to you? — When I got to him, I asked him if he would have some medical advice. He said he had been brutally treated on the way and was severely injured. He said that someone had attempted to murder him, knocked him about, or robbed him or something to that effect. He said there were two people

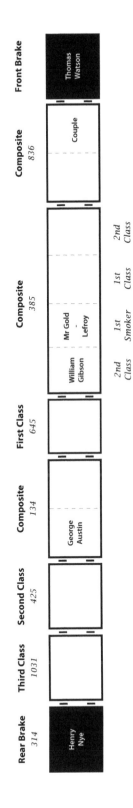

Schematic showing Composition of the 2.00 pm Brighton Express Train.

© Adam Wood

besides himself in the carriage, and they had got out on the way.

Mr Justice COLERIDGE: Did he say whether both of them or only one of them had assaulted him? — He did not say.

The ATTORNEY-GENERAL: In what condition did you find the carriage? — The blinds were up on the near side, but on the off-side one blind was down. On going into the carriage, I saw a lot of blood on the cushions and on the coconut floor matting. There was also blood on the footboard on the off-side of the carriage.

Did you find anything in the carriage? — Not at Preston.

Did you notice anything when you came out of the carriage? — I saw a piece of watch chain [produced] hanging from one of the prisoner's shoes. I said, 'What have you got here?' and at the same time I took hold of the chain and gave it a pull. I then found that a watch was attached to the chain.

What was the length of the piece of chain? — I should say from four to seven inches.

What sort of a watch was it? — It was a gold watch, I noticed.

Was any observation made by the prisoner? — I said to him, 'How do you account for this?' and he replied, 'I know nothing about it.' He then repeated the story about someone having attempted to murder him. I then handed the watch to him, but he took no notice of it, so I placed the piece of chain with the watch attached on the seat of the carriage.

What happened next? — The prisoner returned to the same carriage and travelled to Brighton with Gibson, one of the ticket collectors. At Brighton they alighted and went to the superintendent's office. As soon as we arrived at Brighton, I again visited the carriage in which the prisoner had been riding.

Did you then find anything in the carriage? — I found two sham sovereigns and a white pocket handkerchief, and several pieces of newspaper.

[*The ATTORNEY-GENERAL asked for the coins to be produced, but a policeman said he believed they were given to the prisoner.*]

What did you do with the medals? — I took them up to the superintendent's office and handed them over.

What part of the carriage were they in? — One of the medals was under the seat, and the other in a hole of the coconut matting in the middle of the floor.

Was there blood on the handkerchief? — Yes.

When you got to Mr Anscombe's office, was the prisoner there with a clerk named Hooper? — Yes.

Did you say anything to him about the two medals you found? — I said, 'I have found these two flash sovereigns in the carriage.' He said,

Lefroy.

Thomas
Watson

'They are not mine, I know nothing about them.' I said, 'You had better take them.' He said, 'You had better keep them yourself.' I gave them to the superintendent's clerk.

Did you say anything else to the prisoner? — I said, 'You don't look to me to be hurt much.' He said he was hurt all over, and again I said, 'I don't think you are hurt much'. I remarked to him that it was impossible for anyone to leave the train as it did not stop from Croydon to Preston.

What did he say to that? — He said, 'I don't know where they got out, but they did get out.'

Did the train have an electric communicator running through all the carriages? — Yes.

Was it in good working order? — Yes. I tested it at London Bridge, and also at Croydon, and it worked well.

Where was Mr Gold sitting when you saw him in the carriage at Croydon? — On the off side, facing the engine.

Were there any lights in the carriages? — Yes, all through the train. The carriages were lighted going through the tunnel.

Cross-examined by Mr WILLIAMS.

At Hassock's Gate, how far did you go at the slackened rate? — Not more than ten or fifteen yards.[19]

And then made up speed again? — Yes.

Did you say before the coroner, 'I don't think anyone could have got out there without my seeing them'? — I did so. I felt confident then, and I feel confident now.

When the train stopped at Preston Park, did the prisoner speak to you first? — No, to Gibson.

What did he say? —He said he had travelled from London with a countryman and an elderly gentleman in the same compartment, but he did not know who had assaulted him.

Did you say 'flash' when you said to the prisoner 'I have found these sovereigns in this compartment?' — During the time I was in the office, I did.

[*The depositions were then read but they showed that the witness did not use the word 'flash' to the prisoner at the time.*]

In what you originally stated there is nothing about the word 'flash'. — [*No reply.*]

You, at that time, had the sovereigns in your hand? — Yes.

Did you say, when you were before the magistrates, 'I have read of

---

19 According to the *Manchester Guardian*, 5 November 1881, the train slackened to four miles an hour for about fifty yards.

a person getting out of a train going sixty miles an hour, but not with safety. It is possible for a passenger to walk along the footboard and get from one compartment to another'? — I think it is possible for a man to do so.

When the prisoner got out at Preston, did the employees of the railway gather round him? — Yes. Myself, the station master, and two ticket collectors were there.

Had he a high hat on? — I saw no hat on him.

Re-examined by the ATTORNEY-GENERAL.

How long did the train travel at four miles an hour? — For about twenty-five seconds.

The FOREMAN OF THE JURY: What was the object of slackening the train at Hassock's Gate? — The signals were against us.

JOSEPH STARK, examined by the ATTORNEY-GENERAL.

I am a ticket collector at Preston Park station. I was on duty there on Monday afternoon, 27 July, when the two o'clock express from London arrived at 3.20 pm. I went to the second composite carriage to collect the tickets, and I saw the prisoner sitting there, with his face to the engine. When I opened the door, he said, 'Can I get a policeman or have a wash?' I told him he could see the station master.

Had he a hat on? — No.

Was he wearing a coat? — He had an overcoat on his arm.

Was he wearing a collar? — No.

What state was he in with respect to blood? — His face and neck were smeared with blood, and there was a clot beside his ear. There was also some blood between his fingers.

Was there any blood upon his clothes? — Yes. There was blood on one leg of his trousers above the knee.

Was there any blood upon his handkerchief? — Yes.

Did he get out of the carriage? — Yes.

Did he wear any hat after he got out? — Yes.

What sort of hat? — A low felt hat, I think it was. I did not notice much about it.

What happened next? — When he got out, I called Gibson to him; and Mr Hall, the station master, also came up.

Was there any blood in the carriage? — Yes, a lot. There was a pool of blood upon the floor near the right-hand side door.

Any on the footboard? — Yes, it was splashed with blood.

Did you see any medals in the carriage? — No. I observed no medals in the carriage. Lefroy then went on to Brighton with Gibson.

Lefroy.

Joseph
Stark

Cross-examined by Mr WILLIAMS.

Did you say before the coroner that when you saw the prisoner he had a hat on? — No. I don't remember saying that.

[*Mr WILLIAMS then read the evidence as taken before the coroner and magistrates to the effect that witness said the prisoner had his hat on.*]

The WITNESS: I do not remember saying so.

Mr WILLIAMS: Did you see what became of him after he went off to Brighton? — No. I saw Gibson get in with him to accompany him to Brighton.

Re-examined by the ATTORNEY-GENERAL.

Did any first-class passenger besides Lefroy alight from the train at Preston Park? — No, sir. There was nobody with Lefroy.

Richard
Gibson

RICHARD GEORGE GIBSON, examined.

I live at 23 Blackman Street, Brighton. I am a ticket collector at Preston Park station. On 27 June, I was on the platform for the arrival of the two o'clock express from London. It arrived about 3.15 pm; I don't know the exact time. It is my duty with others to collect the tickets.

As the train passed, did you notice anything? —Yes, I noticed a passenger looking out of a first-class window with no hat on, and he was beckoning.

Do you recognize the man in court today? — The prisoner is the man.

What happened then? —Lefroy got out of the train. Collector Stark got to him first, but I was close behind. He said, 'I have been murderously attacked and fired at. Is there a doctor here? I feel faint, and want some water.' He got out of the carriage just as Mr Hall, the station master, came up.

Did you notice anything else? — Yes; I noticed there was a chain hanging out of his left shoe.

About how much? — Three or four inches.

Look at this chain, and tell me if the chain your saw was or was not similar to that one. — It was very similar. Watson stooped down and picked the chain out of the shoe, and there was a watch attached to it.

You don't know what became of it? — No.

Did the prisoner say anything about the watch? — He said he had put it there for safety.

You are certain of that? — Oh, yes, sir.

There was a considerable quantity of blood upon the prisoner? — Yes. His face, neck and hands were covered in blood.

Had he a collar or necktie? — No.

Did you notice his shirt? — It was unbuttoned at the neck.

First Day – Friday 4 November 1881.

Richard Gibson

And you went into the carriage with the prisoner? — Yes.

Did you there notice any blood? — Yes. It was spread over the inside of the carriage.

Was it a considerable quantity or not? — It was a considerable quantity.

When the prisoner was on the platform, was he wearing a hat? — Yes.

What sort of a hat was it? — It was a high hat. I am certain it was a high silk hat.

You went with the prisoner to Brighton? — Yes.

On the journey, did the prisoner speak further about what had happened to him? — He again complained that he had been murderously attacked and fired at.

Did he say how many times he had been fired at? — He said three or four times.

Did he point to any injuries he had sustained? — He showed me a wound on the top of his head.

Did he say how he got that? — He said he had been struck on the head with a blunt instrument.

Did he in any way describe the person by whom he had been attacked? — He said he was assaulted by a countryman.

Did he say anything about an elderly gentleman? — Yes.

What did he say? — He said there was also an elderly gentleman in the compartment, but that it was not him who assaulted him. I asked him where the countryman got out, telling him that the train had not stopped after leaving Croydon. He replied, 'He got out on the road'. He further said that the elderly gentleman had also got out on the road.

Did he say that he knew the elderly gentleman? — No.

Did you examine his ticket? — Yes. On the way from Preston to Brighton, he handed me his ticket. It was numbered 3181. I gave the ticket afterwards to Mr Hall. I also took his name and address. He gave me the name Arthur Lefroy, 4 Cathcart Road, Wallington, Surrey.

When you got to Brighton what did you do? — We went to the station superintendent's office, where we saw Mr Hooper, the superintendent's clerk. Mr Everett, the platform inspector, came in afterwards. I said to Mr Hooper, 'This gentleman complains of having been assaulted on the two o'clock train from London'. I also said there was blood in the carriage.

Did you then accompany the prisoner to the town hall in Brighton? — Yes. A police constable was sent for, and P.C. Martin and myself went in a cab with the prisoner to the town hall.

Did the prisoner there make a statement? — Yes, his statement was taken down in writing by Mr Thompson, the clerk.

What happened next? — From the town hall we then went to the

Richard Gibson

county hospital, where the prisoner was seen by Mr Hall, the surgeon. His head was dressed. He made a statement to Mr Hall, saying he had been fired at three or four times and that he had been insensible, but came round when he got to Preston.

While at the hospital, did you search the prisoner's overcoat? — Yes. I took a pocket-book from the breast pocket.

Is this it? [*A brown leather pocket-book produced.*] — Something after that style.

Did you find anything in the pocket-book? — One or two pawn tickets. I put the pocket-book back in the coat with its contents.

Whilst at the hospital, was anything said about his remaining? — Constable Martin asked Mr Hall whether he was going to detain the prisoner.

In the prisoner's presence, what did Mr Hall reply? — He said, 'Yes, for the night'.

What did the prisoner say? — He said he could not stop, as he had to be in London at eight o'clock that night.

Was it put to him that he had better stop, and that he ought to stop? — He was advised to stop.

By whom? — By the doctor.

Going from the hospital to the town hall, did the prisoner make any request? — Yes.

What? — He wanted to stop the cab and pull up at a linen draper's shop to buy a collar.

Did Martin purchase the collar for him? — Yes; he asked the size, and the prisoner replied, '14½'. A collar and necktie were bought.

Could you see how much money the prisoner had in his hand? — Yes, about thirteen or fourteen shillings.

Was there any question about paying the cab? — Yes. We had had the cab for two hours, for which the charge was 12s. The prisoner said he had not much money, and that he had to pay his fare back to London. He added that he was about to come into a lot of money soon, and said that he would send myself and Martin a present. Subsequently, he paid for the cab.

From the town hall did you go to the railway station? — Yes.

Did you find anything in the prisoner's pockets? — Yes, various coins.

In the overcoat? — Yes.

Loose? — Yes.

What did you do with them? — I put them back again.

Were they coins of the same description as these [*produced*]? — Yes.

Cross-examined by Mr WILLIAMS.

First Day – Friday 4 November 1881.

You didn't take the watch out of the shoe? It was Watson who took it out? — Yes.

To whom did the prisoner say he had put it there for safety? — To me.

Did you hear Watson say to the prisoner, 'How did this get here?' — No, sir.

And did you hear the prisoner say, 'I know nothing about it'? — No.

Was it immediately after that Watson stooped down and extracted the watch? — Not immediately; it was a few seconds.

How far were you standing from the prisoner? — As near as I am to you [*about three yards*].

Did you hear Hall, the station master, say, 'This is a curious place to carry a watch', and did you hear the prisoner say, 'I don't know how it came there'? — No, sir.

Who else were there at the town hall? — Mr Hooper, Mr Everett, P.C. Martin, the prisoner, and Mr Anscombe. I do not recollect anyone else. Watson came in.

From the time you left the train at Brighton to the time you left the prisoner, have you given the whole of the persons who were there? — Yes.

Is there a police station at the town hall? — Yes.

When did you first see this tall hat on the prisoner's head – was it on the platform? — Yes.

Was he wearing it up to the last time you saw him? — Yes, a hat like that.

Mr Justice COLERIDGE: When did you last see the chain? — When it was taken out of the boot.

Didn't it occur to you, when he said that he had to pay his return fare, to ask him why he didn't take a return fare? — No, my Lord.

Did he tell you why he had come to Brighton? — To see Mrs Nye Chart.

Cross-examined by Mr WILLIAMS.

The last time I saw the watch was in Watson's hand, and at that time it had a piece of chain attached to it.

ALFRED JOSEPH HALL, examined by Mr A. L. SMITH.

I am station master at Preston Park. Collector Stark called me when the two o'clock express from London arrived at the station on 27 June. I walked towards Stark and was met on the platform by the prisoner, who asked me whether I was the station master. I said I was. He said, 'I have been murderously assaulted by a fellow passenger'. He asked me if I could send for a medical man. I said he had better go to the hospital.

Lefroy.

Alfred
Hall

What was his appearance? — He walked with a firm step, but his face was covered with blood. He had neither collar nor necktie.

What was he wearing on his head? — He had a high hat on.

What did you do next? — I walked up the train to where Gibson was standing, opposite a first-class compartment. I turned to the prisoner, who had accompanied me, and said, 'Where is the fellow passenger you spoke about? He is not here.' He said, 'He got out at a station further up the line'. I replied, 'That cannot be, because the train has not stopped after leaving Croydon'. He made no reply to that.

Did you afterwards observe a chain hanging out of the prisoner's shoe? — Yes, and part of the rim of a watch. I said to him, 'You have a watch in your shoe, that's a peculiar place to put it'. He answered, 'I don't know how it came there'. I told him he had better take it out, and the guard Watson took it out.

The chain had a watch attached to it? — Yes. The chain [*produced*] resembles the one in the prisoner's shoe.

Now, did you notice whether there was blood in the carriage? — There was a great deal on the floor, and also on the off-side footboard.

Did you issue any instructions at this time? — I ordered Gibson to go to Brighton with the prisoner, and to take him to Mr Anscombe's office, telling him what he had seen and what he had heard. Gibson returned in the evening, bringing back a first-class single ticket, London to Brighton, number 3181, and an address card, which he said the prisoner had given him.

Mr Justice COLERIDGE: Did you not give any instructions as to the watch? — No, my Lord.

What was your notion as to what had happened? — I thought he had attempted to commit suicide.

Here's a man tells you that he has been murderously assaulted by a fellow passenger, who has left the train somewhere or other. You know the train has not stopped, and you find a watch in the prisoner's shoe, which you say you thought very peculiar, and yet you send him on to Brighton? — I told Gibson to explain everything at the Brighton superintendent's office.

William
Hooper

WILLIAM HOOPER, examined by Mr POLAND.

I am a clerk in the superintendent's office at Brighton railway station. On Monday afternoon, 27 June, the prisoner was brought into my office by Gibson and Watson. He told me he had been shot at and nearly murdered in a first-class carriage. I asked by whom, and he said, 'When I got in at London Bridge, there was an old man and a young man in the carriage. When we were going through the tunnel, I saw a flash, and the young man struck me on the top of the head. I remembered no more till we got to the station we stopped at.' I said that was Preston Park, and he said 'Yes'.

Did you say anything further? — He asked if we could get him a doctor, and I told Gibson to take the prisoner to the town hall.

As he was leaving, did Watson hand you two Hanoverian medals which he had found in the carriage? — Yes. I offered them to the prisoner before he went off with Gibson and P.C. Martin. I said, 'These are your medals, you had better take them'. The prisoner replied, 'They are not mine,' so I gave them to Martin to take to the town hall.

Did you see a pocket-handkerchief? — Yes. It was quite covered with blood. Martin also took the handkerchief with him.

At 6.20 pm, did the prisoner come back to your office? — Yes, with Gibson, Martin, and Holmes.

Was he searched there? — Yes, by Detective Holmes.

What did he find? — A leather pocket-book and a white-faced watch smeared with blood. Holmes gave the watch back to the prisoner, and he placed it in his trousers pocket.

At that time, was there any piece of chain attached to it? — No.

What about the pocket-book? — I gave it back to the prisoner as well. He put it in his side pocket.

Mr Justice COLERIDGE: You heard nothing about the watch being found in the shoe, then? — No, my Lord; not till the next day.

Was it mentioned to the prisoner that the two Hanoverian medals produced were just liked those found upon him? — I believe it was mentioned, but I paid no particular attention.

You seem, all of you, to have 'paid no particular attention' to anything. It was mentioned that the medals picked up, which the prisoner said he knew nothing of, were similar to those found upon him. — Yes, it was. The prisoner said perhaps he took them at whist.

That is, having just said that he knew nothing about them, he next said that perhaps he took them at whist. — [*No reply.*]

Cross-examined by Mr WILLIAMS.

You have told us, to the best of your recollection, all the conversation that took place? — Yes.

OLIVER WESTON, examined by Mr A. L. SMITH.

I am an auctioneer and estate agent at Brighton, and a member of the Brighton Corporation. On 27 June last, I was at the railway station when the express came in at 3.20 pm. I saw the prisoner going into the superintendent's office. His hands, face, and neck were smeared with

Oliver Weston

blood, as were his clothes.

Did you hear him say anything? — I heard him state that he had been assaulted, having been shot at three of four times.

What did you do then? — He was standing on my left and I placed my hand on his forehead, and said, 'I say, my friend, that is not a gunshot wound; this looks more like a prod with an umbrella'.

Did you notice anything about the collar? — He had none. He had a very long neck, and it was bare. I distinctly saw bloody finger marks on the prisoner's neck, and on the right side a thumb mark. I pointed these out to one of the railway servants, saying, 'Look at the finger marks on the throat; it must have been rather hot while it lasted'. I also pointed to the large quantity of blood on the back of his coat.

Did you see any wounds to account for the large quantity of blood about him? — No.

Did you say anything else to the railway officials? — In the course of further conversation, somebody said, 'I should think he is a lunatic'. I said, 'I don't,' and suggested the prisoner should be taken to the police station in a closed fly.[20]

Cross-examined by Mr WILLIAMS.

Where did this conversation take place? — At the entrance to the station superintendent's office.

Whom did you address yourself to when you made the remarks you have mentioned? — To one of the railway servants.

Do you see him here today? — No. but I should know him again if I saw him.

Was there anyone present in the office except the prisoner and Mr Hooper? — No.

To whom, then, did you make the remark? — It was made to someone outside.

[*Two or three of the witnesses were here recalled in order that Mr Weston might identify them, but he did not.*][21]

You put your hands upon the wounds on his head? — Yes.

Did you make a statement about the case to a solicitor at Brighton? — Yes. My statement was that there were no gunshot wounds on the prisoner, and that there were bloody marks upon his neck, which showed that a great struggle had taken place.

In your statement to the solicitor, did you say that if Lefroy was taken

20 Some sources suggest it may have been Weston who opined that Lefroy was a 'lunatic'. See Appendix II.
21 See Appendix II.

to the police station he should be handcuffed on the way? — I did not say that.

If that statement is furnished to me as yours, it is not true? — No.

And I may take it that it never occurred? — No.

Did you tender yourself as a witness before the coroner? — No.

Or before the magistrate at Cuckfield? — No.

When did you make that statement to your solicitor? — Not until a month or six weeks ago. My solicitor wrote to the Treasury about it.

Re-examined by the ATTORNEY-GENERAL.

What did you mean when you said the prisoner should be taken to the police station in a closed fly? — I suggested that because I thought he had committed some crime.

JAMES MARTIN, examined.

I am a police constable in the service of the Brighton and South Coast Railway. About 3.30 pm on the afternoon of Monday 27 June, I was sent for to go to the office of the Brighton station superintendent.

What passed? — The prisoner, Gibson, and other officers were there. I was told to get a cab and take the prisoner to the town hall.

Did you get a carriage? — Yes. Gibson accompanied me and the prisoner. Before I started, Mr Hooper, the clerk, gave me two Hanoverian medals.

Did he give you anything else? — A rolled-up pocket-handkerchief that had been found in the carriage.

Did you take those things with you to the town hall? — Yes.

What did you do with the medals and the handkerchief? — I gave them to Mr Thompson, the police clerk.

Then what happened? — I heard Mr Thompson take down a statement from the prisoner. The latter was then taken up to the hospital, and I went to Mrs Nye Chart. Afterwards. I met up with them at the hospital. On our way back, we stopped at a shop in St James's Street; Lefroy gave me two shillings and I purchased a collar and necktie at his request. I paid 1s 6d for the articles and gave the prisoner sixpence change.

Did you get back the medals? — Yes; they were given to me the next day, and I took them back to the police station.

Where did you leave the handkerchief? — At the superintendent's office.

Mr Justice COLERIDGE: Did you see if the handkerchief was marked? — No, my Lord.

Why in the world didn't you look to see if there was a mark of a name on the handkerchief? — I don't know, my Lord.

Lefroy.

James
Martin

You knew nothing about the case? — No.

Nothing of what had occurred? — No.

No one told you anything about it? — No.

Richard
Gibson

RICHARD GEORGE GIBSON, *recalled and cross-examined*
by Mr WILLIAMS.

I took the prisoner straight from the train to the superintendent's office.

And was Lefroy with you the whole of the time? — Yes.

Did you take him from the platform straight into the office? — Yes.
Inside the superintendent's office there were only Mr Hooper, myself,
and the prisoner.

Did you see – either in or outside the office – the man Oliver Weston?
— Not that I know of.

Did anyone have a conversation with Lefroy on the way to the office?
— Not to my knowledge.

If Weston or anyone else had come up to speak to the prisoner, must
you have seen it? — Yes.

If Weston or anyone else had put his hand on Lefroy's wound, would
you have seen it? — Yes.

Did you, inside or outside the office, say, 'These are not pistol wounds;
they are prods with an umbrella'? — No.

Did any person in your presence and in Lefroy's presence, inside or
outside the office, say, 'It must have been hot while it lasted'? — No.

Did anyone say Lefroy had better be taken to the station in a closed
fly? — No.

Re-examined by the ATTORNEY-GENERAL.

Do you know Mr Weston? — I know him well by sight.

Mr Justice COLERIDGE: Were you present when the prisoner was
searched? — I was not.

Were you present when Holmes gave him back the watch that had
been found in his boot? — I was not.

It is certainly ingenious that while the man who knew nothing about
what had occurred was selected to search the prisoner, those who knew
all about the case were carefully sent away. I do not know what the jury
will think. — [*No reply.*]

Samuel
Thompson

SAMUEL THOMPSON, examined.

I live at 41 Brunswick Place North, Brighton, and am police clerk at
the town hall, Brighton. On Monday 27 June, I saw the prisoner there
about 4.15 in the afternoon. Gibson and Martin were also there. Gibson
said, 'This gentleman (meaning the prisoner) wishes to make a report of

his having been assaulted in a railway carriage'. Then, in my presence, the prisoner made a report which was partly a statement. I am in the habit of taking down reports of this description, and I took down in writing what the prisoner said. The report [*produced*] is the same as I wrote.

JAMES TERRY, examined.

I am Chief Constable of the Brighton police. On Monday afternoon, 27 June, I was fetched to the town hall, where I saw my clerk, the last witness.

Were you shown the report the prisoner had made? — Yes, I was shown the report in the scrap book.

Was the prisoner present at this time? — No, but I saw him at the police station about 5.00 pm, after he had left the hospital. He was accompanied by Gibson and P.C. Martin.

You read certain portions of the report to him? — Yes, and asked him if it was true.

Did he say it was true? — Oh, yes.

What then passed? — I said I would do my best to try and find the men who had assaulted him, and he said, 'I hope you will'.

You asked the prisoner about the Hanoverian coins? — The two coins were lying on the desk, and I asked the prisoner if he knew anything about them. He said they must have been dropped in the carriage by the persons who assaulted him.

Was he further questioned? — Sergeants Howland and Holmes had by that time arrived, and they put several questions to the prisoner as to his name and position at Wallington.

Did you ask him why he came to Brighton? — Yes. He said, 'I came to Brighton expressly to see Mrs Nye Chart'.

Mrs Nye Chart is the proprietress of the Brighton Theatre? — Yes. I said, 'Won't you go and see her now?' to which he replied, 'No, not in this state'. I replied she was a very nice lady, and would not mind seeing him, but he refused to go, as his head was bandaged up. He also stated that he must get back to Croydon as he had important business that evening.

Did you know anything about the case at that time? — No. I heard nothing until 9.45 that night when I heard the body had been found in Balcombe tunnel.

Was anything said to you about the watch and chain? — No.

Was anything said to you about the coins found upon the prisoner at the hospital? — No.

Lefroy.

Benjamin
Hall

BENJAMIN HALL, examined.

I was acting house surgeon at the Sussex County Hospital, Brighton, at the time of this occurrence. I remember the prisoner being brought to me on the afternoon of Monday 27 June. He was suffering from a small contused wound about the size of a shilling above the eyebrow on the right of the forehead. At the back of the right ear was a small grazed wound, and on the crown of the head were six small semi-circular cuts. There was still a little bleeding from two or three of these.

Were those wounds caused by gunshot? — I don't think so. The grazed wound was the only one that might have been caused by gunshot, but I think it is improbable.

What had probably caused them? — They might have been made by a blow from the trigger of a pistol, or by the end of a light umbrella.

Or the barrel of a small pistol? — Yes, perhaps so.

What depth were these wounds on his head? — They extended down only three-eighths of an inch to the lining membrane of the skull. The prisoner's hair was moist with blood, and the neck was smeared with blood as if it had run down from the scalp. The probability is that the blood on his face also came from the wounds on his scalp. The hands were smeared with blood, but it is impossible to say where the blood on the other parts came from. From the quantity, I should say that it came not from him but from someone else.

Were there marks of blood on the clothes? — Yes, they were considerably marked. There was blood on his thighs and legs, and his great coat and vest seemed to be nearly saturated.

In your opinion, was there any indication of drunkenness about him? — No.

Did you make any enquiries of him? — Yes. He said he was in a railway carriage, and that while he was reading his paper quietly in the corner he was shot at. He said he remembered nothing more. He described his assailant as an old man, and said there was also another man in the compartment who looked like a traveller from the country.

Did he say how many persons were in the carriage with him? — He did not speak of any other person.

You dressed the wounds and he left then, I suppose? — Yes. I bandaged the wounds and put some plaster on. I told him he was not fit to be about and had better remain overnight in hospital, but he would not stop, as he said he had important business in London that night.

When did you see the body of Mr Gold? — On the following Wednesday. It was covered with wounds, several of which were incised. [*The witness then read the notes as made by him at the first examination of the body, but he was completely inaudible in the reporters' gallery.*]

First Day – Friday 4 November 1881.

Were you present at the post-mortem examination conducted by Dr Bond? — Yes, I assisted. **Benjamin Hall**

Can you describe the injuries he suffered? — He had sustained a pistol shot in the neck, and there were many gashes on the face and neck, and a fracture of the skull, with various contused wounds which might have been caused by the fall from the carriage. The cut wounds must have been caused by a sharp cutting weapon; there were nine of them altogether.

Was there a wound which you did not, at first, think was a bullet wound? — Yes. The bullet entered behind the right ear and lodged in the second vertebra of the neck, having touched the spine.

To what do you attribute the cause of death? — The immediate cause of death was syncope, or failure of the heart, caused by the loss of blood and the shock to the system resulting from the pistol shot wound.

Mr Justice COLERIDGE: In your opinion, had the pistol been held close to the body when it was fired? — Yes.

Would the effect of that wound be to stun him? — Yes.

And so stop his powers of resistance? — Yes.

Cross-examined by Mr WILLIAMS.

What condition were the prisoner's clothes in? — They were very much torn.

In your opinion, had the wound on Lefroy's head been self-inflicted? — No.

A JUROR: Did you consider that the wounds on the prisoner's head might have made him insensible? — It is impossible to tell from the appearance of the wounds themselves whether they would produce faintness, but, to judge from the amount of blood on him, I should think he would have been faint.

Mr Justice COLERIDGE: Were the wounds on the prisoner sufficient to account for the quantity of blood in the carriage? —No.

But looking at the nature of the wounds on Mr Gold's body, they would be sufficient to cause such a flow of blood? —Certainly.

The court adjourned at 5.35 pm until the next day.

****

Second Day – Saturday 5 November 1881.[22]

HENRY ANSCOMBE, examined by the ATTORNEY-GENERAL.

Henry Anscombe

I am superintendent of the railway station at Brighton. I was at the station on Monday 27 June. The prisoner was brought to my office about 5.40 pm. He was accompanied by Inspector Barnes and Gibson.

Had you any information brought to you before the prisoner arrived? — I had.

When you saw him, you saw his head was completely bandaged? — Yes. I asked him what was the matter, and he said he had been shot at in the railway tunnel. I said 'By whom?' and he said, 'By two parties in the train. One was an old man, and the other a countryman'.

What else? — I said, 'Where are they?' and he said, 'I don't know'. I asked him where it had happened, and he replied that the shots were fired just as they were entering a tunnel. He said he was rendered almost senseless from the time he was shot till he got to the station, where the tickets were taken.

Did you ask him whether he was much injured? — Yes. He said, 'I should think I am, having four or five bullets in my head'.

I think he also said, 'I want a lawyer and I shall offer a reward'? — He did. I said there was no lawyer there.

I believe you enquired whether he had been searched? — Yes, I asked Gibson and Barnes, and Barnes said he did not know. I said to the prisoner, 'Have you anything about you?' He replied, 'What do you mean?' and I said I wished to see if he was carrying a pistol or a knife.

I believe, at this time, he had a light overcoat on his arm? — Yes.

At this point, did Holmes and Howland come into the office? — Yes. I ordered Holmes to search him.

You first saw some money in silver? — Yes. About twelve or fourteen shillings was found in his left-hand pocket, but that was given back to him.

Anything else? — Yes. A small gold watch.

Can you describe the watch that was found? — It was small and common looking, with a white face.

---

22 Transcript of the day's proceedings amalgamated from the *Daily News*, Monday 7 November 1881; *Brighton and Sussex Daily Post*, Monday 7 November 1881; *Maidstone and Kent County Standard*, Saturday 12 November 1881; *Manchester Guardian*, Monday 7 November 1881; *Sussex Evening Times*, Saturday 5 November 1881; *Sussex Evening Times*, Monday 7 November 1881; *West Sussex Journal*, Tuesday 8 November 1881.

Henry Anscombe

Was there any chain attached to it? — No. It was in his trousers pocket, not his waistcoat. It was given back to him.

Were any medals found on him? — Two or three Hanoverian coins were taken from his pocket and put in an envelope. They were of the same character as those produced.

Were they given back or not? — They were handed to Holmes.

Did you make any observation? — I said to the prisoner, 'That looks queer, as some similar medals have been found in the carriage'.

What reply did he make? — He said, 'I know nothing about them. I must have got them when playing whist last night with my friends.'

Was a pocket-book taken by Holmes from the prisoner's pocket? — Yes.

Did the prisoner make any observation? — Yes. Just as Holmes was going to look at it, he said, 'That is my private property,' and Holmes gave it back to him.

Did the prisoner then leave the office? — Yes. He said, 'I must go home. I have business to attend to,' and he left with Howland and Holmes about six o'clock.

At what point did you learn about the body being found? — After they were gone, I saw a message passing through the telegraph instrument that a body had been found in the tunnel. I then telegraphed immediately to the station master at Balcombe.

Cross-examined by Mr WILLIAMS.

Do you know a person at Brighton named Oliver Weston? — Yes. He is a house and estate agent, and a town councillor.

Did you see him near your office that evening? — No.

Was the prisoner thoroughly searched in your presence? — Yes, as far as I could see, but his boots were not taken off.

There was no chain found upon him? — No.

Did you see anything at all of a handkerchief? — No, I cannot say that I did.

Did the prisoner say to you that the two men who were in the carriage with him got in at London Bridge? — I think he did.

William Howland

WILLIAM GODDEN HOWLAND, examined by the ATTORNEY-GENERAL.

I am a detective sergeant in the Metropolitan Police and attached to the London, Brighton and South Coast Railway. From information received, I went down to the police station at the town hall on Monday evening, 27 June. At five o'clock, I saw the prisoner there. He came in shortly after me as he had just returned from the hospital. I afterwards saw the prisoner at the station superintendent's office at the town hall.

By whom was he accompanied? — By P.C. Martin and the witness Gibson.

You took down details of Lefroy's complaint? — Yes, I made a note of what Lefroy said, and it was read over to me in the prisoner's presence by Mr Terry, the Chief Constable.

What was said? — The prisoner said, 'Just as the train entered the first tunnel, a shot was fired. I saw a flash and heard a report, but I did not see any firearms. Then I felt a severe blow on my head, which rendered me insensible. When I recovered consciousness, I was just against Preston Park station.'

Did you put certain questions to him? — Yes.

Did he tell you how he sat? — Yes. He said he sat on the left-hand side of the carriage, facing the engine.

Did you ask him where the two men entered the train? — Yes. He could not say whether both men were in the carriage when he entered the train at London Bridge, but one was. He said both of them were in the carriage when the train started.

Did he give you any description of them? — He said the first one was aged from 'sixty to eighty, with slight grey whiskers and dark clothes'. The second was 'about fifty, with dark whiskers.' He did not give me any description of the second man's clothes. He said the old gent sat in the left hand corner, and he (the prisoner) sat opposite. I asked if he held any conversation with them, and he said, 'No'.

Anything else? — I asked him where he dined, and he replied, 'At the International Restaurant'.

Was the prisoner searched? — Yes, in the superintendent's office at the railway station. I asked him if he had any firearms about him, and he said, 'No, search me if you like'. I said, 'You have given a satisfactory account'. I saw Holmes search him and take a watch out of the prisoner's left hand trousers pocket.

Did the prisoner make any observation? — Yes. He said, 'That is mine; that is my watch'. As to the chain, he said he had lost it, but he did not say where.

Did he say what kind of chain it was? — Yes. A metal cable chain. He said, 'When I recovered, I found the watch on the floor of the carriage, and no one else in it'.

Did you notice whether the watch was given back to him? — I did not notice, but no doubt it was.

Did he say he had lost any money? — Yes, about twenty-five shillings.

Did he wish to return to London? — Yes. He said, 'I want to go back to London, as I have an appointment in the Strand at 8.30 pm'. I

Lefroy.

William
Howland

said, 'Hadn't you better go home to your friends? Me and Holmes will accompany you.' He left for the 6.20 pm train, accompanied by Holmes. He did not tell me who the appointment was with.

Did you see anything of the Hanoverian coins? — No.

Did you afterwards go to the prisoner's house at Wallington? — Yes, with Holmes.

Cross-examined by Mr WILLIAMS.

Had you told him before this conversation who you were? — No.

Just give me your book. Did you make any entry that the prisoner said, 'That watch is mine'? — No.

Why not? — I did not see any necessity for it.

Did you think it of any importance? — No.

You had seen the state the man was in? — I saw him bandaged up.

Had you heard anything about any chain? — I had not.

Did you see any chain? — No.

Was there anyone present when he said 'That watch is mine'? — Yes. I think Sergeant Holmes and Mr Anscombe were there.

Have you said before that they were there? — I believe they were there. I am certain Mr Anscombe was.

Did you think it necessary to write anything down about the chain? — Yes.

And not about his saying 'That watch is mine'? — No.

[*Witness then, at the request of the learned counsel, proceeded to read the actual entries he had made in his pocket-book, which, so far as could be gathered, were as follows: 'After passing Croydon, before entering tunnel, heard report. Felt blows on his head. First man aged sixty. Slight grey whiskers. Second aged fifty; dark whiskers. Sitting left-hand corner, opposite. Did not enter into conversation. Saw flash. Was not looking out of carriage window. Wore metal cable chain. Gold watch on floor.'*]

That is all that you wrote down? — Yes.

With regard to the statement, 'That's my watch': where was that made? At the town hall or at the superintendent's office? — At the superintendent's office.

Did you see anything of any handkerchief? — No.

There was no knife found on him? — No; so far as I am aware.

No firearms? — No.

No cartridges? — Not that I saw.

Have you been engaged in this matter since the committal? Has a thorough search been made to find the pistol? — I have been informed that a thorough search of the line has been made.

You did not think it of sufficient importance to detain the man? — No.

Second Day – Saturday 5 November 1881.

Re-examined by the ATTORNEY-GENERAL.

At that time you made your notes, had you heard about anyone being killed or murdered? — No.

All you put down was an account of what occurred in the carriage? — Yes.

Are you sure that he never said the watch was not his? — No.

There was nothing said about its being anybody else's? — No.

He did not offer to leave it at the office? — No.

Mr Justice COLERIDGE: You were a detective. Did it not occur to you to make some enquiry about the man? — No, my Lord.

Did you ask him why he came to Brighton? — No.

GEORGE HOLMES, examined by the ATTORNEY-GENERAL.

I live at 16 Theobald Street, Southwark. I am a detective sergeant in the Metropolitan Police and in the employ of the London, Brighton and South Coast Railway. About 4.30 pm on 27 June, I received information and proceeded to the town hall at Brighton.

What time did you arrive there? — 4.45 pm.

Did the prisoner come there? — Yes, shortly afterwards. I saw him arrive in a cab with P.C. Martin and others.

Had you previously read the statement by Lefroy in the rough scrap book? — Yes.

Was the prisoner questioned at this time? — Yes, by Sergeant Howland.

Was the prisoner then taken to the railway station? — Yes, in a cab, and we followed afterwards. I then saw Lefroy at Mr Anscombe's office.

You asked him if he had any firearms about him? — Yes. He said, 'No, you can search me if you like'. On searching him, I found 1s 6d and two bronze pennies in one pocket, and about four or five shillings in his vest pocket. In his left hand trousers pocket, I found a gold watch.

Was there any chain attached to it? — No.

Did he say anything about it? — Yes; he said he had lost the chain.

Did he say what it was like? — Yes; he said it was like the one I am wearing – a cable pattern.

Did he say where he had lost it? — In the carriage.

Did you find anything else on him? — Yes, in his overcoat pocket I found two Hanoverian pieces.

What did he say upon that? — He explained that he must have got them when playing whist the previous night.

In the second pocket of the overcoat, did you find a pocket-book similar to this [*produced*]? — Yes.

Did he say anything to that? — Yes. I was about to open it when prisoner said, 'I have something private in there'. I gave it back to him.

Lefroy.

George
Holmes

Was anything said about the prisoner staying the night in Brighton? — Yes, but he said he wished to go back to Wallington.

You left Brighton with the prisoner by the 6.10 pm train? — Yes. I rode with Lefroy in a first-class carriage, and Howland rode in the guard's brake, so as to make enquiries at the stations on the way up.

Did you have any conversation with the prisoner on the way? — Yes. I asked him if he was in the habit of carrying a pistol when he travelled. He said, 'No, I like to keep a good distance from those things'.

I believe you stopped at Balcombe? — We did.

Did you see Howland there? — I did. I looked out of the window, as I had done at all the stations, and Howland was on the platform.

Did he speak to you? — Yes. He told me a body had been found in the tunnel.

Did Mr Brown join you in the carriage? — He did.

Who is he? — He is the station master at Three Bridges.[23]

How did you sit? — The prisoner sat with his back to the engine on the near side of the carriage. I sat directly opposite him. Mr Brown at first sat on the same side as the prisoner on the off side, but afterwards came across to my side and spoke to me.

Did he speak loud enough for the prisoner to hear? — I don't think the prisoner heard anything.

Was there any statement made by Brown which you think the prisoner could have heard? —I don't believe he heard any remark.

On arriving at East Croydon, did you receive a telegram with reference to the gold watch? — I did.

Did you suggest to the prisoner that you should take a cab from East Croydon to West Croydon? — Yes.

I believe the cab was taken all the way to Wallington? — Yes. Lefroy said it would be as well for them to ride all the way to Wallington in the cab, as it was not much farther than West Croydon.

Who paid for it? — Prisoner did.

Four shillings? — Yes.

Did any conversation take place on the way? — Yes. Lefroy said, 'It is a very sad affair, and I hope the man will be caught. The Scotland Yard people should be informed at once'.

You drove up to number 4, and took the prisoner into the house? — Yes.

Did you go into the drawing room with him? — I did.

Did you say anything to him? — I asked him for an account of the affair, which he gave me, and I wrote it down.

---

23   William Harold Brown, who was not called to give evidence at the trial.

Second Day – Saturday 5 November 1881.

Will you produce, please, what you took down? — You have it.

[*The paper was handed to the witness by Mr POLAND.*

Witness then read the following statement:[24] *'Arthur Lefroy, 22, of Cathcart Road, Wallington states, He took the 2.p.m. train from London Bridge to Brighton, riding in 1st compartment. Two more passengers being in the compartment, he, Lefroy, sitting near the platform with face to the engine, the two others sitting opposite. Description of passengers: 1st age about 60, height medium build slight, grey whiskers, dressed in dark clothes. 2nd age about 45 or 50. Height medium, complexion fresh, dark whiskers side of face, no moustache, dressed in dark greyish suit. Neither spoke to him in the train at all, and on arriving at the instance of the first tunnel after passing Croydon he saw a flash and heard a report of fire arms and could not state if revolver or pistol. He half sprang up from his seat. As far as can be remembered, he received a blow on the head, supposed from the younger man, who was sitting in centre of car. Saw a flash on opposite side which rendered him insensible and on recovering consciousness found himself in semi-sitting position. On arriving at Preston Park, he at once called one of the ticket collectors who accompanied him to Brighton Station; from there to Brighton Hospital. Stated to receive six wounds, supposed caused by a gouge to his head. He was accompanied to the Town Hall.'*]

The ATTORNEY-GENERAL: That was the statement so far as it was made by Lefroy himself? — Yes.

In addition you made some slight notes yourself? — Yes.

[*Witness here read various memoranda as to his conversation with Lefroy about the number of the watch, which were quite inaudible in the reporters' gallery.*]

Did you at any time ask him the number of his watch? —Yes, in the drawing-room at Wallington.

Did Mr Clayton, who keeps the house, come into the room? — He did.

Did you ask him as to the number of his watch before or after Clayton came into the room? — I am not certain which.

When you asked the prisoner the number of his watch, what number did he give you? — 56312 was the number he gave me.

Did he try to open the watch? — Yes, but did not do so in the first instance.

What did you do? — I asked Mr Clayton if he could.

Did he succeed? — No; he gave it back to me, and I opened it that time.

---

24   The statement is held at The National Archives (TNA: PRO ASSI 36/26). Punctuation has been added by the editor.

Lefroy.

George
Holmes

Did you then look for the number of the watch? — Yes.

What was it? — 16261.

Did you then make any remark to the prisoner? — I said, 'You have made a mistake'.

What did he say? — 'Oh, yes; I forgot.'

Did you then ask him as to the maker's name? — Yes.

What answer did he give? — He said, 'I don't know. I bought the watch from a friend of mine only a short time ago, and I have not looked.'

What was the maker's name, as a matter of fact? — Griffiths, of Mile End Road, London.

When you were leaving the house, did you say anything to the prisoner? — I said, 'Where shall I see you tomorrow, provided I get any information?' Lefroy replied, 'You will find me here till twelve o'clock, and after that at the United Arts Club, Savoy Street, Strand.'

Where did you go after you left the house? — To the station master at Wallington, where I received a telegram.[25] In consequence of that, I went back to Lefroy's house and stood outside the front door.

Could the prisoner have left from the front of the house without you seeing him? — I don't think so.

How long had you been away? — About six or seven minutes. The station is a few hundred yards from the house.

You did not enter the house, then? — No. I remained outside the house till Detective Howland and Sergeant Tobutt arrived. One of them went to the back of the house, and the other one entered. When they returned, the prisoner was not with them.

Cross-examined by Mr WILLIAMS.

Did the prisoner show you a pocket-book at Wallington? — Yes. The pocket-book produced is the same.

Did the prisoner resist being searched? — No.

You found upon him no knife? — No.

No firearms? — No.

No cartridges? — No.

No chain, no second pocket-book? — No.

No purse? — No.

And no skull cap? — No.

When you passed Three Bridges, did you know as a matter of fact that the body of a dead man had been found in a tunnel? — Yes.

When did you first learn that the watch was missing from Mr Gold's

---

25   A copy of the telegram, which was sent from Three Bridges, is held at The National Archives (TNA: PRO ASSI 36/26) and reads: 'Instruct Holmes to keep the man Lefroy in his safe custody til I arrive. By no means lose sight of him. Urgent.'

Second Day – Saturday 5 November 1881.

body? — At Wallington.

Was it before you questioned the prisoner or after? — Before.

Then you had received a telegram saying that the dead body was watchless, and that you were to take the number and other particulars of the watch of the man you had with you? — Yes; I got that at East Croydon.

[*Mr WILLIAMS then read the telegram, which ran as follows: 'Tell Inspector Holmes to take number of watch on wounded man in 6.10 up train, as man found had no watch.*']

Did Brown speak loudly to you in the train? — Yes, rather loud at first.

And he told you a man had been found dead in the tunnel? — Yes.

That was before you had any conversation about the watch? — Yes.

If prisoner heard it, he made no observation on it? — No.

How many times did you put pencil to paper on this statement? — I wrote it all down before I left.

Did you write any portion of this at Brighton? — No, sir.

Then I may take it that you took no note of any conversation that took place at Brighton? — I did not.

Did you see a portrait of a man who was supposed to have committed the murder in a daily paper? — Yes, I saw the portrait in the *Daily Telegraph* on 1 July. It represented the man as wearing a round felt hat.

Mr Justice COLERIDGE: If this is supposed to have made any difference, I think the jury ought to see it. I have never seen it.

[*The copy of the Daily Telegraph containing the sketch was then produced, and handed to the judge, and afterwards to the jury.*]

Mr WILLIAMS: Have you yourself taken any part in searching for the pistol? — No, sir.

Who was with the prisoner when you left him? — Mr Clayton.

Who told you about the watch being found in the prisoner's boot? — I was not told.

Do you mean to say that, coming from Preston Park that day with the prisoner, you did not know that a watch had been found in the prisoner's shoe? — I knew nothing of it.

It had not been mentioned to you? — No.

Did not Terry or someone else tell you at Brighton? — No.

Tell me. You knew that Lefroy was wounded about the head, and had gone to the hospital to have his wounds dressed? — Yes, I knew that.

You knew that a dead body had been found in a tunnel? — Yes.

You knew that that dead body had no watch upon it? — Yes.

You knew, according to your own account, that Lefroy gave a wrong number to the watch? — Yes.

And, knowing all that, you yet did not take him into custody? — Just so. I did not think it necessary to apprehend him.

Lefroy.

Re-examined by the ATTORNEY-GENERAL.

Did you report the number of the watch that night to your superior officer? — Yes, to Sergeant Moss at Carshalton. The number was then circulated.

Do you know of any source from whence that information could have come, except from your statement? — No.

Mr Justice COLERIDGE: You knew, or you knew just after getting to Wallington, that he had given you the wrong number; you asked for the maker's name and found he did not know it; you heard him say he had bought the watch from a friend; and then you let the matter drop? — Yes, my lord.

You did not ask him from whom he bought the watch? — No, I didn't go into that.

It would have been a very natural question to ask, would it not? — I did not think to do so.

[*The ATTORNEY-GENERAL said he would call Mr Brown, the station master at Three Bridges, in order that the defence might put any questions they liked. Mr Brown was called, but he was not examined by the counsel.*]

WILLIAM MOSS, examined.

I am a police sergeant stationed at Carshalton. I received information from Sergeant Holmes as to the number of the watch on the morning of 28 June.

About what time? — About two o'clock in the morning following the murder.

Did you communicate the maker's name and the number of it to the proper persons to be circulated? — Yes.

Was it circulated throughout the different police stations? — Yes.

What was the number he gave you? — 16261.

What was the maker's name? — Griffiths, of Mile End Road.

THOMAS JENNINGS, examined by Mr POLAND.

I live at Balcombe. I am a platelayer in the service of the London, Brighton and South Coast Railway Company.[26] About four o'clock on the afternoon of Monday 27 June, I was walking through the Balcombe

---

26   According to the 1881 census, twenty year old railway labourer Thomas Jennings lived at Bagpeth's Cottages with his widowed mother. He was the youngest of fourteen children. On Saturday 16 July 1881 – the day after Lefroy's committal hearing began at Cuckfield – he married Sarah Selsby. He gave evidence before the magistrates three days later.

Thomas Jennings

tunnel from Three Bridges to Balcombe.[27] My nephew, William Jennings, was with me.[28]

Did you carry with you a naphtha lamp? — Yes.

Did you find the body of the deceased lying in the middle of the tunnel? —Yes, it was lying in the six foot way, between the two lines.

Was it lying parallel with the rails? — Yes.

Was the body on its back? — Yes, with the head towards Brighton.

Was part of the coat over the face? — Yes.

Did you notice much blood about? —There was blood on the hands and face.

Was the face very much cut about? — Yes.

How were the arms and legs arranged? — The right leg was crossed over the left. The right arm was crossed over the breast, and the left arm was turned under the back.

The body was clear of the rails? — Yes.

Did you examine the body? —Yes. The body of the coat was crumpled up underneath the shoulders. I felt the body outside the shirt, near the breast.

Was it cold? — No, it was middling warm.

Did it appear quite dead? — Yes.

Was the body afterwards taken from the tunnel? — Yes. My nephew went to the signal box and telegraphed that a body had been found. An engine and brake afterwards came from Three Bridges, and the body was put into the brake and taken to Balcombe station. It was then taken to the stables at the Railway Inn, near the station.

Whilst in the tunnel with the body, did you see any marks upon the ground close to where the body was lying? — Yes, I noticed a mark about eighteen yards from where the body was lying, on the London side. It looked as if something had fallen down and removed the dust.

From the place where the dust was removed, did you see any marks between that and the place where the body was lying? — Yes, there were marks in the ballast as if something had been dragged along.

Was there any blood near the body? — Some marks of blood were on one of the sleepers.

The blood you saw appeared to be fresh blood? — Yes.

A little later on, did you find near that place a boot? — Yes. I found

27 Some sources say Jennings was walking from Balcombe to Three Bridges, but as his brother John, the next witness, stated he was walking ahead and from north to south before the body of Mr Gold was found, Thomas Jennings must have been walking behind him, from Three Bridges towards Balcombe.

28 Twelve-year-old William Jennings was the son of the next witness, John Jennings, who at thirty-six was Thomas's second eldest brother (after George, b. 1844).

Lefroy.

Thomas Jennings

a shoe about seven yards south of where the body was lying, towards Brighton. There was only one boot on the body, and this was the missing one. I also found a linen cuff a few yards north of the body. There was no cuff on one wrist of the body. There were two bronze pennies and some keys a short distance from the body, but no hat.

Cross-examined.

The body, was it that of a big heavy man? — Yes.

Did you notice that his clothes were torn all to rags? — No, I did not notice.

Did you search the body? — No, I did not.

John Jennings

JOHN JENNINGS, examined.

I live at Willow Cottage, Balcombe. I am a ganger in the employ of the Railway Company and brother to the last witness. On the Monday in question, I was walking through Balcombe tunnel from north to south. I walked in the six-foot way and I had a light with me. At about 2.30 pm or 2.40 pm, I passed the spot where the body was afterwards found, but it was not there then. Soon after, the two o'clock Brighton express passed me in the tunnel about a quarter of a mile from the south end. Later, I heard a body had been found in the tunnel.

You went there? — Yes; I went back into the tunnel. I there found the body with my brother.

What did you do? — The first thing I did was to trace how it came there. About eighteen yards north of the body, I saw a mark in the ballast, which looked as if something had fallen there very heavily. About eight yards nearer the body, I noticed another mark, as though something like clothes had brushed over the ballast lightly. The mark about eighteen yards from the body was in a position as though something had fallen from a carriage of a down train on the off side into the six foot way.

What time was it when you reached the body? — It was 4.50 pm.

Did you feel the body? — Yes. I felt the body under the waistcoat near the heart, and it felt warm, but there were no signs of movement at all.

George Lewis

GEORGE LEWIS, examined by Mr POLAND.

I am a police constable, stationed at Balcombe. On Monday 27 June, I received information of a body having been found in Balcombe tunnel. At 4.50 pm, I went into the tunnel and got there about 5.30 pm. I saw the body of Mr Gold lying in the six-foot way.

Did you examine the body? — I did. I felt the body at the throat, breast, and hands, and it was quite cold.

You saw the boot and the cuff which have been spoken of? — Yes.

Second Day – Saturday 5 November 1881.

George Lewis

And did you also see a broken eyeglass? — I did.

Where was that? — Two or three yards north of the body.

Did you later see the other part of the eyeglass? — Yes. I afterwards searched the body at the stables at the Railway Inn, and I found the broken piece of eyeglass attached to an elastic cord round the neck.

Did you match it with the other part of the glass? — Yes, it corresponded with the piece found in the tunnel.

In taking the elastic off you broke it? — Yes. It broke near the end as I pulled it from the deceased's neck.

Did you also find this gold chain [*produced*]? — I did. It was round the neck in the ordinary way.

In taking it from the body, did a small piece break off? — About two or three inches broke off.

Did you also find on the body a pocket-book? [*produced*] — Yes. It contained two receipts for flour, two blank cheques, a memorandum book, and a first-class express season ticket for London to Brighton.

Was the deceased wearing a collar? — Yes. It was saturated with blood.

It had Mr Gold's name on it? — Yes.

And was the deceased also wearing a necktie? — Yes. That too was saturated with blood.

Did you notice if the deceased's clothes were damaged? — Yes. The knees of the trousers were cracked across as though he had fallen on the dirt and so cut them. There was blood on them, too.

In what condition was the deceased's head and face? — There was blood and black dirt from the tunnel all over them.

Was he wearing a hat? — No.

Did you order the removal of the body? — Yes. I had the body taken from the tunnel and removed to the Railway Inn at Balcombe.

Cross-examined by Mr WILLIAMS.

Did you notice whether the coat was much torn? — It was not torn at all. [*The coat was here produced.*] I cut it to take it off the body, but it was not torn originally.

Did you find a second pocket-book? — No. I only found one pocket-book.

No purse? — No.

No skull cap? — No.

No little sovereign bag? No.

Canvas bag? — No.

No money on the body except what we have seen here? — No.

Have you helped in the search for a revolver on the line? — Yes. A diligent search has been made by gangs of men.

Lefroy.

George Lewis

And no revolver has been found? — No.

There was a knife found, wasn't there? — I believe so.

[*The ATTORNEY-GENERAL objected to this, saying that the witness did not know of his own knowledge that a knife had been found. As a matter of fact, several knives had been found.*]

John Blunden White

JOHN BLUNDEN WHITE, examined by Mr A. L. SMITH.

I live at 39 London Street, Brighton. I am a carriage inspector at Brighton Station. On Monday 27 June, just after the arrival of the two o'clock express train from London Bridge, I went along the off side and inspected the carriage in which the prisoner travelled. I noticed a great deal of blood on one of the footboards, which had the appearance of having run out under the door of the second compartment. It was fresh blood. Underneath the footboard were marks of fingers which were blood-stained; they were a little beyond the hinges of the door of the compartment. My opinion at the time was that someone had been looking out of the window and had been struck.

Did you open the door? — I took possession of the carriage first. I had the carriage put in a siding, and afterwards I made a closer inspection of it.

What then? — I saw a considerable amount of blood on the floor of the off side of the carriage and on the cushion of the seat facing the engine. There was also blood on the other cushion, and in other parts of the carriage.

Was it fresh blood? — Yes, all of it.

How many bullet marks did you find? — Three in all, but not then.

Where were they? — I found a bullet embedded in the woodwork about seven inches from the bell-pull, on the side of the engine. The bullet is still there; it has not been taken out. Another was in the trimming at the back of the carriage, nearest the engine. The third was on the opposite side to the bell-pull, in the cushion.

Has the one near the bell-pull been taken out? — Yes. Barnes took it out.

I believe the cushion is here? — It is here.

What is the height from the sleeper to the footboard? — Will you allow me to look at my notes? [*Witness looked at his notes.*] From the top of the sleeper to the top of the footboard is 3ft 10½ inches. From the footboard to the floor is 1ft 2in, making just five feet.

Cross-examined by Mr WILLIAMS.

You say there was one bullet in the padding immediately over the corner seat nearest the engine? — Yes.

That would be immediately over the head of a person sitting there? — Yes.

The other was immediately under the alarm bell? — Yes.

Another was in the cushion of the middle seat on the opposite side of the alarm bell? — Yes.

Where was the fourth? — We only found three, as far as we are concerned. There were only three bullet marks.

Re-examined by Mr A. L. SMITH.

Were there other marks? — There were marks as if a struggle had taken place. There were marks underneath each seat.

Mr Justice COLERIDGE: Two of the bullets were on the same side as the bell-pull and one opposite? — Yes.

Mr A. L. SMITH: The bullet mark in the back padding, was that above the off side, or near the side seat of the train coming from London? — Near side. The platform side.

If you were looking towards Brighton would it be the right or left side? — Left-hand side.

[*Mr Justice COLERIDGE here remarked that, if either side wished it, the jury should have an opportunity of inspecting the carriage. Mr WILLIAMS said it would be better for the jury to see the carriage. It was therefore arranged that the jury should see the carriage during luncheon time.*]

The ATTORNEY-GENERAL: The carriage in question is at the London, Chatham and Dover Station close by. After being examined, it was locked up and has been locked ever since.

JOHN BARNES, examined by Mr A. L. SMITH.

I am an inspector at Brighton Railway station and live in Peel Street, Brighton.

On Monday afternoon, 27 June, did you go to see a first-class smoking carriage belonging to the two o'clock train from London? — Yes.

Can you describe what you saw? — I saw a quantity of blood in the carriage. I saw the bullet which was in the panel near the bell-pull. That is there now. I saw the mark of another bullet in the back cushion on the near side of the carriage, and found a bullet.

Was it the same size, as far as you know, as the bullet now produced? — Yes. It was inside the cushion about a quarter of an inch.

Did you take the bullet out? — Yes, I took it into Mr Anscombe's office and gave it to Mr Hooper, his clerk.

John
Blunden
White

John
Barnes

Lefroy.

x

John Barnes

Cross-examined by Mr WILLIAMS.

Do you know where the bullet is now? — It was subsequently given to the magistrates at Cuckfield.

Thomas Bond

THOMAS BOND, examined by Mr POLAND.

I am a fellow of the Royal College of Surgeons, and lecturer on forensic medicine at the Westminster Hospital. I live at 7 The Sanctuary, Westminster Abbey.

You made a post mortem examination of the body of Mr Gold on 1 July? — I did.

At the stable near Balcombe station? — Yes.

Mr Hall and Mr Byass were present? — Yes.

Were you in court when Mr Hall was examined? — I was.

Did you hear the description he gave of the condition of the body? — I did.

Was that correct? — Yes.

Can you describe the condition of the body? — The body was that of a large, well-nourished frame. Decomposition had commenced but not advanced too far. The body had not been opened and not interfered with except the skull cap had been removed, and a piece of skin about the size of a half-a-crown from under the right ear. I proceeded to make external examination.

Did you notice marks of black grease on one of the legs? — I did.

Was the leg injured? — The left leg very much. I found a jagged penetrating wound exposing the bone just above the left knee cap on the left side.

Was the injury likely to be effected by coming in contact with gravel? — Much more likely to have been injured by coming into contact with the wheel of an engine covered with grease. The wound was much blackened by what appeared to be black grease. The grease was in the tissue of the leg. There was no effusion of blood around this wound, but just above it there was a large brown patch (the colour of that book) without any effusion of blood.

Was the right knee injured? — There were two superficial abrasions, and on the inside of the right thigh there was a bruise two inches long. These injuries were accompanied by an effusion of blood into the tissues around.

Were the injuries inflicted before death? — I am certain the injuries to the right leg were done before death. The other injuries were probably caused either after or at the time of death.

Was the left hand injured? — There were slight abrasions on the wrist and contusions on the inside of the arm. There was a deep cut on the

x

inside of the ball of the thumb, extending down to the bone. On the inside of the last joint of the thumb, there was a jagged cut, also down to the bone. On the inside of the fourth finger, close to the last joint, there was a cut. That is, on the inside of each of the four fingers, there was a deep cut close to the last joint. When the fingers were flexed, these cuts all corresponded, and appeared to have been done by one sweep of a knife.

As if the hand had grasped some sharp instrument? — Yes; and the knife drawn through.

Was the right hand injured? — There was a very deep cut extending almost round the thumb, very nearly severing it at the juncture of the thumb with the wrist bones. Opposite the last joint of the thumb, there was also a jagged cut down to the bone. There were abrasions and contusions on the back of the hand, and a severe contusion on the back of the forearm.

Were there any injuries to the face? — There was a curved, jagged incision, extending from the lobe of the right ear down the side of the lower jaw, across the body of the jaw in the left side of the face. This cut followed the lower border of the jaw and at the upper part divided the skin only, but grazing the bone at an angle of the jaw, and underneath laying bare the muscles which form the floor of the mouth. On the right side of the neck, half an inch below the aforementioned cut, was a superficial incision an inch long. On the point of the chin, there was a superficial cut an inch long, dividing the chin only. On the left side of the face was a cut, two inches long, extending from the angle of the mouth across the cheek to within an inch and a half of the left ear. This cut divided all the tissues down to the mucous membrane of the mouth, including the muscles and the facial artery. A quarter of an inch below, and parallel to the above cut, was a deep incision about an inch and a half long, also dividing the tissue down to the mucous membrane. Just above those two cuts, there was a lineal abrasion of the skin extending from the cheek to the lobe of the ear, and slightly wounding the ear. On the bridge of the nose there was a slight contusion. In the corner of the left eye, there was a jagged wound about an inch deep. I could put my little finger into it. There was extensive effusion of blood into and around the eyelid. There was also effusion of blood beneath the conjunctiva of the eye. On the right side, there was another contusion of the eyebrow, and half an inch above it, on the inner side, there was an oblique incision extending nearly down to the bone. Just above this cut, towards the left temple, there was a severe contusion about two inches long and one and a half wide, with a good deal of blood effusion. On the top of the head, there were two abrasions of the skin, and there was also

Lefroy.

Thomas
Bond

contusion, with considerable effusion of blood. On the cartilage of the
right ear, there was a superficial cut

The cuts on the neck and face – had they the appearance of being
inflicted by an assailant? — Yes. I think the wounds on the face must
have been inflicted by a right-handed man attacking from the front, from
right to left. The cuts were done by a sharp instrument. In my opinion,
the cuts showed evidence that they had been aimed at the throat. I judge
of that by their direction. They were not at all like suicidally-inflicted
wounds, and the wounds on the hands coupled with those on the head I
believe to be absolutely incompatible with an attempt at suicide.

All done during life? — They all had the appearance of having been
made during life with the exceptions that I have noted. The injury on the
knee, on the back of the head, and the fracture of the skull, were in my
opinion caused by falling out of the carriage, either after death or at the
time of death.

Can you describe the injuries to the skull? — Dr Byass had divided
the scalp over the top of the head in the usual way to remove the skull
cap. Extending backwards (for Dr Byass cut at a right angle), there was
a jagged cut three inches long. The tissues around were much stained by
infiltration of blood, owing to the dependent position of the cut, but the
edges of the cut showed no sign of effusion with the tissues.

Was it done before death or after death? — I can't say with any
certainty. I am inclined to the opinion that this cut, like the cut on the
knee, happened after death, or at the moment of death.

Was this a fracture as might be caused by coming in contact with the
ground? — Just such a fracture. On turning back the skull cap, I found a
fracture of the bone extending from the vertex forwards and downwards
to the right, through the parietal bone and through the great wing of the
sphenoid bone, thence inwards to the body of the bone. The periosteum
was torn through, but there was no evidence of extravasation of the
blood in the course of the fracture. This injury also, I think, happened at
the moment of, or after, death. In the posterior fossa in the base of the
skull, there was considerable discolouration of the lining membrane, or
dura mata, of the skull.

Can you describe the results of your internal examination? — On
opening the body, I found the right lung healthy; the left lung was
collapsed and adherent to the chest wall. The bag of the heart was also
adherent and the apex of the heart was adherent to the bag. The heart was
large and flabby. None of the cavities of the heart contained any blood
beyond a small clot of fibrin. The valves were all healthy, but there was a
little degeneration of the large artery just above the valves. The abdomen
was very fat and contained a good deal. The stomach was empty; and the

mucous membrane was healthy, but beginning to decompose. The liver was somewhat fatty, and much decomposed; the kidneys were rather small, but not diseased. All the other organs were healthy.

Did you examine the brain? — Yes. It had been removed by Dr Byass, and I replaced it. There was no indication in the brain by which I could form an opinion as to whether it had been injured during life.

Did you cut under the right ear to find the bullet? — Mr Hall had cut the skin away. I traced the hole, and found the bullet embedded in the muscle of the gullet, which I produce. It was just in front of the second vertebra, to the left. The bullet had passed an inch below the right ear, behind the upper part of the lower jaw, close behind the internal artery and striking the vertebra. There was a good deal of effusion of the blood around this fracture, and the fracture extended downwards through the body of the vertebra to its articulation with the third, chipping off the lower half of the anterior part of the vertebra.

What size was the bullet? — It was a small bullet, but I have seen smaller. About the size of a bean.

Was it such a one as to be fired from a revolver? — Yes.

Would such a wound cause insensibility? — I think it would have caused momentary insensibility.

Do you think after the shot a man would have been able to make any resistance? — I think perfectly well.

Was it sufficient in itself? — I think eventually it would cause death.

What do you mean by eventually? — I should say a fortnight or even three months.

In your opinion, can you tell us the cause of death? — The immediate cause of death I believe to have been syncope from the shock of the gunshot wound, and loss of blood.

Cross-examined by Mr WILLIAMS.

Most of the wounds were inflicted during life, and some at the moment of death? — Yes.

Would the bullet cause a great quantity of blood? — No. There would be a great loss of blood from the cuts, but not from the bullet wound.

Mr Justice COLERIDGE: Was there any evidence to lead you to suppose the shot had been fired close to the deceased? — I should say not exactly close, or the skin would have been blown to pieces, but it was sufficiently near to blow the powder into the skin. Mr Hall took a piece of skin off, and on that I found the usual indications of a bullet wound. The wound is very small, and slightly discoloured with powder. The smell had been destroyed by spirit; but there was extravasation of blood into the skin tissue. I should say the weapon was held about a foot

Lefroy.

away. I have seen many bullet wounds. The pistol was not held near enough for the gas to enter the skin, but close enough for the powder to be found on the skin.

WILLIAM WINDSOR, examined by Mr A. L. SMITH.

I am a labourer on the London, Brighton and South Coast Railway.

Do you remember what day it was you noticed the down express to Brighton? — I don't know what day it was.

Do you remember the fact of Mr Gold's body being found? — No.

Do you remember the fact of the express altering its pace at Hassock's Gate? — Yes. It slowed down before reaching the station, and then quickened again.

After the train had passed, did you notice anything on the up line? — Yes, a hat. [*A round bowler hat was produced.*]

Did you see any one get out of the train when it slackened? — No.

Cross-examined by Mr WILLIAMS.

How far was the train on the London side when it slackened? — 400 yards.

Did it slacken up to Hassock's Gate station? — Yes.

How far were you on the London side? — 300 yards.

So the train began to slacken 100 yards before it came up to you? — Yes.

Was the hat you saw on the line there before the train passed? — No.

You are sure of that? — Yes.

GEORGE SHORT, examined by Mr A. L. SMITH.

I was at work on the Brighton line with the witness Windsor.

Did you hear of Mr Gold's body being found on the line? — Yes.

Did you see the down express come? — Yes.

Did it slack its speed? — Yes. It slackened north of Hassock's Gate

Afterwards, did you pick up a hat? — No. I saw one. That is the hat [*produced*].

When the train slackened, did you see anyone get out of the train? — No.

If anyone had got out, must you have seen him? — Yes.

Cross-examined by Mr WILLIAMS.

How far were you from Windsor? — Three yards.

You saw him pick up the hat? — Yes.

It was not on the line before the train passed? — No.

What happened to the hat? — It was given to the station master.

Second Day – Saturday 5 November 1881.

WILLIAM WOOD, examined by Mr A. L. SMITH.

William Wood

I am a corn dealer, living at Hassock's Gate. I am in the habit of travelling by the London, Brighton and South Coast Railway to attend the London Corn Market.

On Monday 27 June, did you travel by the two o'clock express train from London Bridge? — I did.

Did you fall asleep part of the way? — I did. I fell asleep after we left Croydon, and woke up just before we got to Hassock's Gate.

Were you awakened by the train reducing speed? — Yes.

How slow did it get down to? — I could not say. It went very slowly, and then it resumed its speed.

When it was going at its slowest, did you look out of the window or not? — Yes. I looked out of the off-side of the carriage, and noticed a hat lying on the line [*produced*].

Did you see anybody leave the train on that side of the line? — No.

Did you see any men working there? — I saw several men working on the line.

Cross-examined by Mr WILLIAMS.

You live at Hassock's Gate? — Yes.

And the train slackening woke you? — Yes.

It slackened so much that you thought you would get out? — Yes. As I was passing my own house, I hesitated as to whether I should attempt to leave the carriage. I actually moved my bag from one side to the other to do so.

If you had gone on, you would have had to come back from Preston? — Yes.

ROBERT PEEL, examined by Mr POLAND.

Robert Peel

I am an express engine driver in the employ of the Railway Company. I live at 38 Gloucester Road, Brighton. On 27 June, I drove the two o'clock Brighton express. I heard no fog signals. As we approached Hassock's Gate, the distance signal was against me, and I shut the steam off. I did not hear any shots during the journey, or notice anyone get out except at stations. When I backed my engine on to the train at London Bridge, I saw Mr Gold, whom I have known for ten years past. I saw him get into the train. He was wearing a broad brim, high hat like the one produced. I could not say whether he was carrying an umbrella. We did not stop between London and Croydon.

Cross-examined by Mr WILLIAMS.

Between Croydon and Hassock's Gate, did the train slacken to less

Robert Peel

than thirty miles an hour? — No.

Certainly not to less than four miles an hour? — Certainly not.

Re-examined by the ATTORNEY-GENERAL:

How many years have you been a driver in the employ of the company? — Thirty-four years. I make the statement as to the speed of the train after that long experience.

Then my learned friend has brought that out against himself. [*A laugh.*]

Alfred Aylwin

ALFRED AYLWIN, examined.

I am stoker to the last witness. We shut off steam for a few seconds at Hassock's Gate, but did not apply the Westinghouse brake. We could see the signals against us a long while before we came to them, as far as Burgess Hill station. The signals kept dropping as we approached. We did not pass one when it was against us. I was looking ahead, and did not see anyone alight from the train.

Henry Nye

HENRY NYE, examined by Mr POLAND.

I was the rear guard of the Brighton train on 27 June. I remember the train slackening speed.

What speed did it slacken down to? — Four miles an hour for three or four seconds.

Did you see anyone get out of the train then? — No.

When you knew the train would slacken speed, did you look out at all? — Yes, on the near side, and saw along the whole of the train.

Did you see some lads on the line? — Yes.

Did you speak to them? — Yes.

Mrs Nye Chart

MRS NYE CHART, examined by the ATTORNEY-GENERAL.

I am the proprietress of the Brighton Theatre. I am known in the profession by the name of Mrs Nye Chart.[29]

Do you know the prisoner at the bar – Lefroy? — No, I do not.

Had you made any appointment to see him on 27 June? — No.

Had you any knowledge of any business for which he should want to see you? — No, I know of none.

Thomas Picknell

THOMAS PICKNELL, examined by Mr POLAND.

I live at Red Bridge Cottage, Balcombe, and I am a ganger of platelayers employed by the Brighton Railway Company. On Monday

29   Ellen Elizabeth 'Nellie' Nye Chart ran the Theatre Royal, New Road, Brighton from her husband's death in 1876 until her own passing in 1892.

afternoon, 27 June, about a quarter to five, I was about three-quarters of a mile south of Balcombe station when I found the linen collar, the one produced. It was marked 'A'.

Where was it lying? — In the six-foot way between the two roads.[30]

With blood on it? — Yes, the blood was quite red, and the collar was wet with rain.

Was it in the same state as it is now? — Yes, so far as I know.

That was the collar shown to you when you were before the coroner? — Yes.

You had been over the same ground in the morning? — Yes, and it was not there then.

Cross-examined by Mr WILLIAMS.

Was one of the button-holes torn through? — Yes.

EDWARD TULLETT, examined by Mr POLAND.

I am a platelayer, in the service of the Brighton Railway Company. On Monday 27 June, at five minutes past three in the afternoon, I found the tall felt hat produced. It was about half a mile south of Burgess Hill station, between the two rails forming the up-line.

Had you seen the two o'clock train from London to Brighton pass? — Yes.

Was there any hat there before the train passed? — No.

And you found the hat directly after the train passed? — Yes.

What did you do with the hat? — I took it to the Burgess Hill station.

KATE GREENFIELD, examined by Mr POLAND.

I live at Balcombe with my father, George Greenfield. On Sunday 3 July, I was on a visit to a friend at Hassock's Gate.

Do you remember finding a purse [*produced*]? — Yes.

Where was it? — In some grass by the side of the line.

You say it was in the grass? — Yes. I should say it was within throwing distance of the line.

Just describe how it was picked up. — One of the children I was with picked it up. It was empty, as it is now. I took possession of it, and took it home to my father, who was one of the coroner's jury.

What part of the line was it? — About a quarter of a mile north of Hassock's Gate station towards London.

What side of the line was it? — On the right-hand side going from London to Brighton.

Thomas Picknell

Edward Tullett

Kate Greenfield

---

30   The six-foot way is the gap between the two rails.

Lefroy.

Henry Waller

HENRY WALLER, examined by Mr POLAND.

I live at Hassock's Gate and am a ganger in the service of the Brighton Company. On Monday 27 June, I was in the Clayton tunnel about 6.45 pm.

Did you there find the umbrella produced? — Yes.

Where did you find it? — About eleven yards from the north end of the tunnel.

On which side? — The up side close to the wall. I took possession of it, carried it to Hassock's Gate, and gave it to the station master there.

[In reply to his Lordship, it was stated that this was Mr Gold's umbrella.]

Alfred Gilbert

ALFRED GILBERT, *recalled and cross-examined* by Mr WILLIAMS.

Can you tell me whether Mr Gold brought the £38 to the bank in a canvas bag? — I believe it was. I believe I gave him the bag back after taking the money from it, but I cannot say. It is customary to do so.

Was he in a hurry that morning? — Yes, a great hurry, and he was attended to out of his proper turn in consequence.

Mr Justice COLERIDGE: What was his habit? Had he one particular bag? — I could not say.

The Court then adjourned for luncheon at 1.30 pm. Afterwards, the jury went to the London, Chatham and Dover Railway, close by the court, to view the railway carriage in which the murder was committed. The jurymen paid particular attention to the marks on the footboard. Their visit attracted considerable attention.

*

On the court resuming, the first witness called was:

Albert Ellis

ALBERT GEORGE ELLIS, examined by the ATTORNEY-GENERAL.

I carry on business as a stationer at 5 Railway Terrace, Wallington.[31]

Your shop is close to the station? — Yes.

For how long have you known the prisoner at the bar? — About eighteen months. He has dealt with me repeatedly for foolscap paper, et cetera.

Do you also know Mrs Clayton? — Yes. The prisoner is a relative of Mrs Clayton, and he was living at her house in Cathcart Road, Wallington.

You knew the prisoner under the name of Lefroy, I believe? — Yes.

31   Mr Ellis was 23-years-old according to the 1881 census and lived alone.

Second Day – Saturday 5 November 1881.

On Monday 27 June, did you have a letter brought to you by one of Mrs Clayton's children? — Yes.

Is that the letter [*produced*]? — Yes.

Is it in the handwriting of Lefroy? — Yes.

[*The ATTORNEY-GENERAL then read the letter as follows: '27.6.81. Mrs Clayton presents her compliments to Mr Ellis and will feel greatly obliged if he could call upon her at above address some time before 10 30 this morning concerning an order for stationery she wishes to give him.'*][32]

In consequence of that letter, did you go to 4 Cathcart Road? — I did.

What time did you get there? — A few minutes before ten.

That morning? — Yes.

You saw a female servant first? — Yes.

You did not see Mrs Clayton? — I did not.

How long did you wait there? — Five minutes.

Whilst you were waiting, did Mrs Clayton's child bring you that paper? [*produced*] — She did.

Is that also in the handwriting of the prisoner? — It is.

[*The document was then read: 'Kindly get me 1 day ruled copy. Books: 1 copy of Bunyan's P. Progress 2/6, 1 copy of Swiss Family Robinson 1/6, 1 copy of At the End of the World, 1 copy of Love's Labour's Lost.'*][33]

As you were concluding your business, did you see Lefroy leave the house? — Yes. I heard the gate click and I saw the top of Lefroy's hat.

When you returned to your shop, did you receive a communication from the boy who assists you? — Yes.

Is that the lad named Pink? — Yes.

Did he hand to you an envelope with its contents? [*envelope produced*] — Yes.

Was the envelope addressed to you? — Yes.

Is it in the handwriting of the prisoner? — Yes.

What was inside the envelope? — It contained two Hanoverian medals, a shilling, and a blank piece of paper. [*Medals produced.*]

Was the prisoner in your debt? — Yes.

How much? — £1 7s 6d for goods delivered.

The boy made a statement to you as to the manner in which he had received the paper and its contents? — He did. He had given the prisoner change as if the envelope had contained two sovereigns.

Mr Justice COLERIDGE: You will call the boy to prove it was given him by the prisoner?

The ATTORNEY-GENERAL: Yes, my Lord. [*To the witness.*] Upon

Albert Ellis

---

32   Wording taken from a copy of the letter held at The National Archives (ASSI 36/26).
33   Ibid.

Lefroy.

Albert
Ellis

finding what the contents of the envelope were, did you return at once to Cathcart Road? — I sent my lad.

I believe he found the prisoner was not there? — Just so.

Was there nothing passed between you and the prisoner as to the payment of the money due? — Not that I remember.

What took place on the Thursday previous? — Oh, I beg your pardon. I think he promised to pay me on the following Saturday.

Was it the custom of the lad to go to the station to sell newspapers upon arrival of the trains at Wallington? — He sometimes did.

How far is East Croydon from Wallington? — About a mile and a half.

CAPTAIN HARPUR (A Juryman): On the morning you say you saw Lefroy at Wallington, can you tell what kind of hat he had on? — A tall hat.

Frederick
Pink

FREDERICK PINK, examined by Mr POLAND.

I am in the service of Mr Ellis, the last witness.[34]

Did Lefroy, on 27 June, come to your master's shop? — Yes.

What time? — A few minutes past ten o'clock in the morning.

Did you know that Lefroy at that time was indebted to your master? — Yes.

What did he say when he came into the shop? — He asked to pay his bill.

What change did he want? — He wanted thirteen shillings change for two pounds.

When he said that, did he produce anything? — Yes; the envelope.

Did he tell you what the amount of the bill was? — No.

Did you know what the amount of the bill was? — No.

How did you know what change to give him? — I gave him all the change I had in the till, which was thirteen shillings.

Are you often left alone in the shop? — No, sir. [*Laughter.*]

Mr Justice COLERIDGE: Did the prisoner say he wanted more that thirteen shillings change? — Yes.

Did he say why he left with short change? — Because he was in a hurry, as he was going by train.

At what time did he leave the shop? — About 10.05 am.

Mr POLAND: Did you attend at the railway station for the purpose of selling newspapers? — No. The steps leading to the station.

34 17-year-old Frederick Pink lived around the corner from Mr Ellis's shop, at 4 Railway Approach. In the 1881 census he is listed as an 'Errand boy'. He married Elizabeth Saunders in 1885, by which time he had become a baker's assistant, a career he continued until his retirement. The couple had three children. Frederick Pink died in 1919.

Oh! I beg your pardon. Do you sell to the persons leaving by the station? — Yes.

Is there a train leaving Wallington for London at 10.49 am? — Yes.

Did you attend it that morning? — Yes.

Did you see the prisoner that morning after leaving the shop? — Yes.

Cross-examined by Mr WILLIAMS.

When you were before the magistrates, did you say that you attended at the station, that you did not see Lefroy among the passengers leaving by the 10.49 train, and that if he had left by that train you would have seen him? — Yes.

WILLIAM TURPIN, examined by the ATTORNEY-GENERAL.

I am chief inspector on the London, Brighton, and South Coast Railway.

Of course you know this line very well? — Yes.

Do you know Wallington station? — Yes.

Is Waddon nearer to London than Wallington? — Yes.

How far is Waddon from Wallington? — [*Witness looked at his book.*] About three miles.

There is a train leaving Wallington at 10.49, and Waddon at 10.53, which arrives at London Bridge at 11.32? — Yes.

When is the next train after that? — The next train from Wallington to London starts at 11.23, and arrives at London Bridge at 11.56.

Was there an earlier train? — A train starts at 10.39, and arrives in London at 11.12.

Cross-examined by Mr WILLIAMS.

About what is the distance from Wallington to Carshalton? — I should think it is something over a mile.

The nearest station the prisoner could go to would be Wallington? — Yes.

Mr Justice COLERIDGE: What line is the Carshalton station on? — What we call the London, Mitcham and Sutton line. The terminus for these trains is London Bridge or Victoria.

HENRY CREEK, examined by the ATTORNEY-GENERAL.

I am assistant to Messrs Thomas Adams and Co., pawnbrokers, 25 High Street, Borough.[35]

Is it part of your business to take in pledges and advance money on

---

35   The full company name was 'T. Adams & G.J. Hillstead'.

Frederick
Pink

William
Turpin

Henry
Creek

Lefroy.

Henry
Creek

goods? — Yes.

Is there also in your business a lad named Allwright? — Yes.

Was he there in June last? — Yes.

[*Pawn-ticket produced.*] That is a ticket dated 2 June 1881. It is marked 'O'coat'? — Yes.

Does that stand for overcoat? — Yes.

Pawned for ten shillings in the name of William Lee, 8 Southampton Street, Peckham? — Yes.

[*The ATTORNEY-GENERAL asked for the coat to be produced. A minute or two afterwards a policeman returned, and said the door of the cupboard was locked, and the constable had gone away for a few minutes.*] [*Laughter.*]

As a fact, was an overcoat pledged for ten shillings? — Yes.

Is that your handwriting? — Yes.

Is this the coat? [*Light brown overcoat produced.*] — That is it.

That coat was never redeemed? — No.

And it remained in your charge until the commencement of this case? — Yes.

On 11 June, did you advance £1 5s on a gentleman's dress suit? — Allwright did.

Do you produce a dress suit? — Yes.

Were you consulted about the pledge? — Yes, I was. I knew that £1 5s was advanced on the suit.

The next transaction is on 21 June? — Yes.

I believe this ticket [*produced*] is a duplicate, and is returned by the person pledging when it is redeemed? — Yes.

On 21 June, was a revolver pledged at your place of business? — Yes.

How much was advanced upon it? — Five shillings.

What sort of revolver was it, in relation to size? — A small one.

Did you now produce one similar in size? — I have it here. [*A small revolver was produced and handed to the jury.*]

You produce that simply as an example, to show the size of the pistol? — Yes. I borrowed the one now in court in the town, to show the description of the item pledged.

Now, was that pistol taken out of pawn on Monday 27 June? — It was.

When it was pledged on 21 June, what became of the pistol? Was it given to anyone to take away? — It was laid on the back counter, with the duplicate card beside it. Then it was packed up and the ticket pinned on, and taken away.

Who did that? — Allwright.

Where was the pistol when the person came to redeem it on the 27th? — Up in the warehouse.

Did you obtain the pistol yourself, or did you send any one? — I sent Allwright for it.

Where was he when you requested him to get it? — He was down in the cellar. He had to clean lamps and glasses there. He usually goes down into the cellar at about eleven o'clock, and he was in the cellar at the time I called him.

[*The ATTORNEY-GENERAL read the contents of the pawn ticket: '21st of June, 1881. Revolver, 5s. William Lee, 9, Southampton Street, Peckham.' Mr Montagu WILLIAMS drew his Lordship's attention to the fact that the pawn ticket and the ticket supposed to be a duplicate were not the same, but the Attorney-General explained that the one issued to the customer had to contain the full address and the other did not.*]

I want you to go back to 21 June. When that person brought the pistol were any cartridges brought as well? — Yes. He put them on the counter. I said I did not require them.

Was anything said about the pistol? — Yes. I saw that the pistol was loaded and had six chambers. I returned it to him and said, 'We don't take it in like this. If I take it in at all you must unload it.' He unloaded it, and I packed them away in the cartridge box one by one.

How many cartridges were in the box? — The box was full, and contained, I should think, about fifty.

Then he took them away? — Yes. I gave him 5s upon the revolver, and he took away the ticket.

Where was he standing? — In a box. The shop is divided into compartments which we call boxes.

Now, you have seen the prisoner in custody before the magistrates, and also at Lewes Gaol on 12 July? — Yes.

Where was he at Lewes Gaol? — In the corridor.

Anybody with him? — About seven or eight persons.

Were they in prison dress or ordinary clothes? — Ordinary clothes.

Did you or did you not recognise the prisoner? — I did.

Now, what do you say? Is he or is he not the person who pledged the overcoat on the 2nd, and the revolver on 21 June? — I firmly believe he is the same man.

Can you say about what time it was on 27 June that the person you say is the prisoner redeemed the pistol? — Between eleven and twelve o'clock in the forenoon.

Was that person the person who pledged the revolver? — To the best of my belief, he was.

What cause had you to come to the conclusion that he was the prisoner? — Partly from my remembrance of the time, and partly from the fact of the revolver being pledged.

Lefroy.

Who came about this matter to you? — I sent for an inspector detective.

When was it that you made that communication? — I don't know the date, but it was the Thursday week following the Monday.

Your attention had been attracted by what was stated in the newspapers? — Yes.

You have applied your memory as well as you can to the circumstances of the pledges? — Yes. [*The overcoat pledged on 2 June and the dress suit pledged on 11 June were here produced.*]

Cross-examined by Mr WILLIAMS.

It was in consequence of what you had seen and read in the papers that you communicated with the police? — Yes.

And it was after that that you went down to Lewes for the purpose of identifying the prisoner? — Yes.

And after that you were examined before the coroner and the magistrate? — Yes.

I want you to be very accurate. Did you say before the magistrates, 'To the best of my belief, the prisoner is the man who pledged the pistol, but I won't swear to it'? — Yes.

Do you say the same today? — Yes.

Did you also say the same with reference to the man who redeemed it? — Yes.

Do you say the same today? — Yes.

Did you say you could not recollect the hour of pawning the pistol. 'I will not swear it had gone eleven. The transaction was not sufficiently impressed on my mind'? — No. I was not asked the question.

In regard to redeeming, may I take it that you said you would not fix the time for redeeming because it was not fixed on your mind? — Yes.

You say you can't recall how the prisoner was dressed, either at the pawning or the redeeming? — No.

You could not say whether he was wearing a high or a low hat? — No.

Did you go on to say, 'I recognised him, to the best of my belief, as a customer, but I could not say how long he had been a customer'? — Yes.

There are a good many customers at a pawnbroker's? — Yes.

There is some Act of Parliament, though I forget which just now, upon the subject, but pawnbrokers are not very particular about names and addresses, are they? — I can only speak for myself. I am.

Look at the surnames on these tickets. Are they the same? — One is different from the others.

And the Christian names? — There are two different Christian names.

Are the numbers the same in the street? — No; they are all different.

Now, supposing a person came in that you recognised as a customer, you wouldn't ask him his name? — Yes, I would.

You really mean it? — I really mean it.

Now, on a Saturday night you have a great many customers, have you not? — No.

Perhaps you have not a large business? — In that class of business, perhaps it is not.

Perhaps you mean it is not a large business in respect of receiving pledges? — It is not a low class business; it is a high class business. We only take articles in pawn of value over about 5s.

You don't take in such things as flat irons and tin kettles? — No. [*Laughter.*]

Mr Justice COLERIDGE: I suppose that flat irons would not go exactly with a dress suit.

Mr WILLIAMS: If a flat iron came in, would you not take it? — No. We should not take anything under 5s or 6s.

Where is your book? — I did not bring it.

Why? — I was not supposed to bring it.

Would there be any entry in the book as to these things? — There would.

The ATTORNEY-GENERAL: We will telegraph for it at once.

Mr WILLIAMS: Could you by your book tell at what time in the day articles were pledged? — Yes, I could tell you the time an article was pledged, but not the time an article was redeemed.

What time do you close? — Seven.

Always? — Except Saturdays.

Except then, you invariably close at seven o'clock? — Yes.

When you were asked before the magistrates about the pledging of the pistol on the 21st, did you say, 'I may have been out when these goods, alleged to have been his, were pledged on the 11th'? — Yes.

Did you say this? 'I swear it is the same man who pledged these things on the 2nd of June, because the name and address are the same. That is the only reason I can give for believing it is the same man.' — Yes, I did.

Did you see him on the 2nd? — Yes.

And on the 21st? — Yes, as I believe.

You won't pledge yourself that you saw him on the 11th? — No.

You think you saw him on the 2nd? — Yes.

You think you saw him on the 21st? — Yes.

And the reason of that is that the name and address on the tickets is the same? — No.

Did you say with reference to the 21st, 'I don't know whether the boy was in the shop. To the best of my recollection, no one else was in the shop'? — Yes.

Lefroy.

Henry
Creek

I may take it that what you said before the magistrate was that you believed he was the man who pledged the things, but you would not swear to it? — Yes.

You took a pistol to the Cuckfield enquiry? — Yes.

Was it similar to the one alleged to be in the possession of the prisoner? — Yes.

Where did this second pistol come from? — It was one pledged after 27 June. It was brought in by a young man, who wanted 5s for it. That is exactly the amount the prisoner's pistol was pledged for. I eventually took it in, but only because an inspector from Scotland Yard recommended me to take it in pledge.

There was an inspector of police in one of the compartments, and the person who pledged the pistol was in another? — Yes.

What was the name of that inspector? — Jarvis.

Jarvis did not come there for the purpose of pledging? — No.

What did he say to you? — He said, 'Bring it along to London Bridge station'.

When did he say that? — When he was in the shop.

Did you take it along to the solicitor's office at London Bridge? — Yes.

Who did you see? — Some gentleman who took down my statement.

Did he take down any statement as to the pawning of the pistol by the young man? — No.

What did you do with the pistol when you got to London Bridge? — I showed it to the gentleman there, and then took it back to the pawn shop.

That was two days before you went to Cuckfield? — Yes.

Who told you to take it to Cuckfield? — I think somebody told me to take it there.

In whose possession was it at Cuckfield? — My own. It was in my bag.

What examination did they make of it at London Bridge? — They had it in their hands, and they looked at it all over.

Did they examine the size of the muzzle of the pistol? — I don't know.

Who was present during this examination? — I believe Inspector Turpin was in the room when I was there, and Mr Hillstead, one of the partners, was also there. Jarvis was not in the room.

How long where you there? — I was in the room about half an hour.

Did you see any bullets? — Yes.

Where? — At my shop. I mean, subsequently.

Do you know whether any bullets were produced at all? — Where?

At the London Bridge station? — I never saw them.

Re-examined by the ATTORNEY-GENERAL.

Second Day – Saturday 5 November 1881.

On 2 June, you were the person who gave out the ticket for an overcoat? — Yes.

What name did you put down? — Lee.

Did you ask, or were you told, how to spell the name? — No.

So you put down 'Lee' without being told whether it was spelt 'Leigh'? — Yes. I did the same on the other occasions when the prisoner came in to pawn things.

But the third ticket is spelled 'Leigh', is it not? — Yes.

Do you recollect on that occasion being told by anyone how to spell the name? — No.

Do you find sometimes that persons pawn things in assumed names? — Frequently.

Do you take things from persons according to the name and address they give? — Yes.

After 27 June, a person called in at your shop to pledge a pistol, and an inspector happened to be present? — Yes.

You had some doubt about taking the pistol in? — Yes.

Why? — We do not care to take in pistols.

But by Jarvis's advice you took it in? — Yes.

Did he give you a reason for it? — I had told him the revolver was similar to the one that had been previously pledged. It was then that he said to me, 'Bring it along.'

Did you take it to Cuckfield to show how similar it was to the missing pistol? — Yes.

Has it been redeemed now? — No.

[*The ATTORNEY-GENERAL told the witness to bring the books, pistol and duplicate of the second pistol, on Monday morning.*]

ERNEST ALFRED ALLWRIGHT, examined.

I am assistant to Messrs T. Adams and Co. Sometimes I take in goods that are pledged. The 11 June ticket is in my handwriting, and is for a dress suit. Creek saw the person about the dress suit, but he was engaged, and I completed the transaction.

Did you see the person who brought the goods to pledge? — Yes. I wrote out the ticket.

Were you present when the revolver was pledged on the 21st? — I was standing by the counter. I remember the person who pawned the revolver being asked by Creek to take the cartridges out of the pistol.

What do you say? That the prisoner is the person who pledged the coat on 11 June and the revolver on the 21st? Is he or is he not the man? — He is.

Do you speak with doubt or with certainty? — With certainty.

Lefroy.

Ernest Allwright

Do you recollect 27 June, when you were asked to get the revolver? — Yes. I was downstairs in the cellar. I was just going to wash myself to go into the shop. I usually go to do the cleaning work at about twelve o'clock.

Did you see the person who redeemed the pistol? — No.

But you brought the pistol up from the warehouse? — Yes.

At what time? — About twelve o'clock, I should think.

Cross-examined by Mr WILLIAMS.

You saw this other pistol that was pledged? — Yes.

Was it the same pistol that was pledged on the 21st? — No.

Sometimes many people are waiting in the same box to pledge things? — Yes.

When are you busiest? — On Mondays and Saturdays.

Frank Swaisland

FRANK SWAISLAND, examined by the ATTORNEY-GENERAL.

I am employed as assistant to Mr Vaughan, pawnbroker, of 139 Strand.[36] I produce the aluminium watch that was pledged on 30 May last.

This ticket [*produced*] was found in the pocket of the prisoner's coat, at 4 Cathcart Road. Is this ticket one issued by you? — Yes.

[*The ATTORNEY-GENERAL read the contents of the pawn ticket: '30th May, 1881, M (metal) watch, 5s. John Lee, Southampton Street.'*]

Looking now at the prisoner, what do you say as to the identity of the man who pawned the watch? — I should think he was the man.

Cross-examined by Mr WILLIAMS.

Have you seen the prisoner since he pawned the watch? — Not until I saw him in the dock.

What is the number of the watch? — 1135.

George White

GEORGE WHITE, examined.

I am assistant to Mr T. Miller Sutton, pawnbroker, 17 Stockbridge Terrace, Pimlico. The ticket produced was issued by me. It says, 'John Lee, 11 New Street, 16s., two coats and two pairs of trousers' I do not remember the person who pawned the articles.

George Mathews

GEORGE MATHEWS, examined.

I am assistant to Mr Bowman, pawnbroker, of London Road, West

---

36   *The Post Office Directory* 1880 lists Charles B. Vaughan, silversmith, at 39 Strand rather than 139, which was a soap makers'.

Croydon. The ticket produced was issued by us on 22 June 1881. It reads, 'John Lee, Tamworth Road, four plated spoons and a leather bag, 5s.'

Do you remember who pawned them? — No. I have no recollection of that.

CHARLES TOBUTT, examined.

I am a sergeant in the East Sussex Constabulary, stationed at East Grinstead. On Monday night, 27 June, I went with Inspector Turpin to the prisoner's lodgings at 4 Cathcart Road, Wallington. Turpin went upstairs, and I remained below. I received a coat from Turpin which was lying on a table in the hall.

At the time you saw it, was the coat you now produce wet or dry? — It was damp.

Were there any marks upon the coat? — Yes, one arm of the coat was much blood-stained.

Do you produce a pair of trousers? — Yes; the right leg is bloody.

Were they wet or dry? — Damp, but not so damp as the coat.

Was there not also a surgical bandage? — Yes. I produce it. It smelt strongly, as if some kind of liniment had been on it, something similar to Friar's Balsam.

Did you search the pockets of the light coat? — Yes.

Did you find this pocket-book? — Yes, in the breast pocket.

Did you find these five tickets in the pocket-book? — Yes.

What else did you find? — A new registered envelope, unused, with marks of blood on it. There was also a piece of pink writing paper, a piece of blotting paper also blood stained, and a second-class railway ticket from London to East Croydon, dated 24 June, I believe.

GEORGE BERRY, examined.

I am superintendent of the East Sussex police, stationed at East Grinstead.

Did you see the prisoner in Lewes Gaol? — Yes, on 9 July, the day after he was apprehended.

Did he ask you anything? — He asked me who had the pawn tickets which were found in his coat. I told him I had. He asked me for the pawn ticket for his dress suit, as he wished to sell the suit for the purpose of his defence. I declined to give it up.

THOMAS GRAHAM CLAYTON, examined by
the ATTORNEY-GENERAL.

I formerly lived at number 4 Cathcart Road, Wallington.

George Mathews

Charles Tobutt

George Berry

Thomas Clayton

Lefroy.

Thomas Clayton

Did the prisoner lodge in your house last June? — Yes. I knew him by the name of Percy Lefroy Mapleton. He is related to my wife.

How long had he lodged there? — Ever since he came back from Australia, eighteen months ago.[37] He occupied a room jointly with a man named Seale.[38]

What were the rental arrangements? — He paid, as a rule, eight shillings a week, but he was irregular. He had not paid for two or three weeks before 27 June.

Did he borrow money of you? — Not of me, personally.

Do you know if he had a season ticket to London? — At one time he had a second-class season ticket on the Brighton line, from Wallington or Sutton to London, but it had been run out for some time.

What class did he usually travel after that ran out? — I don't know. I never travelled with the prisoner and he never told me what class he usually travelled by.

While he lived with you, was he in any employment? — I believe so.

Where? — I believe he was employed on the staff of a newspaper.

What newspaper? — *The Era.*

What time did you leave the house on the morning of 27 June? — About 8.45 am, to go to my business.[39]

At that time was Lefroy up? — I think not.

Had you seen him before you left? — Yes, in his bedroom.

Did he tell you he was going to Brighton that day? — No.

Did he say what he was going to do that day? — No.

When did you return? — At 6.15 in the evening.

Later in the evening did you see the prisoner? — Yes.

What time? — About 9.00 pm.

Was his head bandaged up? — Yes, with a white bandage.

What did you say to him? — I asked him what was the matter.

What did he say? — He said he had been assaulted by a countryman in the train on his way to Brighton. He said he had been knocked on the head by a gouge. He pointed to blood on his trousers.

Did he say anything about being insensible? — Yes. He said he was insensible by the blow till he arrived at Preston station.

Was Holmes, the police officer, with him? — Yes. He seemed to be telling Holmes what had happened.

What did he say? — He said the men who assaulted him must have got

---

37 In fact, by the time of his trial Lefroy had returned from Australia more than two years previously. However, at the Magistrates' hearing at Cuckfield in July Thomas Clayton again said that Lefroy had returned 'about eighteen months ago', suggesting he was vague as to when his wife's cousin had actually moved in with them.

38 Frank Seale was Ann Clayton's brother, forty years old in 1881.

39 Clayton is listed in the 1881 census as a 'distiller's clerk'.

out of the train as it was going along.

Where did this conversation take place? — At a small table in the front room. Holmes had pencil and paper.

Did Holmes say anything to you? — He said he was trying to get fuller particulars of what had occurred from the prisoner.

What took place then? — The prisoner answered another question, and then Holmes read over what he had written to the prisoner.

What did the prisoner say? — He assented to it, and said it was correct.

Do you recollect something being said as to the prisoner's watch? — Holmes asked the prisoner what the number of his watch was. The prisoner told him a number, but I cannot remember what it was.

Did you see what Holmes did? — He asked the prisoner to let him look at his watch.

Did Holmes try to open it? — Yes. He did not succeed at first, so he handed it to me.

Could you open it? — No. I gave it back to Holmes.

Did he then succeed in opening it? — Yes.

What did he say? — He said to the prisoner, 'You have given me the wrong number.' He mentioned the number, and he said, 'That is a different one to the previous one'.

Did Holmes mention the maker's name and address? — Yes, but I do not remember the name.

What was the address? — To the best of my recollection it was somewhere in Mile End.

Were you in the room all the time with Holmes and the prisoner? — Not all the time.

How long did Holmes stay with the prisoner? — A quarter of an hour.

After Holmes left, did you speak to the prisoner? — Yes.

What did you say? — I said it was a very strange affair.

What did he say? — He said it was, and that he hoped the man would be caught.

Was anything said about his head? — He said he should go to Dr Cressy.

You knew Dr Cressy? — Yes, he is a medical man living in the neighbourhood.[40] He was my wife's doctor.

You afterwards went out, leaving the prisoner there? — Yes.

What time did you return to the house? — A little after ten.

Was the prisoner still there? — No, he had gone out.

And, afterwards, did the police come and search the house? — Yes.

---

40   In 1881 Dr William Cressy practised at "Haysden", Manor Road, Wallington, where he had resided for at least ten years.

Thomas
Clayton
They found the light overcoat? — Yes.

Just look at the light overcoat which was produced by Mr Creek. You saw it before the magistrate on 2 July? — Yes. To the best of my belief, it is the prisoner's overcoat.

You don't know at all about the dress suit? — No.

Just look at the clothes produced, two coats and a pair of trousers. What do you say as to those? — I am not clear as to whose all this clothing is; some of it, I think, is mine.

Just look at the bag [*produced*]. To the best of your belief, is that your bag? — It is.

You missed your bag? — Yes.

Do you know anything of the spoons inside? [*produced*] Just look at them. — No. They are not my property.

The initials on the spoons are 'R.M.O.'. Do you know to whom they refer? — No.

Mr Justice COLERIDGE: Had you any relative in connection with those initials? — No.

The ATTORNEY-GENERAL: When did you first miss your bag? — About the middle of June.

Had the prisoner any watch? — Yes.

Had he an aluminium watch at one time like this one? [*produced*] — He had.

Did he ever have a revolver as far as you know? — Never.

Had Lefroy ever been in Australia? — Yes, about eighteen months ago.

Mr Justice COLERIDGE: Whereabouts in Australia? — Melbourne, I believe.

Cross-examined by Mr WILLIAMS.

Can you say where the prisoner was born? — He was born in the house of my wife's father.

What relation is the prisoner to your wife? — Second cousin.[41]

And how old is the prisoner? — He is twenty-one years of age.

How long have you known the prisoner? — About nine years.

How long has the prisoner resided with you? — All the time, with the exception of a year, when he was in Australia, and a short time that he was at Ventnor.

41 In fact, Percy Lefroy Mapleton and Annie Seale were first cousins. His mother, Mary Trent Seale, was the sister of Archibald Seale, Annie's father. Along with his elder sisters, Lefroy grew up in the home of Archibald and Sarah Seale. He is registered as living in their home in Lewisham in the 1861 census, aged one.

Second Day – Saturday 5 November 1881.

Did he go there for his health? — Yes.

During the time you knew him, was he a sickly, weakly man? — Yes. He frequently complained of ill-health and being consumptive. At times, he was almost prostrate. He frequently had spitting of blood during the time he was lying down.

Do you remember, in the month of June, your wife being confined? — Yes.

What date? — The 23rd. That would be a Thursday.

Do you remember, on the Tuesday previous, what time you left for London? — At my usual time, a quarter to nine.

Had your wife complained of her health? — Yes.

Did the prisoner volunteer to stay with her? — Yes, so that he could fetch the doctor to my wife if necessary, and render any assistance he could in household affairs.

What time did you return? — At about 7.20 pm.

Why do you fix the time at that? — Because I came by the train which arrived at 7.15 pm. Either that or the 7.00 train.

When you came back did you see the prisoner? — Yes.

As soon as you arrived? — Yes.

Who opened the door? — He did.

Is your wife here? — Yes, in the town.

Is she subpoenaed by the Treasury? — Yes.

Re-examined by the ATTORNEY-GENERAL.

You were examined before the magistrates, and also before the coroner? — Yes.

Of course you took a great interest in this case? — Yes.

You knew Mr Dutton? — Not before the case came on.

Did he cross-examine you? — Yes, on the last day of the inquiry.

Did you tell the magistrates that the prisoner was present at your house on the 21st? — No, I was not asked.

When did you first recollect that it was on the 21st that this young man was present in your house on that day? — It has never been absent from my memory.

Then you knew it when you were examined before the magistrates? — Yes.

Did you tell Mr Dutton of it? — No.

Do you mean to say, you have never mentioned it to Mr Dutton? — I have not.

Have you mentioned it to anyone before today? — To my wife only.

Do you know whether your wife had been in communication with Mr Dutton? — I have no doubt she has.

Lefroy.

You had a servant on 21 June? — Yes.

How far did the surgeon live from the house? — About a mile.

Mr Justice COLERIDGE: Mr Creek was examined on 25 July. When were you examined? — I don't remember the date.

The ATTORNEY-GENERAL: You took great interest in the case, did you not? — Yes.

Did you not take the trouble to become acquainted with what occurred at all? — I don't remember the particulars of the evidence.

That is not my question. You took an interest in this case, Creek was examined on the 25th, and you on another day. Had not you made yourself acquainted with the general purport of Creek's examination? — I have no doubt I read it in the paper.

Did you not perceive on 21 July the relevancy of that piece of evidence? Why did you not tell Mr Dutton?— I had no communication with Mr Dutton personally.

Why did you not write to him? — I did not think it necessary until the trial.

You reserved it for the trial? — Yes.

[*The Attorney-General read the evidence given by the witness on a former occasion.*]

Have you any idea where Mr Dutton got the information to put the questions? — I presume from the prisoner.

Further cross-examined by Mr WILLIAMS.

Your wife was not examined as a witness either before the coroner or the magistrates? — No.

As far as you know, any communications passing between your place and Mr Dutton's came through your wife and not through yourself? — Yes.

There was a man lodging at your house named Seale? — Yes.

Do you know if Seale had been in communication with Mr Dutton? — I don't know.

Is it a fact that your child was born on the 23rd? — Yes.[42]

Mr Justice COLERIDGE: I understand you to say that you took a great interest in the case, that you knew the general purport of what Creek said, that you knew the importance of what you have told us on the 21st, and yet you deliberately withheld it, to produce it today? — I was never asked the question.

The ATTORNEY-GENERAL: You told me you withheld it for the trial? — I was not asked it.

Why not? — It did not occur to me.

---

42   Wilfrid Thomas Clayton (1881-1964).

Second Day – Saturday 5 November 1881.

Mr Justice COLERIDGE: You have said you knew of its importance. Why did you not communicate it to someone who could have brought it before the magistrate? Answer that question. — [*The witness remained silent.*]

[*Angrily.*] You cannot answer that; you know you cannot. — No.

No, I know you can't. You had better leave the box. [*Sensation in court. The witness accordingly withdrew.*]

ANN MARGARET CLAYTON, examined
by the ATTORNEY-GENERAL.

What is your name? — Ann Clayton.

The prisoner lived at your house for some years? — Yes.

Take a look at this letter, written to Mr Ellis [*produced*]. We hear that you were in bed at that time unwell? — Yes.

Was that letter in your handwriting? — No.

Was it written with your authority? — No.

Cross-examined by Mr WILLIAMS.

On Tuesday 21 June, did you see the prisoner at the bar? — Yes.

Were you at that time exceedingly ill? — Yes.

Did the prisoner volunteer to remain with you for the purpose of fetching a doctor? — Yes.

Did he remain at your house in Wallington the whole day? — Yes.

Your child was born on the 23rd? — Yes.

Were you upstairs or downstairs on 21 June? — I was downstairs most of the day, but I was not lying down at all. I had a school at that time, and I was teaching that day in the room behind the front drawing-room.[43]

What age are you pupils? — The eldest was thirteen.

I mean, old enough to take a message? — Yes.

Was the prisoner in the schoolroom with you? — No.

How many hours were you occupied in teaching the children? — From ten till twelve, and from two till four.

You had a female servant in the house at this time? — Yes.

I do not wish to go too much into details. Did the prisoner come into the room at all? — Yes. About eleven o'clock. He came in, and asked if I still wished him to remain at home, and I told him I did particularly. I was very nervous of being left alone with the girls.

---

43   The 1881 census records 4 Cathcart Road as a day and boarding school, with Annie Clayton as governess. She had four children boarding on the day the census was taken, 3 April: Alice Bell (thirteen), Agnes Bell (eleven), John Bell (eight) and Harold Rolley (eight).

Lefroy.

Did you subsequently speak to the prisoner at any time during the day? — I went out to speak to him, and during the afternoon school he came in to speak to me.

What did you go out to speak to him for? — To have the comfort of speaking to someone.

But you were teaching the children? — Yes.

Where was he? — He was upstairs.

Recollecting the position you were in, do you mean to represent to the jury that you went upstairs all of a sudden to speak to the prisoner for the comfort of speaking to someone? — Yes.

After four o'clock, were you with the prisoner in the breakfast room? — Yes, he came to speak to me there.

Have you had communications with Mr Dutton? — Yes, several times.

Do you recollect when you first communicated with him? — About August.

You took a strong and painful interest in this case? — Yes.

Did you discuss this matter with your husband? — No. I did not say anything to my husband about this fact till some time ago.

When did you learn the importance attached to the 21st? — Not till two or three weeks ago.

Who called your attention to the importance of the day? — Some friend.

Could you mention the name of the friend? — No, I could not. I have tried to think several times.

In what way was it mentioned as being connected with the transaction? — As being the day on which the pistol was pledged.

You knew of its importance? — Yes.

Can you not now recollect the person who mentioned the importance of this matter to you? — No, I am sorry I cannot.

Re-examined by the ATTORNEY-GENERAL.

What brings it to your mind that it was the 21st, and not the 20th? — I remember that a neighbour was confined on that day.

Did you ever mention this matter to your husband, or your husband to you, before this? Two or three weeks ago? — No.

Did you read portions of the evidence some weeks ago? — Yes.

Did you become aware that the prisoner had pawned certain goods? — Yes.

Did the prisoner at the bar ever communicate to you that he had been at home on 21 June? — No, there was no communication.

Were you ever asked by Mr Dutton or anyone on behalf of the prisoner whether he had stopped at home? — No.

Did this unnamed person ever suggest to you that Lefroy had pledged the pistol? — I think the observation was made that it was pledged a few days before it was redeemed.

You saw the fact in the newspapers that the revolver had been pawned? — Yes.

And then you recollected that he had been at home on the 21st. — Yes.

Further cross-examined by Mr WILLIAMS.

Are you certain the prisoner stayed with you before your confinement? — Yes. I have never had any doubt that the prisoner stayed with me two days before I was confined.

Were you, after your confinement, ill for some considerable time? — Yes.

You recollect the prisoner having tea with you? — Yes. After four o'clock, the prisoner had tea with me in the breakfast room. That was from half past six until seven.

Did the prisoner stay with you after this? — Yes. He was with me until my husband returned at nine o'clock.

Ann Clayton

DR WILLIAM EVERETT CRESSY, examined.

I am a medical practitioner living at Wallington. I attended Mrs Clayton at her confinement.

On the evening of 27 June, did the prisoner call to see you? — No.

Did he ever come to your house? — No.

William Cressy

JOANNA CHAMBERLAIN,[44] examined.

I am a servant to Mr and Mrs Clayton. I remember Mr Ellis coming to the house on 27 June. I showed him into the drawing room.

Joanna Chamberlain

---

44   Although given as 'Johanna' in all newspaper reports, this correct spelling is taken from her signature on her deposition. She was 14 years old at the time of the murder. Joanna Chamberlain went on to lead a tragic life. After working for the Claytons, she appears next in the 1891 census as a housemaid to the Kelsey family in Sydenham. In November that year she gave birth to a daughter, Elizabeth, with no father being named on the baptismal register. The infant died aged just 6 months. A son, Walter, was born in 1893, again with no father named. Joanna married John Patrick Simmons in 1898, the couple having two daughters, Rosie and Kate. However, something went badly wrong. Kate was born in Croydon Workhouse infirmary late in 1900, and Joanna is recorded there in the 1901 census as a pauper along with her three children. Walter was 8, Rose 1 and Kate 4 months. No record of John Simmons' fate can be found, nor Joanna's after her appearance in the 1901 census. In 1911 Rose is recorded as a scholar at The Convent of the Faithful Virgin and Roman Catholic School in Upper Norwood. She emigrated to New Zealand in the early 1930s and married, dying in Wellington in 1999. Kate also emigrated to New Zealand, and died in 1993. Walter Chamberlain died in 1952.

Lefroy.

Joanna
Chamberlain

You told the prisoner Mr Ellis was there? — Yes, sir.

Where was the prisoner at this time? — In the breakfast room.

You know nothing about the papers given to Mr Ellis? — No, only that one of Mr Clayton's little children brought the papers to Mr Ellis.

Do you recollect Lefroy leaving the house that morning? — Yes.

Did he leave while Mr Ellis was in the house? — Yes.

Do you remember him returning in the evening? — Yes, with a stranger.

You observed that he was hurt? — Yes. His head was bandaged. He came into the kitchen and asked for some water.

Did you have any conversation with him? — I asked him what was the matter, and he said he had been assaulted in the train. I asked him if there were many more hurt. He said, 'Yes, five or six killed or robbed'. I said, 'I hope they will soon be caught, sir,' and he said, 'So do I'. Then he said he was going to see Dr Cressy, and then he went out by the area. That was the last I saw of him.

Where is the area? — In front of the kitchen. You have to go up steps to get to the front gate.

Did you see what type of hat he was wearing? — No, I did not notice that.

Was he still wearing a bandage? — Yes.

Do you recollect whether he wore a moustache or not at that time? — I don't recollect.

He went out about half past nine, did he not? — Between half past nine and ten.

Cross-examined by Mr WILLIAMS.

Do you recollect the day Mrs Clayton was confined? — Yes.

Was the prisoner there that day? — Yes.

Do you remember if Lefroy was there two days before or not? — Yes, he was.

Mr Justice COLERIDGE: Has the solicitor for the defence spoken to you before about this? — Yes, my Lord. I was asked two or three weeks ago.

And you said then you had no recollection? — Yes, my Lord.

The ATTORNEY-GENERAL: My Lord, I am afraid that, in opening this case to the jury, I stated that the prisoner left home on the night of the murder by the back way. As the evidence just given now stands, I am bound to withdraw that statement from the jury.

Mr Justice COLERIDGE: Oh, certainly.

[*At this point, his Lordship said to the jury that it was impossible to finish the case that night, as some important – exceedingly important –*

matters yet required attention.]

Mr Justice COLERIDGE: Gentlemen of the jury, I am sorry the necessities of the case should compel your being detained together till Monday, but arrangements have been made for your comfort.

The court then rose, it being 5.45 pm,
to meet again on Monday morning at 10.00 am.

****

Third Day – Monday 7 November 1881.[45]

Henry Creek

HENRY CREEK, *recalled and examined* by the ATTORNEY-GENERAL.

I am assistant to Messrs T. Adams & Co., pawnbrokers, London Bridge. [*He produced his pledge books.*] The pledges are entered in the books, not as they are taken but at various times during the day, but always in the numerical order in which they were issued.

How many pledges did you take in on 21 June? — Nineteen.

And on 19 June? — Forty.

Can you, from that entry, tell us about what time that pistol was pledged? — It is nearly the last entry in the book, so I should say about seven o'clock. No entry in the book would give a clue to the time of redeeming.

As to this second pistol, when was that pawned? — On 13 July.

That would be after the prisoner was in custody? — Yes. [*Pistol produced.*]

Do you know the person who pledged it? — Yes. It was a young man named William Watson,[46] in the railway accounts office at London Bridge.

Jarvis was in your shop at the time? — Yes. When Watson brought it in, I showed it to Jarvis and asked him if he knew anything about it. He said 'No'. I asked the man if it was his own. He said 'Yes'. I understood him to say he had won it in a raffle.

Is this pistol similar to the one pledged on 21 June? — Yes.

Did you say this to Jarvis? — Yes.

What did Jarvis say further to you? — He said, 'Bring it along with you and show it where you are going to'.

Cross-examined by Mr WILLIAMS.

Where is the entry as to the other revolver? — [*Witness makes to hand the book to the learned counsel.*]

Read, if you please, what you have in your book as to the entry of 21

---

45 Transcript of the day's proceedings taken from the *Daily News*, Tuesday 8 November 1881; *Brighton and Sussex Daily Post*, Tuesday 8 November 1881; *Maidstone and Kent County Standard*, Saturday 12 November 1881; *Manchester Guardian*, Tuesday 8 November; *Sussex Evening Times*, Monday 7 November 1881; *West Sussex Journal*, Tuesday 8 November 1881.

46 William Watson, aged twenty, is listed as a 'Railway clerk' in the 1881 census.

Lefroy.

Henry Creek

June. — It runs, 'Price advanced 5s, number of pledge 356, William Lee, 9 Southampton Street, revolver.'

Can you say why the word 'Peckham', which appeared on the duplicate of the ticket after 'Southampton Street', was left out of the book? — There was not room to insert it.

Sarah Bickers

SARAH BICKERS, examined.

I formerly lived at 32 Smith Street, Stepney, and had lived there for nine years.[47]

Up till Thursday 30 June, did you have a bill in your window? — Yes, sir. It said 'Lodgings to Let'.

On that day, the prisoner called at your house? — Yes.

About what hour of the day? — A little after eleven o'clock in the morning.

When he called what did he say? — He asked to see the bedroom for let. I showed him the first room on the first floor. He asked the rent and I told him, 'Six shillings a week'.

Did you make any inquiry as to who he was? — I asked him where he came from, and he said he came from Liverpool.

What name did he give? — In the evening I asked him his name, and he said it was Clark.

What occupation did he say he followed? — That of an engraver.

You asked him if he liked the room? — Yes, and he said he did. He agreed to take the room that day. It was not quite ready, so he said he would go out and return at two o'clock.

Had he any moustaches on his face at that time? — I did not notice any.

Was anything said about his luggage? — He said his luggage was coming from Liverpool next day.

Did he pay anything on account of the rent? — Yes, he paid me 3s 6d in advance.

In the evening, he went out for a short time? — Yes.

On the next day, did he go out? — He went out after breakfast and came back soon after two o'clock.

Did he go out on Friday evening? — I don't remember seeing him go out.

Did he go out on Saturday? — Not in the daytime. He may have gone out in the evening, but I did not hear him.

And on Sunday? — He did not go out at all.

You have other lodgers in the house, I take it? — Yes.

---

47   A report by Inspector Donald Swanson relating to a claim on the reward by Mrs Bickers states that she had moved to nearby 1 Jamaica Street in order to escape the attention of newspaper reporters and onlookers.

Third Day – Monday 7 November 1881.

Is it their habit to dine together on Sundays? — Yes.

Did you make any enquiry whether he would come down to dinner on Sunday? — Yes, and he said he would prefer to dine upstairs, as he was rather busy.

On Sunday, did he take a newspaper out of the parlour to his bedroom? — Yes. It was part of the London *Daily News*. Afterwards I asked him for the paper, as I had heard there had been a dreadful murder on the Brighton line, and I wanted to read it.

Was any observation made at all as to the news of that week? — I asked him if the murderer of Mr Gold had been arrested.

How did he reply? — He said, 'Not that I know of.'

With respect to his going out, did he ever tell you that he was going out? — On the Tuesday morning after he arrived, he told me he was going out to have a bath at five o'clock on Wednesday, but I don't remember him going out at all.

On the morning of Thursday 7 July, did a letter come for him? — Yes. It was addressed to him in the name of Clark, at my house.

What did you do with it? — I took it up to him and put it under his door.

Did the prisoner make any statement as to the number? — He said he had made a mistake in the number and given his address as 33 instead of 32. He asked me if a letter of his might not have been delivered to the house next door.

Did he make that statement after you had placed the letter underneath the door or before? — Before. Subsequently, he went to the next house, number 33, and got another letter which had been sent there in mistake for him.

After he had received that letter did the prisoner ask you to do anything for him? — Yes. I remember him bringing down a telegram on Thursday morning, which he had written out on a plain piece of paper. He asked me to go in a cab to his place of business and get some money for him. I declined to go, and asked him why he did not go himself.

What did he say to that? — He said he had sprained his ankle getting out of bed. Then he said, 'Never mind, Mrs Bickers; if you can't go, try and get a lad to go'.

Did you get someone to go for him? — Yes; I afterwards asked Mr Doyle to go. He is a greengrocer and lives in my street.[48] He came in between twelve and one o'clock. I saw the prisoner give him some money and a piece of paper. Mr Doyle then took the message to the telegraph office for him.

---

48   Although some newspaper reports state Mr Doyle was a baker, Inspector Frederick Jarvis's report confirms that he was a greengrocer.

Lefroy.

Sarah Bickers

Did you read the message? — No, I did not read the paper, but I noticed it was sent to Mr Seale. I did not see any copy of it taken.

The next evening, 8 July, he was arrested? — Yes.

Did the constables search the room? — Yes.

When you let the room were the drawers empty? — Yes.

Did they find one locked? — Yes.

Did you know before the prisoner came of any false whiskers or hair being in the room? — Certainly not.

Did you see the articles which were found in his room? — No.

Did you not see a collar? — No.

As far as you know, you left nothing in the drawers of his room? — No.

Had he any work to do while he was with you? — I never saw him doing any, but he said he did engraving work.

Did anyone visit him while he was staying at your house? — No one visited him.

[*Mr Doyle was the next witness called, but he did not answer to his name.*]

Donald Swanson

DONALD SUTHERLAND SWANSON, examined by Mr POLAND.

I am an inspector of the Criminal Investigation Department, Scotland Yard.

On Friday 8 July, about 7.45 pm, did you go to Mrs Bickers of number 32, Smith Street, Stepney? — I did.

Another officer, Jarvis, was with you? — Yes, and P.C. Hopkins.

Inspector Jarvis remained outside while you went in? — Yes.

Did you go to the first floor? — Yes. I went to the front room on the first floor.

Did you see the prisoner there? — Yes.

What did you say to him? — Addressing him, I said, 'Percy Lefroy Mapleton?' He replied, 'Yes, I expected you'.

What did you say to him then? — I told him I was a police officer, and that I should apprehend him on the charge of wilfully murdering Mr Gold on the Brighton Railway on 27 June. At the same time, I cautioned him that whatever he said I would take down in writing and use in evidence.

What did he say in reply? — He said, 'I am not compelled to make any reply, and I think it better not to make any answer'. I wrote that in my note book as he said it, and read it over to him. When I had done so, prisoner said, 'Well, I will qualify that by saying I am not guilty'.

What happened next? — Inspector Jarvis then came into the room and to him I said, 'This person admits being Lefroy. I have told him the charge and this is his answer.'[49]

Did you and Jarvis then proceed to search the room? — Yes.

Was there a drawer there which was locked? — Yes.

Did you ask the prisoner for a key? — Yes.

What did he say? — That the lock could not be opened, and he did not have a key.

Was the drawer broken open? — Yes.

What was found inside? — Jarvis found a black cloth waistcoat.

Did that appear to be stained? — Yes.

What with? — Blood. [*Waistcoat produced.*] The stain is on the right side.

Was there also a black scarf? — Yes. [*Scarf produced.*]

Was the scarf stained with blood as well? — I did not observe whether it was stained.

Does it appear to be stained now? — Yes, on the inner lining.

Were there also three shirt collars? — Yes. One of them was marked 14, another 14½, and the third was not marked at all.

Were there stains on the collars? — One of them had a light stain of blood.

There was also a portion of a woollen shirt? — Yes, with parts cut away. [*Shirt produced.*] The pieces were found in a cupboard in the room, some being bloodstained.

Were there two cloth caps? — Yes. [*Produced.*]

Are those caps new? — Yes.

Partly worn, I think? — Yes, a little.

Anything else? — There was a pair of false whiskers and moustache combined, a pint bottle of arnica, and a pair of scissors.

Did you hear Jarvis speak to the prisoner about the scissors? — Yes. He said he was desirous of taking all that belonged to him, and asked whether the scissors belonged to him. The prisoner said, 'Yes, I used them to cut my moustache and whiskers off'.

Besides this, was the prisoner personally searched? — Yes.

How much was found upon him? — One shilling.

Which you took possession of, and then took him into custody? — Yes. I took him to Scotland Yard, and eventually brought him down to Lewes, and handed him over to Superintendent Berry.

What hat was he wearing then? — A grey tweed cloth cap.

Did the prisoner make a further statement? — On the way in the cab, I heard the prisoner making a statement. Jarvis took it down.

---

49   Although some reports suggest Swanson cautioned Lefroy while Jarvis was in the
      room, the evidence given by both detectives at the Cuckfield Magistrates' hearing
      confirms that events occurred as given above.

Lefroy.

Afterwards, at Lewes Gaol, did you get from one of the warders the soft hat the prisoner was wearing when you arrested him? — Yes.

What did you do with it? — I got Mr James Hannam, of the High Street, Lewes, to measure it. Afterwards I returned the cap to the gaol.

[*The witness was asked to compare the blood-stained collar found in the tunnel with those found in the prisoner's lodgings.*]

What is the result? — The one covered with blood is slightly smaller than both of those found at the lodgings.

[*The witness was not cross-examined.*]

FREDERICK SMITH JARVIS, examined by Mr POLAND.

I am an inspector of police at Scotland Yard.

We have heard you went with Swanson when the prisoner was arrested? — Yes.

You proceeded to personally search the prisoner? — Yes. I found on him one shilling in silver.

Did you search the room also? — I did. In a chest of drawers, I found one black cloth vest, two caps, three collars, a false moustache and whiskers, and a portion of a coloured flannel shirt. In a cupboard in another part of the room, I found a number of cuttings, similar to the flannel shirt, and a light scarf. On the chest of drawers, I found a pair of scissors, a bottle of arnica, and a briar root pipe.

Did you ask the prisoner about the scissors? — Yes. On seeing the scissors I said, 'Do these belong to you?' He said, 'Yes; I used them for cutting off my moustache'.

The things produced were taken into possession at the time? — Yes.

Did you say anything to him? — I called over the things as I took possession of them, and he said, 'I think that's all'.

Were there any stains on the clothing? — Yes. The waistcoat had blood upon it inside and out, mostly on the right breast. One of the collars has also blood upon it. Some of the clippings of material similar to the shirt are apparently blood-stained.

You and Inspector Swanson took the prisoner to Scotland Yard in a cab? — Yes.[50]

On your way, did the prisoner make a voluntary statement to you? — Yes.

Had the prisoner been cautioned at this point? — Yes. Swanson had cautioned the prisoner in the room in my presence about saying anything before we left.

Did you make a note of it? — When we got to Scotland Yard.

What was it? — He said, 'I am glad you have found me; I am sick of

---

50   Lefroy was taken first to Arbour Square police station and then to Scotland Yard.

it. I should have given myself up in a day or two. I have regretted it ever since that I ran away. It puts such a different complexion on the case, but I could not bear the exposure. I feared certain matters in connection with my family would be made public'. He then said, 'I suppose I shall be allowed to see a lawyer?' I replied, 'Certainly.' He then said, 'I am glad you did not bring any of my so-called friends from Wallington with you'. He was then taken to the station, and detained during that night.

WILLIAM TURPIN, *recalled, and examined by* Mr A. L. SMITH.

On the night of 27 June, I went to Wallington, accompanied by Howland and Tobutt.

Holmes, I believe, was waiting in the road outside? — Yes. He remained outside while I and Tobutt went into the house.

Did you go into Lefroy's room? — Yes. Mr Clayton showed us Lefroy's room.

What did you find? — I found these trousers [*produced*] lying on a chair near the head of Lefroy's bed.

Was there blood on them? — Yes. There was much dry blood on them, and a surgical bandage lying on the floor near the chair.

Did you find that coat which you have in your hand? — Yes, downstairs on a chair in the hall. There was fresh blood all over the right arm, and it felt clammy at the time.

Did Mr Clayton assist you so far as he could? — Yes. He seemed very willing to assist. I asked him if there was a photograph of Lefroy since he had grown up. Clayton searched the place and said there was not.

WILLIAM THOMAS DOYLE, examined
by the ATTORNEY-GENERAL.

I was a neighbour of Mrs Bickers. On Thursday 7 July, I was at her house between twelve and one o'clock.

Did you see the prisoner there? — Yes.

Did he request anything of you? — He asked me if I would take a telegram to the post office for him. He said he was sorry to trouble me, as he had sprained his foot.

Did he give you this piece of paper with writing upon it? — Yes.

[*The ATTORNEY-GENERAL read the telegram as follows: 'From G. Clark, 32 Smith Street, Stepney, to S. Seale, J. T. Hutchinson and Co., 56 Gresham Street, London. Please bring my wages this evening, before eight, without fail. Shall have the flour tomorrow. Not 33.* ']51

---

51   The telegram was intended for Frank Seale, who was employed by Mr Hutchinson, presumably an attempt by Lefroy to establish contact with his cousin. The 'S.' Seale was probably a transcription error on the part of either Mr Doyle or the telegram operator.

Lefroy.

William Doyle

Did he then give you some silver? — He gave me 1s 6d, telling me the telegram would cost 1s, and that the sixpence was for the trouble. I copied the message on to one of the ordinary forms and dispatched it.

Lydia Gold

LYDIA GOLD, *recalled and examined* by the ATTORNEY-GENERAL.

We learned from you on Friday that your husband wore a gold chain attached to his watch? — Yes.

Do you recollect how that was attached to the watch? — By a gold swivel.

Was there any ring attached to the swivel? — The swivel was attached to the chain direct.

Mr Justice COLERIDGE: So it was easy to take the watch off, and throw the chain away, if anyone was minded to do so? — Yes.

Cross-examined by Mr WILLIAMS.

Did Mr Gold's brother collect rents for him at one time? — Yes.

Where did he live? — At Hackney Wick, I believe. He has lived there some time.[52] I have not seen him for about five years.

What was his name? — Thomas.[53]

Why did he cease collecting rents? — Because Mr Gold, having reduced the number of his shops, had time to collect them himself.

Henry Chapman

HENRY CHAPMAN, examined by Mr POLAND.

I am the principal warder of Maidstone Gaol. I have had the prisoner in my charge. I produce the hat the prisoner has been wearing while in gaol. [*A tall silk hat, which was quite new with a white lining, was handed into court.*]

James Hannam

JAMES HANNAM, examined by Mr POLAND.

I live at 186, High Street, Lewes. I am a tailor and hatter.

Were you shown by Inspector Swanson a soft cloth hat? [*produced*] — Yes. That is the one.

Have you carefully measured it? — I have.

What is the size of it? — 6⅞ full.

What do you mean by full? — It is an easy ⅞.

Have you measured the felt hat found on the line? — Yes.

What size is it? — It is 6⅞ bare. It is a hard hat; the other is a soft

---

52   Thomas Gold took over the his brother's premises at 77 Mile End Road following Frederick's relocation to Preston Park, and remained there until at least 1876 (Electoral Registers). In the 1881 census he is recorded with his family at 1 Cadogan Terrace, Hackney.

53   Ten years Frederick Gold's junior, Thomas is recorded in various sources as also working as a baker.

substance.

Look at the tall silk hat; what size is that? — The size is seven.

Do you notice any marks on it where it has been worn? — There is a space of three or four inches where it has not been worn at all.

Mr Justice COLERIDGE: That means that it is a little large? — Yes.

I suppose it all comes to this, that all these hats could be worn by the prisoner and by hundreds of others besides? — Yes.

JOHN FORD, examined by Mr A. L. SMITH.

I am a ticket collector at the London Bridge station. I remember the two o'clock express to Brighton leaving the station on 27 June. I examined the tickets of the passengers in the rear of the train only, but had nothing to do with the front portion. I saw no first-class tickets to Brighton.

JOSEPH EVERETT, called and examined by Mr A. L. SMITH.

Are you a ticket collector at London Bridge? — No.

Then we do not want you. [*Laughter.*]

FREDERICK GRIFFITHS, examined by the ATTORNEY-GENERAL.

I am a jeweller carrying on business at Croydon. My father formerly carried on business as a watchmaker at Mile End. He died about five years ago.[54]

Did he keep any book of sales? — He did not.

If Mr Gold had bought a watch of your father, would it have been booked? — No.

Was Mr Gold a neighbour? — Yes.

Was he a customer of your father? — He was.

WYNNE EDWIN BAXTER, examined by the ATTORNEY-GENERAL.

I am one of the coroners for the county of East Sussex. I presided at the inquest on the body of the late Frederick Isaac Gold, at Balcombe.

Evidence has been given as to a photograph marked B [*produced*], which was shown at the inquest. Do you know what that was? — It was a photograph of a pen and ink sketch of Lefroy which had appeared in a newspaper. [*Photograph of the Daily Telegraph sketch produced.*][55]

---

54   10 August 1876 at 97 Mile End Road.

55   A photograph of the sketch was copyrighted on 4 July 1881 by the London Stereoscopic and Photographic Company of 54 Cheapside. The record of the copyright is held at the National Archives (TNA: PRO COPY 1/54/16), but the image is not attached to the record.

Lefroy.

George
Berry

GEORGE BERRY, *recalled and examined* by
the ATTORNEY-GENERAL.

Since this murder was committed, has a search been made in the neighbourhood of the line? — Yes.

You know the line? — Yes.

There are several ponds on the side of the railway near Three Bridges? — Yes.

Is there underwood? — Yes.

And long grass? — Yes, and flora.

Certain knives have been found, have they not? — Yes. [*Knives produced: two of them old table knives, and one a pocket knife.*]

[*To Mr Justice COLERIDGE.*] My lord, these knives are probably without marks of blood. One has rust upon it, but it is not thought to be blood.

The ATTORNEY-GENERAL: Then, my Lord, on the part of the prosecution, that is the case.

Mr Montagu WILLIAMS: I should like two or three minutes before I begin, my Lord.

Mr Justice COLERIDGE: Then take a quarter of an hour.

[*As the judge was about to leave the bench, Mr Oliver Weston came forward, and in a loud voice addressed his Lordship, saying:*] My Lord, my name is OLIVER WESTON; I beseech that I may speak. I have three witnesses from Brighton to prove what I stated on oath the other day.

Mr Justice COLERIDGE: Mr Weston, I cannot hear you. — I implore your Lordship to hear my witnesses.

I cannot do so. — I beseech your Lordship, in mercy's sake, to hear me.

I cannot. You are not a party to this case. — My Lord, I am ruined if I am not heard.

[*Firmly.*] I cannot help that. I cannot hear you now, and I must have you removed if you persist.

His Lordship then left the court.

The court adjourned.

* * *

Third Day – Monday 7 November 1881.

Speech for the Defence.[56]

*At 12.03 pm, Mr Montagu Williams commenced
his speech for the defence.*

Mr Montagu WILLIAMS: May it please your Lordship, and Gentlemen **Mr Williams**
of the Jury — This is no ordinary case of murder that you are sworn to try.
There is no question here as to degrees of crime. It is not a question of the
sanity or insanity of the person accused. It is not a case in which mercy is
likely to be extended. It is essentially a question of murder, and it is your
duty to inquire into it – a duty which is cast upon you by the obligations
of the oath which you have taken. It is for you to say when this matter is
concluded whether this young man, for young he is – he is only twenty-
one years of age – is to walk out a free and unshackled man into the light
of day, or whether he is to suffer a violent and ignominious death, and be
sent, with all his sins upon him, into the presence of his Maker.

Gentlemen, there have been many witnesses in this case, and I think I
am right in saying that the chain must be a continuous one and a strong
one – so strong that it is your duty in every possible way in favour of life
to try to break it. The material must be such, and it must be forged in such
a manner, as to withstand every possible test; otherwise the prisoner is
entitled to your verdict of 'Not Guilty.' It has been said that there are many
grains of sand in this case, which, taken together, constitute a mound,
such a mound that neither the fury of the storm, nor the strength of the
strongest wave, can scatter it. If, in any particular, it fails in substantiality,
the prisoner is entitled to your verdict.

I have one fault to find with an expression that was used – and it is
the only fault I have to find with the way in which this case has been
conducted. The Attorney-General said that the prisoner is entitled to the
benefit of a doubt. There is no such thing as the benefit of a doubt. There is
no benefit; it is a right to which the prisoner is entitled. If, after reviewing
and carefully reviewing, every particle of evidence brought before you
on the part of the prosecution, you are not absolutely as certain as human
intellect can be certain, that the prisoner at the bar committed this murder,
he is entitled to be acquitted. You are asked by the prosecution to enter
upon a large and serious speculation. I warn you against doing so, lest
you get far beyond your depth, and become utterly submerged.

Now, gentlemen, I submit to you that the very first starting-point of the
chain of evidence is wanting, and, without any preface, I will proceed to
prove it. Mr Gold, the unhappy man who met with his death on 27 June,

---

56 Transcript of Mr Montagu Williams's address to the jury amalgamated from the *Daily News*,
    Tuesday 8 November 1881 and *Leaves of a Life: The Reminiscences of Montagu Williams,
    QC* (Boston and New York: Houghton, Mifflin and Company, 1890), pp. 260—287.

Lefroy.

Mr Williams had been a tradesman. He had been a well-to-do man, and had acquired sufficient property to enable him to retire from business, and to live, as he hoped and believed, the remainder of his days in peace. He was a man of some precision, and his habits were of a very regular character. It was his custom, among other things, to proceed every Monday morning to a shop belonging to him at the East End of London and collect the week's takings. He usually paid this money into the bank, but it was his custom on the Monday preceding the first of every month to bring down for his wife sufficient money for the week's housekeeping, which varied from £12 to £15. In a little sovereign purse, he was in the habit of carrying never less than £2 10s or £3 in gold. It was also his custom to bring down his wife's dividends. These dividends would become due, if they were Consols,[57] in the first week of July; but it was his custom frequently to bring down the money to his wife in advance, that is, a week before the dividends became due.

Now, the week of 27 June would be the last week of the month, and the 27th being a Monday, it would be in the ordinary course of events in the life of this very precise man, that he would bring down the money on that day. Even if he did not bring down the takings at all, he would have upon his body £2 10s in gold, the money for the monthly housekeeping, and he would probably have the dividends, or the amount of the dividends to which his wife was entitled.

Where is there a particle of evidence to show that the prisoner at the bar knew anything of this? Where is the tittle of evidence to show that he ever saw Mr Gold in his life? Where, with all the opportunities the prosecution have had, with all the money they have at their backs, with all the solicitors and solicitors' clerks and counsel whose services they can command – where, I say, have they produced a particle of evidence that the prisoner ever knew one atom of Mr Gold's affairs? Am I right, then, in saying that the first link has failed? Other people may have known Mr Gold's habits and his customs, but not the prisoner at the bar. So far as we can learn, Mr Gold was absolutely and completely a stranger to the prisoner.

The theory of the prosecution is that this was a planned murder – not a plan to take the life of Mr A., B., C. or D.; but a plan to take the life of Mr Gold, at a time when the accused knew that he had money upon him.

I am glad, gentlemen, that I used the word 'theory', for the case against the prisoner is purely theoretical, there not being a single fact to support the case of the prosecution. In the matter of probability or improbability, I say that the question is entirely in favour of the prisoner. The prosecution say that he started on 27 June with the deliberate purpose of murdering

---

57   Consolidated bank annuities.

Montagu Williams QC.

Third Day – Monday 7 November 1881.

Mr Gold, and that he went looking from carriage to carriage for his victim; but there is not a particle of evidence to support that accusation.

Let us look at the probabilities. Do you suppose that a man who intended to commit a murder would do so immediately after committing a fraud? What had he done in the morning? Undoubtedly a shabby trick – a misdemeanour, if you will. He had gone, or sent, to the shop of Mr Ellis for the purpose of changing counterfeit coin – obtaining money under false pretences, and doing that which must fix him upon any question of identity. And, having done this, the prosecution say he committed this murder for the purpose of obtaining money. It is far more probable, I should think, that, if he contemplated anything of the kind, he would have put off committing this murder for another week.

It is a very odd thing, too, that he carried his card in his pocket, and I repeat that, on the question of probabilities, the case is entirely in favour of the accused, and not against him. Nay, more, if he redeemed this pistol on the morning of 27 June, do you think he would carry with him pawn-tickets bearing the same names as those which were found upon him?

His own story is simple. He says: 'I admit obtaining that money that morning, and I admit that I did go down to Brighton on that day. I had an appointment with a young lady, and that was the reason for my looking through the train.' Is that as improbable, gentlemen, as the theory suggested by the prosecution? It may be said: 'What right has a young man who has no money to meet a young lady in this way?' Well, the prisoner is a young man, and you cannot put an old head on young shoulders.

Up to the starting of the train, when you come to the question of probabilities, the probability is in favour of the story told through me today.

I will not now dwell upon the question of the articles found upon Mr Gold, and I will allude to the pistol by-and-by. Mr Gold, be it remembered, had, or would have had, two purses – one purse like that found in the neighbourhood of the line. When I come to the line, I will call your attention to the spot where the purse was found. However, there were two purses. There were also two pocket-books. The purse like that which has been found would have had the £2 10s or £3 in it. The other purse has never been discovered. One pocket-book was found on the body of the unfortunate man; the other is in some watery place.

Then, as to the skull cap, that is an important factor in the case, and will be an important matter when I come to deal with it. But where is that skull cap? When we come to the theory of the third man in the carriage, we shall have to deal with that cap. If the prisoner was alone, and committed the murder in the carriage alone – because that is the suggestion of the

Lefroy.

Mr Williams prosecution; and not only is it their suggestion but their case – where is the second purse, where is the second pocket-book, where is the skull cap belonging to Mr Gold?

The articles on the body of Mr Gold when he left Preston on the morning of the 27th I will refer to later on. There is one other matter to which I will allude, and that is that the widow said he left home in his usual health, and that he was a tall, powerful man.

And now we come to the train. The first witness called – Franks – stated that he was standing at the front part of the train, and that there were only two ticket collectors. That evidence has been contradicted by a witness in another part of the case. He stated, however, that there were two collectors, and that he was one of them. He says that, on the Monday, Lefroy was under his observation. He says, 'I knew Lefroy'. If he knew Lefroy, Lefroy would have known him; and let me observe to you that Franks is absolutely the only witness who proves, if he is to be believed, incontestably that Lefroy and Mr Gold were the only occupants of the carriage – he is absolutely the only witness. Now, is he to be relied upon?

Carry your mind's eye to the station of the London and Brighton Railway at London Bridge and look at the number of trains that are continually going out and arriving. The ticket inspectors look at every ticket before persons are allowed to enter the trains, and will you believe that a ticket collector would be able to tell you, without having any earthly reason for doing so, that, at a particular time, in a particular carriage, he saw two persons sitting? Use your common sense in that matter, gentlemen.

But it is much stronger than that, because this man says that he had no reason for observing Lefroy. Indeed, there is no evidence that he had any reason for observing him. He said, 'Lefroy sat in the far corner of the carriage with his back to the engine'. Now, this man looked at Lefroy carefully. He actually knows how many pockets he had in his coat; at least, I won't say he knows how many, but he knows the exact position of them. He remembers, even, that his left hand was in one of his pockets. He tells you the time he got into the train. He tells you that his overcoat was buttoned. I wonder he does not tell you how many buttons he had on his overcoat! But he does not go so far as that. He tells you his overcoat was buttoned and that his frock coat was buttoned underneath it. The colour of the frock coat was black, and he took his ticket out of a pocket on the right hand side.

Then he goes on to say a number of other things as to the appearance of the prisoner, which I will not call in question, because he had seen him before, and therefore he would know it. But we have it without doubt that, having seen him only for one minute of time, he is enabled to give you accurately all this description of the man. Now, in a question of life

Third Day – Monday 7 November 1881.

or death, where you must weigh everything, and not throw dice upon a man's life but weigh carefully and accurately every single circumstance, can you trust evidence of this sort without fear of the consequences?

Well, now, this witness tells you that Lefroy wore a low felt hat. A most important thing that. Why does he tell you so? He had not a low felt hat. The burden of testimony is overwhelming that he had a high hat. One of your body put a question to Mr Ellis, the answer to which showed that he had no doubt, when Lefroy started from Wallington, he had a high hat on. Every witness proves incontestably that the man had a tall hat on. Then why does Franks, who is so accurate as to other matters, say that he wore a low felt hat? Was there a third person? That is one solution. But I will give you another. That copy of the *Daily Telegraph* containing the picture was published on 1 July. It is quite true, as has been observed, that not every one reads the *Daily Telegraph*, but it has a very large and wide circulation; and do you suppose there was a man in London, when this matter became known at a somewhat dead season, when this sensational occurrence – for it was sensational, though I hate the word – was made public, who had not seen that copy of the *Daily Telegraph*? How unfair it is to the prisoner I will show you by-and-by. Now, why did Franks put this low felt hat on Lefroy, except he had seen this picture with the low felt hat? Either it was the fact that he had seen the picture, or that he became aware of the fact that a low felt hat had been picked up on the line. He says he never saw a copy of the *Daily Telegraph*. Do you believe that? Do you believe that, having heard of this dreadful murder, which is one that appeals to everybody – and there is a great deal of danger to the prisoner in that, for I am always afraid of the argumentum ad hominem, and this is a case that strikes you all, because you are all liable to be railway travellers, and therefore it is a case which presses upon you with more rigidity – do you suppose that this man had not seen a paper? Who are the men, of all others, who are likely to see them but railway ticket collectors and guards? Look at the number of liberal-minded passengers who come up to town every morning by train, and, having read their papers, hand them over to the guard or the collector. It is the commonest thing possible. Go into any of the great stations in London, and you will find the guards and ticket collectors, in their leisure time, reading the newspapers, and ask yourselves whether this man must not have seen the *Daily Telegraph*.

After Mrs Gold came a number of witnesses whom I did not cross-examine, and therefore I do not propose to say much about them. The evidence related to the question as to the identity of the watch. That, I take it, is admitted. There is no doubt whatever that the watch subsequently found in the shoe of Lefroy was Mr Gold's watch. That is not denied, and

Lefroy.

Mr Williams at the proper time I will deal with it.

Then there was a witness named Cross, who stated that the money paid to Mr Gold, the takings of the week, was in a little canvas bag. The other witness was Gilbert, a clerk at the bank, who stated that Mr Gold paid the money into the bank in a bag. It is not, however, absolutely proved that Mr Gold ever had it back. As it is not proved, all I can say is this: under ordinary circumstances, according to the bank clerk, the little canvas bag would be returned to Mr Gold, like the second pocket-book, the second purse, and the skull cap. If it were so returned to Mr Gold, where is it?

The next witness was Sewell, the ticket-clerk. What is his evidence? It was he who, I think, issued a ticket to Lefroy. That is not contradicted. Lefroy could not have gone without a ticket. But he is useful in cross-examination to show that the prosecution has utterly failed to exhaust the tickets. They say there were only so many first-class tickets issued that day. That comes to absolutely nothing, because return tickets from Brighton are available for seven days, and any person having taken a ticket in one of those seven days previous to 27 June could have returned by the two o'clock train upon the 27th with the half of that ticket. So that all traces of the ticket as far as it goes comes to absolutely nothing. The fact of three first-class tickets being issued by that train, therefore, absolutely and positively proves nothing, because we have had proof beyond doubt by Sewell that any person travelling within seven days could have returned with the half of the ticket. There is no means of showing, because the tickets are destroyed, whether any persons so returned by that train. In addition to this, it is proved by Sewell that a ticket to Victoria would be available at London Bridge. The whole theory of tickets, therefore, is dissipated into the thinnest of thin air, and comes to nothing. Sewell said that, to the best of his belief, Lefroy had a high hat on. A high hat again, gentlemen!

The next witnesses were Gardner and Wood, the booking clerks at East Croydon, who endeavoured to prove that two persons got into the train, but they did not prove that Mr Gold and Lefroy were the only persons in the train.

The next witness is one of considerable importance. It is Mr Gibson, the chemist. Mr Gibson was a traveller, with his little son, in the next compartment – a second-class. He tells you it was at Merstham tunnel he heard some shots fired. He is not sure whether he heard shots or fog signals, but it is alleged now on the part of the prosecution that they were shots. Merstham tunnel is seventeen miles from London and is 1,830 yards long. After this tunnel, you pass through Redhill Junction, than which there is no busier station on the line. The bullet having been fired at the entrance to the tunnel, according to the theory of the prosecution, and being at that time in the gullet of Mr Gold, the two men were struggling **Mr Williams** and desperately fighting as they passed through Redhill Junction. After passing through Earlswood, we come to Horley Station, and there have the testimony of two witnesses, Mrs and Miss Brown. We have then this fact – that at Horley, the wound having been inflicted at the entrance to Merstham tunnel, this deadly struggle was still being kept up. The distance to Horley is twenty-five miles and thirty-seven chains; therefore you may take it that from Merstham tunnel to Horley is something like eight miles. Thus, this deadly struggle must have been going on between this stripling and the deceased during all that distance, because the theory of the prosecution is that, if the bullet in Mr Gold's neck produced insensibility at all, it was but a momentary insensibility. If Lefroy had killed him on the spot there would have been no struggle as far as Horley. Whether the struggle was continued further we do not know; but the body was found at Balcombe, which is, in point of fact, thirty-two miles from London. As far, then, as the evidence goes, up to Horley this lad, this sickly, weakly lad – he is before you, and you cannot say he is a powerful man – is supposed to have continued this struggle. Do you believe it, gentlemen? You have it on Dr Bond's authority that the pistol wound, if it produced insensibility at all, only produced momentary insensibility, and that the deceased was perfectly able to struggle for his life. You have a tall, powerful man struggling for eight miles; and yet, gentlemen – I put it to you – there is not a particle of the prisoner's dress torn. As far as the evidence goes, some injuries were found upon him, but these I will account for by-and-by.

We now come to the evidence of Mr Gibson, who tells you that he heard shots in Merstham tunnel, and that he did not notice the slackening of the train.

The next witnesses are the Browns. They were standing at the window of their cottage at Horley, and they say they saw two persons in a carriage, as the train whisked past, standing up as if they were fighting or larking.

The next witness was Watson, the guard, and he contradicts Franks in a certain way. He tells you that, instead of there being two ticket collectors on the platform at London Bridge, there were three or four. He says he does not know how many persons there were in the carriage occupied by Mr Gold, and he tells you this important fact: namely, that in each carriage the door was unlocked on either side. He tells you, also, that at Preston Park he saw a chain hanging out of Lefroy's shoe. Now what is the inference from this on the part of the prosecution? They say that Lefroy, having planned this murder – upon what foundation this allegation is made, I am unable to say – committed the murder, and, having done so, plundered and ransacked his victim, from whom he took a watch. This

Lefroy.

Mr Williams watch, they say, he put into his shoe, and left the chain hanging out as an indication of his guilt, so that everyone should see it – and everyone did see it.

Why did he put the watch in his shoe? In case he was searched? Why, if he were searched, they would take his shoe off. It is idle to say, gentlemen, that, in order to avoid detection, he did such a thing. Then I say this – if he took it for plunder, and it was part of the scheme to rob and murder the poor man, why didn't the murderer put it in his pocket? What was the necessity of putting it in his shoe? And if he did put it there, why leave part of the chain hanging out? I say, again, the probability is much stronger that he would have put it in his pocket. But if another person did it, before escaping from the train, the case is altered. Having got whatever money there was on the body, he fixes the watch – the very thing that would have brought him to the gallows – on the senseless man? Where is the improbability in this? Is it more improbable that the third man should do that, than that the prisoner should put it in his shoe with the chain dangling out? With regard to Watson's evidence, he is the only person who said that, when Lefroy was asked about the watch, he replied that he put it there for safety.[58] Watson was standing by Hall, the stationmaster, and the other man – Gibson, I think; and their evidence is that Lefroy said, referring to the watch, 'I don't know anything at all about it'. I hope you will not let the case rest on Watson's remembrance of the exact words of the conversation. The greater balance of testimony is that Lefroy's utterance was, 'I don't know anything at all about it'. I ask you, is there any reliance to be placed on the evidence that Lefroy said, 'I put it there for safety'?

I will offer you an exemplification of how dangerous it is to rely too much on Watson's evidence or upon his reproduction of the exact words used. After Lefroy had arrived at Brighton, Watson stated that he asked him, 'What about these two flash sovereigns?' I asked him whether he did not say 'these two sovereigns,' without using the word 'flash'. He replied he was not sure he did not. If Watson said merely 'these two sovereigns', not employing the word 'flash', Lefroy's answer is intelligible; for he said, 'I have no sovereigns'. Watson had them in the palm of his hand, and if the heads were turned up they would look like sovereigns. To show, then, how unsubstantial and insecure it is to rely upon every word Watson states, I would remind you that that witness, when pressed, will not swear whether he used the word 'flash' or not. Now, he says 'the train slackened at Hassock's Gate down to four miles an hour', and he is the man who

---

58 Montagu Williams has confused the testimony of Thomas Watson and Richard George Gibson. It was Gibson who claimed that Lefroy had said he put the watch in his shoe for safety.

Third Day – Monday 7 November 1881.

asserts that it is perfectly possible for a person when a train is in motion to pass from one carriage to another. You will see the importance of that by-and-by.

Now, it has not been conclusively proved that there was no third man in the compartment. If there were a third man, and this murder was committed by the third man, then he, first of all having disabled Lefroy in the manner I am suggesting, would have had ample time to get out at Hassock's Gate or to change his carriage. Evidence has been given that the train slackened for 300 or 400 yards.

There must have been somebody who disposed of the various articles on the line. Except the umbrella, all the articles were on the line before Clayton tunnel was reached. Clayton tunnel, I think, is only four or five miles from Preston, where the train stopped. The tunnel itself is 2,252 yards long; and the umbrella was found just as you get into Clayton tunnel. Now, gentlemen, did you see the umbrella? It was a hooked umbrella – a peculiar umbrella; and getting from one carriage to another, would not a man be likely to steady himself with it, and use it for the purpose of catching on? It is just the very thing. It was ready to his hand. Remember, the next compartment was empty. Remember, no one except three ladies got in on the way, and not in that part of the train. The evidence is conclusive that the next compartment was empty. The platelayers affirm that they did not see anybody on the line; but negative evidence is not conclusive.

Well, then, I have got the fact that there was ample opportunity for the man to have changed his carriage. With all their power, the prosecution cannot produce a particle of evidence to show that the next carriage was not empty when it left London Bridge. What more easy than for a man to change his carriage, so as to get away from the blood of the man who lay in the corner, and who sooner or later would recover – as recover he did? He might also have changed his carriage at Preston Park, when the attention of the whole of the people was called to the blood in the carriage, and to the man who was summoning aid and assistance, and in whose boot the watch was subsequently found. What more easy for him than to go on to the terminus at Brighton? By the evidence of the guard, it is quite possible for a person to have moved from one carriage to another, and he shows you the place where he most probably did so.

The Court at this period adjourned for luncheon.
On resuming, Mr Montagu Williams continued his speech as follows:

Here is another thing which is wanting. They have shown, by the issuer, the number of tickets issued to passengers for that two o'clock train, but they have not shown how many tickets were collected at Preston. At Preston, the train stopped for the purpose of collecting tickets, so that any

Lefroy.

Mr Williams person getting out at Brighton would have no need of a ticket. Therefore, it would have been most material in the suggestion that there were three persons in the railway carriage – which is not stated for the first time, which is not a defence raised by me, but which is the prisoner's defence from alpha to omega — from the first to the very last. Not to give that evidence was an omission.

The next witness was a very remarkable one. He was Joseph Stark, the ticket collector at Preston; and low felt hats seem to be catching in that part, for he wants to make out by his evidence that the prisoner was wearing a low felt hat at Preston Station, whereas if you take the guard's evidence, and look at the map before you, you will find that a low felt hat was found upon the line just beyond Burgess Hill, and, therefore, according to him, there must be three hats.

Then there is the evidence of the man Franks, to which I attach great importance, as it will show you at once how unsubstantial upon details he is. You have it proved by Gibson, and by every other person with the exception of Franks and the other extraordinary witness who put a low hat upon the prisoner's head, that he had on a high hat. I shall use his evidence for the purpose of showing you how unreliable he is. My learned friend, the Attorney-General, has endeavoured to put the low hat upon the prisoner's head. A hat, you will observe, is afterwards found, after the train has passed upon the line. Therefore it does not require a great amount of intellect to show that something must have happened. If this second hat belongs to Lefroy, he must have got it after he got into the train at London Bridge. That he had a high hat on his head, then, is proved to demonstration by a question put to a witness by your foreman. Therefore, if this hat is made to fit Lefroy, the suggestion is that Lefroy had two hats. Franks has proved he had a high hat on at London Bridge; if so, another hat was concealed upon his person. That is impossible. It is absolutely and positively impossible. You cannot get a hat into your waistcoat pocket. Franks describes him as having one hand in the pocket of his overcoat, and his other was outside. It is, therefore, perfectly impossible that he should have had two hats.

Having made these observations, I pass on to the next witness, who was called before you. He is a witness of considerable importance – he is the witness Gibson, who was with Lefroy all the time from the time the train left Preston until it got to Brighton, from the time that they went from Mr Anscombe's office till they reached the town hall, and from the time they left the town hall till the time the surgeon dressed Lefroy's wounds, and then again until they returned to Brighton Station. At all events, we have it that Gibson was with Lefroy from Preston to Brighton, from Brighton to the town hall, and from the town hall to the station. He is the man

Third Day – Monday 7 November 1881.

also who says he said to Lefroy, 'Where did the countryman get out?' to which Lefroy said, 'They must have got out on the road'. Then, in answer to a question from me, he stated that he said the prisoner said, 'He must have got out on the road'. That makes a great deal of difference. It was a most natural thing for Lefroy to have said. What was more natural than, having been rendered inanimately faint from his wounds, and knowing that there were two men in the carriage with him, and missing them when he recovered his senses at Preston, that he should say, in answer to the question, that 'they' got out on the road? Supposing any one of you, gentlemen, had been assaulted in a railway carriage, and had known that two persons were in the carriage with you when you became insensible, would you not, if you missed them when you recovered, have naturally said that 'they must have got out on the road'?

Then there is a man who says that the prisoner had a card in his pocket. I have already addressed you upon that. There were either one or two cards with his right name and address upon them. He must have known when he left Wallington that he had the cards in his possession; and would he have gone with a card in his pocket, with his right name and address upon it, for the purpose of being identified if he were about to commit murder?

It appears to me that, in this case, everything that could be lost has been lost; but I make no observation as to that. The handkerchief has been lost, and that would have been a most important piece of evidence, as handkerchiefs are generally marked, and there might have been some mark upon this which would have told to whom it belonged. It is not, however, forthcoming; but I do not for a moment suggest that it has been improperly made away with. I have endeavoured to throw no censure upon any one, and there has been no reason why I should do so.

With regard to the tokens, Lefroy first of all said that they were not his, but subsequently, according to the evidence, he said that they were whist markers. If they were the subject of a fraud, it would not be unnatural that he should deny that they were his. Those coins have not been found. Then again, one of the officials said that he accompanied Lefroy from Preston to Brighton, from Brighton to the town hall, and back to the station, and that it would have been impossible for him to have made away with anything.

Now, my friend asked: 'How was the chain attached to the watch?' And the answer was: 'By a swivel'. It has been said that, when the watch was discovered, a piece of chain was attached. Now, what has become of that piece of chain? The prisoner could not have detached it. Who did?

The next witness I shall call before you is Hooper, who becomes very important by-and-by, when you come to consider the evidence of a man who comes before you as an injured person. As to who is the injured

Lefroy.

Mr Williams person, or rather the person attempted to be injured, I leave you to form an opinion. I mean the man Weston. It seems almost incredible and impossible to believe that anybody can be so diabolically wicked as to come before you and, upon his oath, make a statement of that kind against a man who is on his trial, who has enough against him, Heaven knows, with the vast power of this prosecution. It is almost impossible to believe, I say, that any man can be so vile and wicked as to come forward and state upon oath that which he has stated. But if Hooper and Anscombe are to be believed, and if Gibson is to be believed, that man's statement was, from first to last, absolutely false. Hooper was present in Mr Anscombe's office, and he says there was no such person there as Weston. Now, who is this man? He is a man who I presume is in a position to read the papers, and does read them. This was a matter of common notoriety. Everybody was talking about it; and Mr Weston, with this important evidence within his knowledge and his remembrance, never goes before the coroner, he never goes before the magistrates at Cuckfield, but he subsequently volunteers, some six or seven weeks ago, a statement to some solicitor at Brighton. I do not wish Weston put out of the case. I say, either he is the witness of truth or he is the witness of falsehood. There is no middle course, and it would have been most important if the Solicitor to the Treasury had called that solicitor at Brighton before you, to show what was in the proof of this man's evidence. But I call your attention to what he actually did swear in court yesterday. He said he pointed to the prisoner's eyebrows, and to the cut upon them, and made use of these words: 'That does not look like a gunshot wound. It is more like a prod from an umbrella.' That is the first suggestion of an umbrella. He next said that he said, 'I should take him to the police station,' and that he saw no wound on the prisoner to account for so much blood. Now, that is the statement he makes some five or six weeks ago. I have had, as I expected I should have, the greatest latitude in this case, and I asked my lord if I might have Gibson back, and he at once assented. I asked Gibson if he was with the prisoner continuously all the time at the station, and he said he was. Was Weston there? No. Did Weston say those words about the umbrella, the words about its being 'hot while it lasted', and the words about 'If I were you, I would take him in a cab'? There can be no mistake about this: it is impossible. Another witness – Anscombe – was recalled, and I put this question to him: 'If Weston said this, must you have heard him?' and he replied, 'I must'. Now, let me say that this witness, Weston, is the witness of the prosecution, and another of their witnesses – Gibson – was actually called and said that the story he told was an absolute fabrication. If the observation applied to that case, how much more would it apply to the circumstances of the witness Weston going up to Lefroy and putting his hand upon the prisoner's shoulder, and saying, 'That could not have been a gunshot wound. It is a prod with an umbrella.' I asked Gibson, 'Did any living soul touch the man in your presence?' and the reply was 'No'. There is the evidence of Weston and there is the evidence of Gibson who registered it. If all this is untrue, and it is an invention on the part of Weston, then all I can say is that in my long experience of human life I have never before heard of so monstrous a story.[59]

The next witness called was James Martin, a policeman, who proved nothing so far as my case is concerned; and the next witness, Thompson, was merely called to produce a statement. Terry, the inspector of the Brighton police station, seems to have had no suspicion of the crime.

The next witness is a very important one – it is Mr Benjamin Hall. He was the doctor who examined Lefroy's head at the time he was taken to the hospital. But before I go to his evidence, I prefer to take you to the railway carriage. What is the statement of Lefroy about the matter? He says, 'I got into the railway carriage at London Bridge. Mr Gold' – it turned out to be Mr Gold – 'was in the train, and a third person, a man who looked like a countryman. Mr Gold was sitting reading a newspaper.' We have it from a man at Croydon that he had a handkerchief over his face. He was an oldish man, and it is very likely he may have been going to sleep. Lefroy says, 'As I sat there, there was a flash. I was fired at. I was missed, so far as that went, and I was instantly assaulted with the butt-end of a pistol.'[60] This is important when we come to the question of the wound as spoken to by Mr Hall. 'I was,' says Lefroy, 'rendered insensible by the wounds'. Lefroy was sitting in the corner of the compartment, but what position he was in after the train started we cannot say. Persons shift their places in railway carriages from one cause and another; therefore, we cannot attach much importance to that matter. But if he were sitting there, you know that there is a bullet mark immediately over where his head would be, in the corner. If he was missed, and the man rushed upon him, by that time Mr Gold would be aware of the state of things, and would do the most natural thing – rush to the bell. It is over that bell that there is another bullet shot. If Lefroy is rendered senseless, he can know nothing more about the matter until he wakes up at Preston with a watch in his shoe. Is that impossible? Remember, if the story is true, there is no living man knows the truth about the third person but that third person; and it is for you to say, before consigning a fellow-creature to the grave, that it is impossible that a third person could have been present. The blood on the neck of the prisoner was a consequence which would naturally be anticipated from the wounds upon his head and face. Mr Hall

---

59   See Appendix II.
60   The statement about being 'assaulted with the butt-end of a pistol' is not given in evidence.

Lefroy.

Mr Williams was asked: 'In your opinion, were the wounds sufficient to have caused faintness and insensibility?' His reply was 'Yes', and he added that they must have been inflicted by a pistol, or by the end of an umbrella. The man's head has had plaster upon it, and a white surgical bandage was subsequently found in Lefroy's coat pocket.[61] It was suggested that there was no blood upon it. If the wounds had already been plastered, why should there be blood upon it? But it has been proved that there was blood on the neck and collar, which would naturally be the result of wounds on the head. As to the umbrella, if you struck with that in a struggle, you would strike flat; and with regard to the blood found on the prisoner, if he were attacked, and lay prostrate, and if a struggle were going on between two other persons for some miles, what wonder is there that blood should be discovered?

They say that Brown got into the carriage, and that one of them said, in a loud voice, that a body had been found. 'Hush! you must not speak,' was the answer. Why should not he have heard? The remark was made in such a loud tone of voice – so loud a tone that it called forth the 'Hush!' – therefore you may take it for granted that he did hear, for the first time, of a dead body being found in the tunnel.

Holmes is the man who searched him at Brighton, and here I have to point out that no second pocket-book, no second purse, no skull cap, no canvas bag were found in his possession. If he was the murderer, where were they? If, too, Mr Gold had £2 10s or £3 in his pocket, where was the money? In his possession, when searched, the prisoner had only thirteen shillings. Where, then, was the money? It was not in possession of the prisoner.

Then, as to the pocket-book found upon the prisoner at Brighton, he told the detective that it contained private papers. Duplicates were there, no doubt, but when it was taken from the prisoner at Wallington it was, according to the evidence, in the same state as it was at Brighton.

Holmes is a detective, and goes on with the prisoner to Wallington, and there it is, I say, that, having heard for the first time the evidence against him, however innocent he was, he began to lie. When asked the number of his watch he gives the wrong number. But there is no question put by the Attorney-General as to what became of the watch. The watch was last seen in the room downstairs, at Wallington. Whether Holmes kept possession of that watch, I do not know. I do not say so. I do not think so. From that moment, the prisoner says, he never saw the watch.

The next evidence goes on to show that, some little time after Holmes left, the accused, knowing all the circumstances of the case, left Wallington. If he were an innocent man, why did he fly? You know,

61   William Turpin had testified to finding the bandage 'lying on the floor near the chair'.

gentlemen, we are not all constituted alike. We have men of strong moral **Mr Williams**
courage, and we have men of weak moral courage. We have men of strong
physical courage, and men of weak physical courage. The prisoner said,
'I wish I had remained where I was. I wish I had not gone away.' He had
far better not have gone. He had far better have remained where he was,
and it would have been a mercy to him if, in the discharge of his duty that
night, Holmes had taken him into custody. But he flies. He knows he has
been seen at Brighton, the only occupant of the carriage, deluged with
gore; he knows he has been taken to the hospital, with wounds on his
head; he knows that the body is found in the tunnel; he knows a telegram
is received stating that no watch is upon the body; he knows that Holmes
is a detective officer who is inquiring about a watch; he knows the watch
has been placed by someone in his shoe, and that that watch is found
in his possession. What man is there who would not fear? He tells a lie
about the watch and about the number. The officer leaves the house. The
temptation is too great. Individual safety is the first thing a man thinks
of, and I ask you whether there are not half a dozen men out of a dozen
who would not have done the same? Don't forget that his action must
have been quick. If a guilty man, he knew the duplicates were in his coat
pocket.

Now that finishes the evidence as regards what took place that night.
Moss was the next witness, and Holmes mentioned to him the number of
the watch.

The next witnesses are the Jennings, who found Mr Gold's body; and
Lewis, the constable at Balcombe, who proves the state in which the
body was found, and the absence of the articles Mr Gold is alleged to
have had, not one of which is upon the prisoner. But this witness not
only proved that. He stated that a diligent search had been made for
the revolver, but that no revolver had been found. If there was a third
person, and he escaped, he would have taken the revolver with him, and
that would account for it not being found. They have had gangs of men
from Merstham tunnel to Balcombe tunnel, and from Balcombe tunnel to
Brighton, searching for that pistol. The search is to no avail. My learned
friend, the Attorney-General, asked the question of one of the witnesses:
'Are there not many ponds and marshes on the road?' I dare say you
know the road. I dare say there are ponds and marshes, but it must take
a remarkably good shot to so accurately gauge it that, when a train was
going at full speed, a revolver would fall in a certain place. But there is
not a particle of evidence to show that the prisoner was ever in possession
of a pistol. If it is important to show who offered the pistol in pledge, how
much more important to show that he ever had one in his possession?

Then comes the evidence of Dr Bond, who is a man of the greatest

Lefroy.

Mr Williams possible experience. He tells you that he made a post mortem examination of Mr Gold's body. Mr Bond's scientific opinion is that all the wounds, with the exception of the fracture of the skull, were inflicted during life. He adds that, not only must a pistol have been used, but a knife; because we have not only one wound, but wounds upon both hands and thumbs – deep cuts, such as would make Mr Gold prostrate from loss of blood; and, in point of fact, he died from injuries inflicted upon him by somebody in the railway carriage. Now, where are the knife and pistol? The line has been searched, and these have not been produced. If a life and death struggle took place between these two men, would you not expect to find some marks upon Lefroy's hands? If a terrible conflict were waged for eight miles between a powerful man and this stripling, would you not expect to find some marks or cuts on prisoner's hands, in consequence of Mr Gold trying to get possession of the knife? There are no such marks – not a scratch. But where is the knife? Now, if a third party did the deed, the knife would be where the pistol is – in the possession of the murderer. Two knives were found upon the line. Every inquiry has been made; and it is not suggested for one moment that these knives have anything to do with the case. Has the knife gone the way of the second purse, the skull cap, et cetera? When you are trying the life of a man, surely these things are of the greatest importance.

Now, Mr Bond says Mr Gold was dead before he was thrown out. If so, it cannot be suggested that the marks of blood underneath the footboard were produced by his grasping the board for the purpose of preventing himself being thrown out. How could Lefroy get Mr Gold's body out of the carriage? Lefroy had been wounded himself, and has lost sufficient blood, according to the medical evidence, to render him insensible. Yet the theory is that he lifted the body out! Gentlemen, have you ever tried to lift a person in a swoon! It was a dead weight. The purport of Dr Bond's evidence is that he would expect to find Lefroy in a fainting condition, and yet it is suggested that he threw Mr Gold's body out.

The next batch of witnesses speaks concerning the hat. The proof is clear that the hat I now show you [*holding one up*] came out of the carriage. Whose was it? Lefroy did not have two hats. Then where is the head that fits this hat? It is a most extraordinary thing. This hat is not put before you for the first time. It was produced before the coroner, it was produced before the magistrates, and it is produced before you today. Months have rolled by since this murder. The prisoner was arrested in July; we are now in the month of November, and not a single explanation of any kind is forthcoming as to this hat. The name and address of the maker are in the hat. The address is in the Strand. The prosecution may have the maker here for aught I know. Now, I submit to you that the

Third Day – Monday 7 November 1881.

evidence which this hat discloses is in favour of the doctrine of a third person in the carriage.

The next point in the evidence is the slackening of the train. Then we have the evidence of Mr Wood, the witness who was awoke by the train slackening. It brought him home to his own door, and so slow was the rate at which it was going that he actually picked up his bag with the intention of getting out.

With reference to the collar of Lefroy which was found on the line, my contention is that it was twisted off his neck by his assailant, and that, being wet with blood, it probably stuck to the step, and was afterwards gradually detached by the movement of the train.

With regard to the pistol, the evidence concerning it is chiefly the evidence of pawnbrokers' assistants. One of them, Creek, states that it was pawned on 21 June and released on the 27th. He said that he knew the prisoner as a customer who had been in the habit of pawning articles in the name of Lee, and that, speaking to the best of his belief, he was the person who pawned that revolver, but when cross-examined he could not swear that the prisoner was the person, thus declining to swear that which the prosecution asked the jury to believe. As a rule, pawnbrokers do not take much notice of the people who come to pawn, and have often very good reasons for not doing so; and articles are almost always pawned in false names and addresses. In the hurry of business in a pawnbroker's shop, it is impossible to identify every customer; and the evidence of Creek that Lefroy was the person who pawned the revolver on 21 June cannot be relied upon by you as evidence that should be acted upon against the prisoner. If he did pawn that pistol, do not forget that whoever did so had in his pocket a box of cartridges. With regard to this, the pawnbroker's assistant says: 'I took the shots from the pistol, which I found to be loaded, and put them back in the box.' I did not ask the question whether there was any address on the box, because I thought the witness might very reasonably have forgotten whether there was or not. There is not a particle of evidence to show that you are dealing with the pistol which Lefroy bought, or that he ever bought one or pawned one, except the evidence of a pawnbroker's assistant.

That evidence of the assistant brings us to the evidence of Mr and Mrs Clayton. They were called before you late last night, and is it to be suggested that they came here for the purpose of committing wilful and corrupt perjury? The pawnbroker's assistant says that, from his book, he should say the pistol could not have been pawned on 21 June earlier than nearly seven o'clock. If the Claytons' evidence is correct, it is impossible that the prisoner at the bar could have pawned the pistol. Mr Clayton says, 'I came home by the train which reached Wallington shortly after

Lefroy.

Mr Williams seven, and when I got home the man who opened the door was Lefroy. I swear it.' Nothing could shake him. If that be true, the evidence of the pawnbroker is worthless. And why should it not be? I asked Mr Clayton, 'Why do you remember the 21st?' He gives you an excellent reason – his wife was confined on the 23rd. He himself had gone to town, and Lefroy, who was an idle man, or, at any rate, one whose work was desultory, had no cause to go to London. Mrs Clayton is then called into the witness box, and what story does she give? Nothing is so convincing as her tale. She says, 'I expected my confinement. I was ill. Lefroy had lived with me, or my father, all his life. I was nervous that day.' Gentlemen, women in that state are nervous. She continues, 'I asked him that day, in the morning, if he would stay with me at home, for fear I might want a doctor,' as, of course, she would be unable to send one of her scholars. She goes on, 'During the day I was in the room in which I receive my scholars, but went out of it occasionally to see Lefroy, as I thought it would comfort me'. Is that impossible? Then I ask her, 'When did you have your tea?' 'At six o'clock.' 'Who had tea with you?' 'Lefroy,' is the answer. Is that a tissue of lies from beginning to end? Would you believe against evidence like that, that given by a pawnbroker's clerk, and thus find the prisoner guilty?

The evidence called before you today has been evidence that I have attempted to controvert. It has been simple evidence to show that he tried to disguise himself after having fled. What is more natural than that he should have done so?

I have now exhausted the observations I propose to make to you upon the evidence on the part of the prosecution, and I have to ask you to take that evidence as whole. Before you can convict the prisoner you must be prepared to say that the evidence is conclusive, and that there cannot be a mistake.

Remember, gentlemen, that your verdict is final, and that the question in your hands is one of life and death. Remember that the light of life once extinguished can never be rekindled. You are told that circumstantial evidence is convincing. Now I deny that. Paraphrase it, and what does the statement mean? It means that the human intellect is infallible. I ask you, is that so? Is it to be said that circumstantial evidence has never been wrong? Have not convictions taken place where the evidence has been proved wrong? In our own time you will find that, over and over again, life has been sacrificed by circumstantial evidence; homes have been wrecked by circumstantial evidence; and disgrace and degradation have been brought upon those who came after by reliance having been placed upon circumstantial evidence.

I seek by these words of mine not to endeavour to turn your minds from the straight path. I do not seek to lead you to depart from the sanctity of the oath you have taken; but I do entreat you to judge of every particle of

Third Day – Monday 7 November 1881.

evidence with that ability such as it is in the power of human intellect to bestow.

Gentlemen, you can but do your best. I have discharged the duty cast upon me, and I now leave the matter in your hands.

I can only, in conclusion, pray that, in this terrible hour of your need – for a terrible hour it is for you – that He to whom all hearts are open, and all secrets are known, may guide and conduct you.

Speech for the Prosecution.[62]

The ATTORNEY-GENERAL: My learned friend has told you, and told you rightly, that you are responsible for that man's life. That is true. But you are equally responsible for the performance of your duty, and to take care that if the crime that has been committed by somebody is rightly brought home to the door of that man, its consequences should fall upon him. It is a stern duty that you have to fulfil, and one which, doubtless, you would rather not have cast upon you; but I must point out that it is a duty that must be performed without fear or flinching.

My learned friend has chosen to assume that the evidence in this case is circumstantial evidence. He has told you that circumstantial evidence is misleading. It is true that circumstantial evidence is often misleading, but it very often happens that direct evidence is more misleading than circumstantial evidence. When witnesses are speaking to a fact and are not telling the truth, direct evidence must be the most misleading in the world. But in this case there is a great mass of evidence which I should not have supposed to have been circumstantial evidence. There is direct evidence of the most cogent kind, and which, if unexplained, must lead you to the conclusion that the prisoner is guilty of the crime with which he is charged.

But just before I deal with the explanations my learned friend has placed before you, let me see whether there be not some facts in relation to which there can be no doubt. I think, on looking at the condition of the prisoner before 27 June, we may regard it as an established fact that he was driven by circumstances into a condition of great need, and almost of desperation. We can trace him by the records of these pawn tickets as having placed article after article, articles of the utmost necessity, in pledge. We have him placed under the necessity of depriving a relative of some portion of his property in order that he might retain his power of redeeming his pledges. In addition to that, we have the fact that on 27 June he was driven, in order to obtain the thirteen shillings, to the

---

62   Transcript of the Attorney-General's address to the jury taken from the *Daily News*, Tuesday 8 November 1881.

Lefroy.

commission of a crime which is punishable by law.

Gentlemen, when a man finds cause to commit a crime on account of pecuniary need, it is but a matter of degree what further crime he will commit in order to satisfy his necessities. Do not suppose, of course, that because a man has committed one crime he has such a want of moral sense that he will necessarily commit another. It is simply a matter for your consideration. If want of money will drive men to commit one crime, I say it is possible – I do not say it is either probable or likely, but possible – that that crime will lead a man to commit a more desperate crime.

With this knowledge of the prisoner's condition, the next general fact is that, so far as direct evidence goes, he is in the society of the murdered man at the time that the murdered man commenced his journey. That is admitted. He is found at the termination of the journey alone, with the body of the murdered man lying dead behind him on the line. He is found covered with blood, and proof is given that he must have passed through a struggle for life, and that he had suffered in the course of the struggle. He is found then in the possession of the property of the murdered man. You have him telling falsehood after falsehood in regard to matters that must have been immediately present to his knowledge, and those falsehoods were retained until the last. There was a hue and cry after him; flight was resorted to, and he acted with a knowledge of all the circumstances as a guilty man naturally would.

That, of course, is a very general view of the circumstances of 27 June. The circumstances, therefore, and this evidence, heavily press upon him, and if unexplained, conclusively establish, as I consider it, his guilt. But he has now, through the mouth of his counsel, endeavoured to make these facts consistent with his innocence. Now, I am sure the learned counsel for the defence will not misunderstand me when I say what was said before by a very eminent lawyer, that you never know the strength of a case for the prosecution until you have heard the defence of a prisoner by counsel, and notwithstanding the manner in which my learned friend has fulfilled the difficult task assigned to him he will forgive me if I repeat those words, and say that his endeavour to explain the direct evidence away by theory and hypothesis made for the first time the case for the prosecution present itself in its full strength. It is to the inferences that counsel for the prisoner has drawn from the facts, as we now know them, that I have now to make a reply on the part of the Crown, and I will endeavour to follow my learned friend in the hypotheses he has laid before you.

The question is, what was it led the prisoner to make that journey to Brighton, travelling in a first-class carriage? He has never apparently travelled first-class before. Well, my learned friend has mentioned today

Third Day – Monday 7 November 1881.

what has never been mentioned before. He has said that there was some young lady whom the prisoner had appointed to meet him at London Bridge to accompany him to Brighton. Well, I am speaking in the presence of my learned friend, and of course with full acknowledgement of his right to be the judge of this case; but it does occur to me that if a fact is capable of being proved, a counsel has no right to state simply that fact upon his instructions without some further proof. It is right that we should have in courts of justice the fullest consideration for the feelings of others. But this is a case of life or death, and the man's existence depends upon your verdict. Are we to believe that considerations of delicacy go to this extent: that this young lady, whose friendship was sufficiently strong to accompany him to Brighton, refuses to compromise her character by appearing here to say so? Had she not the common humanity to say that though she might go into court with a blush on her cheek, yet she would dare to come forward and explain the circumstances? Gentlemen, let us hope for the sake of woman's character that this young lady did not exist.

Well, under these circumstances, this journey is commenced. It is of course humanly possible that there may have been a third person present, but what right have you to assume that there was such a person in the carriage when you have all the testimony of the persons who would give you information upon the subject denying the assertion? The evidence went to show that Mr Gold was sitting in the centre seat, and at Croydon he was observed to have a pocket-handkerchief over his head, so that he would not have observed anyone who was about to attack him. So far as we know, no trace can be found of any third person, and I submit to you that the statement of a third person being present cannot be relied on. The theory of the defence is not, I contend, within the range of possibility.

Gentlemen, we have heard that a stranger left the train at some point, and we have heard a great deal about stoppage at Hassock's Gate. The question for your determination is not whether the train was slackened to a speed of four miles an hour, but whether a person could alight from it without observation. According to the hypothesis of the learned gentleman, the supposed stranger – or third person – must have reached Preston Park after the encounter with Mr Gold, and must have borne traces of the blood which poured from the wound. If the prisoner was so much saturated, what must have been the condition of the man who was said to be the real murderer? He must have been a spectacle horrible to look at, and in that condition it is now suggested that he passed unnoticed the scrutiny of ticket collectors, superintendents, passengers, and others. Where, then, was this human being – this third party? Not one of those persons who must have seen him, had he been on the train, has the common love of justice, the human feeling, to come forward and say, 'I

Lefroy.

saw him take to flight. I saw him fleeing from justice.' Whilst, however, the particulars of the case had been scattered over the country, producing – I won't call it prurient curiosity, but attracting an amount of attention which probably would better be employed if directed to other matters – whilst, I say, all this has been going on, not one can be found who will say, 'I am the man'. If the case of my learned friend is that there was such a person, why did he not act upon such a view to the extent of asking the ticket collectors and others whether they saw such a person? Gentlemen, I had no idea that there was any such theory to be brought forward until today – that the supposed murderer had alighted at Preston Park; and therefore I had no reason to ask the witnesses questions on a point which I had not imagined. But why did my learned friend not test the sincerity of his faith by asking witnesses whether they saw such a person? As to the other theory – that the supposed murderer might have passed from one carriage to another – I have an observation to make. Where are the traces of blood that must have been left on the next compartment? Is there to be found one trace of blood in that compartment? No such signs are to be found.

The prisoner, upon his arrival at Brighton, told falsehood after falsehood. My learned friend said that it was at Balcombe, when Mr Brown entered the carriage, that the prisoner commenced to lie – when he knew, according to my friend's statement, that he was likely to be accused of the murder. You will find that, when the watch was first seen at Preston Park, prisoner said, 'That is mine'. My learned friend asks you to come to the conclusion that Howland has perjured himself to convict a man of whom he knows nothing. Howland did not have that in his written statement, because he put down nothing of what occurred at Preston Park, but only the account which the prisoner gave of the journey. Howland saw what took place at Preston Park, and therefore did not want to take it down. When you see the extreme probability there is that the prisoner did make this statement, I regret that my learned friend would have thought it consistent with his duty as an advocate to suggest that.

What is another account the prisoner gave of the watch? He says, 'When I awoke I found it on the floor,' and his own statement was that he put it into his shoe for safety. What right had he to take this watch? Unless you are going to say that those witnesses who have given evidence on this point have without reason perjured themselves, this is a falsehood; and my friend has forgotten these facts when he says that Lefroy began to lie at Balcombe tunnel. You will recollect, too, what occurred about the Hanoverian medals. Two or three are found in the compartment when he arrives at Brighton. He is asked about them, and says, 'I know nothing about them unless they were dropped by the persons who assaulted me'.

Third Day – Monday 7 November 1881.

When pressed to remain at Brighton on account of his condition, Lefroy declared that he must return to London, having an appointment. Now where is the person with whom he made the appointment? Is there any delicacy in this matter?

I think too much importance is attached to the loss of the watch. At Brighton, Lefroy was treated as an innocent man. It was not known at the time that a dead body had been found in Balcombe tunnel. It is important to know what became of the piece of chain attached to the watch. We know it could have been easily removed, being attached by a swivel. When the watch was again seen, the piece of chain was gone. Now, the prisoner must have removed the chain, for nobody else had the watch. Why did he remove it? He saw that the chain would correspond to the chain found on Mr Gold's body.

I must say one word about the evidence of Mr Weston. Having heard my learned friend's attack on him, I was anxious to know to what that attack led. Mr Weston expressed opinions as to the cause of the injuries on Lefroy's head, but those opinions prove nothing. You have the better testimony now – the medical testimony. I can see no reason why such a conversation as Mr Weston describes may not have taken place. It would last only a few seconds, and great excitement prevailed. But it would have been indecent to enter into Mr Weston's matter in Lefroy's trial. If there is any doubt as to Weston being present, then put his evidence altogether aside. What had that evidence to do with the crucial facts, such as the finding of the watch and pawning the pistol?

Passing over less important matters, I go back to the morning of the 27th, on which Mr Gold met his death, and come to the consideration of whether the prisoner had in his possession any weapons to inflict the wounds which caused death. One of these wounds was a shot from a pistol, probably a revolver, of small bore. Mr Gold left London Bridge with the right side of his head turned towards the prisoner, and he was shot on the right side underneath the ear with a bullet which would produce death, or at all events produce such a shock as would be likely to prevent the person wounded from entering into a protracted struggle. Now, it is admitted that on 2 June the prisoner pawned clothes for ten shillings, giving the name of William Lee, 8 Southampton Street, Peckham. In his coat, which was given up by Mrs Clayton, the pawn ticket was found. On 11 June, he pawned a dress suit for £1 5s, giving the name James Leigh. This might be taken to establish that he is the same man. On 30 May, in the name of John Lee, he pawned an aluminium watch for 5s, the ticket for which was found in his pocket. From the defence, it appears that from a coincidence – which I will ask you to declare as to whether it was possible or not – it appears that one man invents for himself a

Lefroy.

perfectly imaginary name and address, namely, Lee, of Southampton Street, Peckham, and another man, whom he does not know, fixes upon exactly the same address. Is this within the bounds of possibility? The tickets being a matter of record and taken as correct makes the assertion that these men of Southampton Street were one and the same more conclusive. Mr Creek, the pawnbroker's assistant, who, I think, is quite right to be extremely cautious when he is giving evidence against a man whose life is at stake, says, 'I believe that is the man'. As a matter of fact, he picked him out from among seven other persons, all of them differently dressed. Is he not worthy of belief because he is cautious? Whilst he acts with caution, there is another young man who is present at the pledging of the dress suit on 11 June. He was also a witness of the cartridge episode in the pledge-shop on the 21st. This young man positively identifies the prisoner at the bar as the pledger. Can you, in the face of the evidence of the men who do this, fail to see your duty? The determination to believe this evidence or not is the crucial test of the case. Are you going to refuse to listen to evidence which, if it be untrue, must be wilfully and intentionally so? I ask you to probe your conscience and say whether you can shrink from coming to the conclusion that the prisoner had this pistol in his possession some time on 27 June. If he had, mark the effect. By a pistol shot, Mr Gold met his death. Someone has that pistol, and from the testimony it appears that at twelve o'clock Lefroy redeemed it. Where is that revolver? If the prisoner had it, what has he done with it? It is humanly possible that he had the revolver, but still did not shoot Mr Gold, but still I cannot help thinking that it is a false theory that he is not the man. Gentlemen, my learned friend has to account for where the pistol is. If it be that he had the pistol, why has he chosen to make away with it?

As to the watch, it has been suggested that it was left at Cathcart Road, and, if so, some of his friends must have kept it out of the way from excess of zeal. If they have done so, why have they not now come forward in the interest of the prisoner, and said that they had concealed the watch with the view of benefitting the prisoner? If they did so, I am sure full forgiveness would be given to them, but in the meantime the prisoner must be answerable. It is the watch of the murdered man, and he may have cast it away that proof of his guilt might not be found. The prisoner did not come out of his hiding place and brave the charge. He did not come forth and play the part of an accuser, and he would never have come forward and met the charge had not the police received information as to his whereabouts.

Complaint has been made because the prosecution brought no evidence to show a knowledge on the part of the prisoner of the habits of Mr Gold.

Third Day – Monday 7 November 1881.

Attorney -General

I do not think that there was any necessity for such evidence, and we could not be supposed to know whether Lefroy knew Mr Gold's habits and ways a fortnight before the day of the murder.

Then as to the articles found, and those that have not been found. I must express my astonishment that so many of them have been brought to light, especially considering the great distance along which they must have been scattered. The prisoner, allow me to observe, was not completely searched. His pockets, it is true, were searched, but his clothes were not, and, probably, if the chain had not worked out of his shoe, the watch would not have been found. Where the watch was, other things could have been put. There are, gentlemen, many minute matters in this case with which I will not trouble you; but I may ask why, if there was a third passenger in the carriage, the countryman of whom you have heard threw out the heavy man and left the light man in the carriage? As to the evidence of the Claytons, you will find that it presents discrepancies, and that it is that of those who have a not unnatural bias towards a relative. Gentlemen, the case is before you. I have not throughout its course been influenced against the accused. At the same time, it would be cowardice and affectation to say that the public are not to be protected by justice being done, and I hope you will yourselves do the utmost, neither leaning to the right hand nor the left, to endeavour to arrive at the verdict which according to the evidence may seem to your judgments fair and just.

Thomas Bond

DR BOND was recalled, and in answer to a question of Mr Justice COLERIDGE whether he had observed any hair on the hands of the deceased, replied in the negative, and said that he did not know whether the body had been washed or not before he examined it.

The court adjourned.

*

Fourth Day – Tuesday 8 November 1881.[63]

Judge's Charge to the Jury.

At 11.00 am, Lord COLERIDGE took his seat upon the bench.

Gentlemen of the jury, you and I have arrived at the stage of this long enquiry with which we have more especially to do, and I need not tell you I am quite certain that long as the enquiry has been, and long as it may be necessary for me, I hope not at any very unreasonable length, to detain you, that no time must be grudged in an enquiry of this kind, because you have been quite truly told that it is the most momentous issue that can be presented to a body of gentlemen to determine upon. You have to pass your judgment upon the life of a fellow-creature, and you have been rightly told that the fellow-creature is a young man, at the threshold of life, and, therefore, if he should be found guilty by you, he will be cut off in the flower of his age; and it is right and fitting that a step of that kind should be taken by you after the gravest and fullest consideration. A great Roman writer, often quoted by our own authors, has said in noble language, 'Nulla unquam de morte hominis cunctatio longa' – no deliberation is long, no hesitation is protracted, which is to end in the death of a fellow-creature. This verdict differs from all others in this. All other verdicts can be reviewed. All mistakes can be, to a certain extent, set straight. In this case, however, a wrong decision may be repented of, but cannot be atoned; and therefore it is right that a decision in a case of this kind should be arrived at after the greatest deliberation which conscientious men can give.

At the same time, I must tell you that it would be unmanly to shrink from duty in this as in any other case, without regard to the probable consequences of it. No man, in the discharge of a public duty, whatever the consequences may be to others persons of the duty which he has to perform, can look, or ought to look, at anything but the simple, solemn, straightforward performance of his duty. The soldier cannot look at the consequences of his acts. No man can look, or ought to look, if he is ordered by proper authority to do a thing, at the consequences of what he does. You and I are instructed, are ordered by the law to make this investigation. The law knows human nature for what it is. It is probable

Lord Coleridge

---

63   Transcript of the day's proceedings taken from the *Daily News*, Wednesday 9 November 1881.

Lefroy.

that we may make mistakes, but that ought not to hinder us, shall not hinder me, and I am sure will not hinder you from the performance of your duty as you understand it. Human nature is fallible, but we have to proceed according to the rules of human nature. One of those rules is that murder, if it is proved, is to be punished by death, and the proof of murder is the same proof as the proof of any other matter. It is true: where the issue is momentous, the deliberation should be most careful; but there is no difference in principle; there is no variety in rule between the investigation into which I now ask you to enter with me than that of any other investigation you may be called on to make when sitting in the jury-box and instructed by a judge.

Now, gentlemen, let me begin by pointing out as shortly as I can the kind of persons with whom in this case we have to deal. They are two – one is an old man, I think sixty-four, a man apparently of good means, retired from business, bringing home from week to week as much as £30 to £40 – a man who was regular in his habits, and apparently in one respect a little unlike other persons, that he was a very silent man, that he shrank from the conversation of others, and was apt in his journeys to separate himself a good deal from the fellow travellers into whose company he fell. He had been undoubtedly a man of great physical strength; he was a large man, a healthy man, and, as far as sixty-four allows of it, he was a man of full vigour of body. Of course, those who are past or approaching to that age know that at sixty-four the body is not quite what it had been, and that a man at the age of sixty-four cannot expect, and if he did, would expect in vain, to be what he was when a young man. Mr Gold was, as far as we know, in the habit of carrying two purses, one for gold, and the other as a rule for silver and copper. He wore a double eye-glass, and carried a watch with a chain that went round his neck instead of being merely attached to his button-hole. According to the evidence of his wife, it appears that he never carried firearms; that he had a dislike to them; and that although he had at one time possession of a firearm of some kind, it had been for many years locked up.

The prisoner at the bar was a person very different in all respects. He was quite a young man, in his twenty-second year. He was a man without money. He was a man curiously erratic in his habits, and was not scrupulous in matters of honesty, as appears by some matters given incidentally in evidence for another purpose in this case; and of his early life – how he was brought up, what occupation he followed, what temptations he was exposed to – of all these we know nothing; and I have mentioned these unfavourable circumstances not at all for the purpose of drawing any such unjust conclusion as that because a man was not unwilling to cheat a tradesman of a few shillings he would murder a man

Mr Justice Coleridge.

Fourth Day – Tuesday 8 November 1881.

with knife and pistol, but merely to show the kind of man he was, the life that he had led, and the temptations – because that will become a matter well worthy of your consideration – to which his condition in life exposed him.

These were the two persons into whose relations we are called on to enquire; and as far as we know the first time upon which they are brought into any relation with one another was on the morning or the noon of 27 June last. On that day, Mr Gold had gone up as usual from Brighton to London for the purpose of getting the weekly takings of the shop which he still possessed in Walworth. He might also have gone up for the purpose of getting other moneys; but, however that may be, we do know for certain that he went to get the weekly takings, and we also know for certain that he was in the habit of bringing with him every week from London to Brighton a very considerable sum of money. He went up dressed as usual, strong and hearty as usual, and in all respects very much as he had done apparently for many weeks before, and might have hoped to do for many weeks to come. It appears from the evidence of Mrs Cross that he went between 10.30 am and 10.40 am to 145 East Street, Walworth, and there got from her in a bag the takings of the week before, amounting to £38 5s 1d; and we have it proved by Mr Alfred Gilbert that, a little after noon, he went to the Whitechapel Branch of the London and Westminster Bank and gave the money into the hands of Mr Gilbert. He took it, undoubtedly, in a bag, and Mr Gilbert is under the impression that he took the bag away, but is not quite certain, and whether he did or not must now remain uncertain. That was a little after 1.00 pm, and at 1.50 pm he is seen by the witness Franks upon the platform of the London Bridge station of the London and Brighton Railway. There, beyond all doubt, he met the prisoner in this sense, that undoubtedly the prisoner was at some time or other on the platform, and undoubtedly he left London and arrived at Brighton by the same train by which Mr Gold left London and did not arrive at Brighton. Now, it is important to consider at this point how it was the prisoner had come there, and it appears to me that it would tend to clearness to take things in their logical order.

To begin with, the earliest thing we know about the prisoner for certain is that on 30 May he had pledged with Mr Swaisland an aluminium watch upon which he had received an advance of 5s, and that he pledged it in the name of John Lee, of Southampton Street. Mr Clayton said he believed the watch was the prisoner's, although he would not swear to it, but undoubtedly the watch of the prisoner which Mr Clayton was acquainted with was an aluminium watch, that an aluminium watch was pledged in the name of John Lee of Southampton Street, and the pawn-ticket is found upon the prisoner. If, therefore, you were simply trying to

Lefroy.

**Lord
Coleridge**

question whether the prisoner did or did not pawn that watch on 30 May, you would not have the slightest hesitation in coming to the conclusion that he had done so. On 2 June, he pledges an overcoat for 10s with a man of the name of Creek. He pledges it in the name of William Lee, of 8 Southampton Street, Peckham. That overcoat is sworn to as being his property, and the pawn-ticket for it is found upon him. On 11 June, at the same pawnbroker's shop in the Borough, he, with another man – I think, strictly speaking, Creek did see something of this, but so little that it is not worth bringing him into the question at all; the transaction was with a witness of the name of Allwright – and on 11 June, through Allwright, he pawns a dress suit, upon which he gets an advance of £1 5s, in the name of James Lee, 8 Southampton Street, and that dress suit is his. The pawn-ticket is found upon him. He himself claimed it, and his claim has been allowed, and that suit beyond all question is his. Now, on 20 June, he pawns with a person of the name of White two coats and some trousers, and upon them he gets 16s advance. He pawns them in the name of John Lee, 11 New Street. This pawn-ticket is also found upon him. Mr White properly says, 'I cannot say. I never saw the man but once, but I cannot say upon recollection that he is the man.' But there is the name, and there is the pawn-ticket, and although I will not go at this moment into the observations I shall have to make later on, but in passing I will observe that in this, as in all cases, whatever a prisoner can prove, not only is he bound to prove it, but there is no longer any hardship in being bound to prove it; because now prisoners can make their defence, if it be relevant to the issue, at the expense of the country, and they only have to say that they want such and such witnesses, and state what they can prove, for the magistrate to bind them over, and the country pays the expense. If, therefore, a pawn-ticket being found upon him in respect of some coats and trousers pawned by John Lee on 20 June – if there was another real John Lee who had through some transaction, which is possible, transferred his pawn-ticket to the prisoner, nothing would be easier for the prisoner to produce John Lee, and if he did choose to produce John Lee, this evidence would at once have vanished from the case, and he would have produced John Lee at the expense of the country. I am therefore justified in saying, in the absence of any such suggestion as I have indicated, that those coats and trousers were pawned by the prisoner on 20 June.

I now omit the 21 June, although it comes chronologically next in order, but I shall have to discuss that date later on. The next thing we know about the matter is 22 June, when he pawns four plated spoons, in a bag, upon which he gets an advance of five shillings with a man named Mathews. These he pawns in the name of John Lee, of Tamworth Road,

Fourth Day – Tuesday 8 November 1881.

Croydon. That he did so is plain. Mr Clayton has been before you, and he says, 'That bag is mine. I gave him no authority to pledge that bag. I missed that bag about the middle of June.' The spoons were marked 'R.M.O.' and were pawned for 5s, and for these articles the pawn ticket was found upon him. We know that the prisoner would not, humanly speaking, have done this unless he had been driven to severe straits for want of money. Who R.M.O. is we don't know, but if R.M.O. is any person on whose behalf this pledge was really made, you must know it. If R.M.O. could have been called, we should have got rid also of that link – small though it may be – but still a link in the chain. R.M.O. is not before you, and you must take the consequences of the absence of the witness who, if he were capable of giving an explanation, could have given it as I have pointed out at the expense of the country. All this is proved, and what is the result of it? The result is this – that he had pledged five sets of things with different people, but all in the name of Lee, of Southampton Street. I am aware that in one case it is Southampton Street without the number, and in one case 8, and in another number 9. If the pawn-tickets had not been found upon him, and any reasonable explanation could be thought of, there would be something in it; but I revert to the statement I make. There are five tickets in the name of Lee, and three of them in the name of Lee, of Southampton Street. Now, did he or did he not pledge on 21 June and redeem on the 27th a revolver for 5s? On the 21st, it appears by the books of Mr Creek that a William Lee of 9 Southampton Street, Peckham, pledged a revolver: a person apparently bearing the same name, and apparently living in Southampton Street, Peckham, pledged a revolver on that day. Now Mr Creek is of the opinion – he will not swear positively, but is strongly of the opinion – that the revolver was pledged by the prisoner at the bar. There was rather more than the usual opportunity of observing the person who pledged it. It becomes important that you should hear the very words in which the matter is sworn to. [His Lordship here read the evidence of Mr Creek, in which he refers to the cartridges, and asked the person pledging the revolver to unload it, and stated that he firmly believed the prisoner to be the man who pledged the clothes and the revolver.]

That is the evidence, I think you will say, of a careful and moderate man as to his belief of the identity of the prisoner with the person who pledged this revolver on 21 June. The man who pledged it took the same name as the prisoner took in undoubted transactions; he took the same street as the prisoner took in undoubted transactions. That is sworn to in the language I have read by a witness as to whose character and credulity you are the judges. But it does not rest there, because the young man Allwright identifies him also. He, who was standing by the side of Mr

Lefroy.

Creek, who had only ten days before had a transaction which we know was with the prisoner, because he has claimed the clothes, says that on the 21st the man who took the same name and place of abode as the prisoner was the prisoner at the bar. Then it is right to read to you how these witnesses were cross-examined. There is a great deal of cross-examination which, in my judgement, it was quite right to administer, because the learned counsel did not know what might come of it, and it was right to abandon it when he saw what came of it – I mean with regard to the second pistol. I may here say I don't think that any time has been wasted in this case. Mr Montagu Williams was quite right in pursuing this matter and in abandoning it when he saw that nothing came of it. The cross-examination of the young man Allwright was confined, as the Attorney-General pointed out yesterday, to a very brief amount of questioning. Now, gentlemen, in those cross-examinations, I must say that it does not suggest the idea of what was stated by Mr and Mrs Clayton. And I may say in passing, for my part, I think that the manly and simple course to take in this, as in other cases, is to open your case in cross-examination. Now, did the prisoner redeem that pistol on the 27th? It is an important question as to the pledging whether he redeemed it on the 27th, in determining whether he pledged it, because it is reasonably clear that the same man who pledged, redeemed. In fact, if you can be sure that he redeemed it, it is a very strong argument indeed that he pledged. I hope you appreciate, gentlemen, what I put. Did he redeem on the 27th? This is what Mr Creek says in cross-examination: 'I believe the man who pawned the revolver on the 21st is also the man who redeemed on the 27th; he did so between 11.00 and 12.00 a.m. I am sure of this partly by my own memory and partly also by the occupation of Allwright at the time.' Then Allwright is called. He says this: 'On the 27th, I remember being asked to bring a pistol which had been put away in the warehouse. I was downstairs. I had been at work, and was going to clean myself, and I stood in the passage with the pistol in my hand.' The effect of this is that Allwright brought up a pistol from the warehouse at the time Creek says the prisoner redeemed one. Now, that seems to be tolerably strong evidence that the person who redeemed the pistol was the prisoner, and that he must also have been the person who pledged it.

Against all that, what is there to be said? There is to be said nothing, it appears to me, except the evidence of Mr and Mrs Clayton. I don't say that the evidence of Mr and Mrs Clayton is to be disbelieved because they are relatives of the prisoner and interested in the matter. I suppose that persons less exalted than Brutus have in hundreds and thousands, in the present as in his own time, told the truth at the risk of doing injury to those they loved. Therefore, from the mere fact that Mr and Mrs Clayton

Fourth Day – Tuesday 8 November 1881.

were persons connected, however remotely, by blood with the prisoner at the bar, there is a reason for looking at their evidence carefully, but it is no reason for disbelieving it. But is the evidence in itself credible? That is a matter for you, but there are these difficulties in the way.

In the first place, not a word was ever said until they came here. They made no suggestion of it before the magistrates, no suggestion before the coroner that the murder could not have been committed with the weapon which was supposed to be connected with it, because that weapon had never belonged to the prisoner, and that the Lee who had pledged it and the Lee who redeemed it could not be the prisoner because the former man was never near the establishment on 21 June. Now, that would have been a most cogent matter to have brought forward at an early stage of this inquiry, and for my own part I am unable to conceive why, if it was true, it was not brought forward. Mr Clayton, whose evidence I will read to you in a moment, said that he knew it all along, that he knew it before the magistrates, that he knew it when he was before the coroner, and also when he heard the evidence of Creek there, who was examined six days before he was. He said he had read the papers and was deeply interested (as of course he was) in the case. He is a clerk and an educated man, his wife keeps a school, and he himself has a head upon his shoulders – in fact, he can put two and two together. He knows what is the relevancy of a piece of evidence, and his evidence was certainly very important if it was true. Why did he not tell that, if he knew it? Mr Williams intimated that he had been a little troubled by the questions put, and had not mentioned it, and had subsequently withheld it for the trial. At any rate, he did withhold it for the trial. It is immaterial, therefore, whether Mr Clayton was or was not embarrassed by the judicial manner of putting questions, as he deliberately withheld a piece of evidence which would have been most material if true. His wife also says that they knew it all along. She is asked, however, 'When did the importance of it first strike you? When did you first mention it?' The answer is, 'Two or three weeks ago; but it passed from my mind, in the first instance, until I talked to a friend'. Who was the friend? 'Well, I have forgotten,' she says. Further, what is the story itself? The story is that the man Clayton had to go to his business when his wife was near having her child, and that she felt ill. The prisoner then volunteered to stay at home, to go for a doctor if a doctor should be needed. There was, however, a very decent, intelligent young woman in the house. Why could she not go? There were also a number of pupils, and why could not they go? Mr Montagu Williams says she could not take one of her pupils for such a purpose; but I cannot see that either their own or their parents' feelings could have been hurt had they gone for a doctor for Mrs Clayton, considering the condition she

Lefroy.

was in. Then again, she went to see the prisoner several times during the day. Nothing that ingenuity or practised experience could bring forward has been wanting on the part of Mr Williams to lay this before you. There is another matter which Mr Williams characterised as a piece of homely evidence – that is, when Mrs Clayton said she remembered the 21st because a neighbour of hers had had a child on that day, and she had said she wished it had been her own. Joanna Chamberlain gives most important evidence when she says that what was done on the 21st was suggested to her only a week or two ago. It is not incredible that when the Claytons became aware of the importance of evidence relating to the date that they should have sent for Joanna Chamberlain and said, 'You remember that Mr Mapleton was at home on the 21st, all day long'. It was in the case of Mr and Mrs Clayton, in the case of their evidence being true, to get an independent person to say, 'I recollect that he was there'. Under the present circumstances, Joanna Chamberlain's evidence positively and negatively goes against them. The question, therefore, before you, is: on which side is the greatest preponderance of evidence? The result of this is an enormous preponderance of evidence, not absolutely uncontradicted, upon the circumstances of the 22nd.

With regard to the second pistol, I think you may dismiss that from your minds altogether.

Now, how was the prisoner at that time as to money? Upon that matter we have the evidence uncontradicted and unchallenged. On that morning, a circumstance took place which I will not enlarge upon in detail, because it might seem to distract your attention and make too much of the act of dishonesty in which the prisoner was concerned. 'Empty bags,' they say, 'cannot stand upright'; and an act of dishonesty many a man has been and will be guilty of who would shrink with horror from the crime of murder. Therefore, it affords no proof at all in the all-important question if did he or did he not murder Mr Gold, and you must cast it out of your mind. However, he, an educated man, did resort to a contrivance to get a few shillings – thirteen or fourteen shillings – but, unfortunately, it does not rest there. It is necessary from one point of view that I should refer to it. How did he cheat? He cheated by the use of two Hanoverian medals of the same kind as those which were found upon him and which were found on the bottom of the carriage which was covered with the blood, at least, of Mr Gold. Therefore, at least, the fact is important, as it places him in possession that morning of coins which have been called Hanoverian sovereigns. I never saw any of those coins before this trial, and why they are considered discreditable in this country I know not. It is important to remember that he had in his possession some of the coins with which he committed a petty fraud upon Mr Ellis, the stationer.

Fourth Day – Tuesday 8 November 1881.

That was the state of things when those two persons started in the train together. Then there is an immense weight of evidence, not absolutely uncontradicted, that the prisoner had a pistol; but there is absolutely uncontradicted evidence that he had Hanoverian medals. There is also strong evidence that he was in pecuniary straits. The two men got into the carriage. That is not disputed. Franks, the ticket inspector, stated that he observed no other person in the carriage. It may be that he has persuaded himself upon that matter, and he had, as you see by the evidence, remembered in detail more than you or I probably would be able to remember. Then, on the other hand, it is his duty to watch and remember these things and to prevent fraud on the railway. It is his function to remember these things. That observation you must take for what it is worth; but I should myself shrink from the recollection of the details which Franks retained in his memory. It is to be observed that people whose duty it is to look after certain and particular things retain a recollection of those things more so than we, probably, whose experience is more general. We rely a good deal upon notes, and so far we spoil our memory a great deal, but these men have to rely upon their memory. This is an observation which, by my experience, I am able to make. However, the two men get into the carriage together, and at Croydon they are seen together. Mr Gold had then his handkerchief over his face and head.

Now the train – I don't forget the slackening, to which I will refer presently – never really stopped between Croydon and Preston. At Preston, the carriage was found with Mr Gold not in it, but with the prisoner in it. Now, if there was no third person – Mr Gold had undoubtedly at that time been murdered and pretty nearly cut to pieces – if there was no third person, either Gold attacked the prisoner or the prisoner attacked Gold. There is no third view possible, if there was no third person. That is a most important question, which has been made important by the very able way in which Mr Williams has laboured to place it before you. He has said upon that point more than I should have thought was possible, and has said it in a way that was likely to impress you, as it impressed me. A judge gets hardened upon these things, but I was impressed upon this matter, and I have no doubt you were also. There is no evidence that there was a third person – that is, except for the suggestion of Mr Montagu Williams on the part of the prisoner, there is no evidence of a third person. No one saw him, and no traces of him are found. There is no actual tangible piece of evidence you can put your finger upon and say, under this piece of evidence lies a third man. Now, first of all, there were only three single first-class tickets issued at London Bridge Station. The numbers of those three first-class tickets are ascertained. Two were issued to a lady, and they have been returned. The third first-class ticket

Lefroy.

Lord Coleridge was issued to the man who it is not too strong to say was the prisoner, because it was found upon him. At Croydon there were only three first-class tickets issued, and they were used by ladies and have been returned. That is, all the first-class tickets issued to Brighton have been returned except the one numbered 3181, which was found upon the prisoner. If the evidence given by Franks and the man at Croydon be true, there were two people and only two people in the carriage in which Mr Gold and the prisoner sat, and the only way in which a third person could have got into the carriage would have been to have got into it either without a ticket or while the train was in motion.

Now, the train was an express train, and it went at express speed – except for slackening at Hassock's Gate – the whole of the way from Croydon to Brighton. But the slackening at Hassock's Gate would not do for getting in, as it is nearer Brighton than any spot where any of the articles were found. It will not do for the third man getting in there, but it might do for his getting out. If he was in the carriage, therefore, the third person must have got in while the express was passing. There is no doubt that it is possible for a person to get out of a train going at any speed, and to pass from one carriage to another. No doubt, as one of the witnesses said, it was a dangerous proceeding for anyone to undertake it who was not used to it. Still, one has heard of such things being done. But I never heard it suggested that anybody could get into a train going at sixty or thirty or even twenty miles an hour, though they might possibly have got out of it without injury either to life or limb. But, then, it is said that there might have been some return ticket issued at Brighton, and that the holder might have got into the train at London Bridge or Croydon, and might have perpetrated the murder somewhere between Croydon and Balcombe, and then have vanished into space. Well, that is possible – I mean the thing is within the bounds of possibility, no doubt. But this, like every other case, is not to be decided by what might be, but by what is the fair and reasonable inference to be drawn from the facts of the case.

Now, one would like to know about this third man, and how some of the difficulties in the way of this case are by any reasoning to be got over. I will assume him in the carriage, and so assuming him I will ask, where did he disappear? He must have been in the train down as far as Clayton tunnel, which is within a few miles of Preston, because just before the tunnel Mr Gold's umbrella is found. That must have been thrown out, and by the person who murdered Mr Gold. Well, the hat which is said to be the prisoner's must have been thrown out by somebody, and if it was thrown out by the supposed third person, that was about half-way between Burgess Hill and Hassock's Gate. Up to that time, the man must have been in the train, for the collar was found, and the prisoner, according to

Fourth Day – Tuesday 8 November 1881.

his own suggestion, did not throw his own collar out, but when he awoke from his swoon he found himself alone in the train, and without his collar. Well, it is suggested that he may have got out at Preston, and here I will make an observation which I was going to make when another suggestion was made, and made for the first time in the very able speech of Mr Montagu Williams. You will understand me as finding no fault with him, because I am quite aware that judges of eminence have sanctioned the practice which he pursued; and it is enough, in my opinion, to vindicate a person in the position of Mr Williams, that a judge of great eminence has distinctly and upon consideration sanctioned the course he took as a professional man. Therefore you will not understand me to make the smallest personal reflection upon him. But, eminent or not eminent, I must express my own opinion about the practice, and for my part, so far as my authority – which no man can undervalue more than myself – and my opportunities, which are not very many, go, I shall most steadily discountenance the practice.

I think it is a bad practice, and I will tell you why. I think this case is a very good evidence of it. You know it is really a suggestion made at the last moment through the lips of counsel, instructed to make it by the prisoner. Now it is open to the great objection, that it gives the prisoner – if it were to be encouraged and allowed, this enormous advantage, this unfair advantage – God forbid that he should not have an advantage, enormous or not, so that it is fair – but it gives him this unfair advantage, that he may say what he likes, not upon oath and without cross-examination. Many and many of us would like to say to him, 'Yes, but how do you account for this, and how do you explain that?' But you cannot, for he is protected from cross-examination. Judges have always permitted an undefended prisoner to say things which a counsel would be at once stopped if he were to say. But it is a very different thing when a counsel goes beyond suggestions – which he has a perfect right to do; he may say that the facts of the case are perfectly consistent with his suggestion – but if he proceeds to say that this or that is what the prisoner states, it appears to me then that he goes beyond the line of his professional duty, and beyond the line which in my judgement ought to be drawn, and I must say that so far as I can prevent it, I will. It leads to this, which in criminal cases is much to be deprecated. It leads of necessity, if the statement is sufficiently bold, to what we had yesterday, which I could not stop, and which I did not desire to stop, viz., a vigorous, argumentative, powerful reply from the counsel for the Crown. The counsel for the Crown must, if a statement is made by the prisoner which he thinks utterly untrue, show to the jury his reasons for disbelieving it. Therefore, it not only gives an unfair advantage to the prisoner, but it leads to a powerful reply from the counsel for the Crown,

Lefroy.

whose duty first of all is not that of the fierce impassioned advocate, but that of one who, in administering justice, endeavours so far as he can to put the case calmly and quietly before you. For these reasons, therefore, I must say that the practice, though it is sanctioned by the eminent and great authority to whom I have alluded, is one which I will never, so far as I can prevent it, permit.

However, the suggestion has been made that the third person got out close by Preston. Now, out of what carriage did he get? He was a man who, by hypothesis or suggestion, had got rid of his hat. Well, then, where did he go? Assuming that there was this third person, and that he was the guilty party, and that the person who did not commit the murder was deluged with blood, how did the person who did commit the murder manage to escape without a trace of blood? If he got out at Preston, where were all the inhabitants of the neighbourhood? Where were their eyes? A man covered with the stains of a tremendous murder – how was it that nobody got hold of him and asked him how he came to have that blood on him, or where his hat was? But more than that, the man must have seen Mr Gold and remarked the fact that he carried a watch and guard; he must have conceived the idea of attacking him, and he must have attacked him in the presence of the prisoner; he must have begun by rendering the prisoner insensible, and then commenced this murderous assault, continued for I do not know how long, upon Mr Gold. He kills Mr Gold, and gets rid of the body; then he gets rid of Mr Gold's hat and his umbrella, his purse, and a variety of other things; he disappears into space at Preston or somewhere else, and the witness, as the prisoner is on this assumption, remains insensible for a distance of something like twenty miles, and revives – comes back to his senses – just as the train arrives at Preston station. The whole thing is over; all the indicia, all the signs of the murder are got rid of, and, just as the train stops at Preston, the stunned and insensible witness awakes. From what are you to believe that there was a third person? There is no evidence. There is only the ingenious and eloquent suggestion of counsel for the defence, and there is this mass of evidence against it. I don't say it is an impossibility, but it is certainly a most extraordinary and remarkable theory.

Now let us go to what are the undoubted facts with regard to this journey. Two persons certainly, Mr Gold and the prisoner at the bar, were in the carriage. Mr Gibson, the chemist, hears at the entrance to the Merstham tunnel four shots. He is certainly right about that, as three bullet marks were found in the carriage and one bullet in Mr Gold's neck. That there were four bullets fired is beyond question. Now, then, that is at the beginning of the Merstham tunnel. That is seventeen miles from London; and between twenty-five and twenty-six miles from London,

Fourth Day – Tuesday 8 November 1881.

the struggle is seen at Horley by Mrs Brown and her daughter. I cannot suggest to you why you should disbelieve their statement. They had no kind of interest in the matter. That the struggle was prolonged is proved, because Mr Gold was a powerful man, and though he was assaulted and had a bullet in him, he was yet to prolong the encounter. If the prisoner was the person, you have the fact that he is a slight, delicate man, and probably not a match at all for Mr Gold without a pistol. But it may be that he was a great deal more than a match for him with the knife and pistol, and that someone used a pistol no one can doubt; and he is hacked to pieces, with fourteen knife wounds in different parts of his body, some of them very deep, and causing a great flow of blood. Now, then, that struggle is seen eight miles from where the report of the pistol was heard; the body, which Mr Bond says must have been thrown out when alive, is cast from the carriage, and the same witness thinks that probably the skull was fractured by the fall. That was at the entrance to Balcombe tunnel, between thirty-one and thirty-two miles from London, so that from seventeen to thirty-one miles from London the struggle was going on. That is an awful thing to consider. You have seen the carriage, and you will be as good judges as I am, probably far better, of the terrible incidents of the struggle. I do not know whether you ever read a great work by a great man, 'The Haunted House', by Thomas Hood. If you ever did, you will see there, told in words of great power, but without the use of a single repulsive or horrible expression, a story of a victim at once caged and haunted. That is by no means an inadequate account of what must have taken place inside the carriage.

The post-mortem examination made shows that fourteen wounds were inflicted besides the fracture, and shows proof of the use of a sharp knife used with relentless fierceness; and the fact of there being so many wounds in such different parts of the body, independent of the place where the body itself was found, and independently of the testimony of the two Browns, shows that the struggle must have been a long and protracted one. Now, Gold was a powerful man though he was an old man, and the other man was young though possibly weak. There is proof, therefore, before you that the struggle began with the discharge of the revolver, because Mr Gibson tells us that he heard four shots in rapid succession. The struggle goes on till there is an end of Mr Gold, and he is cast out, apparently still bleeding, and fighting for his life to the end, as you see by that dreadful piece of evidence of the bloody finger marks under the footboard of the carriage. Well, he dies, and his body is in Balcombe tunnel, and the train arrives at Preston Park, leaving Mr Gold in the tunnel breathing his last and the prisoner alone in the carriage.

From this time forward, everything he does and says becomes worthy

Lefroy.

of the closest attention. As far as I can make out everything that appears to be a datum in this case, almost everything that created suspicion, appears at this time to be passed unsuspected. When there was a fact which those who heard it ought to have communicated to those who could act upon it, it turned out that those who could have acted upon it never heard of the fact, and those who knew the fact never communicated it to those who could make use of it. I do not wish to blame anyone. It is much easier to be wise sitting up here than to be wise when having the conduct of a difficult matter offhand. I quite admit that, but still there is a want of cohesion in this case, from this point at which I have now arrived, which I must leave you to piece out as well as you can. I think it is Gibson who says he saw the watch, and he is told by the station master to tell the authorities at Brighton all about the case, but he never tells them a word about the watch. Still it is proved that the watch was seen, and Mr Williams, in a manly fashion, did not dispute the fact, and also the fact that it was Mr Gold's watch. Watson, the guard, says, when he got to Preston Park, he saw the prisoner standing on the platform, close to the compartment in which he had been riding, and he then goes on to describe what you have heard in evidence. Yet, after all that was then seen in reference to the prisoner's condition, the watch was put on the seat. That seems to me a most extraordinary thing to do.

Then the scene changes to Brighton, to the superintendent's office, where the prisoner was brought, and after what transpired there, it is a most extraordinary thing that Anscombe, who was the superintendent, did not prevent the prisoner's departure – did not say 'No, no; you must not go. You must stay here.' You have got all this important information. Stark, the ticket collector at Preston Park, substantially corroborates what Watson says, though the evidence of these two is not quite similar. Gibson, another ticket collector at Preston Park, makes a statement which, if true, is a most astonishing one, viz., that the prisoner, on being questioned, said he put his watch in his shoe for safety. This witness says Lefroy had a high hat on. The witness previous says a low hat. You cannot expect corroboration on every point. Undoubtedly, Lefroy had on a hat of some kind, and the witnesses had no motive for mentioning one hat in preference to another. When Gibson and Lefroy arrived at Brighton, it is due to the Brighton people to say that Gibson did not say one word about the watch or the countryman. Another point is: why was not Lefroy asked whether he had a return ticket? If he had, as he alleged, an engagement in the evening at his club, why in the name of common sense did he not take a return ticket? Particularly as he was pressed for money. But these questions do not seem to have been asked by anyone. In putting this, I am not conscious of putting anything that is not obvious to the commonest

Fourth Day – Tuesday 8 November 1881.

common sense. One cannot help thinking how these things could escape observation. The two Hanoverian coins found on the floor of the carriage were given back to Lefroy, and nobody troubled to see what became of the pocket-handkerchief. These little things are such as form strong links in a chain of evidence. There is the strongest possible proof that when the prisoner left Preston station in Gibson's company for Brighton, he had the watch, to which was attached a piece of chain, which chain was gone at Brighton. Mrs Gold says her husband wore a chain. If the broken piece of chain were attached to the watch, what has become of it? There seemed to be want of care in this instance. Watson put the watch and chain on the seat of the carriage. Perhaps he did not know enough of the matter to be blamed for what he did. The necessary inference is that the prisoner made away with the piece of chain between Preston and Brighton. In Hooper's evidence, the Hanoverian medals are again mentioned. I have no personal experience of these medals. If the prisoner was in the habit of using them innocently at games of whist, it was an important matter to mention in evidence.

Mr Oliver Weston was then examined. The observations of the Attorney-General with reference to him are worthy of your consideration, but I confess I cannot even now make out why he was called. All he said was that he was of opinion there was something wrong, that he could not account for the large quantity of blood, but he did not add to the case. He introduced a number of facts that were practically or actually contradicted by witnesses who had no interest in the case, any more than he had. Mr Weston is a town councillor of Brighton, and presumably a respectable man. He volunteered his evidence, and says he remarked when he saw the prisoner on the platform that the wound on his head was not a gunshot wound, but like one that would be caused by an umbrella. If he had known that Mr Gold had an umbrella, he might imagine that in his despair he would use it to defend himself against his assailant, but if he knew nothing of Mr Gold, and at the time nothing was known as to Mr Gold's death, and there was not a whisper about an umbrella, it strikes me that it was a very odd observation. There are people who persuade themselves of two things. First of all, that it is an important thing to appear in an important case; and next, that his evidence is the most important feature in it. Mr Weston is possibly a man of some self-importance, and therefore has got himself into this scrape. Mr Williams was quite right in what he said about him, but his evidence does not seem to me to be of any importance, and therefore I will not trouble you with the contradictions.

[*Having referred to the evidence of Martin, the policeman in the service of the Brighton Railway, and of Mr Terry, the Chief Constable, and pointed out that the statement of the prisoner that he had come to*

Lefroy.

*Brighton to see Mrs Nye Chart had been contradicted by that lady, who
knew nothing whatever about him, his Lordship continued:*]

The prisoner's counsel, Mr Williams, says that he went down to meet
a young lady, and that he would not say who she was, and that the young
lady would not come forward. Now, can anyone believe that statement
which the prisoner instructed his counsel to make? First of all, he is
on trial for his life, and it would be something like suicide if, having a
witness whom he might call to an important part of his story, he refused
to call her. But, in the second place, is there any English girl who would
see a man hung sooner than herself come forward to say that he went
to Brighton for the perfectly legitimate purpose of meeting her? I don't
suppose that there is an English girl capable of such conduct, and I don't
believe you do either. But gentlemen, there is an untruth told by the
mouth of his counsel, and it is a libel on Englishwomen.

*His Lordship then read the evidence of Mr Hall, the surgeon,
after which the court adjourned for luncheon.
After the reassembling of the court, his Lordship said:*

There is not very much more of this tiresome work of reading the
evidence to be gone through, because, as soon as I have done with the
Brighton witnesses, I can resume summarising the case to you in my own
language.

[*His Lordship then read the evidence given by Anscombe, Howland,
Tobutt, Berry, Holmes, and other witnesses, and in commenting upon it
said:*]

With regard to the prisoner's statement respecting the watch, we know
he had not lost this watch; nor was it a metal chain, as described by the
prisoner, but a thin gold chain that was attached to it, and which was
broken off Mr Gold's body. There was at one time a question whether the
prisoner heard the remark made by Brown to Holmes about the finding
of the body, but Mr Montagu Williams has elected to assume that it was
heard. The subsequent statement of the prisoner – 'I bought the watch
from a friend of mine some time ago' – was admitted to be untrue. Then,
with regard to the surgical bandage which was round the prisoner's head,
there was no blood on it, although the prisoner represented that he had
been so brutally maltreated, and, you know, when it was produced, I
expressed surprise that there was no blood on it. It is unfortunate that the
persons who saw some of the most important things did not state those
things to people who had to act upon them. The statements to the people
with whom he got into conversation, the statements about the countryman
and about his getting off, the variety of statements about the medals,
Mrs Nye Chart, et cetera: all of these are proved to be untrue. He was

Fourth Day – Tuesday 8 November 1881.

found in the possession of Gold's watch, undoubtedly, and the inference is that he had made away in some way of another with Gold's watch. He had used Hanoverian medals in the morning, and in the afternoon medals of a similar description are found in the railway carriage. It has been endeavoured to instil into your minds that his flight to London and residence with Mrs Bickers was the result of weakness. Well, it might be the result of weakness, but it might equally be the result of guilt. In his flight, he may have thought of the evidence which was being piled up against him, and that the centre of four millions of people was about the best hiding place he could find. But nothing is more useless than to speculate upon motives.

There is one matter which neither learned counsel has been able to show, and that is whether the prisoner at the bar was aware of Mr Gold's habits, or, indeed, knew his person at all. One cannot tell whether he knew Mr Gold in consequence of his being a constant traveller upon the line, or from any other reason. We have no right whatever to make any such presumption against the prisoner. At any rate, if he went to the London Bridge station with a revolver, he could hardly have gone there with an innocent purpose. Whether he went there intending to meet Mr Gold we cannot tell, or whether he went there for the purpose of taking from anybody whom he encountered that money of which he stood so much in need, we cannot tell either.

The question in this, as in every case, is: does the ultimate probability amount to the reasonable certainty which the law expects? It is not that this fact proves it or that that fact proves it, but is the whole story of the evidence against the prisoner fairly reconcilable with his innocence? If it is reasonably reconcilable with innocence, then it is not a question of benefit, as Mr Montagu Williams stated, but a question of right – the prosecution has not fulfilled the duty cast upon them. If there is a reasonable doubt, and it must be reasonable, the person said to be the guilty person must have the benefit; but if, on the other hand, the prosecution have made out their case, you must act as men of honour and men of conscience upon the evidence which reasonably satisfies you. At the end of this long enquiry, gentlemen, I will not make any complimentary remarks. I have seen that you are intelligent men, and I believe you to be men of probity and men of honour. All I can do is to remind you that it is your duty in this case to hold the scales of justice perfectly even as between the prisoner, who is entitled to be acquitted if he has not been proved guilty of this crime, and the Queen, who in this case represents the country, and who has a right to claim at your hands the repression of unbridled violence and the punishment of atrocious crime. The question is: has it been proved that this unbridled violence has been committed by the prisoner? Is it proved,

Lord Coleridge

or not, that this atrocious crime was done by him? If not, he is entitled to be acquitted; if otherwise, he must be found guilty. And, gentlemen, I trust, in a case like this, where the life of a man is at issue, it is not taking the awful name of God in vain to hope that He will guide you rightly.

The Verdict.

At 2.35 pm, the jury retired.
They returned into court at 2.45 pm and answered to their names.

The CLERK OF ARRAIGNS (Mr Read): Gentlemen, are you all agreed upon your verdict?

The FOREMAN OF THE JURY: We are.

The CLERK: Do you find the prisoner guilty or not guilty of the felony and murder with which he stands indicted?

The FOREMAN: Guilty.

The CLERK: You say that he is guilty, and that is the verdict of you all?

The FOREMAN: Yes.

The CLERK: [*Addressing the prisoner, who stood up.*] Percy Lefroy Mapleton, you stand convicted of the wilful murder of Frederick Isaac Gold. Have you or have you not anything to say for yourself why the court should not pass sentence upon you?

The PRISONER [*in a firm voice*]: Merely to thank the jury for the careful -- [*The remainder of the prisoner's remarks, if there were any, was lost in the proclamation of silence while sentence of death was pronounced.*]

Mr Justice COLERIDGE then assumed the black cap and said: Percy Lefroy Mapleton, you have been convicted upon the clearest evidence of a ferocious murder – a murder perpetrated by knife and pistol upon an old man, a harmless man, a man who had done you no harm, and a man who perhaps was altogether unknown to you. You have been justly and rightly convicted, and it is right and just that you should die. The sentence is not the sentence of the weak mortal who utters it, but it is the sentence of the English law, of which he is the minister. I will not harrow you, nor endanger my own self-command, by going into the facts of the murder, and by attempting to estimate your moral guilt. He only who knows the temptation can estimate the sin, and it is not sin, but crime, which I sit here to punish. The law punishes your crime; your sins, whatever they may be, will be judged hereafter. The sentence of the court upon you is that you be taken from hence to the place from whence you came, and from thence to the proper place of execution, and that you be there hanged by the neck until you are dead, and that you be taken to the Sheriff of Sussex for the execution of this sentence. And may God have mercy upon your soul.

Lord Coleridge

SEVERAL OF THE JURORS: Amen!

The PRISONER then turned towards the jury box and said: 'Gentlemen of the jury. Some day, when too late, you will learn that you have murdered me.'

He was then removed from the dock, and the court broke up.

Appendices.

APPENDIX I.

Lefroy's Life in Prison.

————

HER MAJESTY'S PRISON,
MAIDSTONE.

8th Novr. 1881

Sir,

I have the honour to inform you that Percy Lefroy Mapleton alias Arthur Lefroy was this day convicted at the Assizes held here of the Wilful Murder of Frederick Isaac Gold, at Balcombe, Sussex, and sentenced to Death.

He was this afternoon removed to Lewes Prison the place appointed for his execution.

> I have the honour to be
> Sir,
> Your most obedt. servant
> Wm. Green
> Governor

The Right Hon.ble
The Secretary of State
Home Department
Whitehall[64]

————

Lefroy was removed at five o'clock in the evening from Maidstone Gaol to Lewes Gaol, where he will undergo the last penalty of the law. He was accompanied by two warders, and was conveyed in a cab to the South-Eastern Railway station, and on alighting from the vehicle he was hurried handcuffed into the middle compartment of a second-class railway carriage, where four prison officials – two from Lewes and two from Maidstone – took their seats beside him. He was attired in a black frock coat and silk hat, while his handcuffed hands were hidden

64   TNA: PRO HO 144/83/A6404/18.

by a thin overcoat. Reaching the station a few minutes before the train started, the carriage containing him was taken some distance up the line to hide him from the view of the large crowd which had assembled, despite the efforts made to keep his departure secret, and at the time for departure, ten minutes past five o'clock, the carriage was brought back and coupled to the train, and the journey commenced. It was expected that he would change carriages at Tunbridge Wells, but instead of this the South-Eastern carriage was detached and attached to the direct Lewes trains on the Brighton line.

On reaching Lewes Lefroy was at once conveyed to the prison in a cab attended by two warders. A large mob had assembled and they greeted him with groans and jeers.

It is expected that the execution will take place on the 28th or 29th inst.[65]

————

It appears that Lefroy slept well and soundly on Tuesday night.[66] In fact, he was more composed than he appeared at any time during his incarceration in Maidstone Gaol. The execution will take place at Lewes.[67]

————

It appears that so sanguine was Lefroy that a verdict of acquittal would be returned by the jury, that on the morning of the summing up he wrote a note to his sister, who was staying at Maidstone, asking her to have a cab in readiness for him directly after his trial was over, and saying he wished to leave Maidstone at once, and to escape observation as far as possible.

It is stated that the solicitor for the defence is preparing a memorial to the Home Secretary, praying that the extreme sentence may not be carried out on the ground that Lefroy's father and grandfather died insane. It is stated that the execution has been fixed for Tuesday, November 29th, at nine o'clock in the morning. Lefroy is said to be the son of a Captain Mapleton. He was born abroad, and the name 'Lefroy' was given to him at his baptism out of the respect which his father entertained for a brother officer. The convict is an orphan.

Miss Mapleton, the convict's sister, was so overwhelmed that she has since the event temporarily lost her reason, though at the latest report there were hopes that she was recovering.[68]

---

65   *Berrow's Worcester Journal*, 12 November 1881.
66   The night following the closing of the trial.
67   *Reynolds's Newspaper*, 13 November 1881.
68   Presumably Eliza, as Mary had married in 1874, losing the Mapleton surname.

Appendix I.

All the arrangements for the execution of Lefroy are in the hands of Mr. Bull, the under-sheriff; Marwood will be the executioner. The last execution (and the first private one) in Lewes Gaol, was that of Martin Brown in January 1869, for the murder of David Baldy on Newmarket Hill, Sussex.[69]

———————

Yesterday (Saturday) a lengthened letter was received from the convict Lefroy by his sister. The prisoner states that it must be a fearful trouble to his sister and all his relatives. He adds that he learns that efforts are being made to get him respited, and he trusts that the real murderer will be brought to justice. He still declares his innocence. He however admits that he was most ably defended, and expresses his best thanks to all who took an interest on his behalf.

Yesterday morning, Lefroy was visited in his cell by Captain Crickett.[70] He looked extremely pale, and seemed weak. He is reported not to have slept so soundly during the night as previously, but he partook of a hearty breakfast at eight a.m., and afterwards exercised himself a little by walking up and down in his cell, and having his hands folded. During the forenoon he was visited by the prison chaplain, who remained with him some time, and offered up prayers on his behalf. Prisoner, when asked if he had any complaint to make, stated, 'No, dear, no; I am treated here in every way kind. The governor and officials are all very good to me.'

The petition which will be presented to the Home Secretary asking for a respite will be forwarded next week. It will be pointed out that the prisoner's father was comparatively speaking an old man when Lefroy was born, and that he died insane.[71]

———————

The convict Lefroy, now lying in Lewes Gaol, awaiting the execution of the sentence passed upon him as the murderer of Mr Gold, continues in the same demeanour which has characterised his conduct during his long incarceration. Yesterday[72] he was visited by Mr Dutton, his solicitor. He was then occupying the condemned cell in the north-east wing of the prison, and the interview, prolonged as it was, took place in the ordinary apartment in which prisoners are permitted to see their friends. During the interview the prison officials were present, and it is stated that the only alteration in Lefroy's appearance since he left Maidstone after his conviction is due to the fact that he is now attired in convict dress,

69   *Reynolds's Newspaper*, 13 November 1881.
70   George Augustus Crickett, Governor of Lewes Gaol.
71   *Reynolds's Newspaper*, 13 November 1881.
72   17 November 1881.

Lefroy.

instead of the garments which he wore during the trial. Lefroy spoke without hesitation as to his treatment in prison. He expressed his warmest thanks to those who had been attending upon him, and was even glad that the excitement of the trial had passed away. He was perfectly calm and collected, and referred to the murder of Mr Gold as a subject which really did not concern him to any serious degree. He was fully alive to the fact that he had been convicted of Mr Gold's murder, and seemed to be resigned altogether to his fate. In fact when informed that efforts were being made to obtain a respite on the ground of insanity, he persisted as strongly as ever in his innocence, indicating thereby that he wished no such plea to be made on his behalf. Mr Dutton questioned him very closely, the lines of the defence which had been set up at his own request were reviewed from beginning to end, and the unhappy man adhered rigidly to the first statement that he made. There was an object in view when these test questions were put to the convict, and it was singular that he adhered to the original account of the whole transaction almost in the form he instructed his solicitor. In the course of the conversation which took place, Mr Dutton asked Lefroy if he was satisfied with the way in which his defence had been conducted. The culprit answered that he was more than satisfied, and that he believed that everything possible had been done on his behalf. Here, again, Lefroy introduced the subject of the third party, and it is the belief of his friends that he will cling to this idea until the last as the only means of escape. During Mr Dutton's interview he asked Lefroy why, after so patient a trial, he should have turned to the jury, and told them that 'some day, when it was too late, they would learn that they had murdered him'. Lefroy simply replied, 'I could not help it, Mr Dutton'. The same indifference has marked his conduct during the whole time of his imprisonment, but it is thought probably that, although he has so little to say upon the subject of his guilt, he will before the fatal day arrives, make a clear confession.[73]

HIS FAREWELL INTERVIEW WITH MR. AND MRS. CLAYTON

Mr. Clayton and his wife, and their eldest little boy, aged seven,[74] paid a farewell visit to Lefroy at Lewes Prison on Friday afternoon last week.[75] The little boy, who was entirely ignorant of the fate awaiting the condemned man, was present at his special request made at the interview on the previous day. The child was a great favourite of Lefroy's, and it is said that he looked forward to the visit from him with great interest. He was allowed to see the child in his cell, the Deputy-Governor being present for the ten minutes that the interview lasted. Lefroy tenderly caressed the little fellow, and in parting with him appeared to be

[73]   *Daily Chronicle*, 18 November 1881.
[74]   Melville Graham Clayton (1874–1948).
[75]   25 November 1881.

Appendix I.

more moved than since his conviction. Subsequently Lefroy was conducted by warders to the iron cage where prisoners are permitted to receive visits from their relatives and friends. As on the previous day, Mr. and Mrs. Clayton were allowed to converse through a single set of gratings with Lefroy, who had a warder on either side of him, closely watching his every moment. He still maintained his self-possessed and cheerful demeanour, and looked in good health. Although wearing the prison garb, his hair had not been cut nor his moustache removed. He conversed freely, but made not the slightest reference to the crime for which he stood condemned. He requested Mr. Clayton to convey messages of thanks to those persons who had written letters of sympathy to him and subscribed to the fund to defray the expense of his defence. Again he spoke, but with increased hopefulness, of meeting Mr. and Mrs. Clayton in heaven, saying he was quite prepared to die. Just as the interview was about to terminate, Lefroy warmly shook hands with Mr. Clayton; but, before saying farewell to Mrs. Clayton, he kissed her, and appeared to be deeply moved.[76]

———

Mr. Foster, an inhabitant of Hastings, who was tried at the last Quarter Sessions in that town for attempted suicide,[77] and who passed the period intervening between his committal by the Hastings borough magistrates and his trial before the Recorder, in the infirmary cell in Lewes gaol, with Percy Lefroy Mapleton,[78] has, in answer to questions put to him, made the following statement:

Do I hold him to be guilty? Well, as my opinion goes for nothing, and there is no harm in saying so now, I may say that I do. We used to get the newspapers, but before we got them they used to cut everything out about the trial, and Lefroy himself did not seem inclined himself to speak much about it. I was put with him in the infirmary cell and with a young chap named Morris,[79] who got upon

---

76   *The Penny Illustrated Paper*, 3 December 1881.

77   John Foster, a fruiterer, who attempted to commit suicide on a path near Castledown, Hastings on 15 May 1881 (*Hastings and St Leonards Observer*, 21 May 1881). In the *Daily Chronicle* of 12 November 1881, Foster is quoted as saying, 'I was in [Lewes Gaol] for attempting to commit suicide. My wife died, and my daughter also, and on the day she died my goods were seized, and that was how it came about. I am now, thank God, a total abstainer, and some friends are going to help me make a fresh start in life. If I can get a start I have no doubt I can have a good business in a few months. The months I was in prison did me good, as I had time to think of my past life.'

78   This was in the period between Lefroy's own committal and trial.

79   John Morris, who was also charged with 'attempting to commit suicide', appeared before magistrates at Eastbourne Police Court on 8 August 1881. *The Eastbourne Gazette* of 10 August 1881 described him as presenting 'a rather dejected appearance, and looked as if he were really tired of life, and absolutely careless of everything around him'. He was identified as the same man who had also attempted suicide a month earlier by taking poison after losing all his money at the Goodwood races, with the *Brighton Herald* of 30 July 1881 describing the twenty three year old as 'a well-dressed young man, of Jewish cast of features, with a peculiar expression of the eyes'.

Lefroy.

the line at Eastbourne. I went in on July 23 and left on Oct. 18. Morris, I, and Lefroy all slept in the same room. This room contained four beds. I should say the infirmary where we slept was about 80 ft. long by 20 ft. I can assure you we had fine doings. Talk about a prison! If it was not for the confinement, you would hardly think it was one. I scarcely touched prison fare while I was there. Lefroy was kept well supplied with hampers, and all sorts of luxuries, except, of course, alcoholic liquors, and I can tell you, as a fact, that Lefroy is related by marriage to a certain noble earl, from whose cook came an elaborate supply of everything in the shape of eatables.

What sort of a dispositioned young man was he, you ask me? Well, I should say a seemingly more kind-hearted, nice young fellow doesn't breathe. No one could possibly believe him to be guilty of murder. Whatever came into the prison to him was as much ours as his. Of course we did get talking occasionally about the murder, and I put certain questions to him, but, as a rule, he did not seem to care to discuss the matter, although, whenever we spoke of it, he professed his innocence, and seemed confident of getting off. I used to take two or three points, and say to him, 'Well, if you can explain why you went from home that night you ran away, I think you will do'. But he did not like to enter into the matter, and always said, 'We are prepared for that'. He told me also at another time he had heard from his lawyer, Mr Dutton, that they had picked up the pistol half a mile from the railway station, and he used to say that that was in itself conclusive as to his innocence, because no man in his senses could imagine he could have thrown the pistol half a mile from the railway carriages. I repeat he was very lively the whole time we were there, up to a few days before the trial, when his spirits became depressed. But this was owing to a cold which he caught sitting at an open window. He would insist on having that open, and I told him before that just before the time when he wanted his strength most he would be getting a cold. Under this cold he became depressed, but never morose. He might, therefore, [have] seemed to be affected by the trial, when in reality his depression was owing to physical and not to mental causes. He used to have a good many visitors to see him. His sister had been several times, and his solicitor and his solicitor's clerks several times.

We were up to all sorts of tricks in the gaol. You would certainly never think that one of us was a man who stood in peril of his life with a horrible charge of murder hanging over his head, for although we were all as merry as crickets he was the liveliest of the lot. In speaking of crickets, cricket was our chief fun every day. Mr. Clifford Clarke[80] here will tell you that he came one day into the cell and saw Lefroy with me playing cricket. You see this tall hat of mine with the bulges in it? Of course we wore our ordinary clothes, and not the prison dress. We used to make this hat the wicket, get Morris's bolster for the bat, and Lefroy taking off

---

80 Clerk to Lefroy's solicitor, Mr Dutton.

Appendix I.

his stockings, we used to roll them into a ball, and have rare fun. We used to have concerts, too, when we were tired of cricket. Lefroy did not sing, as he was no singer, so I supplied the vocalisation, and we used to make music with our hair combs, putting a piece of paper over the combs, and in this way blowing out jigs and songs to the most capital tunes in the most enjoyable way. Were we never interfered with? No. It is very different with people who are waiting for their trial and those convicted. We were kept right away from them, and the wardens rarely came to see us unless it was in the early morning and late evening, and meal times. We also used as a cricket-bat a piece of one of our bedsteads, which we had skilfully manipulated for the purpose. What do you mean by manipulation! That goes for nothing. You know we are forbidden forks or knives in the place, but I can tell you I made three forks out of three sardine boxes, and at night we used to employ these in eating our food. The warders never knew anything about it, and when we had used them we always hid them away.

Lefroy used to boast considerably that he could easily get out, and that he had instruments about him for the purpose. He used to point to the bars and say it would not be very difficult to get through them. And I do believe he had a notion, for he always had such confidence in himself that he had only to make the attempt to succeed in making his escape. He used to relate many incidents of his former life, and seemed pleased to have listeners, and he told us of the society he had been in both in Australia and this country. Some of these stories, I can assure you, although I don't think he was morally a very dissipated young man, would not bear repeating in the columns of this paper. His greatest weakness seemed to be a love of money and extravagance, for he used to speak of the large sums of money which he used to lay out, in order, as it seemed to me, to make others believe him to be of a higher social position than he really was. He did not appear to think these were weaknesses at all, except on one occasion, when I was saying that drink was my misfortune, he said, 'Ah, drink is not mine, but something else,' from which I concluded that it was a very bad form of dissipation. I know he did not like drink, because we were each of us allowed a pint of beer a day. My allowance took the shape of stout, whilst Lefroy's consisted of ale, and frequently he used to give me his pint without tasting it himself.

He seemed to have had a great deal to do with theatricals, and he was really clever in this. He was a capital reciter, and when we were tired of the cricket and concert of combs, he used to treat us to some recitations, very excellently delivered.

Lefroy was also a capital hand at making cigarettes – in fact, I never knew a better. We used to smoke cigarettes at night-time. You say, how did we get the tobacco? We had none at all, but we had plenty of the very best tea – more than we could use – which was sent in by his high-station friends. He used to take the tea and roll it up in thin paper, and we had splendid cigarettes. During our

Lefroy.

concerts and our recitations we would smoke away in fine style, from eight until ten o'clock, and the warders never came to interrupt us. Although they saw the gas alight in our place, they never interfered with us. I don't mind saying too, now that the case is over, that there was a great deal more in the food which used to be sent in than used always to appear to the eyes of the Governor and the warders. I remember taking up a plumcake one day that had been sent in to Lefroy, and, on breaking it asunder, finding four half-crowns in the centre.

We used to go to bed, as a rule, shortly after ten o'clock, and really I think that the best sleeper of all was Lefroy himself. He seemed to sleep soundly all through the night; in fact, I never knew him to wake up more than once, and then he was very restless in bed. In the morning I asked him if he remembered what he did, and he replied, 'No', and on my telling him he said, 'Oh, I must have been fighting with Watson in my sleep'.

Did he appear as if he had any sense of religion? Well, I can't say that he did, at all events when he first came in; but although you may think that I am not much of a one myself for the Bible, I really think I got him to read it; for I used always to be praising the Book, and saying what a grand Book it was, and that no person came to ill by reading it – and especially I used to point out what beautiful things the Proverbs were, and at last I got him to read the Bible at times. We used to go to chapel every morning. Lefroy never used the Book of Prayer, and he used to say he did not require one. I don't think he attended much to the chaplain's ministrations, for they were not very good friends. A day or two before I left, the chaplain said to him, 'I shall have something to say to you when you come back'. Lefroy took that up as meaning that the chaplain had already condemned him, and afterwards said, 'I would rather chop my hand quite off than speak to him again'. I remember on one occasion – although he held that he would surely disprove his guilt – assuming the probability of his being condemned, and I asked him what he thought about the matter. He said, 'If I am condemned, I will face death like a man; it will not put me out'.

At another time I asked him how he got to London from Wallington, when he left his cousin's house. He said that walk was the worst thing he ever had to endure. During the journey he sat on one of the bridges for four hours, tired and worn out. When he reached London he went to a friend and got some money. He also told me that what he greatly regretted was that he was not able to find his way to Ireland – he was detained in England through want of money – for he felt if only he could had reached there that he would have been quite safe. He used to think it was great fun in deceiving everybody as to his whereabouts when the police were pursuing him, and he used to give me the names of several people whom he stated that he had mystified, and asked me when I got out to call upon them. He particularly asked me to go to Mrs Brown's,[81] at Stepney, to see if they knew

---

81   *Sic*: Mrs Bickers.

Appendix I.

anybody of the name of Clark, an engineer, from Liverpool. That was his way of joking.

Another thing I noticed in his character was that he was very hot-headed, and if you dared him to do a thing that would be the thing he would be most likely to do. I only remember him strange in his manner once, and that was one evening. He then said, 'I feel I must do something serious before I go to sleep'. I replied laughingly, 'Then you had better throw your book – the Bible – through the window'. No sooner said than done, for he did throw the book from him, but whether he intended it to go through the window or not I cannot tell. It broke one or two panes of glass, however. The next day he apologised to the governor for what he had done. He was a most restless fellow, unless when writing or reading. But his restlessness seemed to come from real good nature, and to be a boiling over with a love of saying smart things, and practical joking. One day he got this hat that I am wearing, and he and Morris poured a tin of condensed milk into it; you can see the marks now. That seemed to amuse him mightily. He is undoubtedly a well-educated fellow, and knows how to use his tongue. I can assure you he used to say that in prison he was never more comfortable in life, and as we were carrying on our games, and enjoying all the good things which were sent in to him, he used to say he would not mind having two years of that kind of thing – he was getting used to it. He was very generous, and would give away anything he had. Do you see this collar I am wearing now? Well, this was given to me by Lefroy, and it is the identical collar he had on when he left his cousin's house at Wallington.

Once when we were talking, I asked him how he accounted for the chain. He then spoke more about the murder than he had ever done before. He said there was a third person in the carriage, and the matter of the chain would be explained. I said to him, 'If you can explain this, and one or two other little points, you will get scot-free, but if you cannot you are certainly the man who did it'. He then remarked quietly to me, 'Do I look like it?' I said I did not think so – he was one of the last I should suspect of having done a deed of that kind, and he could not and would not have done it, I am sure unless he was quite out of his mind. I did not attach so much importance to the case while I was in prison, as I find the public have attached to it since I have been out. Lefroy used to have a book sent him containing the evidence, and this I and Morris used to read as well as himself.

He was not a very robust man, and he used to complain very much of spitting blood. On the doctor coming in the morning, he would allow him his handkerchief, on which were marks of blood, but I could not make up my mind whether Lefroy did not put it on, as I did not see any spitting of blood in the day time. His appearance, however, gave one the idea that he was a young man who was in consumption.

Lefroy.

Here is a letter which I have received from him since I have been out. He tells me to 'beware of the vidders'. The meaning of that is that I jokingly told him there were 27 widows in Hastings, each one of whom was anxiously waiting my coming out with the desire to marry me:

Her Majesty's Prison, Maidstone, Kent,
Nov. 1, 1881.

Dear Mr. Foster, — I owe you a very great apology for not answering the very kind note addressed to me by Mr. Clifford Clarke on your behalf, but I really have had so much to think about that I unfortunately left unanswered several letters, and yours amongst the number. I was very glad to hear of your success last week, which, however, was only what I expected. I trust that the testimonial will realise your utmost expectations, and that your kindness of heart and disposition, of which I have had many a proof, will meet with success in all you undertake. You and I have spent many and many an hour together, and I am glad to find there is one man in Sussex who thinks that after all I may not be as black as I am painted. I tried to see your place at East Farleigh, but was not able to identify it from your description. I have not heard from Maurice[82] yet, and need hardly say I shall be glad if you can give me a look in at any time. You did me many little acts of kindness, and whatever faults society at large may impute to me, ingratitude is not one of them. Please remember me to Mr. Savery, whom I have not forgotten, and take this friendly little warning, slightly altered for the occasion – 'Foster, my boy, beware of the vidders.' – Yours very truly,

Mr. J. Foster   PERCY L. MAPLETON

When did I leave Lefroy? I left him on Oct. 18. You see Morris then left to take his trial, and, as they do not permit two persons to be in the cell together, I was taken out also, and placed in a cell by myself. We were parted in the passage after Church. I saw him afterwards in the yard up till the time I came away. I was tried on the 26th.

He was very fond of me, and was like a brother. I told him the history of my life, and he was very interested. I used to look after the food and that. I was like a valet to him, as he did not understand that sort of thing. I wrote a letter to him yesterday (Thursday) morning, and told him our lives would make a very nice history. When they separated us I shook hands and parted from him. In the exercise time he told me he had got some poison – prussic acid, I think it was. At any rate, he said it would kill dogs immediately. You ask, Do I think he is insane? No, I certainly do not. He himself laughed at the idea. He can't bear the chaplain, and I am sure, now that he has gone back to Lewes, he won't have anything to

---

82   *Sic*: Morris

Appendix I.

say to him.[83] I feel rather grieved that he is going to be hung, after living with him over three months. He told me I could make what use I liked of what I heard and saw. He said, 'It can't injure me'. If we did anything in prison he took it upon himself. I do not think that was a sign of insanity; he was too clever to be insane. He never used to say any prayers. He seemed to like getting his name up. I quite liked him after I had been there four or five weeks. I was no more afraid of him than nothing at all. I never feared him. If he tried anything of that sort I should be equal to him. Still he was strong, and had muscles like wire. When he hit the ball, playing at cricket, it came back like a cannon ball, and I used to turn my back to it. He had more strength than I thought he had. That was not quite consistent with the blood-spitting business. I made a spittoon, but I never saw any blood in it. I wrote to him at Maidstone, but I don't think he had the letter, as I saw in the papers that some were kept from him. The reference to my place at East Farleigh means that I told him of a large house at the top of the hill there which would come to me when my cousin dies. When I left I sent word to him by one of the officials that I wished him good-bye.

I never had such a game in my life as I had there. He was always up to something or other. They used to knock my hat about, and they would dress it up and stick it up somewhere. I don't know what the governor thought of it. I shall never forget what I saw there as long as I live. I am sure he was not insane. He used to know which were the best things in the hamper, and I used to think to myself, 'He is no fool'. He hardly ever mentioned Mr Gold, and when he did it was when I brought it up. I could not see how he could get out of the charge, but he used to say he was prepared. He was very fond of music, and if he could hear any in the distance he would get up to the window and open it. They would not shave him, and he asked me to get some paper and singe it off, but that was too warm for him. I should have liked to have done it for the sake of the Governor; he would have wondered how he got his moustache off. I should like to see him once more, after being with him so many weeks. We used to rise at six o'clock, make up our beds, and sweep up the room. We used to take turns in cleaning the room. At eight o'clock the officer used to call with gruel for one and cocoa for two, and bread. Breakfast consisted either of beef or mutton, or ham and eggs with fowl after. Church time was at nine o'clock; at half-past we returned and read the daily news; at half-past ten the doctor called, and the Governor at eleven. Dinner was at twelve, exercise at two, tea at half-past five, and bedtime at nine o'clock. The gas was left on all night so that the night watchman could see through the hole in the wall.[84]

———

83   Although a letter from Lefroy to his cousin Annie Clayton published in the *Daily Chronicle* of 16 November 1881 states: 'I saw the chaplain yesterday for the first time, and like him very well. When General Lefroy was living at Blackheath he (the chaplain) knew him very well'.

84   *Daily Chronicle*, 12 November 1881.

APPENDIX II.

A Defence of Mr Oliver Weston.[85]

———————

No-one enjoys a greater freedom of language than the learned counsel engaged to defend a prisoner arraigned on a capital charge. Not only does he claim for his client the benefits of every doubt which can be thrown upon the facts alleged against him, but he not unfrequently makes 'ducks and drakes' of the reputation of such witnesses as may have advanced testimony to him inconvenient. There is an old saying that:

'Wretches hang that jurymen may dine.'

Similarly, it not unfrequently happens that learned counsel mercilessly gibbet any unfortunate witness that may obstruct the theory they weave out of their ingenuity for the entanglement of the judgement of juries. We had a notable instance of this in the course of the Lefroy trial, in the address made by Mr Montagu Williams on behalf of the prisoner. The Attorney-General, in replying to Mr Williams, felt it necessary to take exemption to the peculiar line of the learned counsel's argument in one particular, and it is our desire to express what must be the feeling of a large number of the public, concerning his treatment of an important witness – Mr Oliver Weston – in regard to another matter. To the learned counsel this witness may be but a name, and his reputation a shuttlecock for the learned counsel's recreation, but we, in Brighton, who know Mr Oliver Weston as a member of the Town Council, and a man whose honourable and upright conduct is a proverb, cannot but feel indignant at the way he has been treated. There is clearly a discrepancy in the evidence of some of the witnesses with regard to what occurred when Lefroy arrived at the Brighton Station, and Mr Oliver Weston's statement of what occurred is contradicted by Mr Anscombe, who denies that he was present at all during the inquiry at the station master's office. Upon this Mr Montagu Williams thought proper to impute to him what amounts to perjury of the worst kind, and to stigmatise it in such brilliant terms as 'diabolically wicked', 'vile', and 'false', 'an invention', and 'monstrous', as it would be, indeed, if the evidence he adduced were not true, for it has a material bearing on the case, and affords a suggestion as to the marks on Lefroy's person which does not appear to have occurred to anyone else.

*

---

85   *The Brighton Gazette*, 10 November 1881.

Lefroy.

Now no-one who knows Mr Oliver Weston will believe either that he is the sort of man that would try to swear away the life of a fellow creature, or that would submit to such an imputation as that cast upon him. He is a man of repute and position, and as a public man his character for veracity has to be maintained. We are not, therefore, surprised to find him taking steps to clear himself from an imputation which is not the less injurious because spoken by a learned counsel in a sensational speech, and intended to strengthen a weak case. In another column we print two affidavits made by persons who prove the presence of Mr Oliver Weston at the station under the circumstances described by him, and we believe other affidavits will follow. Taken altogether, these will, doubtless, clear our fellow-townsman of the aspersions so unworthily cast upon him. It is not for us to explain the discrepancy in the evidence of Mr Anscombe and Mr Gibson, as compared with that of Mr Oliver Weston, but this much we may say: no-one can know better that Mr Weston whether he was there or not: he cannot be mistaken; but the other witnesses might be, and probably are in error as to his having been present. In the confusion and hurry consequent upon the appearance of Lefroy bathed in blood, Mr O. Weston may not have been observed, and his remark passed unnoticed, and this, we think, the most likely solution of the difficulty. At all events, we have no doubt that Mr Oliver Weston will make good any statement, though in the face of great obstacles. Anyway, the circumstances under which the accusation was made against him, and his well-known probity of character, will be sufficient to justify him in the eyes of his fellow towns-men.

* * *

APPLICATIONS ON BEHALF OF MR OLIVER WESTON[86]

Yesterday morning, after the ordinary business had been concluded, at the [Brighton] Borough Police Court —

Mr OLIVER WESTON entered the witness box, and said, 'Gentlemen, may I be permitted to address the magistrates? I want to ask a public question.'

Mr BIGGE – I beg to say that I am not going to hear anything upon that subject from you. I know what you want to say. This court has nothing whatever to do with the subject. You had better go before the County Bench.

Mr WESTON – I shall be able to call persons to make affirmations. I shall also be able to call a public meeting. I have had a deputation waited upon me, and I have had many sympathisers. My good name is my good character. I have been a citizen of Brighton for 35 years, and a Town Councillor for 14 years; and a framer of the laws of that borough. I have got two affirmations made by witnesses, and I ask you to read them over. It is a serious thing, and it has nearly broken me down.

---

86   *The Brighton Gazette*, 10 November 1881.

Appendix II.

I am willing and claim to have a strict investigation of my case.

Mr MARRIAGE WALLIS – Mr Weston, I don't think this matter will hurt you.

Mr WESTON – I have here today two affirmations made, and I have two more when I can get the parties here tomorrow.

Mr W. D. SAVAGE – The unfortunate part of the affair is Mr Anscombe saying he did not see Mr Weston in his office – when he did not happen to be there at the time.

Mr VERRALL (Magistrates' Clerk) – These affirmations are made out by two witnesses, and point out conclusively that Mr Weston was present, and they will be sent to the proper authorities.

The affirmations were then read by the magistrates, and attested by Mr Bigge, as follows:

'I, John Chester Craven, of No. 1, St. Peter's Place, Brighton, Sussex, gentleman, do solemnly and sincerely declare that I was for many years manager of the Locomotive Department of the London, Brighton and South Coast Railway, but retired from that position some years since. That I have been for several years, and am now, a member of the Brighton Town Council, and that I have for many years known, and am well acquainted with Mr Oliver Weston, also a member of said Town Council. That I was a passenger by the 2 pm train from London Bridge to Brighton on the 27th June last. That on the arrival of the train at Brighton Station the man Lefroy was taken by a ticket collector to the office of Mr Anscombe, the station master, and that several persons followed, and were collected at and around the office door; that I saw Mr Oliver Weston amongst those at the doorway, and heard him say something in reference to the man, but what he said I cannot state. – J.C. CRAVEN.'

'I, William Coppard, of No. 17, Albion Cottages, Brighton, Sussex, cab driver, do solemnly declare that I have been a cab driver in the service of one master for seven years. That on the 27th June last I was with my carriage on the first turn from the Portsmouth or western platform of the Brighton Railway Station, and thus within six or seven yards of the entrance to the office of the station master (Mr Anscombe), and where I had a clear view of persons going in or out of such office, or standing at the doorway of it. That I saw the man Lefroy and the ticket collector (Gibson) come across the centre of the station from the east, and go into Mr Anscombe's office; and that I saw Mr Oliver Weston, whom I have known for several years, go also into the office almost immediately after them. That there were several persons then gathered about the office door, and that I saw Mr Weston amongst them. That I heard him talking. That something was said about this

Lefroy.

Lefroy being or not being a lunatic, and that Mr Weston said something on that point. That Mr Weston was there only a few minutes. That I afterwards took Lefroy and Gibson in my cab to the Town Hall, then to the hospital and back, and then back again to the station. – WILLIAM COPPARD.'

APPENDIX III.

Lefroy in Australia.[87]

___

A correspondent writes:

"During my stay Australia, where I was for several years engaged in journalism, I was, on many occasions, brought in contact with the now notorious Arthur Lefroy Mapleton, or, as he calls himself, Arthur Lefroy. He was first pointed out to me in Melbourne by a brother journalist, with a warning – unfortunately only too necessary and common in the colonies with regard to near acquaintances.

At that particular time Mapleton was, according to my informant, gaining a precarious living by writing spicy police reports, and doing other similar work for an obscure Melbourne newspaper. Subsequently I had the misfortune to be brought into more or less personal contact with Mapleton by his becoming a contributor to the journal on the staff of which I was engaged. The first impression he made on many was not unfavourable, especially if the person practised upon was a colonial without any experience of men or manners beyond the limits of the antipodes. His address was winning, when he pleased, and he conversed with an amount of assurance and apparent knowledge well calculated to produce an impression on the unwary. Possessed of a more than ordinarily good knowledge of French, he readily made people believe that the somewhat peculiar alias under which he usually passed was his proper name. As this belongs to a family of repute, it is unnecessary to mention it. Suffice it to say, it was neither Lefroy nor Mapleton. He never, so far as I know, however, attempted to conceal the fact that his real name was Mapleton. He told various stories about his parentage, the favourite one being that his father, who was dead, had been the incumbent of a well-known church in London, and that his mother was a Belgian lady of good family. Another account was that his father had been a partner in an old firm of solicitors in London, in which his place had been taken by his elder brother. When this latter story was told the clergyman would appear as his mother's brother, colour being given to the statement by the fact that the name assumed as an alias was the same as that of a once well-known preacher in the south of London.

He had also an immense fund of secondhand literary gossip. Thus he had the real names of writers under celebrated *nommes de plume* by heart, talked familiarly of a highly popular novelist as his friend, and professed to have a

87   *Daily Telegraph*, 9 July 1881.

personal acquaintance with many well-known authors. Such remarks, which were his stock-in-trade when seeking employment on a newspaper were frequently successful in beguiling country editors in Australia, and sometimes those connected with papers of a higher class. Mapleton managed to obtain employment on one or other of the newspapers in each of the Australian capitals and the various provincial towns which he favoured with his presence. He had chances innumerable, and was more or less notorious in all the capitals, from Brisbane to Adelaide. That he did not succeed was his own fault.

As to Mapleton's general habits, he was what is termed in colonial phrases a bar-loafer. Public houses were practically his home when he was not a strict teetotaller, which, it may said to his credit, he sometimes was for several weeks at a time. For the most part, however, he hung about the various bars, treating others when he had money, either earned by literary work received from home (which was apparently sometimes the case), or being treated in return for his company. It was, in fact, one of his practices to attach himself to some unsophisticated shearer or shepherd and make what he could out of him, and his somewhat stridulous voice was often heard entertaining not very select companions with poetical and dramatic recitations in bar-parlours, while he drank at their expense. His figure was familiar on racecourses where small events came off, and there he mingled with the lower class of betting-men, making a book with more or less success.

He was frequently mixed up with amateur theatrical entertainments, and one occasion, which is singularly illustrative of his consummate aplomb, I remember well. He had made himself useful to a troupe of amateurs in a provincial town, and they in turn tendered him a benefit, at which Mapleton was to give a recitation. He appeared on the platform in a somewhat rough morning suit, and excused himself to the audience for not appearing in evening costume by stating that his landlord had that morning made a demand on him for board and lodging, to satisfy which he had been obliged to pawn his dress clothes! In connection with his love of theatricals, I may mention that, knowing a little personally of Mr George Coppin, the aged and highly respected manager of the Theatre Royal in Melbourne, and actor of no mean repute, and being conversant with theatrical matters generally in that city, I can say with confidence that Mapleton had not the slightest authority for making use of his name in the manner he has, and that no piece of his was ever produced on the boards Mr Coppin's theatre. Mapleton's acquaintance with him is probably much of the same character he professed to have with Mrs Nye-Chart.

From what is known by me of Mapleton I must confess, however, that I feel a certain amount of astonishment he should stand charged with the crime of murder. It is true in the colonies he brought himself on more than one occasion in unpleasant relations with the police, on account of some scurrilous pamphlets which he published when out of other literary employment. But he was of weak

Appendix III.

physique, and in many respects the very last man I should have suspected of being guilty of the daring act committed on the Brighton Railway.

One of your correspondents has, I observe, referred to the fact that on one occasion Mapleton exhibited in his presence a bottle of poison. This was not an uncommon practice with him in the colonies. He there several times when hard up and appealing for a small loan produced a bottle of laudanum, which he announced his intention of drinking that night, in order to put an end to his miserable existence were no help forthcoming. I am a little surprised also that so many persons should have been arrested for the accused man. Despite the fact that his face is possibly one of not infrequent type, he had a peculiar carriage of the head and certain unmistakable mannerisms which any one who had ever seen him or had any accurate description of him could not fail to recognise."

APPENDIX IV.

Discovery of a Revolver.

———

Criminal Investigation
Department
Scotland Yard

24. day of Novr. 1881

I beg to report that at 7.30 a.m. 24th inst a Revolver was found beside the railway in some long grass about 3 miles from Merstham Tunnel where the shots were heard by witness Gibson, by a platelayer belonging to the London Brighton & South Coast Railway. It was brought to this office by Inspector Turpin and on examination it was found to be rusted, the doghead broken and the safety pin gone. By direction I shewed it to the pawnbroker's assistants, Henry Creek and Ernest Allwright. The former said, 'I have seen the Revolver found on the line and although I cannot positively swear that it is the same revolver that I took in pledge because it had no maker's name, still it is of the same make and shape and in every respect similar to the one I took in pledge and which was subsequently redeemed, to the best of my belief to Lefroy'. Ernest Allwright said, 'The Revolver you show me is in every respect the same as the one pledged by Lefroy and which I packed up after being pledged'.

I beg to ask that a copy of this report be given to the Hon. H. Cuffe.[88]

    (sd.) Donald S. Swanson
        Inspr.[89]

———

On Thursday morning,[90] between seven and eight o'clock, a platelayer named Streeter, engaged at work upon the Brighton line, close to Earlswood, discovered a six-chambered revolver lying amongst the grass in a ditch, by the side of the down rails. The exact spot was nearly opposite to the Earlswood Asylum, which is a little on the Brighton side of the station. On finding it, the man immediately took it to the station-master, by whom it was forwarded to London Bridge, where

88   Hon. Hamilton Cuffe, Director of Public Prosecutions.
89   TNA: PRO HO 144/83/A6404/71A.
90   24 November 1881.

it was taken possession of by Inspector Turpin, the chief of the railway police, who handed it to the Scotland Yard authorities.

The weapon, which, as before stated, has six chambers, is a pin-fire old-fashioned revolver of about .300 bore. It is very rusty, and the muzzle is choked with dirt. All the chambers are empty, so that, supposing it to be the pistol used in the murder of Mr. Gold, and that the shots were fired at Merstham, as deposed to by the gentleman in the next carriage, they must have been rapidly emptied before it was thrown from the window to the place where it has now been found. The thumb-piece of the hammer has been broken off, and the rammer used for extracting empty cases and the foresight are gone. The weapon also shows marks of having been knocked about, while amongst the ordinary red rust with which it is covered is some of a blacker tinge, that look like blood marks. This is particularly discernible upon the heel plate. One peculiarity is that there is no trigger guard, and that the trigger turns up under the barrel.

Inspector Swanson, who arrested Lefroy, has since the deposit of the revolver at Scotland Yard, visited the pawnbrokers, Messrs Adams and Hillstead, of High Street, Borough. On arriving there he first asked to be shown the revolver produced at the trial, and this proved to be almost identical with that found in the morning, the only difference being that in the latter the outside of the barrel was cylindrical, and the former sexagonal. He then produced the revolver found in the morning, which he showed to the assistants who gave evidence at Maidstone, and they made the following statements, which the inspector took down in writing:

Henry Creek said: 'I have seen the revolver you produce, and I recognise it was similar in make to the one I describe in my evidence. Of that I have no doubt whatever. It is similar in every respect to the one I took in pledge, and handed back again.'

Ernest Allbright[91] said: 'I have seen the revolver, and have no doubt it is identical in make in every way with the revolver Lefroy pledged, and which I packed up on being pledged.'[92]

---

91 *Sic*: Allwright.
92 *The Surrey Mirror and General County Advertiser*, 26 November 1881.

APPENDIX V.

Appeal for an Enquiry into the Mental Condition of Percy Lefroy Mapleton.

————

40 Churton Street,
Pimlico, S.W.

London, 17th Novr 1881

To the Right Honourable
Sir William Harcourt
Her Majestys[93] Secretary of State for Home Affairs

Sir,   Regina - v - Percy Lefroy Mapleton

The above named Prisoner was found 'Guilty' of the murder of 'Frederick Isaac Gold' on the 8th instant and sentenced to death.

I am preparing a Petition that Her Most Gracious Majesty may be advised to Reprieve that sentence but I shall not be able to leave the papers with you until late on Saturday.

Will you grant permission for Doctors Forbes Winslow and J M. Winn to attend at Lewes Gaol for the purpose of enquiring into the mental condition of the above named Prisoner.

I enclose a copy of a letter which I have this day received from the first-named gentleman -

I have the honour to be Sir –

Your obedient servant
[signed] T. Duerdin Dutton
Solicitor for the Prisoner[94]

*

93   *Sic* in letter.
94   TNA: PRO HO 144/83/A6404/41.

Lefroy.

23 Cavendish Square
W.
Nov 17. 1881

Having had all the facts of the 'Lefroy' case placed before me with a history of his antecedents I am of opinion without expressing any view as to his mental condition that further enquiry is desirable.

L. S. Forbes Winslow[95]

HOME OFFICE
18 NOV
1881[96]

This will be declined of course. Whether a medical inquiry should be ordered will depend on the view the S of S takes of the case. The Statute prescribes:

'If at any time it shall be made to appear to one of HM Principal S of S that there is good reason to believe that any prisoner in confinement under sentence of death is <u>then</u> insane, either by means of a Certificate in writing to that effect in the form given in Schedule A (Cert 1/2 Visiting JJ) transmitted to him by 2 or more of the Visiting JJ of the Prison in which such prisoner under sentence of death is confined <u>or by any other means whatsoever</u> such S of S shall appoint ... 2 medical men.'

GL[97]
18 Nov 1881.

[There was, I believe, no evidence of insanity at the trial, as the line of defence was that he never did the act. It is stated in one of the letters that the Grandfather was insane & I am told the father died of drink – the Petition now being got up will probably contain some details on these points.

Would you wish to ask the Judge, or have a report from the Gov[r]?

Dr Winslow and Winn are the last persons to whom such an inquiry should be intrusted.]

If you determined to have an inquiry, Dr Orange[98] could conveniently go: & the medical officers of the Gaol (if not previously consulted) might act with him.[99]

---

95   TNA: PRO HO 144/83/A6404/41.
96   Date from official Home Office stamp on the document.
97   Assistant Under-Secretary of State Godfrey Lushington.
98   Dr William Orange, medical superintendent at Broadmoor between 1870 and 1886, whose opinion was frequently sought by the Home Office.
99   Handwritten internal civil service advice to Sir William Harcourt on docket containing Dutton's letter requesting permission for Forbes Winslow and Winn to visit Lefroy (TNA: PRO HO 144/83/A6404/41).

Appendix V.

———

Decline this application. I have no facts upon me that would lead me to direct an inquiry under the Statute.

WVH

Nov 18. 81[100]

———

The Central News understands that the Home Secretary has decided against any medical examination of Lefroy on behalf of the convict's relatives. Should Sir W. Harcourt himself have any doubts on this subject he would refer to the prison surgeon's official report. It will be remembered that the Home Secretary was asked to allow Drs. Forbes Winslow and Winn to visit Lefroy; but, as from their published letters, these gentlemen may be regarded as already entertaining strong doubts as to the prisoner's sanity, one of the relatives has suggested that an independent medical gentleman might be sent down to Lewes, and the name of Dr. Graham Bennett, of Hertford Street, Mayfair, has been mentioned in this connection; but it is not considered likely that the Home Secretary will alter his decision on this matter.[101]

———

TO THE EDITOR OF THE DAILY CHRONICLE.

Sir, – I feel bound, in the cause of justice, to make a few remarks on the Lefroy case, as my name had been circulated in connection with it. It is with great regret that I learn from the daily papers that the Home Secretary has determined to let the law take its course without giving the prisoner the benefit of a mental examination by an experienced expert. The facts which have come to light since his incarceration leave no doubt that Lefroy has been for a long period the subject of moral and delusional insanity. Mr. Dutton entreated the Home Secretary that Dr. Forbes Winslow and myself should visit the prisoner and report on his mental condition.

The United States Government has freely given Guiteau[102] the benefit of the opinions of experts. Why then, should our Government deprive the wretched boy

---

100 TNA: PRO HO 144/83/A6404/41.
101 *Sheffield Independent*, 26 November 1881.
102 Charles Guiteau, who assassinated President James A. Garfield on 2 July 1881.

Lefroy of the same privilege?

The facts in support of the plea of insanity are very strong, and are as follows: 1st. Strong hereditary pre-disposition to insanity. His father was insane at the time of his conception, and his mother was in the same condition shortly previous to the birth. 2nd. Marked delusions, chiefly of an exalted kind. Of this there is abundant proof. 3rd. Irrational conduct and behaviour noticed by many of his friends, but whose names have not as yet come before the public. 4th. A murderous act being quite inconsistent with his natural disposition and temperament. 5th. Insolation, or what is as probable an epileptic attack on the race-course at Epsom. 6th. That peculiar feature, so common to the insane, which makes them rather be considered by the world to be criminal, rather than lunatic. From a careful consideration of the case, and perusal of certain documents now in possession of Dr. Forbes Winslow, and not made public (written before the murder, and since his condemnation, facts which can only possibly be known to those who have perused them; data affording invaluable aid in conducting an examination of the prisoner), I am of opinion that competent and experienced experts should have been allowed to examine the unhappy prisoner. – Your obedient servant,

J.M. WINN, M.D,
Harley-street, Cavendish-square, Nov. 25.[103]

––––––––

RECOLLECTIONS OF FORTY YEARS[104]
By Dr L.S. Forbes Winslow (1910)

I was so convinced from a study of the case that Lefroy was not responsible for his actions, that, after another conference with his relations, I decided to agitate in this matter.

Certain documentary evidence was placed in my hands, together with a complete history of the accused. The conclusion I arrived at was that there were sufficient grounds for petitioning the Home Secretary to grant a medical examination of the condemned man. I was informed that I had been appointed to visit Lefroy at the Lewes Gaol, and I immediately telegraphed to the Home Secretary consenting to make the examination, should my request be complied with, in conjunction with a medical Government official appointed by himself. I felt that all England was up in arms against Lefroy, and that public opinion was so great against the plea of irresponsibility that I did not care to take upon myself the sole responsibility of acting as his mental adjudicator in a case of so much public importance and interest. Permission, however, was not granted for me to visit Lefroy. The custom

103 *Daily Chronicle*, 26 November 1881.
104 London: John Ouseley, 1910.

Appendix V.

exists in England that, after condemnation, no outside medical interference is permitted, though previous to the trial, had his friends approached me, I should have been able to have examined him and testified in court as to my opinion upon his mental condition.

*

Lefroy was cunning, as most lunatics are, and this quality was observed throughout the whole of his transactions. His conduct was very peculiar after the murder, but the fact that it was apparently premeditated strengthened the case for the prosecution. But it might be as well to state that most murders committed by lunatics are premeditated, and that insanity and cunning go hand in hand.

*

The case from first to last was a very sensational one, and the attention of London was absorbed in it; but under no pretence whatever was the public executioner to be deprived of his victim.

After these years, and reviewing the case calmly and deliberately, and taking into consideration the history of the case and all the concomitant facts, I am very strongly of the opinion that it would have been to the interests of intelligence, humanity, science, civilisation, Christianity, and justice if a deaf ear had not been turned to the prayer of the unhappy man's family and medical petitioners, simply begging that the Home Secretary would grant them an inquiry into the mental condition of the youth standing on the precipice of his fate. We asked no more than this, and were refused.

APPENDIX VI.

Petition for the Reprieve of Percy Lefroy Mapleton.

———————

40 Churton Street,
Pimlico, S.W.

London, Nov 21st 1881

To the Rt Honble Sir William Harcourt
    H.M. Secretary of State for Home
        Affairs
                Home Office
                    Whitehall

Sir/.

Regina v Percy Lefroy Mapleton

I beg to forward you Petition for the Reprieve of the above named Prisoner who now lies under sentence of death at the Lewes Prison.

The Petitioners comprise a great number of medical men clergymen solicitors tradesmen and members of the aristocracy.

I send therewith copy certificates of death of the Prisoner's mother and father but I am not able to send similar certificates of the death of his grandfather and uncle.

I also send a letter written by the Prisoner to his cousin on March 29th 1878, a certificate of Dr Green dated 26th Oct. 1881, a further certificate of Dr Green dated November 1881, a certificate of Dr Forbes Winslow dated November 19th 1881, & a certificate or opinion of Dr Drysdale dated 19th Novr 1881.

I am in a position to prove the accuracy of the second, third and fourth paragraphs of the Petitioner and shall be pleased to lay such proof before you should you think it necessary that I should do so.

I have the honour to be
        Sir

Your Humble & obt servant
        [signed] T. Duerdin Dutton

*

Lefroy.

To the Right Honorable Sir William Harcourt
Her Majesty's Secretary of State for Home Affairs

A humble Petition that Her Most Gracious Majesty may be
advised to Reprieve the Sentence of Death passed at
Maidstone Assizes on Thursday the 8th instant, by the
Lord Chief Justice of England, upon Percy Lefroy
Mapleton for the murder of Frederick Isaac Gold, on the
27th day of June last.

The grounds of this Petition are as follows:-

1.   That the evidence entirely failed to show the slightest premeditation
and that there is the strongest possible ground for believing that the act was done
under the influence of homicidal mania, there being, as will be subsequently
disclosed, a great predisposition to insanity from the family history of the
accused.

2.   That the defence set up at the trial would have been that the accused
was not responsible for his acts, by reason of the state of his mind, had not his
Solicitor, Mr Dutton, who acted for him throughout, received positive directions
from the accused as to the presence of a third person in the carriage which neither
his said Solicitor, nor his relatives, were, of course, in a position to disregard.

3.   That the Mother of the accused died of Carditis and Consumption
on the 5th day of June in the year of our Lord 1866 and for several months prior
to the birth of the accused on the 23rd day of February 1860 she suffered from
intense Melancholia and Paroxysms of Frenzy.

4.   That the Father was a confirmed Dipsomaniac from the year 1845
until his death of the 5th day of August 1879 and during that period he was subject
to mental delusions, and fits of nervous insanity in one of which he attempted to
smother his Wife and one another occasion attempted to commit suicide.

5.   That his Grandfather, William David Mapleton, also became insane
some time prior to his death which occurred on the 27th day of February in the
year of our Lord 1814 at Jersey, and was under restraint at the time of his death.

6.   That his Father's Brother 'James Mapleton' was of unsound mind
for many months prior to his death and died in that condition at St Helena on the
14th day of March in the year of our Lord 1852.

7.   That the accused himself, who has always been of a weak, sickly
temperament, had a sunstroke whilst standing on the race course on the Derby
Day of 1880, on which occasion he fell down in a fit, and was taken home in a
conveyance, and confined to his bed for several days and has never since been the
same man, having been subject to long and continued fits of despondency and at
the present time and for some years back he had been in a consumption.

Appendix VI.

8.   That the demeanour of the accused, during the continuance of his trial, was one of stolid indifference, and that he seemed in no way either before or after sentence to realize the gravity of his situation which we, your Petitioners, attribute to the diseased condition of his mind.

> Your Petitioners therefore humbly pray that a competent medical inquiry may forthwith be made into the mental condition of the above named Percy Lefroy Mapleton and that should as your Petitioners anticipate, a report be made that he is not, and has not been for some time, responsible for his actions, Her Most Gracious Majesty be advised mercifully to reprieve the sentence of Death passed upon him.

And your Petitioners, as in duty bound, will ever pray.

[signed] T. Duerdin Dutton   40 Churton Street Pimlico S.W   Solicitor[105]

*

SUPERINTENDENT REGISTRAR'S DISTRICT: GREENWICH

1866 DEATHS IN THE DISTRICT OF SAINT PAUL'S DEPTFORD IN THE COUNTIES OF KENT AND SURREY

When and Where Died: Fifth June 1866 / 6 Brighton Terrace New Cross

Name and Surname: Mary Trent Mapleton

Sex: Female

Age: 41 years

Rank of Profession: Wife of Henry Mapleton a Commander Royal Navy

Cause of Death: Carditis 8 days

Certified Signature, Description, and Residence of Informant: A. A. Seale in attendance.[106] 1 Alpha Place, Queen's Road Deptford

When Registered:Sixth June 1866

Signature of Registrar: Thomas Marchant Registrar

*

---

105   What follows are ten signatures, including Drs Forbes Winslow and Winn, but the full list has been detached at some point from the petition, so the exact number of petitioners is unknown.
106   Brother Archibald Seale.

Lefroy.

1879 DEATHS IN THE DISTRICT OF PECKHAM
IN THE COUNTY OF SURREY

When and Where Died: Fifth August 1879 / 38 Philip Road

Name and Surname: Henry Mapleton

Sex: Male

Age: 69 years

Rank or Profession: Staff Commander R.N. (Half Pay)

Cause of Death: Cirrhosis. Jaundice 3 months Exhaustion
Certified by RW Thomas, LRCP

Signature, Description, and Residence of Informant: M.E.B. Brickwood
daughter Present at the Death 38 Philip Road Peckham

When Registered: Seventh August 1879

Signature of Registrar: Josh. S Street Registrar

*

I, Thomas Joseph Green, Member of the Royal College of Surgeons of London
and Licentiate of the Apothecaries Society of London, hereby certify that I was
the regular medical attendant of the late Mr. Mapleton, Father of Percy Lefroy
Mapleton, and that he was an habitual drunkard:-

Also that I attended Mrs. Mapleton, who suffered from mischief of both lungs
and heart:-

Also that I confined Mrs. Mapleton on the 23rd day of February 1860 with Percy
Lefroy Mapleton:-

Also that I attended Percy Lefroy Mapleton during his infancy and boyhood and
that in my opinion he suffers from hereditary lung disease and is physically weak.

Thomas Joseph Green
MRCSL   LSA

26th October 1881.
Parliament House, Peckham S.E.

*

I the undersigned Thomas Joseph Green being a member of the Royal College
of Surgeons of London and Licentiate of the Apothecaries Society of London
hereby certify that I attended Mrs. Mary Trent Mapleton mother of Percy Lefroy
Mapleton for some months before the birth of the said Percy Lefroy Mapleton

Appendix VI.

and that she was suffering from intense Melancholia with Paroxysms of Frenzy.

Thomas J. Green
MR.C.S.L L.S.A.

Parliament House, Peckham
Novr. 18th 1881

*

7 Woburn Place WC

I am of opinion that there are several facts in the history of the convict, Percy Mapleton Lefroy, as testified by his relatives, such as the habitual drunken habits of his father, Captain Mapleton, and that before the birth of the convict, with several delusions which the convict is said to have entertained at different times, which point to the conclusion that his case is one which demands investigation by some persons familiar with the phenomena of insanity. I therefore recommend that a petition to that effect should be signed as numerous as possible & sent in to the Home Secretary at once.

Charles R. Drysdale M.D
Senior Physician to the Metropolitan Free Hosp.
Lond. Nov 19 1881

*

Ventnor
March 29th 1878

Dearest Annie,

You are quite correct when you say I am 'more cheerful'. This is the reason when I first came here, perhaps you may remember that I knew no one. After Christmas I made many acquaintances and I hope a few friends. Of course most of them were young fellows of all ages from 18 to 25. There were of course many good and some I am sorry to say, the reverse. Among the latter set, I should assuredly have fallen, but for the timely advice given me by someone, who was a comparative stranger to me. Four times was I saved from commencing that dreadful course, alas, so familiar to F. James & others. But whenever I was tempted by the devil, those few honest words of advice, coupled with a kindly face I never shall forget brought before me the enormity of the sin I was about to commit and made me throw aside the horrible thoughts in disgust. My last temptation was on Feb. 28. On that date, I had an appointment to keep in the evening at 7-30. All day, God only knows how I prayed & struggled to do the right, but seemingly without avail. At last I made up for the wrong. All the bad arguments had triumphed only too easily. At a few minutes to the appointed time

I walked out of the house, and paused for an instant to look at the lovely sunset. At that minute there was a sudden gust of wind which blew the dust into my eyes. I drew out my handkerchief and something fell to the ground at my feet. I picked it up. It was something which had been given me by the person I have mentioned before. Like lightning I saw my <u>real</u> position that earnest voice rang in my ears, and those clear truthful eyes seemed to look me full in the face, as I stood there in the twilight irresolute. But the night conquered at last, and I was saved. Since then I feel as firm in <u>that</u> way, as I am in total abstinence though very often when now committing smaller sins, one look at my little keepsake and I feel altogether strengthened. That night I made a solemn vow to show my gratitude to the person I have named. Can you wonder that I feel grateful? All this happened before I came up last time. Since then I have had a terrible nightmare. From it I am <u>sure</u> my benefactor is in <u>deadly peril</u>, perhaps of life, and I am as firmly convinced that I shall be enabled to defeat the project, and thus wipe out a <u>little</u> of the debt I owe. I sincerely hope Julia will not come here, as I am not at all up to the mark. Last Wednesday, I was reading, and just happened to look up, when in a minute I saw <u>it</u> and fainted dead away. I hope dear you will excuse these wretched letters, but you must put it down to my having been more <u>out</u> than <u>in</u> my senses for three weeks. I will do as you wish concerning the Wedgwoods. I intend to go there on Monday. With fondest love, Your affectionate cousin <u>Percy L. Mapleton</u>

HOME OFFICE
22 NOV
1881[107]

I don't think there is anything here to warrant medical enquiry. The father was a drunkard & the mother died of consumption & is said to have been subject to fits of melancholy & frenzy while with child of prisoner.[108] Neither of these is insanity. As to the other relations said to have been insane there is not a particle of evidence.

This is the oft repeated case of an afterthought defence not set up at the trial or even suggested & at the last moment fired at the S. of S. as a forlorn hope.

? Nil.
<u>22.11.81</u>[109]

---

107 Date from official Home Office stamp on the document.
108 Inexplicably sic.
109 Note by Sir William Harcourt, Home Secretary.

Appendix VI.

Sir Wm Harcourt says this is to be refused but the letter need not go till Saturday. Say that the S of S having considered his letter & the Petition wh. accompanied it does not find sufficient grounds in them to warrant any interference on his part in Lefroy's case.

<u>22.11.81</u>. AFOL[110]

———————

110   Sir Adolphus Frederick Octavius Liddell, Permanent Under-Secretary to the Home Office 1867-1885. All
       the above from TNA: PRO HO 144/83/A6404/56.

APPENDIX VII.

The Murder of Lieutenant Roper.[111]

———

H.O. 26 Nov. 1881.

Sir W. Harcourt

Mr. Cole the Chaplain of Lewes Gaol called here this morning & made the extraordinary statement to me wh. I requested him to put in writing & wh. is enclosed.

He further told me that the way it came about was as follows: That Mr. Dutton Lefroy's solicitor had an interview with him yesterday in the presence of the Chaplain.

That Dutton told Lefroy that in the course of his enquiries relating to the Brighton Railway case ~~he had~~ several important facts had come to his knowledge on the information of Lefroy's relatives & others which raised a grave suspicion that he was concerned in Roper's murder. Lefroy appeared very excited on hearing this & this morning sent for the Chaplain & made the statement enclosed to him. The facts so disclosed by Dutton are those alluded to by the Chaplain in the latter part of his statement who said to me that he ~~considered~~ he had a difficulty in disclosing those facts considering the peculiar position of Dutton as solicitor for the prisoner & he doubted whether for the present at least he ought not to treat them as confidential. I told him that was a matter for his private judgement but for the present at least he could treat them as confidential if he wished.

He told them to me. They related to Lefroy's conduct & statements at the time of the Chatham murder & to certain articles of clothing having been found with blood stains upon them &c.

It is obvious that this statement may have been made by Lefroy with a view to obtaining a respite from his execution wh. is fixed for Tuesday next.

The only possible use that Lefroy could be wd. be as evidence agst. the soldier, whom he states to have been an accomplice, if Lefroy were to plead guilty & then

---

111 Lieutenant Percy Roper, a young officer with the Royal Engineers, was shot and killed on a staircase outside his rooms at Brompton Barracks, Chatham on 11 February 1881. There were no witnesses, and the popular Roper had no known enemies. A pistol belonging to another officer was found some distance from the body, ruling out suicide. Despite a reward of £500 being offered by the Royal Engineers and another of £100 by the Government, and more than one person confessing to the crime, Roper's murder has never been solved.

be examined as a witness.

But what wd. the value of such evidence be?

I told the Chaplain to say nothing about this confession at present. He promised he would keep it secret and the only other person who knows of it is the governor of the prison.

I think the execution shd. take place & the matter be enquired into afterwards.

AFOL
26.11.81

*

Percy Lefroy Mapleton now under sentence of death in Lewes Prison for the murder of Mr. Gold on the Brighton Railway has this morning communicated to me the following statement:

That previous to the 11th of February last in passing down St James's Street in London he saw two gentlemen standing at the door of a Club and overheard one of them speaking to the other in most disparaging terms of an actress with whom he, Mapleton, was intimately acquainted[112] and that he stopped and demanded that the expressions should be retracted. This was indignantly refused but on Mapleton's insisting on receiving the gentleman's card, he under the advice of his friend gave it and upon it was the name of Lieut Roper of the Royal Engineers quartered at Chatham.

That Mapleton subsequently wrote several letters to him to which he received no reply. That through an acquaintance at Peckham a soldier who knew the barracks at Chatham and the habits of Mr. Roper he obtained the information he desired & not having succeeded in getting a written apology he determined to go down in person and demand it. Accordingly on the evening of the 11th of February he went down, obtained access to Mr. Roper's quarters and finding him there an altercation ensued during which with a pistol which he found on a chair in the room & which Mr. Roper was handling when he came in he shot him in the room.

That at the foot of the stairs his informant and accomplice who was waiting met him and agreed to make everything straight, providing a cab for him & then dragging the body out upon the landing where it was found & scattering about the articles of clothing, pistol, purse, watch &c which were afterwards discovered.

That he Mapleton gave this man a sovereign for his services in the matter.

From facts which have come to my knowledge communicated from without but which I am not enabled at present to treat otherwise than confidential I am aware

---

112   Violet Cameron, the unwitting object of Lefroy's infatuation.

Appendix VII.

of evidence of the most serious character which may substantiate the truth of the confession which the prisoner has made to me today and I thought fit to lose no time therefore in laying this information which I have derived from the prisoner before the proper authorities.

T. H. Cole
Chaplain
H.M. Prison
Lewes

Saturday
November 26/81

———

Sir A Liddell

I entirely concur in the view you take of this confession and that it ought not to stay the execution.

My own impression is that the story is made up as a desperate attempt to postpone the fatal moment. But as you say if it is not that purpose could I award a respite?

WVH[113]
Chatsworth
   Nvr. 27 81[114]

———

To The Right Honourable
The Secretary of State
for the Home Office

H.M. Prison
Lewes

Nov 29th 1881

Sir,

I have the honour to report for your information that the Prisoner Percy Lefroy Mapleton who was executed this morning had before his death made a full confession to me of the murder of Mr. Gold and acknowledged the justice of his sentence. He also entirely retracted the statement which he had made concerning

---

113   William Vernon Harcourt.
114   TNA: PRO HO 144/83/A6404/110a.

Lefroy.

the murder by him of Lieutenant Roper and expressed great regret that, yielding to the pressure of his solicitor and the evidence alleged by him, he had fabricated a confession of a crime of which in reality he knew nothing.

I have the honour to be
Sir
Your obedient servant
T.H. Cole
Chaplain[115]

---

115   TNA: PRO HO 144/83/A6404/110.

APPENDIX VIII.

Declaration of Sheriff and Others.

––––––––––

We, the undersigned, hereby declare that Judgment of Death was this Day executed on Percy Lefroy Mapleton otherwise Arthur Lefroy in Her Majesty's Prison at Lewes in our Presence.

Dated this 29th Day of November 1881

[Signed] Charles Bull	Under Sheriff of Sussex.
[Signed] Robt. Crosskey	Justice of the Peace for Sussex
[Signed] G.A. Crickett	Governor of the said Prison.
[Signed] T.H. Cole	Chaplain of the said Prison.

––––––––––

CERTIFICATE OF SURGEON.

I, Richard Turner the Surgeon of Her Majesty's Prison at Lewes hereby certify that I this Day examined the Body of Percy Lefroy Mapleton otherwise Arthur Lefroy, on whom Judgment of Death was this Day executed in the said Prison; and that on that Examination I found that the said Percy Lefroy Mapleton otherwise Arthur Lefroy was dead.

Dated this 29th Day of November 1881.

(Signature) Richard Turner
Medical Officer
H.M. Civil. Prison Lewes.[116]

––––––––––

116   TNA: PRO HO 144/83/A6404/112.

APPENDIX VIX.

The Long Drop.[117]

––––––––

A rough executioner was Mr Marwood, who for a time officiated for the British Government in these isles.[118] I was present at the execution of Lefroy, and after the body had been "let down," I, in company with Mr Marwood, measured the length of the rope. It was upwards of ten feet and one inch! When, presently, the corpse lay in the coffin, I noticed, in common with the jurors who "sat on the body," that the neck had been dreadfully cut by the tremendous fall. I wonder the head did not come off.

117 *Ross-shire Journal,* 12 October 1888.
118 1872–83.

APPENDIX X.

The Autobiography of Percy Lefroy Mapleton.

———

New Athenaeum Club,
Suffolk Street. Pall Mall. S.W.

Confidential
Nov 30/81

Dear Sir,

The Prisoner Percy Lefroy Mapleton who was executed at Lewes yesterday entrusted to me a M.S. account of his previous life and of the crime for which he suffered, with this request:

That I should revise it according to my discretion & that if it were permitted to be published the proceeds should be applied to his friends in order to assist in defraying their large and serious pecuniary outlay expended in his defence from very limited means.

The account was written day by day since his sentence with my full cognisance and the primary objects which he stated to me were –

1st That he might if possible during the short remainder of his life 'do some little good' by deterring others from the vices of his career.

2ndly That he might do anything in his power to correct the mock heroism which had by the public prints been cast around the case & might present it in a true and proper light to the public.

3rdly That he might make the only reparation left to him exonerating persons whom he had implicated in his various frauds & deceptions & also might clear up all uncertainties & misconceptions surrounding the murder of Mr Gold and give a truthful account of the circumstances of that 'awful' crime and a heartfelt expression of his earnest contrition and lastly, as I have stated, afford any assistance he could to his friends whose means had been crippled for his sake.

I may say that the tone of the M.S. bears out the above named intentions and that I shall be willing if the authorities see fit to exercise the revision requested by the criminal or to deal with the matter in any way they may decide.

Subsequent explanations given to me by him since the account was written would necessitate correction in some of its details, for which reasons the M.S. which I hold would not in its present form (unrevised) represent the final expressions of the writer, if sent for your perusal. The style of the writing although characteristic would in my opinion require considerable modification before publication, not that it is, I am bound to say, in any sense improper.

If you can kindly afford me information to guide me in this matter I shall feel extremely obliged.

I am Dear Sir
Yours very faithfully
T.H. Cole
Chaplain
H.M. Prison Lewes

Capt. Stoppard
Prison Commissioner

––––––––––

H.M. Prison
Lewes
Dec 7/81

Confidential

To Capt. Stoppard
Prison Commissioner &c

I send herewith the M.S. which, on considering a second time, I am bound to think, notwithstanding my desire to further the wishes of the writer as far as practicable, would not be suitable for publication, certainly as a whole.

The exaggerated style and language though quite natural to him & not ill intended seem unfitted to the occasion, and much of the matter is of no general interest and of a highly wrought character.

Although the main purpose of the record was I believe good on his part, especially in the wish to assist his friends, I do not feel able to recommend its disclosure, nor can I vouch for the truth of any of its contents.

On the day before his execution he informed me that the portion of the story inferring a personal acquaintance with 'May Gordon' (Violet Cameron)[119] was a 'romantic delusion' & that he had never spoken to her although he had adopted her as the goal of his ambition! His friends seem to have been aware that some person of the kind was the object of all the scheming & deception of his life, and at the time he wrote to her from this prison I confess that I believed that he was really acquainted with her.

---

119   Violet Cameron [real name Violet Lydia Thompson] (1862–1919), English actress and singer.

Appendix X.

It is only just that I should add that this criminal constantly struggled against his inherent propensity to falsehood and was in his demeanour most humble, submissive and attentive from the time of his trial to his end, doing as much as his extraordinary character was I believe capable of both to realise his awful position and to prepare for another state.

He had no fear whatever of death in itself.

T.H. Cole
Chaplain

HOME OFFICE
1 DEC
1881[120]

If on perusal this manuscript is found unobjectionable I see no reason why it should not be handed to his relatives to do what they please with it.

We can have nothing to do with it.

Sir W. Harcourt
2.12.81

I had better see these papers first.
WVH
Dcr. 5 '88

*

SECRETARY OF STATE
HOME DEPARTMENT

Lefroy.
Mapleton's confession.

This in my opinion should not go further, certainly not be published. It is a curious production, written for effect & with considerable cunning & I believe no small amount of lying. He artfully leaves out that part of his life betwn. his schooltime & going to Australia & leaves it to be inferred that during that time he had met Miss Cameron whom he calls May Gordon & had received some picture from her,[121] whereas I don't believe she ever saw him in her life. Then there are many other persons whose names wd. be brought into unpleasant notoriety if this were published & several imputations of perjury on the witnesses at the trial.

120 Date from official Home Office stamp on the document.
121 In the text, Lefroy indicates that this memento was a lock of hair, rather than a picture.

Lefroy.

The whole story is high flown & sensational & impresses me rather with the notion that vanity & a desire for notoriety more than a wish to tell the naked truth dictated the production of it.

AFOL
8.12.81

Sir Wm. Harcourt.
? If you agree I will lock this up in my secret cupboard.

*

SECRETARY OF STATE
HOME DEPARTMENT

I quite concur in Sir A Liddell's views – this miserable production should not see the light – keep it locked up.

WVH
Decr. 12 81[122]

---

122   TNA: PRO HO 144/83/A6404/112a.

APPENDIX XI.

My Autobiography
By Percy Lefroy Mapleton[123]

Preface

It may be asked by what right and from what motive do I presume to set on paper the story of such a life as mine, and in anticipation of such questions arising I have determined to answer them before they are asked.

Firstly as to my motives which are as follows: that as a great deal of false glamour, mock heroism and falsehood has been thrown over the fearful tragedy of June 27, thereby causing this most awful occurrence to be looked upon in a false light, which may cause untold harm to the unthinking or ignorant in the future, ~~which~~ to prevent which if possible I the only living person who holds the key to the mystery have determined to draw aside the ~~awful~~ drawn down curtain of the past and lay the awful tragedy bare before the world in all its terror, wickedness, and black unfathomable despair.

Secondly: that I most earnestly desire to exonerate from ~~all~~ participation in or knowledge of this crime all those unfortunate persons on whom suspicion or the breath of suspicion has been cast. I need hardly say I refer more particularly to Mr. Thomas Gold and even more as to my noble, devoted, misjudged cousin, Mr. F.W. Seale.

Thirdly. To remove that possibly natural but most injurious idea that because a young man does not drink, smoke, gamble, bet or indulge in acts of profligacy he is never likely to commit any crime. and people who have read of my sin and its consequences together with my poverty have no doubt with a shrug of their shoulders observed "Oh, of course the fellow had been living a fast life" little thinking that to every one of the above indictments I could pleadi~~ng~~ "not guilty" having been practically a teetotaller from my birth, never smoking until last June, and only once in my life having played cards for money three years ago. I have never in my life betted on a race of any sort and no one, whatever may be my faults, has ever accused me of being profligate. And yet in spite of all this I fell.

Fourthly, that in the cause of morality I consider ~~that~~ the ~~causes~~ reasons which led to the committal of this awful crime should have equal publicity with the

---

123 Handwritten manuscript held at The National Archives: PRO HO 144/83/A6404/112a. Lefroy's grammar, spellings and excisions retained.

crime itself.

~~Fifthly and~~ Lastly, that I pen this sad story, this tragedy of real life in the sincere and earnest hope that it may cause some young man, ambitious, careless and unscrupulous as I once was to pause, reflect and ~~pause~~ stop in his Hellbound career, before it be <u>too late</u>. Too late for reparation, too late ~~for~~ to heal the wounded hearts of those you love. Too late for all, for everything but repentance.

One ~~fin~~ word more and I have finished. Every thing mentioned by me hereafter is an <u>incident of my life</u> as it really happened. I have given the real names of persons in every instance but one,[124] and that one is the person I have called "~~Violet~~ May Gordon", which is not her real name.[125] That dear name will go for ever undivulged, and I should consider it little short of profanity to introduce it here. I may mention that I have given everyone their real name not to needlessly drag them into publicity but simply to show that I am relating a romance of <u>real life</u> and not one of fiction. I have endeavoured to avoid wounding the feelings of anyone but at the same time I have only felt it my duty to expose falsehood or misconception wherever it has occurred.

My weary, storm beaten ~~life~~ career is closing fast. Every day my life is drawing nearer to its close and my soul to its Maker. Literally am I now "In the Dark Valley of the Shadow of Death" and that these my dying words of <u>truth and warning</u> may go forth far and wide ~~perhaps~~ somewhere to ripen and bring forth good seed is the last ~~sad~~ sad fervent prayer of

> Percy Lefroy Mapleton
> Lewes Gaol
> Nov 17. 1881

Chapter I

My Birth and Parentage.

In an old fashioned substantial looking house projecting well into the road, with nought but a tiny strip of garden in front I first saw the light on the 23 Feb. 1860. The house was, or rather is, for it stands there now, situate[126] in Queen's Rd Peckham, which twenty years ago was a quiet little suburban road, very

---

124 Not quite true. Lefroy also gives aliases for 'Fielding' in chapters V and VI and 'Lester' in Chapter VI.

125 She was Violet Lydia Thompson (1862–1919), an English actress and singer, who went under the stage name Violet Cameron. She made her stage debut in 1871 playing child pantomime roles at the Drury Lane Theatre. By 1881 she had become quite famous and very successful. It appears Lefroy developed an intense infatuation, almost an obsession, with Violet. According to some newspaper reports, he carried her portrait around with him and claimed to his relatives that he was actually married to her.

126 *Sic* in autobiography.

Appendix XI.

different from the noisy busy London thoroughfare it has since become. At the time I was born there were residing at Alpha Place for so the dear old house was called,[127] seven persons viz. my mother, and my two dear sisters both older than myself, Mary and Julia.[128] My uncle and aunt Captain and Mrs. Archibald Seale and their two remaining children my cousins, both of whose names are only too well known, Mrs. Clayton and Mr. F.W.S. Seale. It may not be out of place here to describe as briefly as possible the above ~~relations~~ and also my father. ~~M~~ The latter, ~~who~~ Captain Henry Mapleton was a Staff Commander in the Royal Navy and also Harbour Master and Colonial Judge in the Island of St. Helena ~~and~~ who at the period of my birth was at sea. He was an officer of great experience and well known and respected in his public capacity. But as a husband and father he was very far from what he should have been. At this period he must have been about five and forty.[129] Leaving him for a moment I must mention that my beloved mother's name was Seale - Mary Trent Seale, her father being Major Seale, an officer in the English army. At my birth she was in extremely delicate health, being in a rapid decline and also suffering from palpitation of the heart. But under all her agonies she was perfectly resigned. Never complaining, never reproachful and unspeakably grateful for the smallest kindness bestowed upon her or those she loved. And in the whole course of my short twenty years life I have never heard ~~and~~ an unkind or harsh word spoken of ~~my~~ her from any living soul. I can sincerely [say] she was beloved by all who had the good fortune to know her.

My parents were at this time very comfortably off, my mother having an estate of her own in St. Helena, and only residing in my uncle's house to be among friends while her husband was away. I will not attempt to describe my dearly loved uncle and aunt, Capt. and Mrs. Seale,[130] too many sad memories of the past crowd over me as I write their names only, to do that, so I will simply say that my uncle was an ex-captain in the Hon. East. Ind. Co's. Service and that my aunt was the daughter of an independent gentleman named Gladwin, of course being only my aunt by marriage. While as for the rest my sisters and cousin Annie were simply three merry school girls, and Frank Seale had but just left Dulwich College. Having thus in a manner introduced my relations I can proceed. For the next 14 years all went on ~~happily~~ quietly enough. My mother now in the last stages of infection,[131] yet bore up bravely, having gone to a house her husband had just taken in New Cross. My sisters of course going with her but I whose life hung in the balance was left in the loving motherly charge of my aunt Mrs. Seale. An arrangement quite agreeable to my father who as long as I was "out of

---

127 The 1861 census lists the address as 1 Alpha Place.
128 Eliza Julia Mapleton.
129 At the time his son was born, Henry Mapleton was fifty-years-old.
130 Archibald Alexander Seale and Sarah Maria Pace.
131 Uncertain reading of this word.

sight" took care I should be "out of mind" also at least as far as he was concerned. But in this year a great momentous change took place in both my uncle's and my father's house. In this ill omened year 1866 my grandmother living with my father died,[132] and then within a very few weeks this was followed by the death of my mother[133] and also of my uncle.[134] I was too young to realise prop the awful shock loss properly then, but I have often done so long since. I remember I mourned for them as deeply as my young buoyant heart would permit, more especially for my uncle, who was cut down by heart disease within half an hour of returning from church. What the shock, this dual shock was to all I need hardly say. For a time they seemed completely crushed by it, more especially as at this time both families suffered great pecuniary losses, and I may here add that my father not long previous to my mother's death had returned from the service on half pay. Just before death my poor mother implored my father to let her baby child be brought up for the next few years at any rate, by her aunt, to which my mother father assented. Thus at this period, the end of /66 we have my uncle and mother dead, both families in rather straitened circumstances, Francis Seale in a good appointment at Kensington my dear cousin Mrs. Clayton engaged as a private governess[135] and I a tiny delicate child of six sleeping beneath the kindly roof of my beloved adopted mother while the future, that glorious word to the young, could not contain all the great happiness that was yet in store for me.

Chapter II

A Brief account of my Schools and Schooldays

About two a year later namely in 1867[136] it was determined that I should go to school and accordingly I was sent to commence my academic course at a little "Establishment for Young Gentlemen"[137] situated nearly exactly opposite and presided over by a little old gentleman and his two maiden sisters named Harding whose great knowledge of the rudiments was only equalled by their kindness of heart and true Christian charity, which principles they endeavoured to inculcate their little scholars with, and I have often thought since then that

---

132 Elizabeth Johnson (1780–1866) married William David Mapleton on 11 August 1801. The union produced three children, Mary (b. 1809), George Henry (b. 1809) and James (b. 1810). She died in the spring of 1866, in her mid-eighties.

133 5 June 1866, aged 41.

134 Cremated 6 August 1866, aged 74.

135 Ann Margaret Seale was still unmarried at this point. She married Thomas Graham Clayton in August 1873.

136 Here Lefroy has changed '68' to '67'.

137 Probably Sherbourne House, 116 Asylum Road, Peckham, a 'Boarding and Day Establishment for Young Gentlemen'.

if a little less theoretical ~~christ~~ and more practical Christianity were taught in schools it would be quite as well. At this quiet little place I stayed long enough to learn to read fluently and was then promoted to the little boys' department of my cousin Annie's school, which she had opened in Alpha Place for young ladies, and already her staff of governors and masters had quite a large number of pupils to attend to, about forty I should think. I was very happy there, very happy. We were admirably taught and considerable attention was paid to all religious matters my cousin and aunt being ardent churchwomen, though of course the latter took no part in the management of the school. One strange little circumstance comes to my mind here which I cannot help relating. We had a particular class there consisting of five or rather six boys. Two of these boys were grandsons of the celebrated Josiah Wedgwood,[138] another is now one of the leading scenic artists in the theatrical world a near relation of the late Sir Arthur Helps. My own particular friend, and a gaunt apparently stupid lad who but a year back however was very high up in the list of Wranglers at Cambridge University were the others. While the head of the class, the "good boy" of the school, (what a satire) was <u>myself</u>. It may be asked here, what was really my character at this time and I will endeavour to answer it truthfully. In school I was the pattern boy, studious, attentive and obedient to all rules. But outside I regret to say the case was slightly altered. I was still the gaunt, nervous child of strong imagination but also one who was early beginning a course which surely ends sooner or later, if not checked, in <u>moral ruin</u>. I mean the habit of deception. I was beginning to lie. In very childish ways but still lie. Owing to my delicate health I was not corrected as a more robust child might have been and slowly but surely the worm entered in my soul. Two happy years passed thus, for the severe and dangerous attacks of bronchitis which occurred in them I did not regard in any way as bars to being happy. Rather the reverse in fact, as when ill everything was done by my devoted relations that money or ~~attention~~ <u>love could do</u> to make me happy, in which they certainly succeeded. At the age of ten it was thought high time I should go to some regular boys school and according[139] I was entered as a pupil on the books of St Mary's College Peckham, a large Church of England School in the Grammar School plan.[140] But I did not long remain there. The boys were (or seemed to be) too rough and I was a delicate timid child. Whatever may have been the case I was very soon after removed from there and placed under the charge of a gentleman who was one of the principal masters at the R.N. School, New Cross. With him I stayed several months eighteen I should think, deriving little benefit from his tuition, ~~for~~ and daily increasing that bad habit (speaking untruthfully) which has been my curse. There was really no discipline, each boy

---

138 The 1871 census shows William and Hubert Wedgwood in attendance.
139 *Sic* in autobiography.
140 Founded in 1868, St Mary's College, Hanover Park, Peckham, was a semi-public middle class school providing commercial and classical education along Church of England principles. It closed in the 1890s.

Lefroy.

did much what he ~~liked~~ pleased and said what he liked. Therefore opening many loopholes for lying and other ill practices. Though in justice to myself I must say that this last did not come from me as I was still looked upon as the "model boy" and every "breaking up" gained the leading prizes for proficiency in lessons. All this time be it remembered my father living, never so much as coming to see me or even writing, and in some degree I attribute my mispent[141] life to the want of proper parental authority at this most critical period of my ~~life~~ career. As I have before said my beloved aunt was in every sense a good and Christian mother to me, but there is not one woman in ten thousand however excellent in every other sense, who can fill a mother and a father's place at one and the same time. And here I have one little digression to make the importance of which will be seen later on. My aunt was a churchwoman and a conservative but at the same time she was rather bigoted on the score of amusements; looking upon theatres and actors as temples and followers of the Devil, never letting her own children go to any and <u>never letting me</u>. This in an otherwise irreproachable character was the one weak point as I shall presently try to show. At this period I used regularly to go to church with my dear cousin Francis Seale, and those Sunday walks to church with him form one of the happiest memories of my young life. He was so kind and loving to me ever ready to tell me meaning of this or that, or do anything for me, and yet never shirking from reproving me gently when I deserved it. He was always like a loving elder brother to me, and even now when I have vowed myself to lay bare the uttermost secrets of my heart, my pen falters as I write of him, and the tears rise unbidden to my weary eyes as I think of the love he bore me, and the past that can never return.

We were living now at Edith Road, Peckham. I and my aunt and cousins being of course together, while my father and sister Mary, now married, were living at West Drayton in Middlesex.[142] My other sister having gone as a lady nurse to a London Hospital. About this time I was fourteen years of age, still very delicate but slightly better than I had been. Very thin, very pale and tall for my age. Knowing little Latin, less Greek, and still less French, but very studious and quick to learn. My old habit of deceiving however was even stronger than before, for my wonderfully fertile imagination (a gift which may prove a blessing or a curse as it is used) fostered this habit immensely. On this point my conscience became daily more and more blunted, until at last telling a lie seemed just as easy as telling the truth. But in spite of this I believe my nature was as loving and as gentle and timid as of old. I was now sent to a large private school in St. Mary's

141 *Sic* in autobiography.
142 At the time of the 1871 census – a little before the period being described by Lefroy – Mary Brickwood, née Mapleton, was living with her husband John and their daughter Mary (aged five months) in Yiewsley, West Drayton. Lefroy's father, Henry, was living with Lefroy's sister, Eliza Julia, at 241 New North Road, Islington. Lefroy was living with his aunt, Sarah, and his cousins, Francis and Ann, at 1 Alexandra Villas, Lausanne Road, just off Queen's Road, Peckham.

Appendix XI.

Rd. Peckham[143] and there I made the greatest possible progress. I entered very low down in the school and when I left I had worked my way right up to the top. By no artifice but by sheer hard work. Among other prizes, including again the one for <u>conduct</u> I gained the Latin prize twice and also ones for French and Mathematics, in addition to prizes for English. To that dear master I owe a debt of the deepest gratitude. He taught or tried to teach, his pupils that honour and truth were something more than words, and those lessons of his while I was with him made a deep impression on me at the time, and to a great extent I was under his Christian influence all the time I remained there. But the best of things must have an end, and in August '76 I left school, with the rudiments of a good education. Undecided in character, delicate in health, tossed on the stormy sea of doubt as to what was right and wrong, no kindly father's hand to guide me, launched on the ~~great sea of t~~ treacherous ocean of the world.

Chapter ~~3~~ III

My Life in Australia

The "Somersetshire" was a slow cumbersome old vessel[144] and it was ~~just~~ nearly two months ~~after~~ before we entered the magnificent natural harbour of Port Philip, Victoria.[145] The voyage had been a singularly uneventful one, without the least gale to stay our progress or iceberg to enliven the daily monotony. It was a strange life to me, this sudden severance from a kind ~~friend~~ home and loving friends, ~~and~~ to be throwning abruptly among a lot of strangers. Old colonials returning from an English trip, ambitious young fellows, men of good family, knowing no calling whatever, resolved to ~~live~~ make their fortunes in a land already overstocked with such as them and of which land they knew absolutely less than nothing. Farmers, medical students and adventurers, these formed my society in the second saloon of the "Somersetshire". Until the vessel was actually out at sea, I seemed to recognise in every man who looked at me a detective, such is the effect of a guilty mind, and ~~when~~ not until the white cliffs of Old England were mere clouds on the horizon did I breathe a sigh of relief and go down to see

143 Almost certainly the Upper School, Peckham, situated at the south end of St Mary's Road. It was founded by Dr John Yeats in 1852, and enjoyed a good reputation for training boys for commercial life. Peckham Rye Common was close by, and used for sports such as cricket and football.

144 The *Somersetshire* was built by Money, Wigram & Sons at Blackwall shipyard on the Thames. She was launched in June 1867.

145 Lefroy is recorded as 'Lefroy Mapleton' in a list of passengers aboard the *Somersetshire*, which departed London on 14 December 1878, arrived in Plymouth on 16 December and, after an overnight stay, left for Australia under the charge of Captain H. Farquhar Holt the following day. Lefroy and his fellow passengers – twenty-nine adults and three children – arrived at Melbourne on 12 February 1879 (Victoria, Australia, Assisted and Unassisted Passenger Lists, 1839–1923).

Lefroy.

that my berth was all right, little dreaming that the quiet elderly gentleman who shared my cabin with me was Detective Hockney of the Lincoln Police in hot pursuit of an absconding bank cashier who had already started for Australia in a sailing vessel![146] On board the "Somersetshire" for the first and last time in my life, I played cards for money and through the means of a game called "nap". I was at the end of the voyage minus nearly seven pounds, by way of commencing "to make my fortune". I was induced to play through the devil's old ally idleness, and continued it with that mad idea, so common to gamblers, of winning back my losses in the end. Gambling has been the ruin of many a young man, and it is the favourite pastime on all large passenger ships, and I would earnestly and sincerely advise all young fellows going out as I did to shun it as they would taking poison, for it is quite as insidious and deadly to the soul. It grows upon one in the most fearful way and the wild fever it kindles in the blood is, as a rule, only quenched by the utter ruin of its victim. Strange to say, I, with all my faults, did not fall a victim to it, not through any merit of my own but simply that I lost so much that it thoroughly disgusted me and I have never since played at anything for a penny. There was not the least attempt at religion on board. Nearly every passenger where I was drank, played cards or otherwise profaned the day of Rest and a better school for condemning religious principles could not possibly have been found for me.

But to return to Australia. On landing at Sandridge[147] the port of Melbourne, I found myself in possession of an excellent outfit in clothes and £35 in hard cash. I was not in particularly good health when landing and also very low spirited at my small capital for I had been informed by everyone "that nothing under fifty pounds was any good." Imbued with this idea I telegraphed home to my friends as follows "Send passage money quickly. Ill." never thinking the pain and anxiety this might cause them, but only looking at my need of money; for of course I told this falsehood as the surest means of getting the money sent out. In the message I put where it was to be sent to and went very contentedly to my lodgings at the Norfolk Hotel,[148] Little Flinders Street, Melbourne. Now in this necessarily brief and imperfect story of my life I shall not attempt to give, as having no bearing on sadder and more recent events, any description of the beautiful Victorian capital,

---

146 Henry Stebbings, a clerk employed by the Lincoln Provident Dispensary, fled to Wellington, New Zealand, on board the *Lorraine* when it was discovered that he had embezzled a total of more than £1,000 from his two employers. Detective Sergeant Hockney of the Lincoln police was dispatched to catch the fugitive, and after arriving in Melbourne on the *Somersetshire* – that is, on the same voyage as Lefroy – he took a steamer to Wellington, where he arrested Stebbings on the evening of 28 February 1878 (*Nottingham Evening Post*, 6 May 1879). Stebbings was returned to England and tried in July 1879, receiving five years' imprisonment (*Sheffield Independent*, 21 July 1879). The passenger list for the *Somersetshire* shows Samuel Hockney, aged forty-one, recorded as an 'Officer'.

147 Renamed Port Melbourne in January 1884.

148 Originally the Ship Inn, the building was renamed the Norfolk Hotel in 1866, and later The Tavistock in 1893. The hotel was closed in 1914 and converted to retail and office premises.

Appendix XI.

this I did to the best of my ability in the "Argosy" for last June, and I mention this fact simply to contradict one ~~of the many~~ among many false newspaper statements about me, ~~i.e.~~ that I did <u>not</u> write the article "A Peep at Melbourne" in the above mentioned magazine for June.[149] Firmly believing that at least forty pounds would be sent, and already having had my eyes opened to the fact that Australia is the very last place for a man without a trade to come to, I determined to pass the necessary interval of waiting for the expected remittance, as pleasantly as possible. I had two good letters of introduction with me, one to the Bishop of Melbourne[150] the other to Mr. Grey Smith, the manager of the National Bank of Australasia,[151] but neither of which I presented, as I did not care to face then the searching questions which I not unnaturally imagined might be put to me, as to my arrival and abrupt departure.

Carrying out this view I stayed on at my lodgings, paying a pound a week for my bedroom and board; for over there of course in the way of provisions ten shillings goes twice as far as it would do in England. My days I passed in reading a great many books, of course having to buy them first; eating, sleeping, attending cricket matches, regattas and the like, while my evenings were passed at one of the numerous Melbourne theatres or in attending a concert or lecture. In short I went everywhere but to church, and to my lasting shame be it said I never once entered God's house while in Australia. I certainly went several times to evangelistic services held at the Opera House but I am afraid more to pass the time than from any right feeling. Drinking, smoking, betting, profligacy or gambling did not form a single element in my life, and yet with all these dangerous vices absent, what a hollow, Godless mockery can be made of anyone's life! Of course in such a mad ~~life~~ career as this my £35 melted like butter in the rays of the sun, and at the end of six or seven weeks when the mail was due I found myself the possessor of about five pounds! The mail came in, and to my dismay there were ~~none~~ letters for me. Nearly mad I rushed off ~~the~~ to the post office and met with the same answer. ~~Greatly~~ Quite crushed by the blow I went home and throwing myself on my bed I racked my brain in puzzling ~~the~~ out the meaning of this apparent ~~unkind~~ cruel neglect. The more I thought of it the less I could make of it, and at last I saw that the only thing I could do was to wait patiently for the next mail due in about a month, and live quietly on the remaining few pounds I had left. No cry to God to forgive and strengthen me, nothing but a blind confidence in my own powers of resisting temptation.

And the result of this was soon seen. At the end of two days my resolve

---

149   The article, 'A Peep at Melbourne in 1881', appeared in *The Argosy*, vol. 31, no. 6, June 1881, attributed to 'Anon'.

150   The Right Rev. Dr James Moorhouse, born in Sheffield, England in 1826. Installed as Bishop of Melbourne in January 1877.

151   Frank Grey Smith (1827-1900), appointed manager of the National Bank in 1871.

to economise my funds melted into thin air and I went on living nearly as extravagantly as before. At the end of a fortnight my five pounds had gone and I was gradually selling my clothes, getting for them about a tenth of their value. At last the long expected mail came in and with a heart filled to overflowing with mingled hopes and fears I went down to the Post Office, and was handed two letters, and in the second I read that which turned my heart to stone and made me feel indeed the desperate condition I was in. These were the words, which were added as a postscript "Captain Symons, in answer to your telegram, dear, has taken a second class passage home for you and you can come by any of Money Wigram's boats."[152] Staggering rather than walking to the shipping office with a dreadful fear at my heart I put the question "when does your next ship leave for England?" and then the answer came "July 4 - "True Briton" for London direct." July 4! nearly seven weeks to wait; what, what was I to do? Nearly penniless, hardly anything of value left, I could not sell my portmanteaux for I owed a weeks rent. What I say was before me? That night I sold the few remaining things I had and paid the rent I owed, thus securing 14 more days food and lodging in which to seek for work. And now in the mad struggle for it I was roaming from morn to night all over the city. Answering advertisements for waiters, shop assistants, cabmen and the like. All failed, and ~~Friday~~ May 23 found me leaving or rather turned out of my lodgings,[153] the Australian winter coming on, without a house or home of any sort, only an old coat and shirt on my back, for my waistcoat had had to go with the rest, penniless, friendless and alone. And for all this I had only to thank my own mad extravagance. But I believed then aye and I believe now that God sent it justly upon me as a punishment for my deceptive conduct and the utterly ungodly life I had led in England.

The first day of my vagrant life passed. I had ~~bread~~ some bread and meat which I had saved from the previous day's dinner, so I did not ~~suffered~~ much from hunger, but it was fearful in the extreme seeing or rather knowing that everyone who passed had a home, however humble, in which to lay their heads. That first night of misery I passed on a bench in the Prince's Park, waking next morning bitterly cold and feeling numbed in every limb. Eating ravenously my last morsel of bread I limped back into the city to try once more for some employment however menial. But my search was futile. "Too delicate" was the answer in one place, "no references" in another, while my pallid face and hacking cough told against me in a third. But this same sickly appearance procured me a meal on several occasions for which however I never asked in any way, for begging was a thing, in all my wretchedness, I never had the effrontery to resort to and I would

---

152 Money, Wigram & Sons, established as Wigram and Green in the early 1800s. The firm built the *Somersetshire*, which had brought Lefroy to Melbourne.

153 Lefroy seems to have his dates mixed up here; he claims to have paid for '14 more days food and lodging' on the night the mail arrived, circa 16 May, but then states that he left his lodgings just a week later, on the 23rd. There remains the possibility that in his rush to tell an enthralling story he has neglected the details.

have starved sooner. But I need not go on detailing the occurences[154] of each of these unhappy days; they were far too commonplace in their abject poverty and want. Every day I was growing thinner, suffering from cold ~~generally~~ always and hunger very often and never knowing from on[155] day to another where I should sleep at night. I have slept on Park seats, by the banks of the Yarra, under some unobserved archway or (when having the unusual good fortune to earn a few pence within the day) I would indulge myself with the unwonted luxury of a common lodging house bed, occasionally reliving[156] the monotony of this by walking ~~out~~ about the deserted streets all night. I may mention here for the benefit of any intending "future seeker" that in the Australian colonies a man has to do one of four things, either to work, beg, steal or die, there is no workhouses ~~or~~ and State charitable relief and consequently no paupers. But this state of things could not last.

One cold, wet stormy night I was walking down Swanston Street: terribly ill and feeble in body but worse, far worse in mind. For nearly two days not an atom of food had passed my lips. I had slept out the night before and got drenched with rain, and now crawling down the lengthy street I came, staggering along catching at iron railings or any other support as I went, deathly cold, and yet burnt up with fever. The shops had been long shut for it was nearly twelve o'clock at night, and consequently but few persons were about.

On, on I went, now walking a few yards and then resting for a minute, ere I proceeded. And where was I going? I was going to do what I had often done before, creep under a small boat which lay bottom upwards in Edwards' boat yard by the river Yarra,[157] and to this cold, miserable shelter I was looking as eagerly forward to, as if I had been going to rest my aching limbs upon the softest bed that that ever mortal laid upon. But even this was denied me, for on reaching the place I found that my boat had been locked up with the rest! It may seem childish, but on learning this I sat down on the wharf and cried like a child. I was so utterly broken down in spirit that this last calamity (for calamity it was to me) seemed more than I could bear.

I had no strength to move from where I was, though it was raining fast and already I was chilled to the bone, but sat there, gazing at the gloomy river at my feet. And as I sat there looking at it a spirit of Satan entered in my heart, whispering first, but getting bolder by degrees, that here in the rushing water at my feet was rest: Horrified at the bare idea I rose to my feet and turned to leave the dangerous spot, but then the thought arose where was I to go? Pass yet another night upon those

---

154 *Sic* in autobiography.
155 *Sic* in autobiography. Should be: one.
156 *Sic* in autobiography. Should be: relieving.
157 Built on the Yarra just upriver from the Princes Bridge in 1857 by Englishman James Edwards, who had been a waterman on the Thames before emigrating in the early 1850s.

dreadful stones, that mocked me to my face, every time they rang out sharply beneath my weary tread? Pass yet another night under the distant stars that shed their light upon me with such cruel coldness, seeming to hold themselves aloof from all the world below, and showing all such abject ones as I our lowliness and sin by virtue of their height? Pass yet another night without a place wherein to lay my head seeing the streets deserted fast and knowing that each person that I passed had got a home, and best of all had rest? No, no, that could not be.

Again I wandered back and looked down, with now a different feeling at my heart and with an oar lying there, tried hard to find the river's depth. Down, down deeper and deeper went the oar and now my hand itself was in the water and I found no depth. Nine good deep feet of rushing water, black as ink and cold as ice and yet they promised rest. Only a little leap, whispered the tempter, a brief struggle and you are at rest. No more hunger, cold or fatigue, but everlasting rest. Only a little leap is wanted. My mind was made up, Yes, yes, it was all true, and never giving a thought to the life <u>beyond the grave</u> where suicides find their pardon, I resolved to plunge into the stream. There was no fear of interruption. No one came this way, and the bridge was too far off in the inky darkness for anyone to see me, though I myself, could see the gas lights on it flicking in the wind. And then getting on the extreme brink I stood upright and took one last sad farewell look upon the world I was so soon to leave.

It was a splendid night for such a deed as this! Oh God, how I can see now that awful picture the boathouse standing out like some great bank of blackness in the air, the pretty bridge throwing its shadows down upon the stream, and making even that look blacker than before. From where I was I could see reflected in the water the ~~reflections~~ yellow of the gas lights and somehow, then, in my half frenzied state, they seemed like eyes that looked at me from far beyond the grave, inviting me to come and share their rest. How the wind howled and shrieked among the gloomy gum trees on the river's bank. Once, even twice, I could have sworn my name was called and turned half guilty and afraid, to find it but the wind. A treacherous, noisy wind it was that drove thick waves of clouds before ~~them~~ it as if to give the stars a curtain that they too might not see the deed of sin below. No thought of those at home once crossed my mind. Nothing but a vague awful longing for rest and black utter despair.

I had taken one last look at the distant lights of the city, held up my hands above my head, so that I might jump out well into the stream; shut my eyes and was bending my body for the leap, when the thought suddenly flashed upon me that I had letters about me which would cause my body when found to be immediately identified. This must not be. I had no hesitation in condemning my friends to years and years of the most awful suspense, but I could not bear that they should know I had committed suicide. So retreating a few paces, I put my hand in the inside pocket of my coat, ~~and~~ pull~~ing~~ed out my pocket book, and proceeded to

Appendix XI.

tear into fragments every atom of paper it contained, throwing them as I did into the gloomy stream below. They were quickly borne away by the rapid current and as I watched them fade into the murky darkness, I envied their good fortune and wished that I was there as well. I was closing the book when I felt my finger touch, in a little pocket I had forgotten, a piece of paper, in which something was wrapped up. Wondering what it could be, I opened it and something small and soft lay in my hand. I was about to throw it away and take the fatal leap, when an extraordinary feeling surely sent by God, impelled me, tired, weary and ill as I was to crawl up to the bridge and there by the lamp light look at what I had found. Yes, there it lay, a tiny golden lock, cut from my darling's hair! Unremembered, indeed as it had been in my madness, it yet was surely sent by God to save my soul from death. As I stood looking at it, feeling as one might feel who was slowly awaking from a trance, the great clock in the city peeled out the hour 1 am. And as the sound reached my ears what a great flood of memories came rushing to my brain. I thought of another chime, that had be rung out in dear old Ventnor when I had won the great first love of a pure and loving heart. I thought of the dear faces ones so far away, and then there came into my ear some a loving voice that said "God bless you and goodbye".

And then as if I had been gradually led up to see it, the awful enormity of the crime I had been about to commit flashed like lightning upon me, and there with my head pillowed upon the cold stone I humbly asked for pardon. Just then I heard footsteps approaching, and saw it was a policeman. "What's the matter, young fellow" he said not unkindly and taking hold of my arm, "Why don't you go home?"

I laughed bitterly. "Home" I said "I have none" and then seeing his compassionate face I told him all concerning my past life, and my miraculous preservation from death. "Well," said the kind hearted constable, "I ain't [a] religious chap I'm sorry to say, but if you're not one then after this night's work, you ought to be. And that's the hair, is it. You It 'ud cheer the pretty head as that came from if she knew what it had done to night. But look here you go tomorrow first thing straight down this St. Kilda Road. About a mile down you'll see a big stone house. They call it the Emigrants' Home and they'll give a decent young chap like you, a rough bed every night, and bread and tea twice a day till your ship goes. And about to night, well this 'ull help you to a bed. Good night." and slipping sixpence into my hand the kind hearted fellow left me. Thanks to his generosity and advice, I got a bed that night with the sixpence and the following day mustered up courage to apply at the emigrant's home, a private refuge for a small number of destitute immigrants supported entirely by private subscriptions.[158] My application was successful and I remained there, treated with every kindness till the ship sailed.

---

158 Possibly the Prince's Bridge Immigrants' Home on St. Kilda Road run by the Immigrants' Aid Society between 1853 and 1902.

Lefroy.

*   *   *

On Friday the 6th of July 1879[159] I bid farewell to Australia thoroughly ashamed of myself and deeply repentant for the past. Of course having no outfit whatever I held a rather invidious position on board, but I did not mind that much. I was so thankful to get home at all. Our ship the "True Briton" did the 12,000 miles in ~~exactly~~ nearly three months, arriving in London on the ~~29~~ 31 of Sept. 1879[160] & thus having been absent nine months and a half, while my actual stay in the colony was limited to barely four months! I did not care to go down to Peckham at once, so went to see my sister Julia at Richmond, and on my way there learnt the terrible news (to me) that "Miss May Gordon was one of our leading exponents of opera bouffe[161] and a very great attraction at the ---------- Theatre."

———————

Chapter IV

A Peep at My Life at Wallington

I was warmly received by my dear sister and from her I learnt that the Claytons had left Peckham for a little place in Surrey called Wallington, and that their address was 4, Cathcart Road, and thither I proceeded after a loving note of welcome from my dearest cousin Annie. As I was journeying down there, my thoughts kept wandering to one subject and that was May. It was quite true that she was rising fast in her profession, for I had been to the theatre [where] she was engaged and seen how popular she was. She seemed just the same, only thinner and possessed of a lovely voice. She was the same, and yet not the same. For if there was a gulf between us when I left, what was there now. She on the high road to name and fortune, I, a wanderer on the face of the earth. No, as I left the theatre, refreshed by a sight of her sweet young face, my mind was made up. She should never know of my return until I could present myself worthily before [her]. No thought of the lingering suspense I was dooming her to entered my mind, for I believed I was doing what was right. At Wallington I was informed of two facts. The first was that, as I have elsewhere said, two summonses were out against me,[162] the other was that my poor father had died a month

---

159   The clipper ship *True Briton* left Melbourne for London on 5 July 1879.

160   Lefroy has given a non-existent date (31 September) for the ship's arrival at Gravesend. It actually arrived on Tuesday, 30 September 1879.

161   French comic operetta, popular in the late nineteenth century.

162   At the magistrates' hearing at Cuckfield, Annie Clayton's husband Thomas was asked whether he knew of the summons which had been issued against Lefroy before his trip to Australia for 'obtaining some pictures by alleged false pretences, and that in consequence of not attending that summons a warrant was issued for his apprehension'. Clayton said he was unaware of the warrant, which was still in force on the day Mr Gold was murdered. Lefroy had also been issued with a warrant for his arrest in connection with the theatre fraud committed by him in 1878. A summons was also issued to a solicitor's clerk involved in the scam, but the case collapsed.

before,[163] and I am afraid the former disquieted me more than the latter. When my father died he had my full forgiveness for his conduct towards [me], and I fervently pray that he found pardon and peace at last above. My life at Wallington was a very happy one for the next few months. I knew no one there but my own relatives, but I was quite content. I was deeply attached to my cousins two dear little children, an[d] led [an] even quiet life. Surely the calm before the awful storm! I rarely, if ever, went to town and then never near any place I was likely to see May. I told my dear cousin a little of the one touch of romance in my life, though of course not all. In her I found, as I have ever found, the sympathy of a dear and loving sister. Christmas passed very happily and I remember very well going to church with dear Seale on the morning of that day.

Then came the General Election of 1880 and being rather in want of funds I by the advice of Mr. Clayton applied for the post of clerk to the local committee "for securing the return of Messrs Stern and Higgins, the Liberal candidates."[164] Mr. Stern was a gentleman of Jewish extraction while Mr. Higgins was the Q.C. of that name. It was very thankless work, there being too much of the "hail-fellow-well-met" sort of thing about it to please me. But the pay was good 35/s a week and I put up with it for that. It was the means however of introducing me to a gentleman of whom I shall have to speak more fully later on. I refer to Mr. W. H. Gutteridge of Wallington. Slowly the months rolled on, and in July I made my first attempt at literary composition, the result being my aforementioned article on Melbourne. Wishing to combine a little amusement with a good object I organised in July a cricket match for the benefit of the Wallington Church Schools, the elevens being Liberals vs Conservatives of Carshalton and district, the admission being sixpence. In a pecuniary sense this match was a decided failure brought chiefly about by my giving all the printing for it to a new man, Mr. C. G. Ellis out of kindness of heart, while the leading printer Mr. Pile (also proprietor of the "Sutton & Wallington Herald")[165] was left out in the cold. So to pacify him and secure his interest, he having a good deal in the neighbourhood, I gave him all the bills to do over again, a proceeding which was quite unnecessary and left, on the affair, a deficit of 35/s. Owing this to Pile worried me a good deal, but he was very kind and allowed me to pay him by contributing to his paper, which I did for some weeks. Up to this time I had earned nothing by my pen, but now a welcome surprise was at hand. I received a commission from Mr. Stanton,[166] the proprietor of the Theatre Royal at Croydon, to write the Christmas piece there, of course a pantomime.[167] I started in October to ~~write~~ commence it,

---

163   On 5 August 1879, at 38 Philip Road, Peckham.

164   Sydney Stern and J. Napier Higgins were the Liberal candidates for Mid Surrey.

165   William Pile, a bookseller and stationer from Sutton who established a printing works in 1878 and was one of the founders of the *Surrey County Herald* newspapers.

166   Alfred Stanton.

167   Lefroy was engaged to supply the words for the Christmas pantomime Robinson Crusoe (*Eastbourne Gazette*, 22 December 1880). Edward Fielding and Miss Fanny Johnson took the two principal parts.

and was getting on famously, when my aunt whom I nearly idolized, died after a painful ilness.[168] She had been long troubled with a racking cough that seemed to shake her terribly, (for she was seventy years of age), but nevertheless she was always gentle and loving to me and ready to take an interest in everything I did. I shall never forget her death. All day long, that fourth of November, she had been lying, gasping for breath, and every now and again in excruciating pain, but towards night that seemed to leave her, and she lay back on her pillow, as cool as if asleep. But towards midnight, a change began to take place, and here I may ask What can be more solemn than a death bed? I know of nothing. Somehow it seems to me that one sees or rather feels the greatness of the Almighty more then than at any other period of life. I was sitting facing the bed on which she lay, while on the one side was her daughter, on the other her son. No one had spoken for sometime, but at last my dear aunt opening her eyes and looking fondly at me, while she clasped her son's hand in hers, said "Promise me that you'll always watch over him." Poor Frank silently pressed her hand and almost heartbroken turned his head away, too overcome to speak. As for me I was in like condition. All the her loving words and deeds, years and years of the purest motherly love, came before my eyes as if I were looking at some great panoramic view of all the past. Oh, how I mourned these for all the careless or ungrateful words I had spoken to her, and then would have given anything to live my young life over once again with her and treat her differently. But vain regrets have never yet stayed for an instant Death's far reaching hand when once the fiat has gone forth. And so it was now. As the dim light fell upon the dying face before me I saw the eyes open[,] give one last loving look, and then they closed for ever on this mortal earth. In an instant I had touched the jet of gas and a flood of light streamed down upon the placid face, but there was suspense. Upon those lips, never more to give me words of loving welcome, there lay a sweet and happy smile, as if she who wore it was only asleep and dreaming of some great and glorious happiness, or perhaps seeing a great and glorious reality. And there we sat, grief stricken and alone, whispering comfort to each other. Whilst I, had I but known what was before me, would have implored the saviour of the world there and then to lay me struck by death's icy hand in rest and innocence beside the one already taken from us.

---

168   *Sic* in autobiography.

Appendix XI.

Chapter ~~5~~ V

The Trail of the Serpent

On the 11th of November they buried my dear adopted mother in the little churchyard at pretty Beddington. Her loss I felt then acutely though now I thank God for taking her away from seeing all the awful tragedy that has brought me here.

However much I felt ~~for~~ her loss, I had in a measure to conceal my feelings, for for the next six weeks I was engaged daily in superintending the rehearsals of my first and last pantomime at the Theatre Royal, Croydon. Boxing night came, all went off swimmingly, the place was crammed, and out of the £90 odd pounds taken at the doors, I had a very nice little percentage myself. The piece ran for a month and when it was withdrawn, I was well contented with the press opinions and pounds I had reaped by it.[169] I now felt that my foot was on the first rung of the ladder, but whatever desires of an ambitious nature I had were never for myself but simply that I might make a name and position worthy to offer May. Her sweet young face was ever in my thoughts, and I had less compunction in not communicating with her, as I knew from several reliable sources that though admired by many she was engaged to none, and ~~kept aloof from~~ had already refused two or three most excellent offers of marriage.

When first entering the literary profession, I did not dare to use my own name on account of its being so familiar to all readers of the "Era"[170] and so adopted instead the nom de plume of "Arthur Lefroy." During the month of January I of course had plenty of money which I was more economical with than usual. During this month, my kind friend Mr. Pile of Wallington offered me an engagement on his paper "The Herald and Mid Surrey Advertiser." I accepted this offer at once and remained with him for some months. The work was light, not above a column of matter, and the pay very fair, a guinea a week. But with this rise my ambition rose also. I went up to town very frequently now to see May at the theatre, not to speak to her, but only to see her dear face at a distance, ~~and~~ coming away happier than before, and yet seeing more and more each time how slowly I was bridging over the gulf between us. It was so hard this bitter fight for bread and fame that I was now engaged in. Writing early, writing late, sending manuscripts here and manuscripts there, but nearly always to be returned and ~~unused~~ not used. Of course, as a young beginner I could not have expected anything better, but this I did not think of then. At last the thought occurred to me that <u>interest</u> was what I wanted to get a fair start, but where to obtain this I knew not. At last when utterly

---

169   However, the pantomime was plagued with misfortune: Miss Fanny Johnson (Robinson Crusoe) became 'dangerously ill' and her understudy had to take over; severe weather operated against the house in the last few days and Mr Stanton was probably unable to recoup his expenditure (*The Era*, 29 January 1881).

170   *The Era* had exposed Lefroy's theatre scam of 1878.

beaten it struck me that I might obtain a little more consideration from editors if I represented by letter that I was a relation of some person well known to them, but who of course was dead. I had a good many pricks of conscience over this, but I quieted them at last by reasoning that I should injure no one in any way, and perhaps benefit myself greatly. In pursuance of this mad idea I wrote letters to several influential people in the literary and political world, asking them to consider any article I might send them as "I was a relative of the late Richard Cobden."[171] Among those I addressed were Messrs. John Bright, Ashton Dilke,[172] J. Cowen,[173] Passmore Edwards, L. Lawson,[174] and John Latey. Mr. Bright did not even answer my letter (which perhaps was quite as well for me), Messrs. Dilke and Edwards gave me leave to contribute to their papers "on approval", and Messrs. Cowen, Latey and Lawson were unable even to do this.

In a week I saw this plan would by no means answer, so determined to go on an entirely new tack altogether. I think at this time I must have been slightly insane or I should not have done what I did do. I wrote letters to several well known gentlemen such as Messrs. Burnand,[175] Charles Dickens, and others, couched in the same strain as before, but being now I was related to the late eminent actor, Mr. Charles Harcourt.[176] But over this however I burnt my fingers nicely for I had to go and see Mrs. Harcourt and the late Mr. Charles Harcourt's bosom friend Mr. Thomas Mowbray. They of course plied me with all sorts of questions to which I naturally had to give lying answers, only backing out of the difficulty by promising to lay before them the proofs of my identity when the July mail arrived from Sydney, of course trusting that by that time I might find a way of escape. About this time (the end of February), I came into possession of about thirty pounds odd, the balance of a small legacy of a few hundreds left me by my mother. This money was of course very acceptable, but what with paying one or two old debts and buying myself plenty of good clothes and a gold watch, not an aluminium one, it soon went, and by the end of March I had little more than what was coming from the paper. But just I was still as ambitious and uneasy as ever, for every day May's popularity seemed increasing, which only made me more desperate, when had I but had the sense to write to her and explain my position I might not have been in this awful position now.

The above hare brained schemes having signally failed I determined to have recourse to a more roundabout but perhaps rather more feasible idea, viz to get

---

171 Richard Cobden (1804–1865), Liberal statesman best known as a parliamentary reformer and free trade campaigner active in the fight for the repeal of the Corn Laws in 1846.
172 Member of Parliament for Newcastle. His wife Maye was a prominent campaigner for female equality, writing *Women's Suffrage* in 1885.
173 Joseph Cowen (1829–1900), Liberal politician and journalist.
174 Edward Levy-Lawson, 1st Baron Burnham (1833–1916), newspaper proprietor.
175 Francis Cowley Burnand (1836–1917), English playwright.
176 No relation to Sir William Harcourt, the Home Secretary, who refused a reprieve for Lefroy.

acquainted (in my own person) with the leading literary and dramatic people and to gradually gain their esteem and perhaps through this a more substantial benefit in the way of a play accepted or an article published. This was my chief thought, but another very important consideration was that I should get thoroughly into May's own "set", hear all about her, and be at hand whenever the favourable opportunity came to present myself to her and claim the redemption of her promise.

My first step was to write to the "Era" under the name of Arthur Lefroy stating "that I was in a position to inform the numerous readers of the "Era" that Mr. Frank Coppin[177] of Melbourne, a great Australian capitalist had some years before purchased an unpublished comic opera written by Offenbach entitled Lucette". In conclusion I said that it was thought by the few good judges who knew of its existence to be one of his happiest efforts, and that I believed the London musical public would have an opportunity of forming their own opinions of it in the autumn. This letter I threw out as a sort of feeler, not stating I was "Mr. Coppin's" agent but letting the public infer I ~~was a~~ held that position.[178]

At the end of three weeks I wrote to ~~two~~ some gentlemen (whose real names I shall give to show those persons, who knew of my acquaintance with them, how it came about, and that it <u>was initiated by me not them</u>.) Mr. G. W. Royce of the Gaiety Theatre, and Mr. George Grossmith of the Savoy, and last but by no means least, Mr. Henry Bracy[179] of the Comedy Theatre. I don't think Mr. Grossmith replied immediately to my letter, but the other two did, the one making an appointment at his private residence, the other doing so at the Globe Theatre where he was then engaged. To both gentlemen I made nearly the same offer, that they should manage a London theatre and produce "Lucette" for my employer, Mr. Coppin of Melbourne. Mr. Royce whom I saw first was excessively kind and treated me more like an old friend that a stranger. I stayed there a long time, Mr. Royce promising to seriously consider my offer [and] introducing me before I left to a talented lady whose name is a household word when "the sacred lamp of burlesque" burns.[180] Early the same afternoon I called upon Mr. Bracy at the

---

177   Frank Coppin appears to have been a character completely invented by Lefroy. Possibly he was based on George Coppin (1819–1906), an English comedian and theatrical manager who left for Australia in the 1840s. Lefroy claimed Frank Coppin was a 'wealthy sheep farmer and an illiterate man' (*Daily Gazette for Middlesbrough* 29 June 1881).

178   In his letter to *The Era* (22 March 1881), Lefroy claimed *Lucette* was a three-part opera comique written by Offenbach in 1869 and only 'known to half a dozen persons'. In fact, no such work exists. Lefroy would certainly have been aware that Offenbach died in October 1880, which would have made the deception easier to pull off.

179   Henry Bracy (1846–1917), opera producer, manager of the Globe and an established principal tenor on the London stage.

180   Possibly a reference to the famous English actress and singer Nellie Farren (1848–1904), noted for her roles as the 'principal' boy in musical burlesques at the Gaiety Theatre.

Lefroy.

Globe and directly I saw his happy, genial face, my heart reproached me bitterly for the deception I was practising. To cut a long story short before we had been talking half an hour I conceived a great liking for the handsome, kindly young actor. He was well known in Melbourne having often acted there, so I had to be very cautious in playing the difficult rôle of a native Australian, but thanks to my excellent memory and early training in deceit, I got through my task, though not without several times wishing I could muster up courage to confess the truth and earnestly ask for his friendship and forgiveness. However, by the time I left, there was no retreat open and the deadly game once commenced I had [to] carry it through even to the bitter end. Mr Bracy. I must say all this while, believed me to be by documentary and verbal evidence the secretary of Mr. Coppin, and a young colonial journalist of some little position. Every day the plot thickened. Bracy and I often saw each other, not unfrequently[181] lunching together, and I can honestly say I never endeavoured to obtain money from him at these or any other times.

So far, this ~~second~~ third scheme had succeeded. I was daily getting to know more and more literary men and actors of repute, and consequently hoped very soon to obtain some substantial benefit from this knowledge. I had asked Mr. Bracy, as stage manager of the Globe, to try and get a little comedietta of mine played, and with I believe the most genuine kindness he promised to try his utmost to do so. Of course this false life was very expensive to me, for "sponging" (if I may be pardoned for using this slangy but expressive word here) was ~~not~~ never one of my faults, and consequently I was living very much more extravagantly than I ought to have done. But the thought that I was getting nearer to May buoyed me up, and I was never happier than when hearing her praised and adored. For all I knew, she believed me still in Australia, and though I had often several narrow escapes of being "introduced" to her, I always escaped in time, and we had never seen each other since that gloomy winter's morning nearly four years before. But a terrible change was at hand.

One very hot evening in May I was sitting with a friend (whom I shall call Fielding) in the nearly deserted smoking room of the Junior Garrick Club, of which club he was a member, talking on various subjects theatric, when he said rather abruptly (anent a particular lady), "I don't think much of her. Give me Lord —— 's fiancé[182] for that." "Who is she?" I asked, cautiously looking at the blue rings of smoke that went curling up to the ceiling. "Why, May Gordon, of course. I thought every one knew that."

*   *

---

181 *Sic* in autobiography.
182 *Sic* in autobiography. Should read: 'fiancée'.

Appendix XI.

That night I walked aimlessly up and down the Embankment for hours, letting the ~~cool~~ soft night air play upon my heated brow and wishing that it might cool also the flames of maddening jealousy and despair that were raging in my heart and soul.

Chapter ~~6~~ VI

The Lights of London

To say that for the next day or two I was utterly demented, would be I am sure no mere figure of speech. I could do nothing, think of nothing but May. For two whole days I stayed at home never going out except at night and then only to wander up and down some gloomy road where I could think of all that I had lost and loved. Fielding's words I found (as I thought) to be quite true, for had I not seen her twice talking merrily to a well dressed rather effeminate looking young man who walking with herself and mother, and whom I learned was a frequent visitor at their pretty little suburban villa. What did it matter to ~~that~~ me that his "lordship" was known to them as plain "Mr. Harrison", it only made the matter worse in my eyes, for before ~~should~~ any breath of scandal should touch my darling through his conduct, I would shout him down and give my own life to save her fair name. Now that my eyes were opened I saw how cruelly neglectful I had been to my darling in never once letting her know that I was dead or alive. All the these years[183] she had been faithful to me, and now was it to [be] wondered at that she sould[184] seek for honest love elsewhere. If I could not beat my adversary ~~on~~ with his own weapons falsehood, I would give in brokenhearted and despairing though I might be, to his marrying her in his own name. But let him once approach her with any other offer and his life should pay the penalty. ~~of the law I should~~[185] What happened to me I cared not. If my life could save her honour I should be well content.

So in my delirium I went to Vaughan's the gunsmiths in the Strand and purchased a six chambered revolver,[186] bought cartridges elsewhere, loaded it, and went about my daily avocations with the deadly weapon ever ready at my hand. It was no mere jealousy of my rival that prompted this. If he married her, and legitimately beat me in the unequal contest of rank and wealth versus poverty and obscurity - well and good, I should have accepted my fate, though life would

183 *Sic* in autobiography. Should read: 'All these years'.
184 *Sic* in autobiography. Presumably should read: 'should'.
185 Uncertain reading due to the obliteration of these words.
186 Presumably the same Charles Vaughan at 39 Strand, where Lefroy pledged an aluminium watch a month earlier.

have seemed to have lost all charm for me, but if he adopted another course, then let his blood be upon his own head. Those were my thoughts and may God in his infinite mercy forgive my entertaining them for an instant.

Having a pretty fertile imagination I was not long in hitting upon the only way in which I could possibly meet Lord —— at all. His rank of course I could not imitate, though as that was unknown to May, I was not so concerned about it, but his wealth I could counterfeit possibly. I had hit upon no definite scheme when one day I accidentally heard that Bracy was a sort of relative of Mrs. Gordon[187] and possessed very great influence with both May and her mother. This decided me at once. That evening I wrote a letter to Mr. Bracy, apologising for not having done so before, and telling him I had received a great shock in just learning by Telegram that my old friend and employer Mr. Coppin (who was travelling to England with the score of the opera) via San Francisco had just died of appoplexy[188] leaving me the opera and £1000 a year which was to be increased to £10,000 per annum when I married. After a going on to express (my really genuine) liking for him, I concluded by asking him to accept the opera as a slight tribute of friendship and regard. My objects being to make our interests identical, and to get him through feelings of gratitude to aid me in my fight against my rival. Of course he [was] to present me in the name of Lefroy and in the position of a wealthy man to let May believe I had changed my name by Mr. Coppin's wish, and then to do my utmost to win back her love once more. A very insane reckless scheme on paper, and yet [not] really quite so mad as it seemed. I should not have to place the opera, or rather an opera, in Bracy's hands before two months had expired. And my assumed rôle, except for the want of the main thing - money, was not a difficult one. I was well educated, had a fair superficial knowledge of most subjects, was well dressed, accustomed to good society and by birth a gentleman. Not by any means the combination of card sharper, shopman and pickpocket that has occasionally been represented.

But the great stumbling block was how to keep up the character of a wealthy man? For the next month or so I might excuse myself from doing this, but not yet[189] longer for suspicion once aroused I knew I should be lost. But with a vain hope like Mr. Micawber that something would "turn up" I rushed in desperation headlong to my doom. All this time my dear friends were naturally anxious as to what made me go to town nearly every day, and remain so late at night so again I do add another lie to the already fearfully long list and say I was engaged on the staff of the "Era" at four guineas a week paid monthly which would not fall due until the last Saturday in June. This I enduced[190] them to believe and so I put

---

187 Mary Josephine Thompson (née Brougham).
188 *Sic* in autobiography.
189 Uncertain reading of this word.
190 *Sic* in autobiography.

it out of their reach to help me at all. Thus I was leading or beginning to lead a double life, impersonating not only two characters but both at the same time. In May I severed my connection with the "Herald" the proprietor naturally being annoyed at the careless way in which I worked for him. So at the end of May I should have been entirely without means had not my article on Melbourne been accepted by a London magazine the Argosy, for which I received £8.10. All this time Bracy and I were becoming daily more intimate. I can truly say I was deeply attached [to] him and should he ever read this I trust he will believe that even I was <u>not all</u> bad. We often dined together sometimes at his club, the United Arts, ~~and~~ or at his house where I met his wife and was treated by her with the greatest kindness. Bracy's gratitude for my generous kindness, as he called it, used to cut me to the heart, and had it not been for my hopeless love for May I should have thrown off the acted lie with horror and disgust. But my astonishment may be imagined when one day I found that my "rival" was but a nightmare no designing peer, but ~~and~~ ol[191] friend of Mrs. Gordon's but was very unpopular with May! And so I had to keep up the imposture without having to fight any opponent at all. And now my affairs were truly becoming desperate. Very often of an evening I would drop in to the Strand theatre for half an hours chat with Bracy or Messrs Marius, Ashley[192] or Cox[193], whoever might be off the stage for the times. These ~~gentlemen~~ were all very kind, genial men particularly M. Marius and I got to like him only secondly to Bracy.[194] One hot evening at the beginning of June while sitting there talking I challenged the Strand Theatre Cricket Club to play a match at their ground St. John's Wood against eleven colonial journalists selected by me. This was at once accepted by letter and I think June 17 was the day fixed for the match. It must not be thought that this was ~~digressing~~ diverging from my scheme, on the contrary I relied upon it to strengthen the already good feeling existing between Bracy and myself, for the instant I placed the forged opera (by a well known English comic opera composer however) in his hands I intended to ask him to introduce me to May. On the 24th instant I was promised a loan of £100 (to be paid ~~and~~ in monthly installments of £5) by a person in whom I had the greatest confidence, so I had no fear for myself after the end of the month. But how to get over my present necessities was the thing, so I determined ~~and~~ with a good deal of reluctance and horror at my deceit to ask for a loan of six pounds from my earliest Wallington friend Mr. W. H Gutteridge. He lent it me willingly, believing me to be in a good appointment and on the understanding that I should pay at least half of it <u>by the end of June</u>. The day for the cricket match came and went. We had a most enjoyable day, ~~and~~ no one there would have imagined the awful heartsickness I was suffering from. My eleven consisted of various

191   *Sic* in autobiography. Lefroy, getting excited, has transposed the *d* from 'old' onto 'an'.
192   Henry Ashley.
193   Harry Cox.
194   Claude Marius (1850-1896), French actor and stage manager.

Lefroy.

personal friends of my own including Messrs Loridan and Parry then of the Strand Theatre who filled up two vacancies in the eleven, while our opponents were Messrs Marius, R. Reece, Bracy, Ashley, Hiller &c &c several well known gentlemen. We won the match and then to my horror I found that my bag had been cut open and money taken from it, and to get home I had to borrow a few shillings from Bracy.[195] I need hardly say the things pawned by me represent the various stages of desperation I passed into. And so the month went on. I owed money right and left and had it not been for the hundred pounds I was to receive at the end of the month I should have been utterly lost. I need hardly say that such a life as I was living was most terribly trying,[196] and I felt utterly broken down as the mental strain was so great. At last the prayed for 24th of June arrived and my liabilities were as follows. I owed about 30/s to Bracy, three pounds to Mr. Gutteridge, a pound owed to my cousins. I had all my clothes to redeem, Bracy believed I was entering on possession of my thousand a year on the following Monday. June 27. In a day or two I had to put without fail (if I wished to keep up my false position) the opera in Bracy's hands and I could not do this unless I handed over to the composer £50 before the 28th of June while as if this was not enough I owed my subscription of three guineas to the United Arts Club of which I had been elected a member. It will thus be seen that in the event of my failing to satisfy nearly all these persons, utter ruin must have followed. The falsehood of my life would have been seen through and May and I would have been parted without doubt for ever. And so I say the most momentous day of my life dawned and in high spirits I went up to Charing Cross station to meet my friend (Lester I will call him) in the first class waiting room there. When I entered he was sitting near the door a couple of portmanteaux at his side labelled "Paris", where I remembered he had told me he was going en route for Madrid. I may say here that I had lent him when I came into my £35 pounds ten guineas, and he had promised to pay it several times, at last when my patience was almost wearied he wrote to me saying he should come into a couple of thousand pounds at the end of June and if I would wait a few weeks longer, he would pay me on the 24th what he owed and would moreover lend me any sum up to a hundred I might require. As I entered, Lester rose hastily. "There you are my boy, rather late, but never mind. Here's your cheque. I know you'll pay it off as quick as you can. Wish you luck. Good bye, take care of yourself" and so saying he shook my hand warmly and

---

195 A slightly different version of events, which includes the snippet that Lefroy's eleven actually *lost* the match, is reported in the *Bolton Evening News* for 29 June 1881: 'Lefroy got up an eleven at a cricket match, his contingent being understood to be colonial journalists, while on the other side were several well-known theatrical gentlemen. Lefroy's eleven lost, and when wickets were drawn and he was required to pay his quota towards the expenses he excused himself on the ground that his bag had been cut open and his purse extracted. It was subsequently found that other bags had been cut in a similar way, but whether anything was missing from them is uncertain.'

196 Text reads: 'a most terribly trying'.

pressed into it a piece of paper and was gone. He had been so quick that I had scarcely time to thank him, but the feeling of intense relief at my heart drove all other feelings away as walking hastily down the Strand I turned into Child's bank with the cheque and had it instantly returned marked "no effects".

*   *

What followed I can never remember with distinctiveness. I remember[197] going and sitting for hours in St. James Park watching the morning turn into evening, and the evening into night. I remember getting up and staggering through the noisy streets about 11 o'clock to catch the last train for Wallington. People spoke to me at home, but I don't remember what they said. I went to bed, and all last that lonely Sunday I went about like a man in a dream, thinking of nothing but my utter ruin. In the evening I walked down with Seale at his own request to his mother's grave and there with the shadows falling round us we shed bitter tears for her we had loved so well. By the time we reached home my heart was filled again with blackness and despair. I sat up in the darkened parlour looking out upon the glorious summer night while slowly and surely the tempter of all took possession of my heart, slowly whispering, whispering to me that I must get at least ten pounds by tomorrow night and that the only way of getting it was by force. Murder was only dreadful in name, when it was done I should feel just as usual for had not my favourite writer George R. Sims said so in the Referee[198] that murderers walked and talked and felt just as any other man might do, and that the brand of Cain and all that was nonsense. Besides, there need not be any murder only a shot to disable and then robbery was easy, especially in a railway carriage argued the tempter. Say in an express train going to Brighton, surely plenty of wealthy people would be in it. There could [be] no failure. No deadly struggle would result. One shot and all would be done. A mere moment[199] of the finger, and I had the the means of staving off discovery. Of course went on the evil one it would perhaps take the matter into the regions of moral certainty if you took some other weapon with you, <u>say a razor</u>. Muster up courage and May Gordon can shall yet be yours. Give in, and I leave you to your fate. Exposed, ruined and disgraced, the law will be put in motion against you and the girl you love shall recoil from you with horror. Even now I can hear the hellish words ringing in upon my ear as terror struck I recoiled in horror from my own blackest thoughts, but alas! it was the old story of Faust and Mephistopheles over again. And I sold my soul for the promise of a woman's love. As the miserable compact was signed and sealed, a strange, and sad voice called twice my name. I rushed to the windows but there was no one there, nothing to be seen but the evening sky

---

197   Text reads: 'rememember'.
198   Sunday sports and entertainments newspaper. Sims wrote a regular column for the paper.
199   *Sic* in autobiography. Lefroy presumably meant to write 'movement'.

reddened in the distance by ~~glare~~ the light of London, which fell upon the somber clouds like the reflection of a mighty fire. ~~There in that great city~~

Chapter ~~6~~ VII

June 27

The morning of last day of my holding out dawned. Just before my cousin Mr. Clayton left he came into my room where I was in bed and asked me when I was going to give him up three things belonging to him which I had pledged. Wearily turning my face to the wall I said "To night, without fail" and he left me. I had already promised Seale to pay him what I owed him this same evening. Soon after nine I got up went downstairs and in pursuance of my plan conceived the night before I wrote the note purporting to come from Mrs. Clayton and sent it to Mr. Ellis. My dear little cousins came into the room,[200] but I did not play with them as was my wont, for I hardly saw them, my very habit seemed gone and in its place a raging spirit lay concealed and moved me as he pleased. My cousins little pupils entered, and one of them said "You do look strange. Don't you feel well." "Well," and then I rushed upstairs with yet [another] echo ringing in my heart. At last Ellis came. I rushed madly from the house, into his shop obtained the money, said good bye to my cousin, feeling as if I should never see her again, and then walked as fast as I could to Waddon station, where I caught the 10.50 from Wallington. London Bridge was soon reached. Out of the carriage, down the steps, strait[201] along the street and then into a gloomy door over which hung three golden balls.[202] No delay anywhere, all ready, everything favourable for no more willing servant is there than the Devil, when by it he gains a complete mastery afterwards. It did not take long to redeem the revolver and there I had it once more in my hands. One shot and all would be over, so argued the Spirit of Darkness and you will be free once more from this awful poverty. But I had something more to do yet: I had not sufficient for my fare to Brighton, so going to the office of a friend, not Seale let it be most distinctly understood, I borrowed five shillings and with that and the money already in my possession I had funds to lunch at the International restaurant in the Approach and enter London Bridge station. And now that I have bared thus far the most awful secret of my heart I will repeat step by step the awful tragedy, what I did, what I felt, and what I thought, shall all be exposed for the first time to the world. Supposition and uncertainty shall cease, and all I ask that these poor words of ~~mine~~ a dying and <u>most earnestly repentant man</u> may be implicitly believed, however I may ask my readers to discount the

200   Melville (b.1874), Elsie (b.1878) and Ashley (b.1879).
201   *Sic* in autobiography: should be 'straight', and Lefroy uses this more familiar spelling elsewhere.
202   This was the pawnbrokers Adams & Hillstead, 25 High Street, Borough.

Appendix XI.

evidence of certain witnesses. Let it be remembered moreover that I am the only living person that can clear up the mystery and intend doing so in every way. And to depict the occurences[203] of this awful day more vivid I shall avail myself of a literary license and do so in the first person.

*   *

The first thing was to get my ticket. Tending 12/6 to the clerk, (not a sovereign for I had none about me) I got my ticket and left the window there being no ladies anywhere near at any time I was there. Going into the waiting room my next proceeding was to load the revolver which I did under cover of a newspaper. This done, after cocking it and feeling that the razor was secure in my pocket I made[204] my way on to the platform. It was now just three minutes to two. Walking past the first first class carriage I looked in and saw to my great satisfaction that one compartment was occupied by only a single passenger. After entering and as I put my head out of the window to shut the door, I saw an old gentleman getting into a carriage someway down the train. Sitting down, with my face to the engine on the near side, I drew out my paper and under cover of it proceed[205] to carefully scrutinise my companion. ~~What's that he's got in that bag?~~ He had a paper bag of fruit with him, strawberries I thought and he apparently did not like me to see him eating them for he put them in the rack above as I entered. Somehow the tempter did not seem to have got such a hold on me when the train started for I shuddered instinctively at the bare idea of shooting ~~him~~ the unconscious man opposite. Very well, said the Devil, how are you going to get back from Brighton if you don't get some money on the road? I looked at him again. He was a short slight man about forty with dark hair and whiskers, and every now and then he would look at me in ~~that~~ a very peculiar way? Could he have known what I've come for? He had a gold watch I could see that and rings, but I did not like his looks. He seemed as if he knew I came to murder him. I ~~discovered~~ looked out of the windows. We were coming to a station, East Croydon. Now should I try or not. I wondered if - But there, he was looking steadily at me again, and his eyes seemed to pierce into my soul. I could stand it no longer and got out of the compartment, my companion little thinking that to his inquisitive looks he probably owed his life.[206] As I was walking down all the carriages, looking in at the windows to see if any first class passenger was by himself, there came in to my heart once more those living and "God bless you and good bye". But this time they found no response. The person hearing them was not in soul the ~~person~~ one to whom they were first spoken.

---

203   *Sic* in autobiography.

204   Lefroy wrote 'made' over the word 'make'. His earlier pledge to tell the story in the first person was meaningless – the whole document is in the first person – but he no doubt intended to announce a plan to use the present tense. He immediately omitted to do so, and then remembered, and, realising that he had got into a muddle, corrected subsequent present tense verbs by converting them into the past tense.

205   Lefroy forgot to convert this noun into the past tense.

206   See Appendix XII.

Lefroy.

No, no, this man with murder in his mind was someone else in my poor earthly form, and so the mocking laugh that came unheeded to my lips, consigned those loving words to the bleak and bitter Hades in my heart to be devoured, spurned and lost by all the evil spirits raging there. At this moment in passing a first class compartment I saw it was tenanted by only one person, whether young or old I could not tell, for his head was completely covered with a handkerchief, which as I entered he removed, and I saw before me for the first time in my life Mr. Gold. He was then sitting nearly in the middle seat with his back to the engine, I nearly ~~facing~~ in front of him, facing the engine in the near corner. When the train started Mr. Gold was looking out of the window and I was ostensibly reading the paper. On, on through the dear familiar scenery rushed the train, reminding me, had I been really there, of many and many a cherished walk with those I loved. But of none of those things was I thinking now, as I sat there with fixed and staring eyes, my hand slowling[207] drawing the deadly weapon from its hiding place. Every minute of waiting seemed ~~and~~ hour. ~~Were~~ were dashing now through Stoats Nest and I knew that soon the yawning gulf of blackness would be upon us. The pistol was now in my right hand, loaded, cocked and <u>levelled</u>. Oh God! How can I write what follows! Quicker and quicker flew the train, higher and higher rose the chalky walls on either side, and fiercer and fiercer raged a battle in my heart not yet long commenced, but which, in these few seconds, was to decide my earthly fate for ever. Which was it to be, a pistol and money and happiness? Or innocence and all my false and hollow life laid bare? Quick, no time for reflection. Higher and higher rose the walls of chalk, shutting out all sight of heaven and telling me that now I must decide for once, for ever. Nearer and nearer, closer and closer, the yawning mouth was close upon us. Fifty yards, thirty, ten, 5 we were in! Slowly I closed my eyes, extend my arm and fired, and e'er the trigger fell, the engine gave an awful shriek, like the last bitter cry of my good spirit as it flew in horror from me, and I was in darkness, both of soul and body. As the report died away I sprang to my feet and peered into the ~~darkness~~ gloom where my unoffending victim had been sitting. Had I killed him? No, no, for in an instant he was upon me, not before though in my madness I had discharged three or four more shots at him. Oh merciful Father give me strength to finish now. In an instant I was extended on the ground up against the farthest door, keeping at bay as well as I could the justly infuriated man, who with one hand grasped me by the throat and with the other struck me savagely upon the head with the revolver, which he grasped by the handle, striking me with the end of the muzzle. Not a word was uttered and there in the darkness of the tunnel that death struggle commenced. The awful ~~gloom~~ blackness of the tunnel without, the air laden with the fearful smell of powder, the half gloom of that living grave, only made visible by the ~~passing~~ feeble light above which shed its sickly light upon the livid face that finally looked in mine, made such a fearful impression

---

207   *Sic* in autobiography. Should read: 'slowly'.

on me that never, if I lived a thousand years, could I forget it. Poor Mr. Gold who might have been unconcerned for any effect it ~~showed~~ had upon him then could easily have pulled the communicator a dozen times, ~~and~~ had he wished to do so, but he never appeared to think of it. As for me I was a mere child in his hands and I had as much as I could do to save myself from being throttled when he threw the pistol on one side and tried to grasp my throat with both his hands.

And so the time sped on, and our positions never changed, he pinioning me to the ground whilst I as strenuously resisted, neither being armed and both being on the floor of [the] carriage at the same end as the door he entered at London Bridge. Never once was there any "scuffling or fighting" standing up from the time the first shot was fired until within a few miles of Balcombe. Mrs. Brown and her daughter must be either gravely mistaken as to the train, or telling a willful falsehood. At last the sense[208] of the deadly struggle changed. All at once, as if by mutual agreement, we released each other, both maddened with fury and both believing they were fighting for their lives. I had still the same utter soulessness[209], if I may use the expression, but this was also increased by a fresh feeling, that of mad desperation. I knew that if we both arrived at Brighton, my fate was sealed, and I did not know but what we might be quite close there, for every minute that had passed had seemed, at least to me, as if it was freighted with the weight of years. And now before Mr. Gold could prevent me I had sprung up and throwing open the door, called to him in a voice as of some demon fresh from Hell below, that made me start and tremble when I heard it, to jump from the train or I'd shoot him, at the same time snatching up the pistol. And then with the train flying along at fifty miles an hour, the door wide open and the floor already slippery with blood, the awful ending came. A mad refusal, high words, a pull at a brittle chain, heaving backwards and forward, turning and twisting, blade against pistol, another shriek from the engine, black, bitter darkness, a sudden jerk, an awful cry, a door quickly shut and I found myself alone.

Alone, my God, alone. When every foot of space was peopled with fierce, bloody faces that glared at me which ever way I looked. When every stroke the engine piston made shrieked murder, a cry re-echoed and re-echoed back and back again by twenty thousand fiendish voices in my ears. ~~As~~ When bleeding hands were on my throat, not once or twice but twenty times a minute, hands that when I beat them off returned more madly to the charge than ever. When every sound was lulled by wild deafening cries that seemed to come from out the yawning abyss at my feet, cries that were taken up by ~~twenty thousand~~ grinning imps and fiendish voices as some wild mighty chorus to their song of murder. Was I alone when pistol shots were crashing on my ears and going like a death knell to my heart? Was I alone or was I not in some great endless gulf that led to Hell, where

---

208 Uncertain reading of this word.
209 *Sic* in autobiography.

all was gloomy blackness and these ghastly spectres but the messengers of Satan sent to lead me on? Was I alone I ask when every shadow on the wall and puff of ghastly steam cried "murderer" and did its best to hunt me down. Was this I ask all this alone?

When everything I touched gave forth hot blood that lay in stagnant pools beneath my feet, or fell unceasingly upon my face like rain and would not be removed. When every breath of foul mephitic air was filled with blood, and left it in the shape of gory spray upon my face. When even now the blackness had a crimson tinge from out which ever and anon ~~white fi~~ some pair of hands came forth and tried to pull me down to that great gory thing below. Should I no more see daylight but as my doom be forced to stand here till the last great day, gazing with staring eyes into the devil haunted gloom beyond. ~~But as the train left the tunnel, the phantoms vanished and as the light of God streamed back into my soul I groped madly around me and fell unconscious to the ground.~~ Why even now the carriage door was full of them, all trying to get in and pull me out, and all had ghastly faces stained with blood that rushed and poured from hideous gaping wounds, and as it flowed it seemed to be alive with many thousand tiny hands that clenched and struck and clawed at me as if to pull me down and down to them. When even now the walls, roof, the seats were running blood, no gentle murmur but a mighty roar of gore that as it fell and rose again like some great crimson tide, sang nought but murder! From side to side I looked but no escape, for everywhere, before, behind, in front were bleeding hands that tried to seize me and to pull me down, while the Dark Dead was acted there before my eyes a score of times a second, and every time the Body fell in to the dark abyss, they shrieked and howled into my ear that I was theirs for ever. Look, how the[210]crimson tide in which I stood was mounting! Higher and higher it came, and there I stood at the window as if spell bound. Hark, how it surged against my legs and crept and crept much nearer to my face. Was there no escape? Was I to wait and be submerged in that ensanguined stream that now had got so close that there reflected in its awful face I saw the hideous ghastly Thing below. My God, reflected did I say? With frenzied eyes and heart that seemed of stone, I saw it was no reflection but the Thing itself, that now was floating up from where it lay with staring eyes and bloodstained blackened face to hold me in a mad embrace and claim me for its own. Nearer and nearer it comes, I could not move but simply went on staring at the dreadful stream that now was close up to my breast, and I could feel it now dashing in hot waves around my throat and those great awful arms were opening for that last embrace. Nearer, near, and nearer they came, they were open now and pulling my face down on to the awful one beneath when there was a loud shriek from the engine, a sudden burst of glorious light and I fell unconscious to the ground.

---

210   Text reads 'the the'.

Appendix XI.

Chapter XII[211]

From Balcombe to Wallington

I could not have been insensible more than a minute or two I think, ~~and~~ but my feelings when I recovered were utterly impossible to describe. I seemed to have been awakened from some most awful dream but the terrible aspect of the carriage soon showed the fearful reality. The most awful horror and remorse seized my soul and I firmly believe that from the previous Sunday night until this moment I had been as insane for the time as any homicidal maniac in Broadmoor. I am not in any way desirous of hiding my guilt but I know then and I know now that my supposition was correct. I felt at this moment as a person of gentle disposition and naturally kindhearted might do if he returned home and was informed that a most atrocious and cold blooded murder had been committed by some one exactly resembling him. Of course now my first thought was self preservation, and to improve my chances of safety I knew I must dispose of the various articles left by Mr. Gold in the carriage. The first thing I hauled out was the revolver which fell in some underwood close to the bridge not very far from the tunnel, on the same side as that on which the other articles were found, but strange to say the razor and a stray cartridge I put in to my side overcoat pocket. On the floor was Mr. Gold's watch with a small piece of chain attached to it, while on the seat where he had been sitting was the handkerchief he had pulled out of his pocket soon after starting I suppose. What should I do with the watch, put it in my pocket? No, I might be searched, so hastily I ~~put~~ slipped it in my shoe and proceeded to open the purse which I found to contain barely half a sovereign. This then was my gold mine, the harvest that was reward [for] my guilty act, ~~and~~ old fashioned watch and ten shillings! As I put the empty purse in my pocket there slowly came into my mind those awful words "What shall it profit a man if he gain the <u>whole world</u> and lose his own soul." I looked in the glass, and my heart sank as I saw my appearance, ghastly face and covered in blood (for I may say that in spite of insinuations to the contrary nearly all the blood upon my head, neck and coat came from my raw wounds). In this state how could I help being suspected and detained. I could hide the bloody coat by taking it off and throwing it over my arm which I did, but this course did not hide the state of my trousers and face. Somehow it seemed to me that my bloodstained collar would attract more attention than anything else, so hastily I tore it off and cast it from the window. I was just congratulating myself that I had got rid of ~~any~~ every thing when to my horror I saw lying in the rack poor Mr. Gold's umbrella. I was about to hurl it from the window when I felt the train perceptibly slacking speed.

---

211   Lefroy has misnumbered the chapter. It should read VIII.

Lefroy.

Terrified lest this should be Brighton, I thrust my head from the window and saw that we were rapidly drawing up at a station platform, and when the train came to a dead standstill (which it did for at least a quarter of a minute), I knew from a board nearly opposite that the station was Hassock's Gate. Now was the time to alight, but before I could carry out my purpose it the train was rapidly quickening speed and soon was flying along as fast as ever. With a groan of despair I sank back in the seat, resolved if at all suspected to make a clean breast of the whole thing. A minute after we entered Clayton Tunnel this momentary good purpose had fled, and I resolved to fight for my life even to the bitter end and in the coming ordeal at the station to use all the Devil's weapons I possessed to blind them as to what I really was.

On the arrival of the train at Preston I saw at once that all tickets would be collected there, so knew that now the struggle must commence. Before the man who opened the door I had had time to comment on the state of the carriage I asked him "if I could see a doctor anywhere" and followed this up by telling Gibson, who came up then that time that I had been murderously attacked, and by him I was referred to the station master. I could see that all three had some suspicions of something being wrong, and so when the station master suggested I should go to Brighton I at once assented. I was greatly alarmed however by Watson the guard picking the watch by the chain from my shoe and asking me how I it got there, to which I replied "that I knew nothing about it." The guard then placed it on the seat by my side, and left me. I do not think either Mr. Hall or Gibson saw the watch until it was taken out, and I know that they never spoke a word to me on the subject at all, Watson being the only one who did so. Collector Gibson was sent with me to Brighton, he sitting exactly opposite to me, in the near corner with his back to the engine. He asked me for my name and address, I of course as a matter of course policy giving it correctly. I was greatly concerned to get rid of the bit of chain, so on the way I called his attention to the beautiful scenery out of the further window, and threw the chain out of the other without in any way attracting his attention. To do this thing however was not by any means so easy as Lord Coleridge suggested. I am quite ready to believe that poor Mrs. Gold made a mistake, but the chain was not attached to the watch by a swivel but instead the watch ring and a link of the chain were united together in an extraordinary way, so that not knowing the spring I had to tear them asunder by main force. We arrived at Brighton and went by Gibson's advice straight to the superintendent's office. I, to escape observation walking as quickly as possible about a couple of feet in advance of Gibson. No one spoke a word to me prior to my reaching the office and then only the clerk. No one touched me in any way or came within several feet. There was a gentleman sitting waiting in the office, but he left almost directly I entered. And what Mr. Weston swore at my trial on God's Holy word to be the truth, the whole truth and nothing but the truth was a series of cold, deliberate and cruel lies, and I only hope God will forgive him as readily

Appendix XI.

as a poor sinning mortal like myself does. I do not believe ~~Weston~~ he intended to do me harm ~~by~~ but solely wanted a little cheap notoriety at the[212] expense of committing perjury.

I believe I succeeded in satisfying Mr. Hooper's suspicions, and in company with Watson and Gibson went to the Town Hall. I expressed my satisfaction at being able to communicate with the police, but I kept on begging for, and really needed, a doctor, for I felt terribly weak and faint from loss of blood. While I was at the Town Hall waiting for a surgeon I, happening to put my hand in my overcoat pocket, found to my intense horror, I had still in my possession the razor and Mr. Gold's purse. (I may say here once and for all that the only things I had at any time in my possession belonging to the deceased were the watch, bit of chain and purse with a few shillings. The purse found on the line <u>was not his</u>, and I take this opportunity of assuring Mrs. Gold on the word of a dying man that my hands never once entered her husband's pockets and anything else that may be missing must either have been appropriated by those who found the body or else must have been lost in London. He dropped no scull[213] cap and certainly no "second pocket book".)

But to return. On finding this damning evidence in my pocket I at once requested to be shown the lavatory, Martin and an old man accompanying me. Martin, according to his evidence, must have slept all the while, for instead of going <u>near</u> where he says I did, I proceeded to a closet and stayed there nearly five minutes during which time I was actively engaged in ramming the razor and purse down the pipe, where for all I know they may still remain. Coming out I found Martin outside staring at the door. No doctor coming I proceeded to the Hospital, Martin and Gibson going with me, though for what reason I am convinced none of them knew. Neither of them are what I should term intellectual men, though Martin had a very dull elaborate sort of cunning, which consisted chiefly of vague doubts of "something wrong" which doubts always being urged in ~~as~~ audible whispers, aided me rather than the reverse. My head was examined by Dr. Hall, the wounds being first covered with lint <u>and then the bandage produced in court wrapped round them</u>, which also I think disputes an illusion of Lord Coleridge's, who let the jury infer (without ever putting a question to Mr. Hall) that my wounds ~~could~~ must have been mere scratches as <u>the bandage was unstained</u>![214]

After leaving the Hospital we returned to the Town Hall, and on the way there I accidentally found a cartridge in my trousers' pocket, which in desperation I dropped on the floor of the cab well underneath the seat. I was now presented to

---

212   The text reads: "the the".

213   *Sic* in autobiography.

214   Lefroy's defence counsel addressed this point. In his closing speech, Montagu Williams explained that the bandage was free of blood because the wounds had already been plastered by Dr Hall.

Lefroy.

Mr. Terry. I assumed the rôle of a deeply injured man, expressed my indignation, complained of my treatment, and was politely ushered out by ~~Mr. Terry~~ him but not before guessing that the two shabbily dressed men who took down my answers were detectives. However, without intending to wound the feelings of Holmes and Howland in the least, they neither appeared men likely to possess much penetration or shrewdness in the matter. At last I reached the station again, saw Mr. Anscombe, and on being asked "if I was much hurt" replied not as he swore viz "I should think I was having <u>five or six</u> bullets in my head" but instead "having five or six <u>wounds</u> in my head". Here I was searched, of course nothing found beyond the watch, which I certainly did <u>not</u> tell Howland was mine. My sole reason for not letting Holmes see the pocket book was that I did not wish him to see the pawn tickets in it. We left for London. On the way up Mr. Brown entered, talked with Holmes but I never heard a word about the body being found, ~~and~~ never dreaming the hideous secret would be revealed so soon! In fact I had a wild idea that possibly it might not be found for days little thinking that tunnels were such thoroughfares as they evidently are.

On reaching Croydon I got Holmes to let me drive to Wallington as I did not wish anyone I knew in Croydon to see me in the terrible state I was in. The telegram received by the detective at E. Croydon made me still more ~~suspicious~~ anxious and when I reached Wallington I did my utmost to dispel any suspicions he might have of the truth by inviting him cordially in and offering to give him every assistance in my power. He took down my statement and then to my alarm Ɨ asked for the number of my watch. What followed is now so well known that I need not gnaw over it again here. The instant the detective went I ran upstairs, changed my clothes, said good bye to my cousin, had something to eat and <u>fully twenty minutes</u> after Holmes had gone I went softly out at the front gate (there being no on[e] in sight) and turned my back weary and sick at heart upon the dear old place for ever.

Conclusion

I walked from Wallington to London via Thornton Heath, Streatham & Kennington and arrived at the Sussex Hotel, Bouverie St. Fleet St. about 1 a.m. where I slept for the night in the name of "Lee". All next day I was wandering about Victoria Park but at night I walked down to Blackfriars and slept at a coffee house near the bridge. The following day I spent on Blackheath and in Greenwhich[215] Park returning at night to London, throwing poor Mr. Gold's watch over the middle arch of Blackfriars Bridge and sleeping at a coffee tavern near the obelisk, and on Thursday I went to Mrs. Bickers' where I remained until arrested in July.

215 *Sic* in transcript.

Appendix XI.

The revolver I bought early in June at Vaughan's in the Strand ~~and the pistol of~~ and the one found on the line has nothing to do with me whatever as mine was a six chambered one thrown out the right towards Balcombe tunnel and this I understand has only four chambers and was found near Earlswood. As to the hat found on the line I know nothing of it. I had only one "low felt hat" and that besides being a very much better hat than the one produced at Maidstone was worn by me the night I left Wallington, to be afterwards exchanged for a different sort of hat.

I have one word to say in conclusion. I freely and sincerely as I hope for mercy myself forgive the ticket collector Frank[216] the awful deliberate ~~falsehoods~~ misstatements he told at my trial. He knows (and perhaps some day on his death bed he will confess it) that nearly every word of his evidence was incorrect. He never saw me get into Mr. Gold's carriage at London Bridge, for I got in there at Croydon, and my ticket was never even examined by him but the other collector rather. What his motive was I cannot guess, but I sincerely trust that should the gentleman with whom I rode to Croydon ever see this, he will corroborate me in this particular.[217] I never saw or heard of Mr. Thomas Gold or any member of poor Mr. Gold's family in my life, and no living soul but myself knew of my going to Brighton, or any intention to going. ~~I will not insult poor Mrs. Gold by asking her to forgive me~~ but I will however ask her to believe in the truth of what I have written and in my sincere and lasting repentance for the awful crime I have committed. Had I ten thousand lives I would give them willingly to bring poor Mr. Gold once more to life. As that however is beyond my power I can only humbly confess my fault, and seek forgiveness of Almighty God. I was very, very wicked to accuse myself of murdering poor Lieut. Roper but I did so in the belief that it might postpone my execution, and now on the word of one whose life is ebbing fast I ask all who read this to believe me when I say that I had no knowledge of or hand in the poor young officer's death. On the very threshold of life I go to my grave with a hope that is ever getting stronger that even I may find in the mercy of Christ that peace and forgiveness to [which] I have been so long a stranger. Ambition (not one of the so called vices) has been my ruin on earth coupled with a fearful habit of deception, and I would earnestly pray that all parents would check the first lie in a child as they would the first symptom of a deadly disease. No one gets wicked all at once, they go step by step, the road daily becomes more easy until at last they can go no further but find themselves engulfed for ~~ever~~ Eternity in the awful ruin of Everlasting Death.

I am deeply sensible of the Christian charity of Mrs. Gold for extending to me under such circumstances her freest[218] forgiveness for ~~of~~ the incalculable wrong

---

216 Should read: Franks.
217 See Appendix XII.
218 Uncertain reading of this word.

Lefroy.

which I have done her and I sincerely regret that I am unable to give her any
further information than I have done.

*

I wish this M.S. story of my life to be read and examined by the chaplain who is
to have the sole right of saying whether it is to be published or no. If he thinks fit
to have it published I should like him to act in the matter with Mr. T.G. Clayton
of Wallington, who would represent my relatives. In the event of the M.S. being
published it must be printed in its entirety as it leaves the hands of the chaplain,
with the addition of a preface to it written by him. Should it be published all
profits accruing from its sale are to be devoted to paying the cost of my defence.

Percy L Mapleton

Nov. 28 1881

APPENDIX XII.

On the Verge of a Tragedy:
A True Narrative
By George Austin.[219]

———

"Lefroy's account of the events that preceded the assassination of Mr Gold, has perhaps never been surpassed in the thrilling history of murder. He says that the whole of the day on which the crime was perpetrated, from the time be left Wallington, the Devil was with him. While he was in the station before the train started, he put the question to the Devil which it was to be — Poverty and Honour, or Wealth and Dishonour — and while he was debating this choice, the Devil suggested the latter; whereupon he walked up the platform and got into a carriage in which there happened to be a passenger, alone. It was into this Lefroy entered, and not, as stated by the railway witness, that in which Mr Gold was sitting. When he entered, the passenger apparently not caring that Lefroy should see him eating strawberries, put the fruit on the hat-rail, and taking out his newspaper began to read. As he did so, Lefroy also took out his own paper, still however keeping an eye upon his fellow-passenger. Meanwhile he cautiously drew his revolver out of his pocket, concealing it under his paper to discover whether it was properly loaded, and this being ascertained, he then 'full cocked' it. He actually intended to take this gentleman's life; but every time Lefroy looked up from his paper, he found his companion — to use his own words — staring at him as much as to say, 'I know what you are about.' So near was this traveller to being a victim in the place of Mr Gold!" — *Daily Telegraph*, November 28th, 1882.

[If any apology were required for introducing to the reader the following true narrative, I think it would be found in the fact of some of the incidents related being of an extremely unusual and remarkable character. I may also add that I have been strongly urged, both by friends and strangers to whom I have related the story, to place it before the public.]

It was on a hot summer day, some few years ago, that, after a fatiguing morning's work in the City, I was about to travel from London, by an early afternoon express train, to Brighton. Being somewhat exhausted by the heat of the weather, and with a parched throat, I had, before starting, purchased a basket of strawberries as a substitute tor lunch. I had arrived at the station early, and having rather a desire

---

219 *The Temple Bar*, Vol. 76 January 1886.

Lefroy.

to be alone, with a view to the enjoyment of a quiet siesta, 1 entered a first-class compartment otherwise unoccupied. At the last moment before the train was set in motion, the carriage door was suddenly opened, and a tallish, slight, young man sprang rapidly in, and placed himself in the corner seat on the opposite side of the carriage and farthest from me.

According to my casual observation, he was a man of not ungentlemanly mien, but conveyed the impression of one who was accustomed to late hours spent in a vitiated atmosphere.

I had just begun to eat my strawberries. My first impulse was to invite my fellow passenger to partake of the fruit, but for some undefined reason I abstained from doing so.

I have often since been compelled to account for the origin of my second impulse; and have been compelled to arrive at the humiliating conclusion that it must have been attributable to nothing more nor less than greediness. If I had been half-way through the strawberries, I should in all probability have obeyed the impulse of hospitality, but I was not self-sacrificing enough to let a stranger "revel free" amongst the larger specimens of fruit with which our fruiterers with commendable liberality invariably bait the top of the basket.

I was however so far sensitive on the subject, that I could not continue to enjoy the strawberries alone, and therefore placed the basket in the rack above my head, intending to resume my feast at a later period. It is important to mention this incident of the strawberries, because, as will be seen hereafter, it has a very significant bearing upon my narrative.

I then occupied myself with my newspaper, my fellow-traveller being apparently similarly engaged. It is necessary to state here that 1 am short-sighted, so that beyond a certain distance, say about eight or ten feet, according to the amount of light, I do not clearly recognise features, unless aided by glasses, which I do not always use.

My readers may doubtless be aware that persons afflicted with short-sight, have often apparently a habit of staring or gazing intently at the object which they are endeavouring to see. This is pre-eminently the case with me; so much so indeed that acquaintances have often indignantly exclaimed, "Why, I met you the other day in the street, you stared me out of countenance, and then passed on as if you did not know me!" — the real state of the case being that I had not recognised them at all. To resume my narrative, I recollect that I occasionally glanced at the stranger, who was just within the range of my vision, and that he appeared to be looking at me with a glittering eye; a fact to which I did not attach any importance at the time, and which would not have left any impression on my mind but for subsequent events.

Appendix XII.

The train stopped at Croydon Station (about ten miles from London), and there my fellow-passenger abruptly quitted the carriage, no conversation whatever having passed between us. I proceeded on my journey, and in due time arrived at Brighton, some fifty odd miles from London, and did not, during that day, hear of anything unusual having happened.[220]

On the following morning I was again in the train accompanied by some friends travelling to London. On opening our newspapers we were much startled at reading:

> "DREADFUL MURDER OF A GENTLEMAN YESTERDAY
> AFTERNOON ON THE BRIGHTON RAILWAY.
> BODY FOUND IN BALCOMBE TUNNEL."

Then followed an account of a passenger alighting at Preston Station (which is within a short distance of Brighton) in a terribly shattered and forlorn condition; whose clothes were smeared with blood, whose general appearance indicated that he had been engaged in a struggle of a very severe and sanguinary nature, and who stated that he had been brutally attacked and robbed by a man in the carriage, who had then escaped while the train was still in motion.

His story being believed by the railway officials, although there were many circumstances which should have made them suspicious as to the truth of it, he was allowed to take his departure.

A few hours later, however, a report was received of the body of a gentleman having been found in Balcombe Tunnel, who, judging from his general appearance, had evidently been murdered.

The real state of the case appears then to have dawned upon the acute minds of the railway officials, who arrived at the intelligent conclusion that, instead of having been attacked, the dilapidated man who alighted at Preston Station, and whom they had so innocently allowed to depart, was, in fact, the murderer of the unfortunate gentleman whose body had been found in Balcombe Tunnel.

The newspaper report then proceeded to give a description of his personal appearance, height, dress, &c, and other particulars, to facilitate the endeavours of the police to effect his capture.

When I read this statement I was struck with amazement, and exclaimed, "Why, that is the exact description of the passenger in whose company I travelled yesterday afternoon, and by the train named, as far as Croydon Station!" I then

---

220   With Lefroy claiming that he left the carriage and immediately entered the one containing Mr Gold, George Austin travelled on the same train on which the murder was committed but seems to have been completely unaware of anything unusual happening on the journey apart from presumably a delay at Preston Park while Lefroy was attended to.

related to my friends the incident of the strawberries, and my greediness in connection therewith.

The murder naturally became the all-engrossing topic of conversation for several days, especially amongst those who were accustomed to travel on the Brighton Railway, and their friends; and a panic with regard to railway travelling with one other passenger only in the same carriage, took, for some time, possession of the mind of the public; and there arose considerable discussion, as to whether it would not be advantageous, for the general safely, to adopt the American system, and to abolish compartments, thus throwing open all the carriages from one end of the train to the other. This idea however was soon abandoned, as the majority were of opinion that the luxury of our present system of comparative privacy is preferable. Moreover it must be remembered that no murder in a railway carriage had taken place for the previous seventeen years, and therefore that the chances against such an occurrence are many millions to one.

The story of my having travelled, as I believed, as far as Croydon Station with the suspected man, whose name turned out to be Lefroy, was not unnaturally often repeated in my family circle, and amongst my club, and other friends.

After the lapse of many days, Lefroy was traced to, and arrested in, an obscure lodging in the east of London, and in a very abject and dejected condition. He was then charged with the murder of the gentleman whose body had been found in Balcombe Tunnel, and evidence was taken in the usual way before a magistrate.

The ticket inspector at the London terminus swore that he knew the person of the prisoner very well, and that he put him into a carriage at that station with the gentleman whom he was charged with having murdered, and with whose personal appearance he was also perfectly well acquainted, as he was a constant traveller on the line. He likewise stated that the prisoner had on a "bowler hat."

When I read that piece of evidence, I was compelled to come to the conclusion that the belief that I had travelled with the accused as far as Croydon Station was incorrect, as *my* fellow passenger wore a "tall silk hat," and that the similarity of dress and appearance in other respects was simply a coincidence, which however in any case would have been somewhat singular, as there were very few first-class passengers on that day in the train by which we travelled. On reading further however, I observed that the officials at Preston Station, where the prisoner alighted, swore that he wore a "tall silk hat."

This evidence forcibly brought back my original impressions as to the identity of the man, and I was so much interested in the matter, that I took the trouble to seek out the ticket inspector at the London terminus, and asked him how he accounted for the discrepancy between his evidence, and that of the officials at Preston Station, with regard to the hat.

Appendix XII.

"Well, sir," he said, "I may have possibly made a mistake about the hat, but I am *positive* that I put the accused into the carriage with the murdered gentleman at this station."

Although, of course, somewhat shaken in my conviction by this renewed and unequivocal assertion of the ticket inspector, I nevertheless continued to entertain a strong instinctive feeling, almost amounting to certainty, of the correctness of my first impression.

I was never however sufficiently interested in the matter — and this may appear strange to many of my readers — to be induced to make a personal inspection of the prisoner, which fact was probably in a great degree attributable to the doubts which had been raised in my mind by the very positive assertions of the ticket inspector; moreover he would have been attired in such very different clothing to that in which my fellow-passenger was dressed, that it would most likely have been difficult to recognise him with any degree of certainty; and furthermore, any evidence which I could give would have been of no practical value, in addition to which police and criminal courts of law have never had any great attraction for me.

The result of the evidence was that the accused man Lefroy was committed for trial, which did not take place for some months afterwards, and in the crowd of events which are always so rapidly following each other, the matter was temporarily forgotten.

When however the time arrived for the trial to take place, the subject again occupied the attention of the public in a very intense degree. The trial lasted for some days, and terminated by the prisoner being found guilty, and sentence of death being passed upon him.

A day or two before that appointed for the execution, I was relating to my children the story of the murder, in the summer of 1864, and also in a railway carriage, of a gentleman named Briggs, the chief clerk in the bank of Messrs Robarts, by a German named Müller. This murder created intense excitement at the time, as the murderer evaded the pursuit of the police, and actually escaped to America, where, however, he was arrested on arrival, and given up under the extradition treaty, brought back to this country, tried, condemned, and hanged. It is somewhere singular that a hat also played a prominent part in that tragedy. Up till the last moment, Müller asserted his innocence, even until the rope was actually round his neck, when, in answer to the last appeal of the German clergyman who was in attendance upon him, and who earnestly implored him not to rush into the presence of his Maker with a lie upon his lips, the unhappy man exclaimed, *"Ich habe es gethan!"* (I did it.)

"Now," said I, "the condemned man Lefroy may be equally obstinate; but should he make a detailed confession, I shall be very curious to see the particulars,

Lefroy.

as the conviction is still as strong as ever on my mind that I did travel in the same carriage with him on the day of the murder as far as Croydon Station, notwithstanding the evidence of the railway officials to the contrary."

On the following afternoon, the day preceding that on which Lefroy was appointed to be hanged, on entering my club, the first man I saw was our cheery messmate, Captain Aquinas, distinguished for the dulcet tones in which he mastheads us when we revoke or trump his best card, or fail to see his "Peter" at whist.

Said he, "Do you remember the story you told us on the day after the murder, expressing your belief that you had been a fellow-passenger with the murderer as far as Croydon Station, and your greediness about the strawberries?" (Alas, nobody ever seems to forget that unhappy admission of mine!)

"Certainly," replied I. "Perfectly well."

"Well," said he, "if you read the *Daily Telegraph*, you will see that Lefroy has made a statement in which he fully confirms your story."

I accordingly sought out the statement in the *Telegraph*, and there, sure enough, the prisoner made particular mention of the fact of his fellow-passenger having a basket of strawberries, and of his evident disinclination to continue eating them in his presence, and how he therefore placed them in the rack at the back of the carriage; how he then devoted himself to the perusal of his newspaper; how he, the prisoner, also had a newspaper, behind which he had a loaded revolver, cocked and ready for use; how he had been more of less under the influence of the *Evil Fiend* from the time he arose from his bed that morning, and how he had resolved to murder his fellow-passenger; but somehow, whenever he looked at him, the gentleman always appeared to be staring at him most intently, as much as to say, "I know what you are about," and that he, in consequence, became so unnerved that he felt quite incapable of carrying out his intention; and, on the arrival of the train at Croydon Station, he rushed from the carriage, and got into another, in which there was only one other passenger, whom he eventually murderer, casting the body into Balcombe Tunnel.

Poor unhappy wretch! Here was a man looking at him only occasionally, with indistinct and imperfect vision, and not having the most remote idea that he had any sinister intention in his mind; whilst the intending murderer in his distracted and guilty conscience, actually becomes impressed with the idea that the eye of that man is piercing him to the very soul! Why, if it were not a matter of such solemnity it would be almost ludicrous. But I will not attempt to solve this enigma. It affords at least an additional illustration that

> "Men are the sport of circumstances, when
> The circumstances seem the sport of men."

I cannot quit this part of my narrative without dwelling for a moment on an

Appendix XII.

episode in it which to my mind affords another singular subject for reflection; as indicating how in this world of anomalies, tragedy and farce may be in close proximity to each other, and even be mistaken one for the other.

Lefroy leaves me in the railway carriage perfectly unconscious of the peril which had been hanging over me, and while I am calmly and placidly, and slumberingly proceeding on my journey, he in the course of a few minutes, and within a few compartments from me, becomes engaged in a frightful struggle with the unfortunate gentleman whom he finally murders. This death struggle is observed by a woman and her daughter from the window of a cottage standing close to the railway; and they seeing the figures moving rapidly about in the carriage, are amused at what they believed to be two passengers engaged in skylarking. They looked upon a *tragedy* and absolutely believed it to be a *farce*!

The perusal of this statement of the condemned man in the columns of the *Daily Telegraph*, naturally created much excitement amongst those of my relations and friends who had become acquainted with my original story, and it was the unanimously expressed opinion being that my preservation was attributable to my being short-sighted.

I certainly do not claim to possess a greater amount of physical courage, or indifference to danger than most men, and I suppose I may not be an imaginative man, for the terrible fate I so narrowly escaped has never given me any shock, or prevented a night's rest, whilst another person, though only a slight acquaintance, on hearing of my fortunate escape from a cruel death, was so agitated as to be unable to sleep the whole night after hearing my narrative.

One of the most remarkable incidents connected with my narrative, is the fact that I had nearly forty pounds in my purse, of which the murderer might have possessed himself with very little difficulty had he remained in the carriage with me, as I should undoubtedly have slumbered during the journey between Croydon and Brighton; whereas he did not obtain as much as twenty shillings from the unfortunate gentleman whom he so cruelly slaughtered; and the fact of his being so short of money was the immediate cause of his being traced and arrested.

There is still another singular incident to relate, remarkable on account of the way in which it presented itself being purely accidental, and which would almost seem to be furnished for the purpose of supplying the final link in the chain of evidence which proves the truth and completeness of my story.

About a week after the unfortunate man was executed, a friend came to me and said, "A curious thing has happened this morning. I was walking in East Street, when I met my old friend, the Reverend Mr Cole,* who is chaplain of Lewes Gaol,

---

* Since writing this narrative I have seen the chaplain, and in the course of conversation he mentioned, as a

Lefroy.

in which Lefroy was imprisoned and hanged. We naturally spoke of the recent event, and of the wretched man with whom the reverend gentleman had had the misfortune to be in such close association. I casually remarked, 'By the way, there is a man in my club who was the passenger who travelled with Lefroy on the day of the murder as far as Croydon Station.' 'Indeed,' exclaimed the chaplain, 'that is very extraordinary! What is the name of that gentleman? I must ask you to place me in communication with him, as I have something very important to say to him.' In reply to a letter of mine to Mr Cole, I received the following communication:

H.M. Prison, Lewes,
Dec. 15, 1881.

Dear Sir,

I am very glad to receive your letter, which corroborates most remarkably a statement made to me by the criminal Percy Lefroy Mapleton, after his sentence, that he entered at London Bridge, on the 27th of June last, a carriage occupied by a gentleman who was eating strawberries at the time, and who placed them in the rack above his head as he entered.

He described the gentleman to me as apparently about forty years of age, slight, with dark hair, and with eyes which appeared to him so searching in their character that he felt obliged to abandon his intention of robbery and violence, and to change carriages at Croydon. The evidence of the ticket collector, Franks, was so positive that Lefroy entered the carriage with Mr Gold at London Bridge, that the prisoner's unsupported declaration to the contrary could only be accepted by me with reservation, but your testimony now offered, and corresponding as it does in minute particulars with his account, leaves no doubt in my mind as to his actually having been your fellow passenger as far as Croydon, and I am also now aware that previous to his trial and long before the newspaper report appeared, he had given the same information for purposes of his defence whilst he was in close custody here, and therefore unable to hear, without the cognisance of the authorities, either directly or indirectly from yourself on the subject.

It is a great satisfaction to me to be able by your aid thus to test the truthfulness of one of the statements of the dying man, as it leads me to hope that his account to me generally of the details of his terrible crime may have been equally truthful.

noteworthy circumstance, that until meeting our mutual friend in East Street, he had not seen him for some years, and he had not met him since. So that if one or other had passed a certain point a minute sooner or later, I should, in all probability, never hve been brought into communication with the reverend gentleman, and should thus have been deprived of his most important testimony, which has contributed so largely to prove the truth of my narrative, and he would not have been afforded the opportunity of complying with the injunctions of the dying man.

Appendix XII.

I offer you my earnest congratulations on what I now fully believe to have been a providential escape, and I think it is only due to you that I should afford you the information which you request.

I am, dear Sir,
Yours very faithfully,
(Signed) T.H. Cole
(Chaplain)

George Austin, Esq,
  Brighton.

My friend then arranged that he and I should pay a visit to the reverend gentleman, and we accordingly went over to Lewes on the following day.

The chaplain requested me first to relate my version of the story, having heard which, he was able, from written statements of the condemned man, to confirm fully each detail of the occurrences which I had described, and especially the fact that the fixed and piercing manner in which he imagined his fellow-traveller was looking at him utterly unnerved him, and compelled him to abandon the intention which he had formed to assassinate and rob him.

The chaplain also possessed so accurate a description of my personal appearance, that my identity as the fellow-traveller of the murderer was established beyond question, and he moreover confided to me the following information.

Shortly before the unhappy man was hanged, when he had abandoned all hope of his life being spared, and he was, in fact, making his confession, he was very anxious to convince me that he was not utterly incapable of speaking the truth. He was, moreover, very angry (although acknowledging the justice of the sentence passed upon him) at the inaccurate evidence of the ticket inspector, who so positively swore that he put him into the carriage with Mr Gold at the London terminus. He then told me the story of riding with the passenger who was eating strawberries, as far as Croydon Station, and how, under the influence of his searching gaze, as he said, he rushed from the carriage in a state of distraction and panic, perfectly incapable of carrying out the crime which he had contemplated. He implored me, if ever I should meet that gentleman, to ascertain from him the truth of these assertions made by him, the condemned man.

There is therefore no doubt that my short-sight was, under the providence of God, the means of my preservation from a horrible fate.

It will be remembered that I have stated, that so long as the sworn evidence of the railway official was opposed to, and apparently disproved, my theory of having ridden with the murderer, I was never induced to make a journey for the purpose of seeing him. But as soon as the announcement was made of the confession

Lefroy.

which confirmed my version of the matter, I conceived a strong wish to have a personal view of him; it was however too late, as he was to be hanged on the following morning.

Within a few days it was advertised that the effigy of the criminal was being exhibited at Madame Tussaud's.

Knowing how lifelike are the representations at that establishment, I was seized with an irresistible desire to see in *wax* the figure which I had not had the curiosity to inspect in the flesh.

I accordingly took the earliest opportunity of visiting Madame Tussaud's, and there, in gazing on the features of the waxen image, I had additional confirmation of the correctness of my original belief. There, beyond a doubt, was the likeness of the man who had looked at me with a glittering eye!

As I stood in that grim chamber of horrors amongst the crowd of spectators, none of whom probably were more interested in the figure of Lefroy than in any of the other surrounding effigies of murderers, I could not help speculating on the reflections regarding him which might be passing through their minds, as compared with those which occupied my own!

APPENDIX XIII.

Three Terrible Nights:
A Story of the Stage
By Arthur Lefroy,

Now in Prison, charged with the murder of Mr. Gold.[221]

––––––––––

PREFACE.

It is a popular fallacy that curiosity which has crime or criminals for its object, is necessarily morbid. Moral disease cries as loudly for scientific investigation; its development and extension is as much a matter of public interest and as fitted for curious investigation as physical disease is; and everything that is extraordinary in the one or the other is equally legitimately and wholesomely a matter of general interest and great public importance.

We shall make no excuse for publishing the following pages.

As a near neighbour of Mrs Clayton, in Peckham, we frequently heard the school-children speak of Percy Mapleton (Arthur Lefroy), as a shy, gentle, timid, good-natured boy, of a strongly romantic disposition, whose chief delight was to shut himself up alone with a book. His friends and relatives were all very fond of him, and their chief cause of anxiety was the thought that the delicate state of his health and the weakness of his constitution unfitted him for either hard study or physical labour.

His family is one of high respectability.

Some short time since he wrote to us as Editor of one of the best known weekly magazines, asking if we could make use of a story he had written; and, in reply, we told him it was a Christmas story, too late for Christmas, but promised that we would keep it by us, and, when we saw an opportunity, print it.

That story we now place before the reader, in the following pages.

THE EDITOR.

––––––––––

221   A booklet published by T. H. Roberts and Co., 42 & 43 Essex Street, Strand, London. 1881. A copy held in the British Library is annotated by hand: 'James W. Sewell. 22nd July 1881.'

Lefroy.

THREE BOXING NIGHTS.[222]

Christmas time! There was no doubt about it. Everything and everybody savoured of it. The light of Christmas fires shone through and gleamed behind the closely-curtained windows, with merry leaps, sending showers of golden sparks up dark chimneys, to emerge more bright and dazzling than ever in the clear frosty air, like fleeting souls hastening through the gloom and cares of life to shine in higher regions.

"Christmas!" cried the bells, as they pealed softly through the still night air – "Christmas! merry Christmas! – Christmas! merry Christmas!" so merrily and cheerfully that he must have been a man of stony heart who did not echo it, too, from sheer sympathy. "Christmas!" murmured the dark river, as it lapped against the buttresses of the old stone bridge, and then sped away with many a secret in its gloomy bosom to the sea, where, in company with many others of its race, it murmured still of Christmas; and "Christmas time!" pleaded inebriated gentlemen when questioned by stern policemen as to why they were sitting in frozen gutters at midnight. For that one day a sort of universal truce seemed to be established. Creditors forgot their debtors, debtors forgot their creditors; wives forgot to scold, husbands to abuse, and young husbands forgot their mothers-in-law, which was perhaps hardest of all. Conservatives and Liberals, Churchmen and Dissenters, "old boy'd" and "old fellow'd" each other to their heart's content, and the plea for all was – Christmas! But when the world got up next day what a change was to be seen! Closed blinds, no church bells, shops shut – just as if everyone was ashamed of his or her last night's festivity.

There wasn't much going on indoors to-day, for it was Boxing Day – that day sacred to Christmas-boxes, bills, and last, but by no means least, pantomimes. And to go to one of these last the children were mad with hope long deferred. Papa and mamma affected not to like or care for such trivial amusements at all, but the children – sly dogs, those children! – knew that when once within the cosy recesses of that "lovely private box," no one would cry "bravo" more loudly or clap his hands more vehemently than papa. And what a lot of pantomimes there were, too! Just look at the various hoardings: "Robinson Crusoe," "Jack the Giant Killer," "Aladdin," and many other well-known stories had been made to contribute to the common good. But first and foremost among the brightly-coloured bills was one that informed the reader "that on Boxing Night would be produced at the Rotunda Theatre" the grand Christmas pantomime, "Jack and the Beanstalk." Then followed the list of characters, scenery, &c., and at the end, in large letters, Clown – Jolly Joe Jeffs.

The Rotunda must have been a well-known theatre for pantomime, for that

---

222   In his memoirs *Leaves of a Life*, published in 1890, Lefroy's counsel Montagu Williams includes the story under the title 'Two Boxing Nights'.

Appendix XIII.

night it was crammed from floor to ceiling. Everything had gone off without a hitch. The music was pretty, scenery magnificent, and the grand ballet had been pronounced by the crutch-and-toothpick genus in the stalls to be "splendid," and by an old lady in the pit to be "beastly."

And now, out of breath with honest laughter, warm, thirsty, and packed like sardines in a box, the great audience sat anxiously waiting for the "grandest transformation scene ever attempted at the Rotunda," *vide* bills. If there was excitement in front, so there was behind. Everyone busy, excited, and nervous, the manager and stage-manager not being by any means in that happy condition described by the immortal Mrs. Jarley as "cool, calm, and classical."

Inside one of the principal dressing-rooms was a man, clad in a clown's dress, pacing moodily up and down, and listening with feverish impatience for a footstep which never came. It was Joe Jeffs, and the person he was waiting for was his wife. And she was a wife worth waiting for, too. Young, pretty, and loving, Nellie Raynor, then only – and, indeed, up to within a week or so of the present time – a ballet-girl at a West-end theatre, had brought some new joy and life to honest, hard-working Joe Jeffs, who, though nearly fifteen years her senior, loved her with a strong and passionate love, and would cheerfully have laid down his life if it had been necessary to save her from harm. And this winter, when Nellie through her husband's influence got engaged at the Rotunda as columbine, Joe Jeffs thought that his cup of happiness was full to the brim.

A knock at the door. "Come in," cried the clown. Mr. Flies, the stage-manager, entered. Flies was a little short man, with a round red face, with very short black hair, so short that it always stood on end as if each hair was desirous of looking over its neighbour's head.

"I'm very sorry, Mr. Flies," said the clown, humbly, "very sorry; but Nellie told me to-night she wasn't well, and would lie down for a bit, and would come later on. I sent a boy to our place some time ago, and she must be here in a minute."

"Minute!" roared Mr. Flies, "what's the good of a minute? I – who the devil's that?" as a hand was laid on his arm.

It was the harlequin, in the bills Roberto Taylori; out of them, Bob Taylor, an old friend of the clown's.

"I've got an idea," said the harlequin, giving a kindly, unseen nod to his friend. "Say a few words to the public, and let my girl Bella go on for the part to-night; she's about Mrs. Jeff's size, and I've taught her the trip long ago."

Miss Bella Taylori was in the front row of the ballet, consequently could dance well and look pretty; but, best of all, was there on the spot, so to speak. The stage-manager didn't take long to make up his mind.

"Bob," he said, to the harlequin, "you're a brick. The very thing. Get the girl dressed at once, and I'll get the guv'nor to speak to them." *Them* being the audience, who were now in a state of noisy impatience. Mr. Flies hurried off.

"Tell your missus it's all right, old man," said the friendly harlequin, as he hurried away.

The clown was about to reply, when a light footstep was heard approaching. A happy smile lighted up his face. "At last," he said, with a sigh of relief, as the footsteps neared the door. Quickly he turned the handle and threw it wide open, but only to start back with a cry of disappointment, for the new-comer was not his wife, but the boy he had sent an hour previously. "Well," cried the clown, "what did she say?"

The boy shook his head stolidly.

"I didn't see her, sir," he said, "only the landlady, and she guv me this." The clown held out his hand, and into it the boy put a tiny note, on which was written, in a woman's hand, "To be given to my husband."

"You can go," said Joe Jeffs, in a voice which was so hoarse and strange that for a moment it startled the lad. When the door was again closed the clown looked at the tiny missive. Was she frightened he would be angry with her for remaining so long behind the time, and so did not care to come at all, but wrote instead? That must be it. With trembling hands he hastily tore it open, and read: "Husband, good-bye, I shall never see you any more. I am going away with someone that loves me very much. You were always too good for me. May God forgive your poor lost Nellie!" Nothing more. Only an old, old story, with a vulgar clown and his wife as hero and heroine.

Joe Jeffs raised his head. Was it paint alone that gave that awful deathly look to his face and fixed glassy eyes? Was it clowning that caused the strong man's hands to shake as if he were suffering from the palsy? And, above all, was it art or nature which made that bitter cry of agony arise from the uttermost depths of a broken heart?

At that minute the call-boy's shrill voice was heard, "Mr. Jeffs, the stage waits!" Mechanically the clown reeled to the door and opened it, down the narrow, dark passage, and staggered through the wing on to the brilliantly-lighted stage, and then, in a voice more resembling the croak of a raven that the utterance of a human being, gave vent to the time-honoured utterance, "Here we are again!"

How the house roared at the strange voice and staggering gait! Such quiet humour! So dry, very dry! And then, after such a capital commencement, the great audience settled down with keen anticipation for the fun that was to come. And come it did. With what zest did Jolly Joe Jeffs trip up the policeman, steal the sausages, and go through the hundred and one odd tricks which go to make up the sum total of a harlequinade! The "gods" were in one continual roar; even the stalls and circle were mildly excited, while as for the pit, the opinion of that black, seething mass of humanity may be briefly summed up in the words of an excited old gentleman, who, carried away by his enthusiasm, flung his neighbour's hat into the air, crying, "Splendid, sir, splendid! Grimaldi was a fool to Jolly Joe!" And tumbling, grimacing, tripping up, now dancing on a spade, a minute later cracking sly jokes, the clown went through it. Only the clown, though, for God's beautiful creation – man, was gone. When his poor, aching head swam for a moment, and he fell heavily to the ground, what a shout went up! Droll fellow, that Jeff – very droll! And their laughter reached its culminating point when, during a hornpipe by the pretty columbine, two large tears stole down the clown's painted face, as he, in burlesque fashion, attempted to imitate it. "He's a-crying with laughter!" roared the excited gallery, and they cheered him to the echo for entering so heartily into the spirit of the thing. At last the end came. One last wild trick, clouds of smoke from the coloured fires, a last mad "rally," and, amidst tremendous applause, the pantomime was over. As the band commenced to play the National Anthem, Jolly Joe Jeffs staggered off the stage, as he had staggered on. Ere he could reach his dressing-room two men stopped him. One was Mr. Flies, the other Mortimer, the manager. "My boy," said the latter, taking him by both hands and shaking them warmly, "you've surpassed yourself. If only your wife could have seen you!" That was enough. For a minute Jolly Joe stood erect, and then, with a wild, gasping cry, fell heavily to the ground. The clown was gone, but the man was there.

NIGHT THE SECOND.

Ten years rolled by. Ten long, weary years they had been to Joe Jeffs, who had never given up the search for his lost darling. A few weeks after his great loss, an old relative had died, leaving him a small annuity. On this he had lived, or rather existed, wandering aimlessly about the country in the hope of one day finding his wife, whom, in spite of all, he loved as fondly as ever.

And this Boxing Night, he was walking down the little High Street of Milford, weary, hopeless, and sick at heart, to all appearance a bent, careworn, old man, a mere wreck of the merry fellow who ten years before had made a great theatre resound with peals of laughter at his drollery. Quickly the clown walked on, for the night was cold, and the biting east wind seemed to pierce his bones to the very marrow. When within a few years of the little inn at which he was staying, his arm was touched.

"Buy a box of lights, sir; do buy a box, please?"

He turned. A woman, wretchedly clad, and with death stamped in every feature, stood at his elbow.

"No," answered the clown, roughly; "I don't want any," and he walked on.

But the beggar was not so easily shaken off. She detained him again, as the wind lulled for a minute, her voice rang in his ear –

"Buy a box, sir; just one box!"

At the sound Joe Jeffs turned.

"Let me see your face," he cried, hoarsely; then, as the pale light of the moon fell upon it – "Nelly, dearie, don't you know me? – Joe, your husband!"

But there was no reply, for his long-lost wife lay insensible in his arms.

* * * *

She was dying, the doctors said – dying of cold and want. So they told her husband, sitting by her bedside in the little inn.

"Can nothing save her?" asked the clown.

"Nothing on earth, my poor fellow – nothing on earth." And the old doctor looked out of the window and blew his nose violently, for a kind-hearted old man was the doctor, and knew something of poor Joe's story, and felt for him.

"Joe."

"Yes, darling."

"Are you sure you quite forgive me?"

A loving kiss was the only answer.

"Nellie, I won't be long," cried the clown.

"Listen!" And by a great effort the dying woman raised herself up – then suddenly,-

"Joe, dear, what day is it?"

"Christmas Day, Nell."

"Ah! so it is. More light, for God's sake, more light!"

The doctor made a movement of his hand, and the attendant drew back the curtains from the little window which looked upon the sea, on which lay a broad path of gold, formed of the last rays of the setting sun upon the water.

"How bright it all is, Joe," cried the dying woman, as she sank back upon her pillow. "At last, at last! Joe, darling husband! good-bye!"

And with a sweet and happy smile upon her face, Nellie went down with the sun.

Joe Jeffs still lives at Milford, but he is wonderfully changed, though. People say he is mad, and so he is, in a sad, harmless way. For as sure as Boxing Night comes round, he paints his face and dresses just as clowns do, and there in the little tap-room of the "Red Lion" he sings "Hot Codlins" in a little, thin, cracked voice, and tumbles in a mild and feeble way, and plays a few clownish tricks. How the villagers laugh! They know he is mad, but that doesn't take away from their enjoyment, and one of old Joe's funniest tricks is to address them all as "ladies and gentlemen," and apologise for the non-appearance of the columbine. But when all the merriment is over, old Joe, with the clown's dress still upon him, creeps down, whatever the weather may be, to the little churchyard, where, with his poor old grey head pillowed on a little marble slab inscribed "Nellie," he pours out a bitter prayer that heaven may take him soon to her he loved so well, and ere he leaves the tomb, with great tears upon his painted face, he softly prays for Nellie too. But the end must soon come.

Each Boxing Night old Joe goes through the same performance, and the people laugh as vociferously as before. But every year he gets more feeble. He can't tumble as he used to, and his sight and memory seem failing fast, and the absent look in his face seems to denote that his thoughts are far away.

And now when people meet old Joe Jeffs, they shake their heads sadly, for they know that soon, very soon, the curtain must fall.

Arthur Lefroy
4 Cathcart Rd
Wallington – Surrey

APPENDIX XIV.

Survivors' Tales of Famous Crimes:
The Brighton Railway Murder[223]
By Walter Wood

———

[In 1881 a profound sensation was caused throughout the country by the murder of Mr Frederick Isaac Gold in a first-class compartment of an express train from London Bridge Station to Brighton. The murderer, Percy Lefroy, alias Mapleton, escaped from custody in the most astonishing manner, and remained in hiding for more than a week. His arrest was a matter of such intense interest that it was made known at the Lord Mayor's banquet and in the House of Commons. An important witness in the case was Mr Thomas Picknell, and this is his story of the crime.][224]

Just on this spot where we are standing — in the six-foot way — I picked up a collar on the afternoon of June 27th, 1881. It was an ordinary turn-down collar of the type very common in those days, but there was an extraordinary thing about it, and it was this: the collar was covered with blood. I examined the collar, and so did my mate, who was with me. Having done so, I let it drop back into the six-foot way.

I was a ganger at that time, and it was my duty to examine a certain section of the line twice every weekday and once every Sunday. I was carrying out that task when I found the collar.

In spite of the stains I did not think much of the discovery, for I supposed that a passenger had scratched his neck and had taken the collar off and thrown it out

---

223 Chapter VII of *Survivors' Tales of Famous Crimes* by Walter Wood (London : Cassell & Co. Ltd, 1916).

224 Thomas Picknell was born in Ardingly, Sussex, in 1840. He married Ellen Thomas at East Grinstead in January 1862, the couple going on to have nine children: William (1863–63), Elizabeth (1864–1950), George (1867–1941), Ellen Jr (b1869), Thomas Jr (1871–88), Alfred (1874–1933), Charles (1876–1918), Albert (1881–1917) and Rose (1883–1962). Thomas was working as a railway labourer by the 1871 census, and at the time of the murder was living at No. 4 Tunnel Cottages, Balcombe. By 1891 the Picknells were living alongside John Jennings and his family at Red Bridge, Balcombe. Thomas Picknell continued to work as a railway platelayer for more than twenty years. He was 76 at the time of this interview with Walter Wood, and died at Balcombe on 19 January 1929, aged 89.

of the window of a passing train. All sorts of odd things are disposed of in this manner. After throwing the collar back into the six-foot way we walked on to Balcombe Station, about three-quarters of a mile away, and there I was startled to hear that another mate of mine, named Thomas Jennings, had found the dead body of a man in Balcombe Tunnel. Balcombe, as you see, is a quiet little country place, with not much going on, but it suddenly became very busy and famous, for a crime had been committed which filled the country with horror and was the thing that was mostly talked about for many a long day.

I soon learned what had happened. Jennings had walked through the tunnel to do some haymaking, and, having finished, he was walking back towards the station, carrying a naphtha lamp with him. He had got almost exactly in the middle of the tunnel when he found the body laying in the six-foot way — that is, of course, the space between the two sets of metals. At that time the cause of death was not known, and I don't suppose that any time was lost in trying to find out. The main thing was to report the affair at the station and get the body out of the tunnel.

There was great excitement all at once. An engine and a brake were got — a brake such as a guard uses on a goods train — and the engine took a number of us into the tunnel to get the body up and bring it on to Balcombe. It was a gloomy business, and a strange scene it was as we gathered round the body in the six-foot way, working by the lights of our naphtha lamps — just the sort of lamps you see at fairs and lighting costers' carts at night. The task was very difficult, too, because of the constant traffic through the tunnel, which caused us time after time to get into the manholes for shelter.

We were in the tunnel about an hour, because we had to wait for a policeman. At the end of that time we had got the body into the brake, and it was drawn by the engine to the station and carried to the Railway Inn, where it was put in the coach-house.

When we first saw the body it was lying on its back, with the head towards Brighton. Even in the gloomy light of the tunnel it was evident that terrible injuries had been caused, for the face was covered with blood, and on this the black dust from passing engines and the ballast had settled thickly, making the features look as dark as a negro's. It was clear enough that murder had been done, and that there had been a long and fierce struggle before Mr Gold was lying in the middle of Balcombe tunnel.

I first picked the collar up — it was soon secured, of course, in view of the discovery of the body — at about a quarter to five. By that time an extraordinary thing had happened at Preston Park Station, just outside Brighton.

A ticket-collector, on opening the door of a first-class compartment, found a young man in it who had neither hat nor collar, who was covered with blood, and who was looking as if he had been badly knocked about. Blood was spattered all

Appendix XIV.

over the compartment, and the young man, Percy Lefroy, asked for a policeman to be sent for. When one came he declared that when he left London Bridge two men were in the compartment with him, one of them an elderly person, and the other looking like a countryman.

Lefroy said that on entering a tunnel he was murderously assaulted by one of the men and became insensible, and that he knew nothing more until he reached Preston Park. While he was telling his tale it was noticed that a watch-chain was hanging from his shoe, and on his attention being called to this circumstance he explained that he had put his watch there for safety.

Lefroy was allowed to keep the watch and chain and to go on to Brighton, the policeman being with him. He was taken to the Town Hall, where he made a statement, and he was then removed to the hospital, where his injuries were attended to. He showed a keen wish to get away, saying he wished to return to his home at Wallington, near Croydon, where he lived with a second cousin. He was given permission to go back, but the case looked very suspicious, and two railway policemen accompanied him. On the journey, at one of the stopping-places, the party learned that Mr Gold's body had been found. This was stated by an official of the company, and Lefroy heard it; but it does not seem that he was greatly upset by the tidings. He reached Wallington and the cousin's house; then he told the police that he was going out to see a doctor. Amazing as it seems, he was allowed to go, and from that moment, for more than a week, all trace of him was lost.

An inquest was held — a tremendous affair it was for a little place like Balcombe, special wires being fitted so that long telegrams could be sent off to the newspapers — and a verdict of wilful murder was returned against Lefroy. A reward, too, was offered for his arrest, and the whole country was thrown into a state of the most intense excitement and a lot of people were quite unnerved when it came to a question of travelling by train.

I spent many weary days at the inquest, at the police court proceedings, and at the trial at the assizes, so that every detail of the case became familiar to me, and I remember them pretty well even now.

[Here Picknell recounts full details of the case.]

It was on Gunpowder Plot Day that the trial before the Lord Chief Justice began. By that time Lefroy had improved very much in looks and had had time to pull himself together. Considering the nature of the evidence against him and the almost utter hopelessness of an acquittal, he was amazingly cool; in fact, he seemed to be about the most unaffected person in court. There was no doubt that he had a mania for attracting public attention, and he made the extraordinary request that he should be allowed to get a dress suit out of pawn and wear it

Lefroy.

in the dock. This fancy was not gratified, but the young man made the best of his chances and was particularly attentive to a silk hat which he wore. Each morning when he was brought up into the dock from the cells below he bowed ceremoniously to the judge and the court generally. It seemed as if the prisoner's great object was to attract attention, and I was astonished that a man who stood in such peril of his life could find time or inclination for such trifles. But the fact was that to the very last moment Lefroy believed that he would be acquitted, and there were other people who actually persuaded themselves that he would be found not guilty. It may have been that they credited the story of the third man in the compartment, the person who looked like a countryman. All I can say on that point is that if there really was a third party in the compartment it was the Devil himself.

I got weary of the whole business long before it was finished — though we had a day off in the course of the trial. That was on Lord Mayor's Day, when the judge had to go to London to take part in the ceremonies.

On the afternoon of the fourth day of the trial the judge had finished his long summing-up, and the jury retired to consider their verdict. That took them only a few minutes; they found Lefroy guilty, and he was sentenced to death. When he had been condemned he told the jury that some day they would learn that they had murdered an innocent man.

It was an odd circumstance that, after being so closely connected with the case for so long, I was not present in court when Lefroy was found guilty and sentenced. I had got tired of the oft-told story and the stuffy atmosphere, and when the summing up was going on I was wandering round the prison walls examining them. When I got back to the court all was over. Lefroy had been removed, and soon afterwards he was taken, handcuffed and under a strong police escort, to Lewes Gaol.

Even in the condemned cell Lefroy did not abandon hope, and he wrote a letter in which he asked for a file and a small saw to be sent to him concealed in the crust of a meat pie, his object evidently being to try and break out of prison, though how he expected to do that, when he was constantly guarded, is a mystery. He also tried to get poison sent in to him, but these attempts were fruitless.

A petition for a reprieve was signed, but no notice was taken of it. When, at the very last, Lefroy knew that his doom was certain he confessed to the murder. He said that he was so desperately in need of money that he was determined to go to any length to get it, even to the extent of murder. He walked up and down on the platform at London Bridge in the hope of finding a woman alone in a compartment. In that case he would have got in and demanded money from her, hoping that he would be able to escape and that it would not be necessary to do more than stun her. There was not, mercifully, any such solitary woman, and seeing Mr Gold alone, and noticing that he looked prosperous, Lefroy jumped into the compartment just before the train started. The watch which he had in his shoe at Preston Park was Mr Gold's. Before being arrested Lefroy threw the watch over Blackfriars Bridge.

Lefroy was hanged at Lewes by Marwood on November 29th, almost exactly five months after he murdered Mr Gold.

I don't know what became of the collar. I saw it at the inquest and at the trial, but not afterwards; and I didn't wish to see it, for I had had enough of it.

As to the revolver, the police made a long and tiring search on the line and elsewhere, but they were not successful. After Lefroy was hanged a ganger found a revolver in a little hole at Earlswood, and that was supposed to be the weapon which was used. I dare say there are many relics of the terrible affair; but most of the people who were connected with the trial have died. Of all the local people, I think I am the only one left, though Jennings is, I believe, still alive somewhere in America.[225]

Well, that's the story of the famous Brighton train murder. Here we are on the very spot where I found the collar. Now we can go on picking primroses on the embankment. They're beautiful, aren't they? Balcombe primroses are said to be the finest in England, and, being a Balcombe man for fifty years, I honestly believe it.

---

225 John Jennings died in 1909, so Picknell must be talking about his brother Thomas, who discovered the body of Mr Gold. No trace of Thomas Jennings can be found after the 1901 census; he is not listed with his wife Sarah in the 1911 census, although she describes herself as 'married' and not a widow. She was working at this time as a housemaid to a solicitor in East Grinstead. No record of the Balcombe Thomas Jennings travelling to America has yet been located.

APPENDIX XV.

The Plea of Insanity in the Case of Lefroy.
By Dr Forbes Winslow[226]

Having expressed an opinion a few days after Lefroy was condemned to death that there were sufficient grounds to justify the Home Secretary in granting a medical inquiry, and no response having been made to an appeal so numerously signed, we have thought it desirable to discuss "The Plea of Insanity" in this unfortunate case. Having been concerned in the matter we feel it an imperative duty we owe to ourselves, the public, and to the friends of the young man now gone over to join the great majority, to give the following particulars.

Within a few days of the termination of the trial we were consulted by some relatives of Lefroy with reference to our forming a conclusion on his state of mind. Certain documentary evidence was placed in our hands, and family histories were disclosed, all bearing directly on the case. Having carefully perused these we expressed an opinion that there were sufficient grounds for petitioning the Home Secretary to grant a medical examination of the condemned man. A few days subsequently we had occasion to go into the country, and on our way down in the train we read in the morning's paper that we had been appointed to visit Lefroy at Lewes Gaol. Upon arrival at our destination we immediately telegraphed to the Home Secretary, expressing our desire that if such were the case we would rather make the examination in conjunction with a medical Government official appointed by himself. This wish was also subsequently expressed by us at the Home Office. We felt that public opinion was so great against the condemned man that we did not care to take upon ourselves the responsibility of acting as mental adjudicator in a case of so much public importance and interest. We only saw the friends on one occasion. We have never seen or had any communication with Mr Dutton, the solicitor for the defence, beyond telegraphing to him on the day before the execution, and also signing the petition presented to us by his clerk, not asking for a reprieve, but simply praying that the Home authorities would sanction an inquiry into Lefroy's mental state. This petition was subsequently signed by upwards of one hundred medical men.

Three years ago a young man presented himself at the house of a consulting

---

226 *Journal of Psychological Medicine and Mental Pathology* 1882 April 8 (Part 1): 122-127. Although the article is unsigned, Forbes Winslow was the *Journal*'s editor at this time.

Lefroy.

physician in Brook Street, giving the name of Percy Lefroy Mapleton. This circumstance had escaped the memory of the medical man whom Lefroy then saw, until hearing of the murder, when, upon reference to his note book, the following entry was seen attached to the name, "This person is evidently insane." Lefroy, inheriting insanity on the side of both father and mother, commenced his career with anything but a hopeful future. His mother dies before he reaches the age of five; his father suffers from softening of the brain for some years previous to his death, which only occurred recently. His natural disposition is described as being gentle in the extreme, and he is reported as abhorring all crime and vice. Of the early life of Lefroy we know but little. He was sent to Australia, and returned a short time back, but whilst on his passage home he conducted himself in such a strange manner as to necessitate being placed under absolute restraint - the captain and officers of the ship can testify to this.[227] If, therefore, his real state of mind had been properly recognised by his family at this period of his history, a terrible calamity would have been averted. We hear of his going into theatrical speculations with an imaginary opera bouffe, supposed to have been written by Offenbach, which he called "Lucette," but which had no reality beyond his own morbid imagination. The extraordinary statements, founded on fabrication, which from time to time have been called "lies," were, in our opinion, delusions, existing only in his diseased mind. We have had in our possession, and we deposited at the Home Office, a letter written to a friend of his, in which he stated that he had come into a property of £10,000 per annum for life, and that he was going in for "parliamentary honours." Does this look like the saying of a man in his right mind? The letter to which we refer is dated May of last year. Within a few weeks of his penning this epistle he commits the murder for which he has met the death of a wilful criminal. Cunning is conspicuous in lunatics, and this quality had been shown throughout the whole of the transaction. Commencing the crime with Hanoverian medals in his possession; the endeavour to conceal the watch in his boots; sending one of these counterfeit pieces to the post office, and expecting to receive a sovereign in exchange for it. His conduct was very peculiar after the murder. It may be alleged on the other hand that there was distinct premeditation, but this is no argument against his insanity. Surely, many of the murders committed by lunatics are premeditated, and suicidal insanity is nearly always so. His method was not that of a sane man. With regard to his confessions, they appear to be nothing but a tissue of crazy incoherencies. He

---

227 No official document has been discovered which confirms this claim, but the following report appeared in the *Morning Post* of 24 November 1881: "The statement which was made to Mr Dutton, Lefroy's solicitor, by a steward who was in the employ of the Peninsular and Oriental Company, as to Lefroy's erratic conduct on board the *Peshawur* on his return journey from Australia, has been fully verified. He was for a considerable time under restraint, and was constantly watched by officers of the ship, and the dates of the sailing from Galle and the arrival of the steamer at Southampton have been fixed and correspond with the account given by the steward." However, as has been seen, Lefroy returned to England on the *True Briton*.

admits one crime after another. It is said that he did this to obtain a reprieve, so as to give time to investigate the truth of his statement. This opinion was eagerly grasped by those desirous of hurrying the victim into eternity. What possible evidence have we that these statements were not positive delusions, emanating from one, who at the time he is reported to have uttered this, was described as "raving like a lunatic and foaming at the mouth?" We could adduce from the other documents we have had in our possession in further proof of what we urged to the Home Secretary, that there were sufficient data for an inquiry to be held. It would be as absurd to consult a medical man upon some knotty legal question as it would be to ask a lawyer to solve some psychological problem. Why then, in the name of justice and common sense, were not those experienced in insanity called in to report on his mental state? The only official opinion as yet published was Marwood's, who considered him sane, and the press grasped this opinion as carrying weight, and sent it forth to the world. In our opinion Lefroy was subject to paroxysms of homicidal impulse, in addition to other marked symptoms of insanity.

In homicidal insanity it requires one especially conversant with the subject to detect mental aberration. A visit to Broadmoor will convince anyone of this fact. Here we see persons convicted of murder, but subsequently acquitted on the ground of insanity, who since their confinement have been of sound mind; but they are, and rightly so, detained during Her Majesty's pleasure. "Homicidal impulse" is often recurrent, and it is never known when a fresh paroxysm may occur, and what the result of such outbreak may involve. It is not connected with any special type of mental aberration, and is generally associated with monomania. The insanity here is often of so superficial a kind that it is most difficult of detection, the intellectual powers remaining seemingly intact throughout the disease. Persons so afflicted are liable to sudden paroxysms of mental excitement and murderous desire. No reason can, as a rule, be detected for the perpetration of the deed, and the crime is apparently quite motiveless. Many homicidal lunatics destroy the lives of those they love most dear. Some victims to this homicidal tendency are quiet, morose, and gloomy in their nature; they are naturally a most dangerous class of humanity, and too often it happens that their real condition is not detected until some crime has been committed which brings their actions under the immediate attention of the authorities. Unnatural cruelties, impulsive desires are also present; the reasoning power, judgment, and ordinary mental symptoms remain intact, the chief characteristic being a morbid and irresistible wish to commit extravagant and murderous acts, no positive delusion being present. It belongs to a class of in sanity called "moral insanity," and one under which Lefroy laboured, the symptoms we have just enumerated being all present. His love affair, which was so conspicuously, we regret to say, brought prominently forward, had not the slightest foundation, but was purely an hallucination of his disordered fancy. According to the law of England, if it can be conclusively established that a prisoner knows the difference between right and wrong, he is therefore held legally responsible. This is a monstrous doctrine. If we examine one hundred ordinary lunatics in any asylum, not, of course, including the demented and absolutely idiotic inmates, we find that quite ninety of this number are able to discriminate between right and wrong; and yet, according to the rule of law now laid down, these persons must be regarded as responsible beings, who, if they aggress, must pay the penalty for so doing. The opinion we originally entertained that a medical examination should have been granted by the Home Secretary is universally held by all those medical men with whom we have discussed the case. As far as the unhappy man himself is concerned, it may perhaps be a mercy that he is spared incarceration as a criminal lunatic for life; but in discussing a case of this nature we should not heed the popular cry for vengeance towards a condemned man. It is to the immediate relatives and those with whom he has been all through life associated that we must extend our pity, and by whom sympathy was doubtless deeply felt for the family of Mr Gold. It is the opinion of many individuals that insanity, if clearly established, should not exempt a criminal from the extreme penalty of the law. We do not, however, for one moment, endorse this, or credit that such a monstrous and unchristian doctrine should be tolerated by the more enlightened members of our community. There are undoubtedly some individuals among both the legal and scientific sections of society who entertain extreme views respecting crime and punishment - men not deficient in natural sagacity, and not uninfluenced by feelings of humanity, who, being educated in the spirit and prejudices of the old school, consider the throne, the seat of justice, and the State in danger if any undue mercy is extended towards those who violate the sacred majesty of the law.

"Not hang a lunatic!" they exclaim, "who has committed the crime of murder! Not hand over to the tender mercies of Marwood an insane person who has imbrued his hands in the blood of a fellow creature? If doctrines like these are promulgated, if such principles are allowed to interfere with the legitimate administration of justice, who will answer for the safety of society, or the security of the State? "We have the happiness, however, of living in an age when such obsolete doctrines can exercise no influence upon the understanding, the humanity, character, and conduct of those placed in positions of great legal trust and responsibility. It may be asked, Why was the plea of insanity not raised at the trial of Lefroy? But with this we have nothing to do. It was our opinion from the first that it ought to have been. Again, Why were the officials, on pain of dismissal, not allowed to divulge anything that occurred within the precincts of the gaol for twenty-four hours previous to the execution, in reference either to the prisoner's conversation or demeanour? The case, from first to last, was a sensational one; and under no pretence whatever could the public executioner be deprived of his victim. Reviewing the case calmly and deliberately, and taking into consideration all the concomitant facts, it would have furthered the interests of intelligence, humanity,

Appendix XV.

science, civilisation, Christianity, and justice if a deaf ear had not been turned to the prayer of these petitioners, simply begging that the Home Secretary would grant a medical inquiry into the mental state of the youth then standing on the precipice of his fate - Ed.

APPENDIX XVI.

Police Work From Within[228]
By Hargrave L. Adam.

The sketch [used as the basis of the *Daily Telegraph* published likeness] was made by a man who had known Lefroy for some time quite intimately. I was recently discussing the case with a friend of mine who had known both the artist and Lefroy. It was generally supposed, at the time the crime was committed, that this was the only occasion on which the man had "gone wrong," that otherwise he had always been quite a worthy member of society, and had been driven to the commission of the crime from sheer want. In this way a good deal of sympathy was worked up for him. As a matter of fact this was entirely wrong, as he was known generally by his acquaintances to be an inveterate thief and a worthless individual altogether. Everybody who knew him suspected him – nobody trusted him. He would steal from anybody, even his own "chums". He used to play cricket, not so much for the love of the sport as for the opportunity it gave him of getting into the tents or pavilion while the players were on the field and rifling their pockets – they having changed into "flannels". He had also been known even to break open their bags, removing anything portable and of value. In fact he was a thoroughly bad lot.

228 London: Holden and Hardingham (1914).

INDEX.

Index.

Index.

Index.

Index.

Index.

Index.

Index.

Index.

Index.

NOTABLE BRITISH TRIALS SERIES.

Notable British Trials Series.

Notable British Trials Series.

* New series.

In preparation:

Henry Hunt (ed. Caitlin Kitchener)

Ronald Light (ed. Sally Smith, Q.C.)

The Mannings (ed. Linda Stratmann)

John Selby Watson (ed. Molly Whittington-Egan)

Lightning Source UK Ltd.
Milton Keynes UK
UKHW021818060619

343997UK00007B/158/P

9 781911 273608